ASSESSMENT IN PRACTICE

ASSESSMENT IN PRACTICE

Putting Principles to Work on College Campuses

Trudy W. Banta
Jon P. Lund
Karen E. Black
Frances W. Oblander

Jossey-Bass Publishers
San Francisco

Substantial discounts on bulk quantities of Jossey-Bass books are available to corporations, professional associations, and other organizations. For details and discount information, contact the special sales department at Jossey-Bass Inc., Publishers.
(415) 433–1740; Fax (800) 605–2665.

For sales outside the United States, please contact your local Simon & Schuster International Office.

Manufactured in the United States of America. Nearly all Jossey-Bass books and jackets are printed on recycled paper that contains at least 50 percent recycled waste, including 10 percent postconsumer waste. Many of our materials are printed with either soy- or vegetable-based ink; during the printing process these inks emit fewer volatile organic compounds (VOCs) than petroleum-based inks. VOCs contribute to the formation of smog.

Library of Congress Cataloging-in-Publication Data

Assessment in practice: putting principles to work on college
    campuses / Trudy W. Banta . . . [et al.]. — 1st ed.
      p.   cm. — (The Jossey-Bass higher and adult education series)
    Includes bibliographical references and index.
    ISBN 0-7879-0134-2
    1. Universities and colleges—United States—Examinations.
    2. College students—United States—Rating of. I. Banta, Trudy W.
    II. Series.
    LB2366.2.A88   1996
    378.1′664—dc20
                                           95-18627

FIRST EDITION
PB Printing 10 9 8 7 6 5 4 3 2

The Jossey-Bass
Higher and Adult Education Series

CONTENTS

PREFACE

Assessment in Practice has been written by faculty and student affairs profession-als who are engaged in assessment for their colleagues who are just beginning to think about assessment or who are interested in improving their own prac-tice. At the present time, well into this country's second decade of emphasis on educational outcomes by state agencies, accreditors, and more recently the fed-eral government, it is a fact that *most* faculty still have not considered the assess-ment of student outcomes seriously. But every day, more pressures—now coming from students and parents and from trustees and employers as well as from state governors, legislators, and coordinating board members—are being applied to convince academics that they need to provide tangible, systematic evidence of what students know and can do as a result of their collective college experiences. Thus, questions about how to think about assessment and what methods to use are being asked by more people and with more intensity than ever before. Every week, an assessment process gets underway for the first time in another depart-ment on another campus, and faculty and administrators who initiated assess-ment programs years ago remain interested in continuous improvement of their practice.

"How do I get started in outcomes assessment? Who is doing good work?" "Can you give me some examples of assessment methods in my discipline?" "How are other colleges like mine assessing their general education program?" "What about affective outcomes—how do we assess those?" "Now that we have been doing assessment for a few years, how do we maintain our momentum? Where can we get some fresh ideas?" These are the questions we hear most often at con-ferences or when people call us to talk about assessment. Therefore, these are the questions *Assessment in Practice: Putting Principles to Work on College Campuses* is designed to answer.

Good practice in assessment is occurring on hundreds of campuses across the United States. Unfortunately, most of this work goes unchronicled, and the accounts that have been written are widely dispersed because they are published in the literature of dozens of academic disciplines. In *Assessment Update,* the bimonthly Jossey-Bass periodical that we edit, we can tell half a dozen stories in some detail in each issue, and at least mention about six more, amounting to some seventy examples of practice in a year, but even that is just scratching the surface of the rich experience in assessment that is now taking place on campuses around the globe.

We began the research for this book by writing to hundreds of people to ask for examples of "assessment strategies that work." The first letters went to the individuals who have contributed to *Assessment Update* since that publication was inaugurated in 1989. Then we consulted lists of institutions sending representatives to recent national conferences on assessment and wrote to the assessment coordinator at each of the 375 institutions that seemed most involved by virtue of having sent multiple representatives over time. These contacts produced others, and we followed up with additional letters to the individuals and institutions suggested by respondents to the initial mailings. Altogether, we sent out approximately 750 letters. Eventually, almost 200 case outlines were submitted, and in this book, we draw upon 165 fully developed one- to five-page descriptions of campus assessment practices.

After the 165 cases were assembled, we were confronted with the formidable task of organizing them into categories. It was clear that we should have sections on assessment in the major field and in general education, because those are the areas that concern most faculty initially and about which they ask the largest number of questions. After more study of the materials, we decided to add a third section on student development, conceived broadly as cognitive and affective growth that might occur in the classroom or in other settings that could be considered part of the campus experience. After that decision, three other divisions of the materials occurred rather naturally: classroom assessment, faculty development experiences designed to prepare instructors to do assessment, and overall institutional effectiveness.

That breakdown gave us six sections altogether. But even organizing the cases in these categories, each with its own loosely structured framework, did not reduce the complexity of our collection sufficiently. Typifying the dizzying diversity and complexity of American higher education, each case depicts a practice or set of practices that has been successful in a particular setting. How could we go beyond the individual cases to draw generalizations—principles of good practice—that could provide guidance for those who might seek assistance in such a volume?

At this point, it occurred to us that one set of such principles had already been published, as *Principles of Good Practice for Assessing Student Learning* (American Association for Higher Education, 1992). We asked ourselves, "Why not take that list of principles and show how each is illustrated in the body of practice we have assembled?"

Thus, we have produced a book in two parts. The first part is organized according to the nine principles of good practice published by AAHE—plus a tenth principle that we added based on our experience of analyzing the cases we collected. Each principle is fully explained in its own chapter (Chapters One through Ten), and each explanation is followed by illustrations of the principle drawn from some of the 165 cases. As we point out in the introduction to Part One, the AAHE principles themselves initially were derived from observation of and participation in good practice in assessment taking place on campuses across the United States. Our experience in reviewing current campus practice confirms that the nine principles do characterize good practice. We leave it to our readers to decide whether or not our tenth principle represents a valid addition.

Part Two presents 86 full cases of assessment practice, in the words of the faculty, student affairs professionals, and campus assessment administrators who developed the procedures. The cases are grouped in Chapters Eleven through Sixteen, in the six ways we described earlier, ways we hope will have meaning for readers seeking examples in a specific area of practice.

Most faculty and administrators are interested in learning first about assessment experience in a two-year or four-year, public or private, large or small institution; that is, a setting as much like their own as possible. Thus, each chapter in Part Two begins with a "Chapter Guide" that briefly describes the size and type of institution in which each case originated. We have used the Carnegie Classification (see Resource A) throughout to describe institutional types. Each chapter guide also contains other information about the chapter contents, such as the types of assessment methods represented in the cases.

Following the chapter guide, a narrative introduction called the "Chapter Overview" describes the rationale for subgroupings of cases and for the overall sequencing of cases within the chapter. Finally, each case is introduced individually in a "look for" statement, which provides highlights that distinguish the case and make it an example of good practice.

The body of each case is presented according to a common outline. To place the case in context, it begins with a brief background description and/or statement of purpose, followed by a full account of the assessment method used, the findings that method has yielded, and the uses that have been made of the findings. Most cases conclude with a success factors section, which responds to the question, Why did this assessment strategy work (or not work)?

Following the concluding chapter (Chapter Seventeen), which discusses whether assessment is making a difference for institutions and their students, the reader will find two resource sections. Resource A contains the Carnegie Classification Definition of Categories. Resource B lists the case authors from both Parts

One and Two. Following these resources, the References list all works cited in both parts. Finally, the index provides comprehensive cross-references for the contents of all chapters and cases.

The two parts of *Assessment in Practice*, presenting institutional examples of practice in two different contexts, should maximize the book's usefulness for its intended audience: faculty, academic and student services administrators, and assessment specialists in all types of postsecondary education. Those who are interested in general principles of good practice in assessment will find these generalizations in Part One. Those who seek specific examples, with full details of their development, can turn immediately to Part Two. However the reader chooses to approach *Assessment in Practice*, it is the intention of all who have contributed to it that the principles and practices it combines in a single volume will extend and improve assessment practice in the United States and around the world in the years to come.

Acknowledgments

We are indebted to all the generous faculty and administrators who were willing to share their experiences with assessment with a larger audience.

We would also like to thank the two individuals who reviewed the original manuscript. Their thoughtful and detailed comments challenged us to think more deeply and, thus, strengthened our work.

In addition, Barbara Gushrowski's unfailing patience, commitment, and invaluable work in preparing the manuscript made the production of this book possible. She, Linda Durr, and Nancy Morales have worked tirelessly to attend to the countless small details of producing such a lengthy volume with so many elements. At the same time, they have continued to make our office an enjoyable place to be. For all their contributions, we are deeply grateful.

Indianapolis   Trudy W. Banta
September 1995   Jon P. Lund
                                                                                  Karen E. Black
                                                                          Frances W. Oblander

THE AUTHORS

Trudy W. Banta is professor of higher education and vice chancellor for planning and institutional improvement at Indiana University-Purdue University Indianapolis (IUPUI). Before assuming that position in 1992, she was professor of education and founding director of the Center for Assessment Research and Development at the University of Tennessee, Knoxville. Banta has written or edited seven books, contributed fifteen chapters to other works, and has published more than 130 journal articles, monographs, and research reports. She has addressed meetings in twenty-one states on the topic of outcomes assessment and visited campuses in thirty states to assist faculty in establishing assessment programs. Banta has coordinated eight national conferences and cosponsored six international conferences on assessing quality in higher education. She has given invited addresses on this topic in China and in several European countries. In 1988, Banta was honored by the American Association for Higher Education for her contributions to the field of assessment in higher education. In 1989, she became founding editor of *Assessment Update*, a bimonthly Jossey-Bass publication. Her baccalaureate degree in education (with majors in biology and history) and master's degree in counseling were earned at the University of Kentucky. Her doctorate in educational psychology was awarded by the University of Tennessee.

Jon P. Lund is director of residence life at Luther College. Previously, he served as a graduate assistant in the Office of the Vice Chancellor for Planning and Institutional Improvement at Indiana University-Purdue University Indianapolis and worked in various student affairs positions at the University of Delaware, Michigan State University, and Saint Olaf College. Lund received his

B.A. degree (1986) in biology and religion from Saint Olaf College, his M.A. degree (1990) in college and university administration from Michigan State University, and is currently a doctoral candidate in higher education and sociology at Indiana University Bloomington. He is the coauthor of a chapter on the student outcomes associated with involvement in student government and a monograph on student learning outside the classroom. In 1992, he received the Annuit Coeptis Emerging Professional Award from the American College Personnel Association.

Karen E. Black is the assistant to the vice chancellor for planning and institutional improvement at Indiana University-Purdue University Indianapolis. For the past three years, she has been managing editor of *Assessment Update*. She has assisted in the development and coordination of three national conferences and three international conferences on assessment. In 1993, she attended the Summer Institute for Women in Higher Education Administration, at Bryn Mawr College. Black holds a B.A. degree (1982) in English and an M.S. degree (1985) in college student personnel administration from Indiana University. She is currently seeking a Ph.D. degree in higher education and inquiry at Indiana University.

Frances W. Oblander is an educational consultant based in Owensboro, Kentucky. Formerly director of student services in the School of Education at Indiana University-Purdue University Indianapolis, she has over fifteen years experience in student affairs and academic administration. She was involved in campus assessment activities at IUPUI for nine years. For the past three years, she has been assistant editor of *Assessment Update*. In 1990, she attended the Summer Institute for Women in Higher Education Administration, at Bryn Mawr College. She has a B.S. degree (1976) in zoology from Colorado State University, an M.A. degree (1979) in college student personnel administration from Michigan State University, and an Ed.D. degree (1986) in higher education administration with a cognate in evaluation from Indiana University. She has served as an evaluation consultant to the Indiana Department of Education and the Indiana Center for Evaluation.

ASSESSMENT IN PRACTICE

PART ONE

PRINCIPLES OF GOOD PRACTICE IN ASSESSMENT

As is the case with so many important projects in higher education, the initial development of principles of good practice in higher education assessment was supported by a grant from the Fund for the Improvement of Postsecondary Education (FIPSE). With FIPSE funding, Theodore J. Marchese and Pat Hutchings at the American Association for Higher Education (AAHE) established the Assessment Forum, and as one of the Forum's activities, they began in 1989 to bring together for periodic meetings a dozen "practitioner-students of assessment" from across the country. In addition to Marchese and Hutchings, the group included Alexander W. Astin, University of California-Los Angeles; Trudy W. Banta, then at the University of Tennessee, Knoxville and later at Indiana University-Purdue University Indianapolis; K. Patricia Cross, University of California-Berkeley; Elaine El-Khawas, American Council on Education; Peter T. Ewell, National Center for Higher Educa-

tion Management Systems; Kay M. McClenney, Education Commission of the States; Marcia Mentkowski, Alverno College; Margaret A. Miller, State Council of Higher Education for Virginia; E. Thomas Moran, State University of New York at Plattsburgh; and Barbara D. Wright, University of Connecticut and the AAHE Assessment Forum.

One of the tasks this group set for itself was to develop a set of assessment principles, which it published as *Principles of Good Practice for Assessing Student Learning* (American Association for Higher Education, 1992), patterned on Chickering and Gamson's influential "Seven Principles of Good Practice in Undergraduate Education" (1987). The AAHE assessment principles, listed below, attempted to bring together for the first time in a single document the generalizations about effective assessment practice that the Forum members had drawn from their own campus experiences and those of others.

The Principles of Good Practice for Assessing Student Learning

1. The assessment of student learning begins with educational values.
2. Assessment is most effective when it reflects an understanding of learning as multidimensional, integrated, and revealed in performance over time.
3. Assessment works best when the programs it seeks to improve have clear, explicitly stated purposes.
4. Assessment requires attention to outcomes but also and equally to the experiences that lead to those outcomes.
5. Assessment works best when it is ongoing, not episodic.
6. Assessment fosters wider improvement when representatives from across the educational community are involved.
7. Assessment makes a difference when it begins with issues of use and illuminates questions that people really care about.
8. Assessment is most likely to lead to improvement when it is part of a larger set of conditions that promote change.
9. Through assessment, educators meet responsibilities to students and to the public [AAHE, 1992, pp. 2–3].

Each of the chapters in Part One begins with the statement of a principle. Then a full examination of the underlying assumptions and rationale for the principle, based on current literature, is presented. The next section of each chapter, "The Principle in Practice," contains illustrative materials drawn from some of the 165 individual descriptions of campus assessment practice assembled for this book. When the case appears in full in Part Two, a cross-reference (by chapter and case number) to the complete description is provided. The authors for all the cases—whether they appear only in Part One, only in Part Two, or in both parts—are listed in Resource B, along with the positions they hold and the names of their institutions.

The last chapter in Part One proposes a tenth principle. Most of our 165 cases contain a section entitled "Success Factors." In these sections, the authors state why they believe their assessment strategies have worked. As we read those sections, we noted some characteristics of successful practice that were repeated with such frequency that we felt they deserved to be summarized in a new principle. We advance this additional principle for consideration by our fellow practitioner-students of assessment.

CHAPTER ONE

ASSESSMENT: IT STARTS WITH WHAT MATTERS MOST

Principle One

*The assessment of student learning begins with educational values. Assessment is not an end in itself but a vehicle for educational improvement. Its effective practice, then, begins with and enacts a vision of the kinds of learning we most value for students and strive to help them achieve. Educational values should drive not only **what** we choose to assess but also **how** we do so. Where questions about educational mission and values are skipped over, assessment threatens to be an exercise in measuring what's easy, rather than a process of improving what we really care about (AAHE, 1992, p. 2).*

The Principle in Context

An endless array of studies, reports, and articles highlights the importance of higher education to both the individual and society (for example, Bowen, 1977; Leslie and Brinkman, 1988). At the same time, many of these documents challenge educators and policy makers to improve education at all levels. The recent focus on higher education and the need for reform is evident from publications such as *Involvement in Learning* (Study Group on the Conditions of Excellence in American Higher Education, 1984), *College: The Undergraduate Experience in America* (Boyer, 1987), *Education Counts* (Special Study Panel on Education Indicators for the National Center for Education Statistics, 1991), and most recently, *An American Imperative: Higher Expectations for Higher Education* (Wingspread Group on Higher Education, 1993). These analyses suggest, among a number of other reforms, the use of assessment and feedback as tools to direct educational improvement. Furthermore, a general theme running throughout these appeals for reform is the need for institutions to focus their assessment efforts on what matters most.

Assessment has the greatest chance for success when it is based on educational values. This means that for assessment to be truly effective—from an institutional perspective—in improving that which is important, institutional agents including trustees, administrators, faculty, staff, students, and outside publics must first have a shared conception as to what the institution is, what it values, and what it aspires to be. This is not an easy task, for there is perhaps no more important, nor difficult, undertaking than grappling with issues of mission and purpose. This is especially true in today's diverse and fluid higher education environment.

From its inception, higher education in this country has had to grapple with issues of mission and purpose. Postsecondary institutions have paused to look inward to examine teaching and learning—the heart of the educational enterprise—and have attempted to define the programs and services they offer on behalf of students. In addition, these institutions have had to look outward to examine and define the links between higher education and society. Such self-examination is indeed appropriate and important in that postsecondary institutions have an obligation to society, particularly with respect to the education of young adults who will one day assume crucial roles in the community. In both instances, the institutional mission statement is a collective means through which to communicate an educational vision and purpose.

However, issues of identity, purpose, and educational values transcend the common notion of institutional mission statements. Many college and university mission statements fail to capture the true purposes of their institutions. Their broad overview of purpose, most often encompassing the areas of teaching, research, and service, makes them generally ineffective instruments for directing institutional decision making and improvement. Too often, these statements fail to say much about students or student learning. Instead, they focus on what faculty and administrators do rather than on what students will learn. They become nothing more than communications to external constituencies, their purpose being to define the institution so broadly as to keep open the institutional door to a steady stream of resources (Davies, 1986).

At other colleges and universities, mission statements do adequately express institutional values. Small church-affiliated colleges, for example, often express their missions in documents that suggest these colleges know why they exist and what impact they hope to have on students, especially with respect to intellectual, spiritual, and psychosocial learning (Brandt, 1994). These carefully crafted mission statements truly reflect what matters most (that is, student learning) and become solid foundations upon which to build assessment programs.

The reality, then, is that the presence of a strong institutional mission statement provides an invaluable starting point for assessment. The absence of this starting point, however, does not mean that assessment efforts are destined to fail. But it does mean that extra care must be taken to craft assessment initiatives around shared institutional values, goals, and vision. It means that assessment specialists, faculty, student affairs staff, and others who are interested in assessment must pay attention to what matters to students and to the institution's internal and external publics and use this information to provide direction for assessment and improvement. It also means that assessment can be successfully accomplished at the classroom, departmental, unit, divisional, or school level, as long as it focuses on the underlying educational values or shared goals at that level. A clear institutional mission statement is therefore helpful as a foundation for assessment but is not entirely necessary, and certainly not sufficient, to ensure success.

In short, assessment cannot and should not take place in the absence of a clear sense as to what matters most at the institution. Indeed, in order for assessment to lead to improvements, it must reflect what people are passionate about, committed to, and value. Or stated another way, institutional assessment efforts should not be concerned about valuing what can be measured but, instead, about measuring that which is valued (Astin, 1991). The following examples highlight the many ways in which faculty and administrators at a number of colleges and universities address the issues of improvement, reform, and accountability by implementing assessment strategies designed around what matters most.

The Principle in Practice

Central Piedmont Community College (CPCC), an Associate of Arts institution with 17,000 students, found itself faced with a variety of new challenges during the 1989–90 academic year, challenges resulting from the fast-paced, complex, and interconnected world into which its students graduate. In the midst of this complexity, the college was still guided by a mission statement that had changed little since 1969. CPCC desired a mission statement that would provide strategic direction for the institution and its assessment efforts. As a beginning phase for the assessment process, CPCC entered into consideration and discussion of the following questions:

> How do community colleges maintain excellence as they adapt to new demands brought about by a changing, technically advanced, interdependent, and complex world? How do colleges nurture greater numbers of students to higher levels of intellectual functioning? How do they promote cultural understanding and prepare students to work cooperatively? And how do colleges meet society's call for action, and give evidence that the new challenges are being addressed?

The quest for answers to these critical questions often leads colleges to reassess their fundamental statement of purpose—the college mission.

John W. Quinley

Similarly, Avila College, a Catholic Master's I college with 1,400 students, was forced to examine its mission in light of demographic changes in the student body. The college had, for more than seventy-five years, attempted to provide a value-based education using the concept of a community of learners. Over the past two decades, the composition of the student body has shifted, and the college has responded by offering classes during the day, in the evening, and on the weekend. As a means of gaining a deeper understanding of how the members of the newly composed student body perceive their college experience, Avila College faculty employ an assessment framework based on the school's concept of community. Using a survey instrument, faculty measure student satisfaction with the various elements of community considered important in characterizing the college mission.

In 1990, the Carnegie Foundation for the Advancement of Teaching published *Campus Life: In Search of Community*. In that publication, the authors identified six elements essential for community on a college campus. The college must be purposeful, open, just, disciplined, caring, and celebrative. The correspondence between these elements and the values underlying the Avila community experience caused us to choose to use these six "elements of community" as a model to better understand how Avila College students in each of the student subgroups perceive and measure their experience of community.

Marie Joan Harris

Gainesville College, an Associate of Arts nonresidential unit of the University System of Georgia, enrolls 2,600 students. A substantial portion of its mission involves the preparation of students for transfer to the university system. Accordingly, the college emphasizes liberal arts programs in its curriculum to reflect the core curriculum of the entire university system. To assess its own programs, Gainesville College relies heavily on its strategic planning document, which outlines the mission of the institution.

In 1990, extensive efforts were made to involve the faculty and staff in the development and refinement of the college's first formal strategic plan. At the same time, the campus was similarly engaged in developing a shared vision statement, which outlines a number of points/goals intended to provide direction to the faculty and staff for the college's second quarter century. The goals enumerated in the shared vision and statement of purpose form the basis for institutional planning and the assessment of institutional effectiveness.

Thomas D. Webb

The University of Memphis, a public Doctoral I metropolitan university, has an enrollment of 20,300 students. The university uses a broad conception of its mission—particularly with respect to preparing students for active participation in society—as the foundation for evaluating the effectiveness of its general education program.

> The role of general education in the contemporary university is central because it can form the basis of a shared intellectual life in an academic community. The linkage between active participation in an academic community through general education and later participation in the democratic society finds expression in the goals of many collegiate general education programs. At the University of Memphis, above all, the general education program is intended to make available to students the tools and awareness necessary for active, lifelong learning and for active, literate participation in society.
>
> Todd M. Davis, Patricia H. Murrell

A number of institutions utilize the mission review process as a stepping-stone in the development of assessment measures aimed at discerning progress toward fulfilling the institutional mission. For example, Midlands Technical College, a public Associate of Arts college of approximately 9,100 students, is involved in the institutional effectiveness movement as a strategy for institutional renewal. Faculty and administrators examine three important questions related to their mission: What is the principal mission of the college? What results can be expected from mission achievement? And what measurements will serve as adequate evidence that the mission has been achieved? Six areas critical to institutional success form the basic components in addressing these questions and measuring the college's effectiveness in attaining its stated mission:

> (1) Accessible, comprehensive programs of high quality; (2) student satisfaction and retention; (3) posteducation satisfaction and success; (4) economic development and community involvement; (5) sound, effective resource management; and (6) dynamic organizational involvement and development [see Chapter Sixteen, Case 79].
>
> James L. Hudgins, Dorcas A. Kitchings, Starnell K. Williams

Chicago State University, an urban commuter Master's I university with a predominately African American population and 9,500 students, incorporates a significant aspect of its mission in its assessment program. The university is committed to providing services and programs that help students persist to completion of their educational objectives. Accordingly, the university relies on its assessment program to provide information regarding the extent to which the university is meeting this particular aspect of its mission.

Chicago State University's comprehensive assessment program includes an assessment of entry-level basic skills, and outcomes assessment of general education, the major, and academic support programs. The emphasis on assessment is closely linked to the institution's commitment to improving the retention and academic success of a large number of first-year students who are at risk of dropping out of college. Multiple assessments are used in academic and support programs to identify students' knowledge and abilities, attitudes, and patterns of behavior in order to provide the appropriate academic and personal interventions tailored to this particular student population.

Delores Lipscomb

King's College, a private Baccalaureate II college of 2,400 students, uses assessment not only as a tool to measure learning but also as an important process through which individual learning and personal development occurs. This focus on the individual is central to the mission of King's College. One important assessment strategy used is the Sophomore-Junior Diagnostic Project, which consists of a unique assignment embedded in a required course offered early in the major. The diagnostic projects vary greatly among departments. The English department, on the one hand, uses portfolio assessment as a means of determining the thinking and writing abilities of its students. The human resources management department, on the other hand, relies on case studies as a way to measure critical thinking and writing skills. In both departments, the Sophomore-Junior Diagnostic Projects enable faculty members to gain valuable assessment information about their students, provide an avenue through which students gain greater insights into their own learning, and serve as a visible reflection of the institutional focus on student learning.

As a result of the Sophomore-Junior Diagnostic Projects, students gain insight into the cumulative nature of learning. That is, students realize that the faculty in their majors expect them to build upon the material learned in their general education classes and that faculty expectations of student performance will increase as students progress through the curriculum. Additionally, students appreciate the fact that faculty in their majors care about the development of the knowledge and abilities necessary for students to be successful during and after their tenure at King's College. This appreciation happens whether students are given very favorable feedback or whether they are referred to appropriate resources such as the Writing Center.

Stephanie L. Bressler, John F. Ennis, Mark Michael, Jean P. O'Brien

Finally, the efforts of the School for New Learning at DePaul University, a private Doctoral II institution with 16,500 students, demonstrate the use of a colloquium to focus the attention of master's degree students on the school's mission to integrate classroom with workplace learning, liberal learning skills with technical or professional expertise, and theoretical concepts with practical application.

The Assessment Colloquium creates a forum for students to develop attitudes and skills of reflective practice in order to inform their own learning, improve performance by integrating liberal learning skills with professional development, and engage in collaborative learning through feedback from student peers regarding individual development. Program objectives of the colloquium include promoting assessment as part of the learning process, obtaining feedback and evidence on the extent to which the learning/learner objectives are being met, and gathering information needed for interventions and/or program improvements [see Chapter Eleven, Case 14].

Catherine Marienau, Morris Fiddler

Conclusion

In a time of constrained resources and demands for improvement, the college mission must be understood not just by the school's faculty and staff but also by its students and the community it serves. Institutions must reexamine and communicate the important educational values that define their existence and implement strategies to assess student and institutional performance with respect to those values. Assessment must be based on that which is truly important.

CHAPTER TWO

AN IMAGINATIVE CONSIDERATION
OF LEARNING

Principle Two

A ssessment is most effective when it reflects an understanding of learning as multidimensional, integrated, and revealed in performance over time. Learning is a complex process. It entails not only what students know but what they can do with what they know; it involves not only knowledge and abilities but values, attitudes, and habits of mind that affect both academic success and performance beyond the classroom. Assessment should reflect these understandings by employing a diverse array of methods, including those that call for actual performance, using them over time so as to reveal change, growth, and increasing degrees of integration. Such an approach aims for a more complete and accurate picture of learning, and therefore firmer bases for improving our students' educational experience (AAHE, 1992, p. 2).

The Principle in Context

Learning is indeed a complex, creative, and dynamic process. In many respects, learning is analogous to the experience of admiring the geometric figures in an M. C. Escher drawing. The meaning and impact of the experience are very different for each observer, dependant as they are on the observer's angle of observation, the factors that draw the observer's attention, and the observer's previous exposure to works of art. So, too, it is with learning; so, too, it should be with assessment.

For years, educators have recognized the vibrancy of learning, yet at the same time, many learning assessment strategies have failed to move beyond evaluations characterized by rote repetition of facts and unimaginative application. Colleges and universities, as Alfred North Whitehead ([1928] 1967) asserted decades ago, exist to foster learning "by uniting the young and the old in the imaginative consideration of learning. The university imparts information, but it imparts it imaginatively. . . . This atmosphere of excitement, arising from imaginative consideration, transforms knowledge. A fact is no longer a bare fact; it is invested with all its possibilities. It is no longer a burden on the memory; it is energizing as the poet of our dreams, and as the architect of our purposes" (p. 93).

Effective assessment programs reflect the imaginative, creative, and energizing aspects of learning, not only so as to more accurately measure the breadth and depth of the learning experience but also to contribute to the ongoing spirit of inquiry, reflection, and growth that characterize the university as an institution. Unfortunately, traditional measurement and assessment strategies have tended to reduce or ignore the complexities of the learning process. This tendency, combined with the realities of little time, scarce resources, and limited access to students throughout the learning experience, makes the assessment of student learning challenging indeed.

Learning itself might well be conceptualized in three ways. First, learning is embodied in the concept of "core content," which refers to the traditional facts and knowledge defined by subject areas such as science, mathematics, English, or the liberal arts. Second, learning is "integrative reasoning," a concept that focuses on the skills that process knowledge and facts into applications for work or daily living. Finally, learning is "attitudes and dispositions," a concept representing the character and qualities society hopes students will attain and demonstrate as good citizens (Special Study Panel on Education Indicators for the National Center for Education Statistics, 1991).

Successful assessment programs take into consideration all three of these concepts of learning through the application of a variety of methods intended to provide an accurate and multidimensional picture of learning. They also focus on the application of assessment methods at different levels in students' college careers and at different points in the learning process. While assessment should begin by addressing the important questions embodied in the institutional mission, it must, at the same time, pay attention to the sought-after outcomes of a variety of majors and areas of study.

This does not imply that educators should assess everything, all the time. Instead, we must consider the various resources available for assessment (for example, time, money, and staff) and develop assessment strategies that are best able to measure student learning fully given these constraints.

Finally, in order to assess learning in its full complexity, educators are forced to consider the reliability and validity of their assessment methods. The questions of reliability and validity center around building confidence in assessment findings, determining the applicability of the findings to improving the educational experience, and assuring some level of precision or consistency with respect to replication. A full treatment of validity and reliability, though important, is beyond the scope of this book. Suffice it to say that a number of publications exist, which the interested reader is encouraged to consult (for example, Borg, Gall, and Gall, 1993; Erwin, 1991).

The Principle in Practice

A variety of institutions have developed and implemented assessment programs that attempt to capture the complex and multidimensional nature of learning. The creativity and variety of many of these strategies is amazing. Ursuline College, for example, a Catholic Baccalaureate II college enrolling 1,600 students, bases its assessment program upon the school's core curriculum. The curriculum has been developed around the stage theories of women's development, in which women move from being passive learners to individuals capable of constructing their own knowledge. The assessment program attempts to capture this learning by using paper-and-pencil instruments and in-depth interviews.

> A group consisting of ten trained faculty assesses the impact of the curriculum on students using a combination of personal interviews and written instruments geared to measure developmental stages that correspond with those described by Belenky, Clinchy, Goldberger, and Tarule in *Women's Ways of Knowing* (1986). The interview schedule they describe is used in student interviews. During campus visits, the authors of *Women's Ways of Knowing* have trained the faculty in methods of conducting and analyzing interviews. Additionally, a companion instrument called the Measure of Epistemological Reflection (MER)(Baxter Magolda, 1992) is used to triangulate the research through the use of a second method.
>
> Rosemarie Carfagna

Likewise, educators at Northeast Missouri State University (NMSU), a public Master's I institution of 6,200 students, rely on the concept of triangulation to arrive at a more complete picture of student learning. Specifically, information gained from a multiple methods assessment format is used to promote the continuous improvement of student learning.

> All seniors sit for a nationally normed examination. Faculty choose the examination they think best measures their graduates' learning. Students receive individual scores, and faculty receive individual score reports for all graduating

seniors. Faculty also receive aggregate data on the percentage of students above the 50th percentile and the percentage of students above the 80th percentile. In many instances, testing companies also provide information about student performance in discipline subfields, and NMSU aggregates student performance, comparing it with that of students from other universities.

All seniors must complete a graduating student questionnaire regarding their satisfaction with resources, processes, and learning outcomes. Departmental results are reported in a comparative format with the university averages.

Each major program requires students to complete a capstone experience as part of the curriculum. Faculty in each major determine the content of the course, and a number of models have emerged. Students might take a seminar on classic works in the field, or they might write a thesis. Some majors require that students sit for a locally developed comprehensive exam, some require students to report research at an undergraduate research conference, some ask students to give a research presentation before an external examiner, and some require students to give a speech to an outside group [see Chapter Eleven, Case 7].

Candace Cartwright Young

The Department of Communication Studies at the University of Missouri-Kansas City uses a variety of assessment tools embedded in student portfolios to supplement assessment data collected by the field test for the major. This public Doctoral I institution of approximately 9,800 students employs portfolio assessment to provide information on student learning, to increase dialogue across courses on learning outcomes, and to prepare students for career entry. Students are required to have a portfolio on file with the department at the time they declare a major.

The following suggestions are made to students regarding the types of items to include in the portfolio (a minimum of three are required): an updated résumé and cover letter; the student's professional goals for graduation and five and ten years later; an example of written work from employment or internship experiences; a research paper from the capstone course or other upper-level course; a self-assessment of communication competencies; an example of written work other than term papers (speech manuscript, newspaper article, advertisement, television script, and so on); a well-written essay test; an essay on the student's personal theory of communication; an explanation of coursework completed outside the department and its benefits; a discussion of a valuable theory of communication; a letter of reference from an employer; a list of classical and contemporary fiction and nonfiction read in the last two years; and/or a list of periodicals and magazines regularly read (and why).

Joan E. Aitken

The Department of Music at Virginia Polytechnic Institute and State University, a publicly funded Research I university of 26,000 students, routinely employs multiple assessment techniques for student evaluation. The department has structured its assessment efforts to reflect the public performance that is an essential part of the study of music.

The Department of Music routinely employs multiple assessment techniques for student evaluation and guidance. Included among these are music performance auditions and competitions, nationally standardized tests, faculty-constructed examinations, music performance jury examinations, recital hearings, concert reviews, and informal communications with alumni. These assessment procedures are conducted in three basic areas: music performance, music theory, and music literature. Each faculty member is involved in one or more aspects of the evaluations, and outside experts such as local music educators (who are often alumni) and regional symphony members also serve as evaluators.

Vernon Burnsed, John A. Muffo

James Madison University (JMU), a Master's I public university of 11,500 students, has a well-established assessment program with strong central support from measurement specialists who assist faculty in developing reliable and valid methods for assessment. JMU ensures that the assessment activities are directed toward areas of primary concern to the institution by relying heavily on locally developed measures using a variety of methods.

A major dividend of ongoing assessment has been greater faculty involvement in the design of innovative assessment methodologies that impact the curriculum. This ensures that curriculum decisions remain in the able hands of those who deliver the curriculum. Over 90 percent of JMU assessment methods in the major have been locally developed, and 100 percent of the liberal studies assessment methods have been developed by the faculty. We have witnessed a creative expansion of methodologies employed, such as personal artistic performance histories, computer science novel program-problem-solving exercises, oral comprehensive examinations (using locally developed scales that assess program goals and objectives), reviews of student research and position papers (employing locally developed scales), student focus groups, employer satisfaction surveys, student self-assessments, portfolio reviews, student interviews, performance critiques, external advisory council reviews of assessment designs and student products, and external supervisor ratings of internship and student teaching experiences.

Donna L. Sundre

One way to obtain diverse and broadly illustrative data is to survey various institutional groups. At private Liberty University, a Christian Master's I institution with 9,200 students, the assessment focus has been on obtaining a variety of perspectives from different stakeholders on core values and assumptions. One important area of inquiry for the institution is student perception of academic and student services. In order to capture the many dimensions of the student experience, Liberty University examines the perspectives of a number of different constituency groups.

> Our approach to assessing academic and student services features surveys of former students and students currently enrolled. In all of the surveys, we retain a core of questions to permit a view of these services from a variety of perspectives. Students submit a course completion survey for each course. Phone surveys have been utilized as well as written surveys. When students are in residence, extensive testing with nationally normed instruments and in-house instruments occurs.
>
> David E. Towles, Ellen Lowrie Black

The University of Tennessee, Knoxville is a public Research I land-grant institution of 25,900 students. The institution has combined quantitative and qualitative methods to measure learning outcomes in both knowledge acquisition and practical application.

> The original assessment procedure was designed to address student learning in terms of content and application with equal emphasis. Based on advice from consultants, a faculty committee in the College of Social Work constructed the *content* portion of the procedure, a paper-and-pencil test composed of 100 multiple-choice items. Each question was worth one point. The committee discussed and analyzed the items and sought guidance from other faculty. Discussion focused on matching questions to the program's mission and goals. After numerous revisions, the first draft was pretested by a group of graduate social work students, and an item analysis was performed.
>
> Attention to the *application of knowledge* was emphasized in the second component of the procedure. The college had earlier developed a portfolio assignment as a culminating activity for graduating seniors. The committee decided to clarify the expectations for the assignment and to develop a more programmatic process for assessment. In the past, the portfolio was an addendum to the curriculum; a requirement for graduation but not part of a specific course. Now, the portfolio is identified as the primary assignment of a newly developed required seminar for seniors.
>
> Frank J. Spicuzza

Because it is highly informative to assess student performance over time, ongoing assessment is a crucial component of successful assessment programs. The Department of Radio/Television Production Technology at Virginia Western

Community College (VWCC), a public Associate of Arts institution with an average enrollment of 6,500, employs several methods to assess the outcomes of its two-year program.

> The radio/TV production program head has developed and implemented a comprehensive student assessment model using the following measures, most of which have become an ongoing part of the program: (1) jury review of student projects in a capstone course; (2) internship evaluations by students and supervisors; and (3) a comprehensive exit test. The program's advisory committee has played a key role in these assessment efforts by helping to develop program objectives, assessment criteria, and performance-based measures. Each assessment measure is based on a list of objectives and "key elements" developed by the advisory committee and program head.
>
> David C. Hanson

Finally, occupational therapy faculty at Kean College of New Jersey, a state-supported Master's I college enrolling 11,900 students, employ a longitudinal design to gain a deeper understanding of student attitudinal changes over time. Specifically, the faculty are interested in examining the way in which students' preferences for various aspects of occupational therapy change during the college experience. In order to accomplish this task, the faculty explore student perceptions over time using a number of instruments.

> Three questionnaires have been designed to explore the students' practice preferences at different points in their educational experiences. Questions focus on whether students have a practice preference, whether their preferences have changed or remained the same during their participation in the occupational therapy program, and if preferences have changed, what influenced that change. Students are surveyed at three points in the college experience: during the junior year when they enter the professional phase of the program; at the end of the senior year when they complete the academic phase of their training; and at the completion of the fieldwork experience, which involves a minimum of six months of full-time internship in at least two areas of practice.
>
> Paula Kramer, Karen Stern

Conclusion

As evidenced by these case excerpts, successful assessment techniques embody creativity, adaptability, reliability, and validity. Through the use of multiple methods, triangulation, and the measurement of knowledge and performance over time, effective assessment techniques can begin to capture and reflect the complex nature of learning. Assessment is truly an imaginative process.

CHAPTER THREE

THE ROAD TO SUCCESS IS PAVED WITH GOALS

Principle Three

A *ssessment works best when the programs it seeks to improve have clear, explicitly stated purposes. Assessment is a goal-oriented process. It entails comparing educational performance with educational purposes and expectations—these derived from the institution's mission, from faculty intentions in program and course design, and from knowledge of students' own goals. Where program purposes lack specificity or agreement, assessment as a process pushes a campus toward clarity about where to aim and what standards to apply; assessment also prompts attention to where and how program goals will be taught and learned. Clear, shared, implementable goals are the cornerstone for assessment that is focused and useful (AAHE, 1992, p. 2).*

The Principle in Context

A clear understanding of an institution's mission and values, though a critical prerequisite, is not in itself sufficient for developing a comprehensive assessment program. The mission and values must be translated into meaningful, specific, and realistic goals for each academic program and student service. These goals represent the direction in which faculty, administrators, and staff wish to see students grow and develop with respect to the desired college outcomes. The process of transforming the college mission into specific goals is both internally important, in terms of linking assessment efforts to improvement, and externally important, in light of calls for educational renewal and accountability.

The call to focus on goals has come from a number of sources. It appears in its broadest and most sweeping form in *America 2000* (1991). Goal 5.5 in that report challenges colleges and universities to focus on student ability to "think critically, communicate effectively, and solve problems" (p. 64). Although this goal expresses what for many are obvious intended outcomes of education, its practical utility for providing direction for assessment programs is limited by its breadth and lack of specificity.

In contrast, the Wingspread Group on Higher Education (1993) organizes the call for educational reform around a different, and in many respects more pragmatic, set of challenges. The group's report suggests that educators, among other things, should (1) develop "a clear public definition of what students should know and be able to do at each educational level"; (2) create "standards of entry *and exit* for higher education"; (3) strive to increase "the use of assessment to diagnose learning needs and enhance student achievement"; and (4) attempt to improve "both the theory and practice of teaching and learning" (p. 20).

But how can both the *America 2000* goal and the Wingspread set of goals be applied in meaningful ways on campus? Creating clarity for learning goals in the midst of the complexity of learning is no small task. After achieving consensus on their institutional mission, educators must ask themselves such questions as these: What are the goals and objectives of a college education at this institution? Given these goals, what are the critical components that students ought to learn from general education, the major, and the minor? How can student services assist in fostering student learning and development?

Discussion and debate on these fundamental questions and many more like them may lead to the development of learning outcomes or taxonomies. Many institutions have adopted Bloom's taxonomy (1956) or other cognitive development frameworks to guide the development of outcomes (for example, Gilligan, 1982; Perry, 1970). Other institutions have identified abilities or competencies that students are expected to demonstrate at different points in their academic programs and at graduation (Farmer, 1988; Loacker and Mentkowski, 1993). In contrast, at yet other institutions, assessment efforts have occurred at the grassroots level, and assessment has been driven more by individual interests than overarching institutional goals. For example, a faculty member may design a classroom-based assessment strategy, or a member of the student affairs division may survey students' satisfaction with co-curricular offerings. Even when motivated by individual interests, though, implementable goals must provide the foundation for assessment.

The Principle in Practice

Practices at several institutions illustrate the importance of linking assessment to broad institutional goals as well as to specific program goals. At Southern Illinois University at Edwardsville, a public Master's I institution of 11,300 students, the Committee on Assessment (COA) serves as the coordinating mechanism through which institutional assessment efforts are managed. Although each department is responsible for the assessment carried out through the Senior Assignments (SRAs), the COA helps to ensure that the assessment is directed toward the larger goals for student learning valued by the institution.

> The role of COA has been to assist each department to (1) formulate a statement of student learning objectives and (2) approve only those SRA plans that can measure corresponding student achievement. Regarding the first part of the role, COA received departmental statements containing various mixes of universitywide and discipline-specific ideals. These statements reflect many exercises in thought, argument, and negotiation. A composite example might include: (1) student should have baccalaureate-level knowledge of the major discipline; (2) student should be able to examine independently the research literature and report on a topic within the major discipline; (3) student should be able to explain orally, using speech free of jargon, a technical topic in the discipline to a lay audience; and (4) student should be able to explain new developments in the discipline in terms of their ethical impact on society [see Chapter Eleven, Case 3].
>
> Douglas J. Eder

In a more specific application of departmental goals at Southern Illinois University at Edwardsville, faculty members in the Department of Chemistry have designed their Senior Assignment to assess students' ability to conduct both laboratory and library research, their mastery of presentation skills, and their ability to defend work orally. The specific activities upon which students are assessed include:

> (1) A literature review, through which students demonstrate their ability to search a current chemistry topic by using resources such as *Chemical Abstracts* and the *Chemical Abstract Service Online;* (2) an independent examination of the research literature, which demonstrates not only a mere reading of the research literature but also critical thinking skills such as analysis and evaluation of data and formulation of conclusions; (3) a summary and written presentation, through which students demonstrate their ability to use the correct, standard scientific format and convey a topical application of their research to society

· and the environment; and (4) an oral explanation and defense, through which
students demonstrate their ability to give a coherent speech in front of others
and answer questions appropriately.

Nahid Shabestary, Douglas J. Eder

In order for goals to be effective, they must be related to overall institutional
and program-specific missions. Several institutions provide good examples of
the way in which goals and mission may be linked. Faculty members in the College of Business at Ball State University, a public Doctoral I university of 20,700
students, began the process of developing goals by first developing a mission. Based
on this mission, a logical progression to the more specific departmental goals
followed.

As the first step in the process, the department chairs met with the dean to
develop a mission statement. This statement reflects the applied nature of
research we expect of faculty as well as the emphasis on excellence in undergraduate teaching that is the distinguishing characteristic of Ball State University. In a next step, the Curriculum Committee met with department chairs to
brainstorm objectives in each of the content areas in the mission statement.
The resulting list was circulated to participants, who rated the objectives as to
their importance. The objectives were then condensed into a list of skills,
knowledge, and values all College of Business graduates were expected to have.
Emphasis was placed on behavioral objectives related to student performance
rather than on teacher activities.

During the 1992–93 year, professors teaching each of the core courses
were asked to describe the objectives they were trying to achieve in those
courses. Forms were developed to help them identify behavioral goals and the
instructional activities and media used to teach the goals. These goal statements were collected by the department chairs and reviewed by the Curriculum Committee. Then these professors met with members of the Curriculum
Committee and the dean's staff to condense the goals and review the statements of current practice [see Chapter Eleven, Case 1].

Inga Baird Hill

Faculty in the Department of Physiology and Health Science at Ball State
University have attempted to examine program goals beyond departmental goals
through their assessment efforts. Specifically, faculty have designed their assessments to examine the extent to which each general studies course offered through
the department contributes to the goals of the university's general studies program.

The initial purpose of this assessment effort has been to evaluate the impact
and effectiveness of each general studies course. Equally important has been
the need to determine how well each course contributes to the goals and objec-

tives of the general studies program. Ultimately, departments must be able to show that their general studies course deserves to be retained in the general studies program.

Dale B. Hahn

Peace College, a private Associate of Arts institution enrolling 500 women, provides another illustration of the way mission and goals can be linked through assessment. The college administers the Academic Performance Survey (APS), a locally developed instrument designed to elicit information from students on their academic preparation and values, perceptions about their academic strengths and weaknesses, and progress in a variety of academic areas.

The types of learning assessed are related to our educational goals, including writing, reading comprehension, public speaking, library research, critical thinking, and quantitative and computer skills. In addition, students report on behaviors related to academic success, including their goals for a college education, their work habits, and their participation in events and activities that strengthen or weaken their chances for academic success. The baseline measure is obtained from freshmen during orientation. Data are then collected from graduating students in April prior to graduation and compared with the freshman data to note improvement.

Korrel W. Kanoy

Education faculty at Indiana University of Pennsylvania, a public Doctoral I university with a student enrollment of 14,000, believe in the importance of linking knowledge and theory in the classroom with actual field application. Accordingly, they have designed an assessment strategy around this goal by creating a simulation exercise for graduate students in the teaching profession.

Getting experienced teachers to question the relevance of the content material in their basal texts and of their own graduate classes is one of the reasons that I developed authentic simulations for my graduate classes. Although there are many effective ways to get teachers to begin questioning and thinking about the applicability of course content, I have found that assessment simulations provide experiences that not only give new meaning to classroom teaching strategies, but also enhance skills in communication, leadership, judgment, sensitivity, innovativeness, and decision making. For example, I developed a simulation designed to promote these skills called the Keystone Simulation. This simulation requires teachers, working in co-op groups, to compete for a $10,000 grant. The simulation is intended to support a project that enhances student learning, student self-perception, multicultural concepts, and sensitivity toward at-risk students.

Robert E. Millward

Finally, Old Dominion University, a public Doctoral I institution of 16,000 students, uses assessment data to drive improvements in an area of particular concern, its persistence rates. Since it is imperative that students stay in school in order to obtain the benefits that accrue from a college education, the university has intentionally designed an assessment strategy focused on this one goal. Using information from surveys completed under the aegis of the Cooperative Institutional Research Program (Astin, Green, and Korn, 1987), as well as data from locally developed instruments, a new assessment tool has been created.

[Researchers have developed] the Old Dominion University Freshman Survey (Pickering, Calliotte, and McAuliffe, 1992) to (Phase I) improve predictions of academic performance at the end of the freshman year and persistence into the second year over what was possible with existing cognitive and demographic data, and (Phase II) identify at entry a group of freshmen who exhibited a greater potential for academic difficulty and/or attrition, and design interventions for them based on this research. Phase III involved full incorporation of this research into the academic advising and assessment programs, and Phase IV involves norming our freshman survey on freshmen at other institutions and on subpopulations . . . at Old Dominion University [see Chapter Thirteen, Case 55].

James W. Pickering, James A. Calliotte

Conclusion

Assessment is most effective when it is based on clear and focused goals and objectives. It is from these goals that educators fashion the coherent frameworks around which they can carry out inquiry. When such frameworks are not constructed, assessment outcomes fall short of providing the direction necessary to improve programs.

CHAPTER FOUR

IT'S NOT ONLY WHERE THEY END UP, BUT HOW THEY GET THERE

Principle Four

*A*ssessment requires attention to outcomes but also and equally to the ex-*periences that lead to those outcomes.* *Information about outcomes is of high importance; where students "end up" matters greatly. But to improve outcomes, we need to know about student experience along the way—about the curricula, teaching, and kind of student effort that lead to particular outcomes. Assessment can help us understand which students learn best under what conditions; with such knowledge comes the capacity to improve the whole of their learning (AAHE, 1992, p. 2).*

The Principle in Context

Assessment of outcomes is important, but so, too, is assessment of the teaching and learning processes that lead to those outcomes. It would be of little value to gather information on student outcomes without gathering and utilizing the equally important information on the student experiences, classroom teaching techniques, and institutional and environmental conditions that lead to the outcomes. Processes, in a sense, are the road maps that enable educators to retrace the college experiences of students. Paying attention to processes thus helps make improvement possible. Analyzing the pathways, detours, and conditions that improve the higher education journey provides invaluable material to educators as they attempt to chart richer and more potent educational experiences for students.

One of the most influential of the reports calling for improvements in higher education is that of the Study Group on the Conditions of Excellence in American Higher Education (1984). This work clearly emphasizes the crucial role of processes as means of creating excellence in higher education. Specifically, the report discusses the conditions under which student learning and growth can be maximized. These conditions include student involvement, high expectations, and the use of assessment and feedback. The authors suggest that undergraduate education can be improved by encouraging student involvement and active student engagement in learning and development, by establishing and sharing clear expectations and standards for student performance, and by providing regular assessment and feedback to improve teaching and learning.

Building upon the work of that study group, Chickering and Gamson (1987) provide more specific guidance regarding effective educational processes. Their "Seven Principles for Good Practice in Undergraduate Education" distills findings from research on student experiences into clearly articulated and focused principles of good practice in undergraduate learning. The principles encompass a wide range of educational processes that improve education. Chickering and Gamson assert that good practice (1) encourages student-faculty contact, (2) encourages cooperation among students, (3) encourages active learning, (4) gives prompt feedback, (5) emphasizes time on task, (6) communicates high expectations, and (7) respects diverse talents and ways of learning. In short, they suggest that the improvement of undergraduate education occurs through focused attention to the good teaching and learning practices that lead to greater learning.

Processes in and of themselves are of limited use in improving student learning if they have not been demonstrably linked to the outcomes they purport to improve. Fortunately, we do have research that provides guidance regarding good practices. Research suggests, for example, that student learning is enhanced when teachers "(1) have a good command of the subject matter and are enthusiastic in its presentation, (2) are clear in their explanation of concepts, (3) structure and organize class time well, (4) present unambiguous learning stimuli to students (for example, use examples and analogies to identify key points, signal a topic transition clearly), (5) avoid vague terms and language mazes, and (6) have good rapport with students in class" (Pascarella and Terenzini, 1991, p. 110).

Research also suggests that increased learning occurs not only through teacher behaviors but also through student behaviors. Students learn more when they are actively engaged in meaningful interactions with peers and faculty members (Astin, 1977, 1993), or more generally, when the extent and quality of their effort increase (Pace, 1984).

In order to assess processes meaningfully, indicators of accomplishments are necessary. Increasingly, educators and researchers within the higher education community have advocated the use of process indicators as a means of assessing student learning (Banta, 1993b; Ewell and Jones, 1993; National Center for Higher Education Management Systems, 1993). This focus on the process indicators that lead to student learning (for example, the amount of time students spend studying, the frequency of student-faculty interactions, and the extent of student involvement in collaborative activities) has materialized as a result of the difficulty, expense, and imprecision of using locally developed and standardized tests to assess student achievement (Banta, 1993b, 1993c). In contrast to the more traditional outcome measures of student progress, process indicators have the advantage of being less difficult and expensive to develop and implement, action oriented in the sense that they can be applied directly to policy decisions, and readily related to improvements in student learning (Ewell and Jones, 1993; National Center for Higher Education Management Systems, 1993).

Focusing on processes in higher education is not new; instructors and students have recognized for centuries, for example, the simple fact that the more one studies, the more one tends to learn. Intentionally assessing and establishing conditions under which learning and teaching processes can be improved, however, is relatively new. A recently developed method for improving the classroom experience for students is "classroom assessment" (Angelo and Cross, 1993; Cross and Angelo, 1988), which focuses on teaching and learning at the most basic (that is, classroom) level and attempts to discover information with respect to what, how, and how well students learn (Angelo, 1991, 1994). It focuses on teaching and learning processes as well as outcomes and on how both can be improved.

It is perhaps no coincidence that the concern for processes in higher education has arisen at the same time as a growing awareness of their importance in business. Awareness of processes is a defining feature of the "quality movement," known commonly as Total Quality Management (TQM) or Continuous Quality Improvement (CQI) (Ewell and Jones, 1993).

One of the key principles of the quality movement as enunciated by its guru, W. Edwards Deming (1986), is that organizations should "improve constantly and forever the system of production and service" (p. 49). For Deming, the value in studying and improving processes in order to achieve a better product was paramount. His writings on this subject, though directed toward business, apply with some modifications to higher education: "Every product [student] should be regarded as one of a kind; there is only one chance for optimum success" (p. 49). Processes provide a means for ensuring that success. Equally important for assessment purposes is Deming's belief that "quality comes not from inspection, but from improvements in the . . . process" (p. 29). Clearly, outcomes should not be the only concern.

The strategies that follow detail the variety of ways in which diverse higher education institutions use a number of processes (such as student involvement, quality of effort, self-assessment and feedback) to evaluate and improve teaching, learning, and educational outcomes.

The Principle in Practice

Ohio University, a public Research II institution of 19,000 students, conducts an annual study of student involvement as part of its ongoing Institutional Impact Project (IIP). The Student Involvement Study consists of a four-page questionnaire administered to all first-year students living in the residence halls on this predominately residential campus. The survey collects information on students' academic involvement, social involvement, and commitment to and satisfaction with the university. It exemplifies a research-based assessment strategy that is concerned not only about outcomes but equally about educational processes. The strategy is based on the premise that student involvement has a close relationship with the quality of undergraduate education.

> Research has shown that in comparison with peers, students who are more involved in activities related to their formal education grow more as individuals, are more satisfied with their education, persist in their education to graduation, and continue their learning after college. . . . By assessing student involvement, Ohio University identifies one aspect of the university's impact on its undergraduates [see Chapter Thirteen, Case 57].
>
> A. Michael Williford, Gary O. Moden

Student involvement is also an area of concern at Santa Barbara City College (SBCC), an Associate of Arts commuter institution of 11,200 students. As a result of their mission and facilities, community colleges face a number of specific hurdles with respect to encouraging involvement (for example, residence facilities are usually not available and the amount of time students spend on campus may be limited). In an effort to assess the extent of student involvement, SBCC administers the Community College Student Experiences Questionnaire (CCSEQ). The college is interested in increasing the number of students who successfully complete their educational objectives, and views assessment data on student involvement, as measured by the CCSEQ, as one source of the information necessary to improve this important process.

Findings from the CCSEQ at Santa Barbara City College suggest that:

> There is a strong relationship between student involvement and student progress in . . . achievement of educational objectives. Additionally, there is a strong relationship between student involvement and student satisfaction with the institution. And finally, the findings suggest specific areas in which student involvement is highly related to student success and areas in which the institution needs to do more to encourage student involvement.
>
> Jack Friedlander, Peter R. MacDougall

The College Student Experiences Questionnaire (CSEQ), an instrument similar to the CCSEQ, is used in a different manner at the University of Memphis (public, metropolitan, Doctoral I, 20,300 graduate and undergraduate students). The university uses the CSEQ to assess the quality of effort students exert in their collegiate experience. Specifically, the instrument assesses the impact of pilot general education courses as compared to matched traditional courses. One of the most notable results has been the influence of the CSEQ findings on teaching processes.

> The findings of the survey have been presented both to the teaching general education faculty and to the university administration. Based partially on the apparent success of the pilot curriculum, the general education core at the University of Memphis has been completely revised. While this is an important outcome of the study, what is most gratifying is the impact of the CSEQ results on the faculty and their teaching. Faculty have described three broad outcomes. First, some faculty note that the instrument (CSEQ) and related concepts of student effort provide a new way of thinking about general education and that the discussions about the nature of general education have evolved from the results. Second, several faculty members have reexamined their own teaching to help ensure that students have greater opportunities for active involvement. Finally, the process has given faculty a window into student perceptions of the campus ethos and a fresh look at how students view particular instructional activities.
>
> Todd M. Davis, Patricia H. Murrell

Specific teaching techniques have been implemented at some institutions to improve the learning process. One of these techniques is problem-based learning (PBL). PBL is designed to promote the development of effective self-directed learning skills, increase student motivation for learning, and help bridge the gap between knowledge and practical application. The School for New Learning at DePaul University (private, Doctoral II, 16,500 students) is one place in which PBL concepts inform the teaching/learning process. The School for New Learning's curriculum is geared toward adult students. Accordingly:

> PBL is well suited for the college's learner- and learning-centered curriculum, particularly as a means to guide independent studies and interactive techniques in the classroom. Among the assumptions upon which "learner-centeredness" rests are (1) adult learners can access materials through their base of experiences; (2) recognition of what a learner already knows about a problem or question can elevate her or his expectations to go beyond the current level of knowledge; (3) assessment is an integral part of the learning process; and (4) an overall objective of learning is to build a base for further learning. These assumptions lead to a number of principles for instructional strategies and techniques: (1) a learner's current level of knowledge should be assessed at early stages of the learning endeavor; (2) learners should have the opportunity to

pursue avenues of learning that are generated through their curiosity and interests; (3) self-assessment and feedback should be built into the learning process; and (4) elements of "learning to learn" should be embedded in the learning experience.

Catherine Marienau, Morris Fiddler

Finally, teaching and learning processes may be incorporated in the types of information that institutions gather and utilize. Winona State University (WSU), a public Master's I university of 7,200 students, is incorporating process indicators in its assessment database. The university will use the database to gauge institutional progress toward providing a quality education for its students. In addition to the process indicators, the database contains outcomes information, such as ACT College Outcome Measures Project (COMP) scores.

Data currently being collected on 150 quality indicators will provide WSU with a comprehensive set of baseline data that will be used to evaluate and improve all aspects of the educational process. Information on students, faculty, staff, administration, budgets, facilities, educational climate, and numerous other areas will be collected and analyzed over time. Internal and external benchmarks will be established, and processes will be analyzed and adjusted for improved performance. Primary areas for improvement will be on student learning activities. Indicator measures based on "Seven Principles for Good Practice in Undergraduate Education" (Chickering and Gamson, 1987) and learning outcomes identified in the WSU mission statement will help focus the university's efforts as we utilize some of our initial findings to improve learning processes and outcomes. Additional information from indicator measures will be analyzed and used to improve the educational environment and enhance interpersonal relations among faculty, administration, staff, and students [see Chapter Sixteen, Case 80].

Dennis C. Martin

Conclusion

Effective assessment strategies, then, pay attention to process. Whether the outcome is increasing students' critical thinking skills, equipping them to interact in an increasingly diverse world, helping them develop basic library research skills, or preparing them for licensure or certification examinations for work, educational processes are essential to the attainment of that outcome. In short, successful assessment practitioners understand that how students get there matters.

CHAPTER FIVE

ASSESSMENT DOESN'T JUST HAPPEN, IT EVOLVES

Principle Five

*A*ssessment works best when it is ongoing, not episodic. *Assessment is a process whose power is cumulative. Though isolated, "one-shot" assessment can be better than none, improvement is best fostered when assessment entails a linked series of activities undertaken over time. This may mean tracking the progress of individual students, or of cohorts of students; it may mean collecting the same examples of student performance or using the same instrument semester after semester. The point is to monitor progress toward intended goals in a spirit of continuous improvement. Along the way, the assessment process itself should be evaluated and refined in light of emerging insights (AAHE, 1992, p. 2).*

The Principle in Context

An old Jewish proverb suggests that the accomplishment of a number of specific tasks in life can be used as a measure of success. Individuals are admonished to plant a tree, write a book, and raise a child. In each case, success is bound up in enduring and ongoing processes; processes that require constant attention, nurturance, and patience as the product of one's efforts comes to fruition. Successful assessment efforts are no different.

Successful assessment is an ongoing, iterative process. It is undertaken with the knowledge that the assessment process itself will be constantly updated and adapted to meet the changing needs of the institution, students, faculty, and the public. It recognizes the importance of reflecting on, learning, and then improving the processes through which assessment occurs. It focuses on examining learning and teaching over time. And its objective is to provide valuable information directed toward current needs as well as future demands.

In many respects, this notion of assessment as a process of continuous change and improvement echoes the Japanese outlook on improvement known as *kaizen*—a philosophy of continuous improvement with a two-hundred-year view of the future (Banta, 1993a). Although it is probably not necessary—or possible—to view assessment within a two-hundred-year framework, it is possible and important at least to take a perspective that incorporates the possibility of assessment changes and improvement over time.

Unfortunately, assessment and institutional improvement are often perceived as exercises to be implemented in order to meet an urgent need. Perhaps assessment becomes a central focus as a result of public calls for accountability. Perhaps it arises in order to meet the demands of accreditation bodies. In either case, as Wolff notes (1992), successful "assessment is not something that can get started along with the beginning of a self-study process. It is only effective if ongoing and continuous. Too often I see institutions treat assessment as an accreditation mandate that only needs to be taken seriously episodically. . . . The kinds of assessment projects that are effective within institutions . . . take years" (p. 80).

Effective assessment programs become embedded in the institutional culture. They are acknowledged, discussed, deliberated, reviewed, and refined. Effective assessment is perceived as an integral part of the overall educational mission. And it focuses, very simply, on learning. The questions important to address in assessment concern: What should be learned? How will this learning occur? And what will be done with that which has been learned? (Pace, 1985). In this context, assessment becomes one of the driving forces in creating what Peter Senge (1990) calls "'learning organizations,' organizations where people continually expand their capacity to create the results they truly desire, where new and expansive patterns of thinking are nurtured, where collective aspiration is set free, and where people are continually learning how to learn together" (p. 3). Assessment at its best is all of these things—and more.

The strategies that follow detail a number of ways in which institutions take advantage of the cumulative power of assessment, both to improve student learning as well as to improve the assessment process itself.

The Principle in Practice

Midlands Technical College (MTC) (public, Associate of Arts, 9,100 students), conceptualizes the process of assessment as a seven-step model. The steps illuminate the important components of assessment at MTC, and highlight in a general fashion the many different considerations inherent in effective assessment programs. They also call attention to the evolutionary nature of assessment.

> While the process of developing or operationalizing institutional effectiveness programs in higher education varies, it usually contains seven basic steps: (1) articulate the mission; (2) establish a planning mechanism; (3) develop an evaluation system that tells if the college is doing what it says it does; (4) identify critical areas of success; (5) establish priority standards upon which the college can judge its effectiveness in the identified critical areas; (6) determine mechanisms for documenting if established standards have been met; . . . (7) utilize results of assessment for decision making [see Chapter Sixteen, Case 79].
>
> James L. Hudgins, Dorcas A. Kitchings, Starnell K. Williams

The School of Nursing at Ball State University (public, Doctoral I, 20,700 students) uses the Content-Input-Process-Product (CIPP) model (Stufflebeam, 1983) as the framework around which to develop its assessment program. The model is used to ensure that student outcomes are monitored and improved, nursing standards met, and accreditation criteria documented. In short, it provides the conceptual map around which the assessment process is charted. It also helps to define the program improvements undertaken at the institution.

> Content evaluation is used to compare outcomes of our program with criteria gleaned from external authorities such as the National League of Nursing, State Board of Nursing, and the American Academy of Nursing. The focus of evaluation is on the identification of the strengths and weaknesses of the program. Input from outside sources provides the data for decision making. The process phase addresses the ongoing success of the evaluation plan. Evidence of outcomes is both formative and summative. The nature, scope, and volume of evidence from the process allow for curricular planning and revision. This is accomplished through the curriculum and evaluation committees. Product evaluation follows for those final crucial decisions related to continuing, expanding, or totally revising the program. Program revisions include such things as (1) coordinating curricular course concepts; (2) reevaluating clinical experiences to include assessment skills, clinical skills, client documentation skills, and principles of pathology; (3) reinforcing nursing concepts and application of nursing diagnoses; and (4) reviewing concepts related to critical thinking and evaluating nursing interventions.
>
> Marilyn E. Ryan, Nancy L. Dillard, Kay E. Hodson

The School for New Learning at DePaul University (private, Doctoral II, 16,500 students) views its assessment program as part of the learning process at the institution. Faculty feedback, student feedback, and feedback from the

Committee for the Assessment of Student Competence (CASC) all form the backbone of the assessment program. CASC occupies a central role in providing quality control in terms of the consistency and administration of the student assessment program. The committee specifically oversees the assessment of students' prior and independent learning for consideration of transfer credit.

> This ongoing assessment process by a standing committee in the college results in (1) improved efficiency of the administrative procedures associated with prior and independent learning assessment; (2) increased consistency in the interpretation of transfer coursework for its applicability to specific competencies in the college's curriculum; (3) development of criteria for the documentation of noncredit learning activities; (4) collection of examples that "test" the current interpretation of learning that is appropriate for students' demonstration of competence; and (5) identification of conflicts among the faculty in their interpretation of the competencies and associated criteria for assessing student submissions.
>
> Catherine Marienau, Morris Fiddler

Ohio University (public, Research II, 19,000 students) uses its multifaceted assessment program known as the Institutional Impact Project as the basis of ongoing assessment focused on continuous improvement.

> The Student Treatment Study is one of several studies in Ohio University's multidimensional Institutional Impact Project, which was developed in 1981 by a task force of Ohio University faculty and staff at the request of the university's president. It is an ongoing program of assessment of institutional impact, outcomes, and continuous improvement. The Student Treatment Study is used to measure student satisfaction in all areas of campus life, collecting information on the attitudes and perceptions of new freshmen after one quarter of enrollment. It assesses how freshmen feel they are treated by the staff of various areas or offices, how they rate the quality of information they receive from these staff or offices, and their perceptions of and reactions to various processes they go through [see Chapter Thirteen, Case 56].
>
> A. Michael Williford, Gary O. Moden

Successful assessment strategies also incorporate longitudinal designs. Assessment at Cumberland University, a private Baccalaureate II college of 1,000 students, focuses on institutional effectiveness, an approach that links the institutional mission, educational programs, and services with ongoing assessment using longitudinal data. The specific assessment strategy consists of the repeated use, over time, of a survey designed to assess teaching and learning. The strategy has three objectives:

First, in the near term, it is intended to satisfy partially the assessment requirements of a Southern Association reaccreditation visit. Second, it is intended to involve faculty actively in dialogue around teaching, learning, and institutional renewal. Finally, it is hoped that over the long term, through repeated administration of the instrument, a longitudinal database will be created to inform administrative policies and procedures and serve as a basis for ongoing program improvement.

Todd M. Davis, Patricia H. Murrell

Ideally, assessment becomes refined and incorporated into the general institutional culture. At James Madison University (state-supported, Master's I, 11,500 students), assessment days have become a regular feature of the institution's calendar. Assessment days are designated in the school calendar solely for the purpose of assessment. One day is set aside just prior to the beginning of fall classes to gather information on students. During the spring semester, another assessment day allows for the collection of additional student information. Assessment is thus conceived as a continual process occurring throughout the school year.

The implementation and continued support of assessment days on campus has been successful because it serves not only as a symbol, but also as a part of a larger institutional commitment to assessment. It is not merely a commitment to assessment, though. It is also a commitment to our students; the creation of a pervasive ethos that values student learning and development enough to work toward what is often referred to as an "assessment culture." Like Total Quality Management and Continuous Quality Improvement, excellence in assessment of teaching and learning does not happen by simply declaring or wishing it; it takes time and concerted effort.

Donna L. Sundre

In addition, ongoing assessment at its best results in specific program improvements. At the United States Air Force Academy, a service academy of 4,200 students, for example, a new test for French minors was developed and administered in 1993. The new instrument replaces an existing test that did not allow students to demonstrate their French proficiency on an authentic task. Results from the first administration of the new test have been used to improve the French program for minors and to establish a baseline against which to assess future students.

Because this was the first time we had administered the new exam, we did not use it as a basis for granting or denying anyone a minor in French. We did, however, use the results to test the test and to examine our curriculum. In terms of testing the test, we looked carefully at cadet responses to items on both the test and the follow-up survey to decide whether or not the tasks were appropriate. . . . Additionally, the cadets' responses provided us with a window on course articulation. Did any "holes" exist in our curriculum? Was there anything that the cadets could not do that they should have been able to do in order to earn a minor in French? . . . In the future, we will compare the results with those of upcoming classes to help us determine the degree to which any changes that may be made in the French curriculum lead to improvements in production skills [see Chapter Eleven, Case 9].

Judith E. Brisbois

Finally, a capstone course at Ball State University, entitled New Venture Creation, has been modified as a result of assessment. The course in the College of Business has been used for student evaluation purposes (to assess learning from the course) and for program improvement purposes. A number of specific course and program improvements have been introduced, some of which involve a board of professionals, a group of consultants, venture capitalists, investment bankers, and entrepreneurs who are active in this assessment initiative.

As a direct result of this course, continuous improvement has been applied to the course itself as well as within the overall business major. During the last ten years, the following changes have been introduced as a direct result of this course: (1) a new course, Creative Financing for Emerging Ventures, was developed and is now taught by one of the board members . . . in order to enhance students' financial understanding. (2) The Ernst & Young accounting firm has volunteered two workshops for the students to help them prepare their financial statements. (3) A number of board members now serve as either mentors or speakers for the class, depending on their expertise. . . . (4) The makeup of each evaluation team has been improved to include a successful graduate of the entrepreneurship program. . . . (5) Communication skills of students are stressed more now than in earlier years. This is a direct result of the evaluation process's uncovering a weakness [see Chapter Eleven, Case 19].

Donald F. Kuratko

Conclusion

Successful assessment programs do not spring up overnight. Instead, they grow and mature as a result of the constant attention and effort of a number of individuals. Assessment strategies must be continually nurtured, evaluated, and refined in order to ensure success.

CHAPTER SIX

INVOLVEMENT IN ASSESSMENT: A COLLABORATIVE ENDEAVOR

Principle Six

Assessment fosters wider improvement when representatives from across the educational community are involved. Student learning is a campus-wide responsibility, and assessment is a way of enacting that responsibility. Thus, while assessment efforts may start small, the aim over time is to involve people from across the educational community. Faculty play an especially important role, but assessment's questions can't be fully addressed without participation by student affairs educators, librarians, administrators, and students. Assessment may also involve individuals from beyond the campus (alumni/ae, trustees, employers) whose experience can enrich the sense of appropriate aims and standards for learning. Thus understood, assessment is not a task for small groups of experts but a collaborative activity; its aim is wider, better-informed attention to student learning by all parties with a stake in its improvement (AAHE, 1992, p. 3).

The Principle in Context

There is, perhaps, no more important principle in the assessment literature than this: successful assessment requires collaborative efforts. Assessment is no less a collective endeavor than is a choir performance. Both require interaction, participation, direction, and the joining together of different voices in common song. Designing assessment programs to examine complex issues such as students' critical thinking skills or values and attitudes is not an easy task. Accordingly, team effort is required to ensure success.

Institutions with long histories of successful assessment programs (the University of Tennessee, Alverno College, and Northeast Missouri State University) all credit the importance of wide constituency participation for much of their success. As Banta (1985) notes regarding the assessment experience of the University of Tennessee, Knoxville (UTK), "perhaps the greatest strength of the assessment program at UTK lies in the extent to which it has involved virtually every major unit of the university and personnel at every level, ranging from students to the chancellor" (p. 24).

Ewell (1988), in his discussion of the implications of assessment practices based on the results of the National Center for Higher Education Management Systems/Kellogg Student Outcomes Project at twenty-two public and private institutions, suggests that involvement and participation are important lessons learned from the project. In addition, results of a recent study of fifteen pilot assessment projects undertaken between 1986 and 1990 on campuses of the California State University system show that faculty participation and administrative support were important indicators of successful assessment (Riggs and Worthley, 1992).

Across a spectrum of institutions, then, widespread involvement in assessment is a crucial factor. Involvement may not ensure success, because a number of other factors are important, such as planning, preparation, and the presence of a receptive institutional culture for assessment. But it does increase the likelihood of achieving the desired results.

Developers of effective assessment programs are concerned about involvement at two levels: first, key individuals and groups within the institution (for example, faculty, students, student affairs staff, and administrators) and, second, groups external to the institution (for example, parents, alumni, employers, trustees, and members of accrediting bodies). Of these various groups, faculty members play the single most important role. Successful assessment programs create an atmosphere in which faculty not only learn about but take ownership of institutional assessment efforts. However, as noted in an influential Carnegie Foundation report (Boyer, 1987), many faculty members are simply not well prepared to assume the difficult tasks of assessment. Accordingly, institutional resources must be devoted to faculty development seminars and colloquia on topics related to assessment.

Finally, participation in assessment is a means of " 'giving voice' to groups that historically have been excluded from the planning, implementation, and evaluation processes of our colleges and universities" (Terenzini, 1993, p. 4). Participation in assessment ensures a wide hearing of the various issues and agendas present on diverse and complex campuses.

Wide constituency involvement in assessment pays off in a number of ways. One benefit is that it helps to lessen resistance to curricular and institutional changes that may come as a result of the assessment efforts. Involvement in assessment may also lead to increased communication within and between diverse departments, units, and external groups and may awaken a desire for further collaborative efforts on other important campus priorities and goals. In addition, involvement in assessment activities may lead to unintended benefits, such as increased faculty enthusiasm for teaching and learning. And finally, as Mentkowski and Doherty (1984) report, based on a study at Alverno College, faculty involvement in longitudinal assessment of student learning leads to discussion about and support of assessment itself.

Involvement in assessment can also be viewed as a form of faculty development. "When faculty devote the time to become fully involved in assessment, they create and become active participants in their own program of professional growth and development. Products of this effort can include stronger curricula, more effective classroom instruction, increased student-faculty interaction, and enhanced student motivation" (Banta, in press).

Faculty development is not enough, however, to get faculty fully involved in assessment. Visible incentives should be provided to encourage faculty to develop the necessary skills to undertake assessment efforts as a means of improving the teaching and learning on campuses. The way to make a functional connection between assessment and improvements in teaching and learning "is to insure that faculty have a proprietary interest in the assessment process . . . such involvement will help faculty to specify—far more precisely than they do at present—the outcomes they expect from individual courses and academic programs. And the more precisely they can specify the outcomes, the more likely they are to match teaching approaches to those ends" (Study Group on the Conditions of Excellence in American Higher Education, 1984, p. 45).

Involvement in assessment goes beyond the notion of simply improving a specific assessment program or strategy. Assessment may, in and of itself, foster learning by providing "feedback to increase the involvement of students and faculty members and to develop their talents as completely as possible. Such assessment is active, rather than passive, since it is designed to facilitate and improve performance" (Astin, 1985, p. 168).

The Principle in Practice

One widely used method to encourage involvement is the creation of one or more committees to shepherd the campus assessment process. Ball State University (public, Doctoral I, 20,700 students) uses a special Alumni Survey Steering Committee to provide direction for the development of an alumni assessment instrument.

In spring 1991, the Ball State Alumni Survey Steering Committee was formed to guide the development of a new, short-term alumni survey. The purpose of the survey was to provide assessment information for departments and for the university as a whole. The steering committee was selected by the Office of Academic Assessment to be representative of the university. The committee included members from each college and representatives from student affairs and other administrative units.

Brian K. Pickerill

The formation of a committee was also important to the success of the assessment program at the University of Wisconsin-River Falls, a public Master's I university of 5,200 students. The steering committee at the institution is responsible for guiding the administration of the College Student Experiences Questionnaire (CSEQ) to explore the depth and breadth of students' experiences on campus.

The preparatory work that is done prior to the administration of the CSEQ is integral to its success. This includes enlisting the support of the chief academic officer and the academic deans; forming a steering committee representative of faculty, students, and staff; ensuring widespread dissemination of information about the instrument to the campus community; and arranging a presentation to faculty and staff on the uses of CSEQ results at other campuses. It is also important that there is early and repeated contact with faculty who are involved in administering the instrument in their classes.

Roger A. Ballou, Lisa K. Reavill, Brian L. Schultz

Faculty involvement at the departmental level is essential for the successful assessment of learning. Rhode Island College (RIC), a public Master's I college of 9,500 students, has established departmental projects in seven academic departments, using grant money obtained from the Fund for the Improvement of Postsecondary Education. The money is used to fund faculty development related to an investigation of the link between rewards for good teaching and improvements in student learning. Through collaborative efforts within several RIC departments, some faculty have created locally developed tests; others have relied on standardized tests. In both cases, faculty participation at the departmental level determines the type of assessment strategies to be undertaken. A notable finding from the case study is that:

The inclusion of "home-grown" strategies, created through collaborative efforts of department faculty, helps to engender the project's success. In sociology and chemistry, for example, department faculty participate in the selection and creation of evaluation devices; they have created some strategies that are designed to test the unique contributions of their particular program in sociology or chemistry. Imported, normed techniques are also part of the evaluation battery. In social work, management, and nursing, each department, as a whole, meets to collaborate on the evaluation strategies. Departmental approval of the special "skills lab" evaluation in social work, the objectives method in management, and the professional competencies developed through the Delphi method in nursing affirms the faculty belief in the utility of these site-developed instruments. Groups of faculty have become invested in the use of these evaluation strategies.

Pamela Irving Jackson, Roger D. Clark, Rachel Filinson

Communication is one means through which active participation is promoted. At Kean College of New Jersey (public, Master's I, 11,900 students), open communication is used to encourage faculty participation in assessment by acquainting faculty, staff, and students with the principles and purposes of assessment. The intent is to diminish the fear and resistance that normally accompanies the introduction of new ideas and programs. Assessment personnel at Kean College use periodic reports to the faculty, presentations, workshops, and publications to communicate the importance of assessment and the benefits of involvement.

Stimulating participation and involvement of faculty is one of the goals of any campuswide project. Open communication has proven to be a means of enhancing faculty understanding of assessment's contribution to teaching and curriculum development. It emphasizes the fact that involvement in assessment affords opportunities for personal and professional growth. Assessment coordinators can promote participation and involvement by regularly reporting to the faculty about the progress of all activities and by responding to all questions. The individual faculty members responsible for the direction of the assessment efforts in their academic programs can report regularly at departmental meetings, so that all program faculty are aware of developments that will affect their major. At information-sharing sessions open to the college community, these faculty can share their experiences in planning and implementing the various stages of outcomes assessment. Such sessions provide faculty with opportunities to share ideas and participate in cross-discipline exchanges [see Chapter Sixteen, Case 82].

Denise Gallaro, Gail Cooper Deutsch, Donald Lumsden, Michael E. Knight

The Department of Communications and Theatre at Kean College taps another important source in gathering its assessment information. The department gathers information about the progress and future prospects of its public relations majors by surveying graduates and their employers. The faculty use a survey to assess the types of material that alumni and potential employers feel should be included in student portfolios and the criteria by which portfolios should be judged. Information gathered from the survey is used to improve the senior portfolio assessment program.

> During the fall 1991 semester, a survey of thirty public relations practitioners in New York and New Jersey (the most frequent job markets for graduates) was administered. The respondents included alumni of the program now in management positions, managers who hire our graduates, managers who accept our cooperative education interns, and managers who serve as guest lecturers in public relations classes. The survey asked respondents to indicate what items should be included in the portfolios of entry-job applicants and to list the criteria on which respondents evaluate portfolios. The surveys were anonymous, but return envelopes were coded to indicate the area of public relations in which the respondent works. Follow-up telephone calls stressing the importance of the study were made one week after the surveys were mailed.
>
> Cathleen M. Londino, Freda L. Remmers

Another important and sometimes overlooked group in assessment development is students. Although students are often thought of only as recipients of assessment, they can also be important contributors. At the College of William and Mary, a public Doctoral I institution with an enrollment of 7,500, students have intentionally been incorporated into the assessment process. Graduate and undergraduate students take roles as "assessors." As a result of their involvement, students benefit from the improvements made in teaching and learning on campus, while at the same time learning about the assessment process itself.

> In the early 1990s, state-mandated assessment at William and Mary was directed by a faculty steering committee chaired by the faculty assessment coordinator and supported by two part-time assistants. The coordinator saw practical advantages in introducing assessment research into the curriculum, and equally important, opportunities for students to participate in inherently interesting projects. The coordinator integrated general education assessment into the course outlines: graduate students would assist with instrument design and undergraduates with pretesting and conducting telephone interviews.
>
> Susan Lovegren Bosworth

Several institutions have extended the notion of involvement to include constituency groups external to the campus. Community involvement is a central feature of assessment at the University of Tennessee, Knoxville (public, Research I, 25,900 students). The human service education program at UTK makes a significant effort to prepare marketable graduates for careers in a variety of helping agencies and organizations. As a means of adapting the curriculum of the program to be more responsive to the changing needs of the job market, UTK relies on a survey to tap a crucial source—employers of human service graduates—to assist in predicting future human service needs and in evaluating the performance of students and graduates.

> Sixteen agency supervisors who hire human service graduates have participated in the study. They have been invited to participate in two ways. A survey instructs informants to indicate how valuable given areas of preparation are to successful job performance, and to speculate on the value of those areas in five years. Courses in foreign languages, internships, co-op or field experiences, computer experiences, and grade point averages are examples of the eighteen areas in this section. The survey also asks informants to rate the importance of twenty-one traits to successful job performance, as well as to rate students/ graduates with whom they have worked in the past on those traits. This part of the survey includes items such as speaking effectively, thinking creatively, working cooperatively, and working with people from diverse backgrounds. The second part of the study consists of an interview that allows respondents to elaborate on their responses to the survey and to identify the problems and clients they expect to encounter in the 1990s.
>
> Tricia McClam

Virginia Polytechnic Institute and State University (publicly funded, Research I, 26,000 students) combines internal and external evaluators to assess the learning of its theatre arts students, as well as to gain valuable information about the curriculum. A major feature of the assessment program in theatre arts is its use of outside reviewers. The success of this type of assessment is attributable to the outside reviewers' knowledge of the program and the discipline and to their objectivity in observation because of their distance from the actual learning environment.

> The department conducts senior exit interviews with its graduating seniors. The interviews are conducted by three knowledgeable individuals who are not faculty members in the department. Each session is videotaped for review by the theatre faculty. In an attempt to ensure a degree of honesty from student interviewees, students are promised that the videotapes will not be reviewed until the September following graduation in May. The outside evaluators, although not faculty members in the department, have expertise in the field of theatre. One is a faculty member from another department within Virginia Tech, who has substantial experience as an amateur thespian and director, while the other two are from outside the university. One of the external interviewers is an assistant professor with a specialization in technical theatre at a neighboring university. The other is the associate artistic director of a respected professional theatre in the region.
>
> Gregory W. Justice, John A. Muffo

Conclusion

As these case studies suggest, successful assessment is dependent upon the involvement of many individuals. Each person contributes his or her knowledge, expertise, and perspectives, thereby enhancing the overall assessment program. Assessment therefore works best when it is conceptualized as a group effort.

CHAPTER SEVEN

MAKING DATA MEANINGFUL

Principle Seven

*A*ssessment makes a difference when it begins with issues of use and illuminates questions that people really care about. *Assessment recognizes
the value of information in the process of improvement. But to be useful, information must be connected to issues or questions that people really care about.
This implies assessment approaches that produce evidence that relevant parties
will find credible, suggestive, and applicable to decisions that need to be made.
It means thinking in advance about how the information will be used, and by
whom. The point of assessment is not to gather data and return "results"; it is
a process that starts with the questions of decision makers, that involves them
in the gathering and interpreting of data, and that informs and helps guide
continuous improvement (AAHE, 1992, p. 3).*

The Principle in Context

For many institutions, lack of data is not a barrier to implementing assessment.
In fact, a great number of institutions find themselves awash in data. The data
collected include everything from pre-entry test scores to surveys of student satisfaction with the general college environment. Many colleges and universities are
unaware of the rich sources of information that they currently possess about their

students (for example, student background characteristics, enrollment data, and course-taking patterns). Data are there to be found if one searches, yet they must be organized, manipulated, and applied in meaningful ways. Moreover, those collecting and using the data must not lose sight of the critical issues and needs driving the assessment efforts. Very simply, institutions need to value the data they have and collection needs to be purposeful as they transform the data into useful information; "they should make a conscientious effort to acquire and use better information about student learning, the effects of courses, and the impact of programs" (Study Group on the Conditions of Excellence in American Higher Education, 1984, p. 21).

The challenge for assessment specialists, faculty, and administrators, then, is not collecting data but connecting them. Care must be taken to connect pieces of data that are often drawn from very different sources so that they say something meaningful (Jones, 1982) and are made useful (Knight, Lumsden, and Gallaro, 1991). Care must also be taken to ensure that the research design facilitates the collection of that which is needed (Light, Singer, and Willett, 1990). In other words, as Wright (1993) suggests: "detailed, provocative evidence is . . . far more useful than percentages or percentile scores alone in stimulating faculty discussion" (p. 9).

The information that results from data collection must illuminate issues that are critical to the institution. Several obstacles exist that make this seemingly straightforward proposition difficult. As Kinnick (1985) asserts, a common barrier to information use is that institutions organize "reports around data, not around issues. Too many reports are data driven rather than directed toward concrete problems or established institutional processes" (p. 97). Likewise, Ewell (1984) stresses the notion of standards of relevance. Data must be transformed into policy-relevant information upon which decisions regarding teaching and learning can be meaningfully based.

In the end, key decision makers must value and use the carefully collected data to guide their decisions (Jacobi, Astin, and Ayala, 1987). They must also pay attention to and respect the diverse perspectives found on campuses in order to ensure that recommendations for change are believable and practical (Wright, 1993). In today's higher education environment, characterized by pressure for accountability, efficiency, and productivity, the meaningful use of information may perhaps be one of the most effective tools for institutions seeking to achieve quality with limited resources.

Finally, once the data have been gathered and connected, they still must be reported in compelling ways. There are a number of reporting options, such as newsletters, reports, electronic media, faculty forums, and student leadership workshops. The key is to report the results in ways meaningful to the campus community. Kinnick (1985) illustrates four strategies through which this reporting can be accomplished: (1) disaggregate data, reporting them not only at the campus level but also at a level that meets the needs of individual campus units (departments, service units, and classrooms for example); (2) report data using graphics and comparative formats (illustrate trends for example); (3) publish short issue-specific reports or research briefs on selected topics; and (4) combine outcomes information with other data.

The excerpts that follow detail the many ways in which institutions apply and report valued information toward purposeful ends.

The Principle in Practice

One of the first steps in using data is to inventory, or at least gain a general sense of, the types and sources of information that currently exist at an institution. Oakton Community College, a public Associate of Arts college of 12,800 students, began its assessment process by conducting an audit of institutional data. The audit was motivated by an interest in improving educational programs and services and by an awareness of accreditation reporting needs.

> The assessment audit was designed to compile baseline information about what sorts of data and information about students were being gathered; how these data were stored, accessed, analyzed, and used; and the extent to which duplicative or potentially complementary assessments existed in isolation from each other [see Chapter Sixteen, Case 78].
>
> Trudy Bers, Mary L. Mittler

Similarly, Gainesville College (public, 2,600 students, Associate of Arts) in the University System of Georgia began its assessment program by conducting an inventory of existing data. The intent of the audit was not only to determine what data were already available but also to project future data needs for decision making.

> In 1987, an ad hoc Committee on Institutional Effectiveness was formed to provide leadership in addressing the issue of assessing the college's effectiveness. One of its first major tasks was to inventory the types of data, assessment methods, and assessment instruments already being used. Information was gathered from all academic divisions and cost centers, and a list of more than thirty assessment "methods and inventories" was compiled by the committee. The work of the committee culminated with the establishment in 1988 of the Office of Planning and Institutional Research, whose primary functions are to provide leadership in the development of a more formal and systematic assessment plan and to generate additional data and information required for effective decision making and planning.
>
> Thomas D. Webb

The result of gathering both existing and new information from a variety of campus sources is the creation of a more complete picture of student learning and development. Even within a single department, the collection of data can present a unique snapshot of student learning and departmental effectiveness. At Oklahoma State University, a public land-grant Research II institution of 19,000 students, the collection of departmental data led one faculty member to comment, in a published report then quoted in the case study:

> When all of the [outcomes assessment] data were assembled, a picture quickly developed, much to my surprise, that revealed, at a glance, our strengths and weaknesses. My attitude about the value and usefulness of program outcomes assessment changed completely, and I am now a strong proponent of the process. . . . There is no question in my mind that program outcomes assessment is a valuable tool for identifying program strengths and weaknesses. It won't correct the problems, but it tells you where to start [Hughes, 1993, p. 4] [see Chapter Sixteen, Case 81].
>
> Ben F. Shaw, Jr., Kenneth H. McKinley, Stephen P. Robinson

At some institutions, a single office may be responsible for collecting assessment data. At Ohio University (public, Research II, 19,000 students), one of the offices responsible for data gathering collects information useful to a wide range of constituencies.

> Alumni research collects both general and program-specific information, often simultaneously. The key to using these data successfully is flexibility in meeting and melding a variety of information needs. Through careful coordination with many campus constituencies, this information has been applied to a variety of programs. The colleges, planning groups, individual departments, and university trustees have come to rely on information provided in the alumni research program and use it in both near-term and long-term planning and decision making at Ohio University [see Chapter Thirteen, Case 63].
>
> Gary O. Moden, A. Michael Williford

The meaningful use of data is an important component of the assessment program at the University of North Dakota. This Doctoral II institution of 12,000 students bases its assessment program on the search for answers to important and interesting questions on student learning and institutional effectiveness.

> One effective assessment strategy is to engage questions that are important and interesting. People are motivated to a greater extent when the questions being addressed by assessment seem to be genuinely important. This is one reason, for example, why qualitative, rather than standardized, assessment instruments form the foundation of the assessment program. Additionally, discussions

within the assessment subcommittee reflect the genuine interest of participants. Discussions are often quite spirited, engaging, and even intellectually stimulating—a far cry from the perception that assessment has to be an obscure, technical matter left to institutional research staff and other supposed experts.

Daniel R. Rice, James H. Larson

Shorter College, a private Baccalaureate II college enrolling over 1,200 students and affiliated with the Georgia Baptist Convention, provides another good illustration of an institution that uses data toward meaningful ends. Faculty members in the Division of Mathematics and Computer Science, using results of a program review of the mathematics curriculum, have updated the existing assessment program by providing more direct evidence of student learning through the use of existing data (for example, algorithmic aspects of problem solving and knowledge of vocabulary) embedded within traditional course examinations.

The difficulty is not that faculty do not assess student progress and do not use the results for improvement; in fact, this is traditional in several areas. The difficulty is that in a very small college setting where faculty actually talk about the educational progress of individual students, it is difficult for faculty to appreciate the need to aggregate assessment data across students and courses. In addition, faculty carry a very heavy teaching load of fifteen hours per semester and need assessment methods that add as little as possible to their load. In this setting, the four members of the Division of Mathematics and Computer Science have adopted an assessment method that aggregates data across courses by re-examining data generated by their usual course examinations.

Richard E. Cowan, Patricia DeWitt

Assessment data should be used to improve services. The assessment specialists and library personnel at Liberty University (private, Christian, Master's I, 9,200 students) use a faculty survey, as well as a short student survey, to acquire information on the utilization of library services. The assessment strategy is driven by the belief that library usage is a meaningful measure of student academic integration. The challenge for this particular strategy is to collect the important data in a manageable fashion.

The focus of the study is on obtaining as much information as possible to support efforts toward improving services, while also demonstrating to outside state and accreditation agencies that current services are adequate. Unchecked, this bifurcation of focus might well lead to the development of instruments that are too long and, hence, excessively time consuming for respondents. Efforts are made to keep surveys as short as possible while still gathering a significant amount of important information.

Ellen Lowrie Black, David E. Towles

The reporting format of data is also an important consideration. A number of institutions rely on newsletters, progress reports, and faculty development sessions to make data more meaningful. Assessment specialists at West Georgia College, a Master's I state institution enrolling 7,900 students, employ a number of strategies to encourage the use of data.

> In order to address the need from the academic departments and units for planning information, departmental facts sheets have been developed that display data on the number of quarter credit hours earned and course sections taught, number of full-time equivalent (FTE) students taught, number of academic majors, number of degrees awarded, and grade distribution of majors. In addition, to address the need for more institutional research-related information, the institutional research office has initiated a quarterly newsletter to keep faculty and staff informed of enrollment trends, assessment activity and results, and environmental conditions that may affect institutional research and planning activities.
>
> Charles F. Harrington

Finally, successful assessment programs apply data in policy-relevant ways. Assessment is used as another component of the decision-making process. At Maricopa Community Colleges, a public multisite Associate of Arts institution of 95,000 students, both oral and written reports have been used to provide baseline data on student academic advising. The data are used to establish benchmarks against which progress toward improving advising may be judged.

> The first component of the benchmark-setting exercise was a survey of, and an oral report by, all of the colleges' advising center coordinators. The questions, developed by the DAAC [District Academic Advising Council], were both quantitative and qualitative. A follow-up meeting was then held in which the advising center coordinators discussed their responses with council members. A report was then written to summarize the status of advising programs throughout the district. This report was used in at least three important ways. First, it was shared with the Chancellor's Executive Council, composed of the vice chancellors and college presidents of the Maricopa colleges. Second, the results were used, and continue to be used, to gauge progress made in enhancing advising services at the ten colleges. Third, the report was used to raise the level of governing board and key administrator awareness and concern about the quality of academic advising in the district [see Chapter Thirteen, Case 51].
>
> Michael Rooney, Maria Harper-Marinick

Conclusion

Successful assessment programs know how to use data. As the excerpts in this chapter have suggested, assessment makes a difference when meaningful data are collected, connected, and applied creatively to illuminate questions and provide a basis for decision making. Only then can data guide continuous improvement.

CHAPTER EIGHT

THE IMPORTANT PART IS WHAT YOU DO WITH IT

Principle Eight

*A*ssessment is most likely to lead to improvement when it is part of a *larger set of conditions that promote change.* *Assessment alone changes little. Its greatest contribution comes on campuses where the quality of teaching and learning is visibly valued and worked at. On such campuses, the push to improve educational performance is a visible and primary goal of leadership; improving the quality of undergraduate education is central to the institution's planning, budgeting, and personnel decisions. On such campuses, information about learning outcomes is seen as an integral part of decision making, and avidly sought (AAHE, 1992, p. 3).*

The Principle in Context

Assessment and decision making should go hand in hand. Indeed, as embodied in a number of the cases we have used to illustrate the first seven chapters, assessment and decision making must occur in concert in order for improvements to ensue. In essence, assessment and improvement are often separated by a single important point: assessment focuses on the *what,* improvement on the *what-you-do-with-it.* Linking the two may very well be the most crucial aspect of successful assessment practice. This linking occurs through the process of decision making.

An abundance of research and commentary exists supporting the importance of linking assessment and improvement. Pascarella and Terenzini (1991), in their massive synthesis of research on college outcomes over the last twenty years, urge decision makers to practice what they refer to as "learning-centered management." This management style is characterized by "an orientation to decision making that consistently and systematically takes into account the potential consequences of alternative courses of administrative action for student learning" (p. 656). Noting that financial concerns can be neither ignored nor perceived as the sole determinant in improvement efforts, they stress the need for administrators and faculty to consider carefully the impact of policy decisions on student learning. Colleges and universities, they contend, have an obligation to focus efforts continually on their common mission of facilitating and improving learning.

Other educators, researchers, and assessment specialists echo the sentiments of Pascarella and Terenzini by calling for the intentional and systematic application of assessment data to improve student learning, academic programs, and student services (Astin, 1985; Erwin, 1991; Ewell and Jones, 1994; Study Group on the Conditions of Excellence in American Higher Education, 1984). Given this abundance of advice, it is all the more surprising that as recently as 1992, barely half of the administrators questioned in the American Council on Education's *Campus Trends* survey believed that assessment offered a way to significantly improve undergraduate education (El-Khawas, 1992). In part, this finding reflects the suspicion many administrators have with respect to the misuse of data by external agencies. Despite administrators' views of assessment, it does appear that assessment is catching on, both for accountability and improvement purposes (El-Khawas, 1992).

The degree to which administrators and faculty members perceive assessment information as crucial to their decision making determines the amount of support that an institution allocates to assessment programs (Erwin, 1991). If administrators and policy makers assign only a minor role to data collection and analysis in the planning and operation of an institution, few resources will be allocated to the assessment process. Conversely, if decision makers value the information, resources will follow. Additionally, in difficult financial times, neither states nor institutions feel they can afford assessment that is not clearly connected to decision making. Thus, assessment "must more fully 'enter the institutional bloodstream' to be effective" (Ewell, 1991a, p. 12).

Institutions widely regarded for their assessment programs, such as Kean College of New Jersey, Alverno College, and Northeast Missouri State University, have long histories of using assessment information to guide decision making on matters of the curriculum and resource allocation (Banta and Associates, 1993; Ewell, 1984). Assessment at these institutions has been woven into their decision-making fabric and is a valuable part of their efforts to improve teaching, learning, and the efficient use of institutional resources. These institutions already apply what other institutions are just now learning: "We must cease to rely on intuition alone and begin to be systematic in using data to direct improvements" (Banta, 1993a, p. 153).

Across a wide spectrum of institutions, faculty members and administrators are applying assessment results in meaningful ways focused on improvement. The excerpts that follow highlight institutional improvements occurring both inside and outside the classroom, with respect to the total institutional environment as well as to courses and curricula.

The Principle in Practice

Faculty members in the Department of Communications and Theatre at Kean College of New Jersey (public, Master's I, 11,900 students) incorporate assessment findings in program evaluation. Based on information gathered from student writing samples, speaking, and small-group communications, the faculty have been able to delineate a number of program improvements.

> As a result of assessment, we have recommended the following changes in our program of teaching methods: (1) constantly reinforce, in each course, the concepts and skills taught in the seven departmental core courses; (2) include critical thinking, public speaking, and writing assignments in every course; (3) provide end-of-course written evaluations of each student; (4) revise advisement procedures to clarify each student's specific goals, review feedback forms, and provide early help where deficiencies are noted; (5) clarify objectives at the beginning of every class period and review those objectives during the next class period; (6) adopt a stylebook as a requirement in every course; (7) increase the use in courses of projects that provide services to community groups; (8) expand international studies and cooperative education; (9) develop new courses and restructure existing courses geared toward new and emerging career fields; (10) design a capstone senior seminar course; and (11) design new assessment instruments such as a public relations portfolio.
>
> Cathleen M. Londino, Freda L. Remmers

Likewise, faculty members in the School of Nursing at Tennessee Technological University, a public Master's I university of 8,300 students, promote continuous improvement through the intentional use of outcomes information that includes student and graduate evaluations as well as scores on standardized tests.

> Combining the National League for Nursing Achievement Test and Mosby AssessTest scores gives invaluable direction for curricular development and revision. Assessment data have strengthened the entire program from specific topics to general concepts that thread throughout a single course or several courses. Specific topics that have been identified as deficits by the class as a

whole are reevaluated and restructured by individual faculty. Courses that include general nursing concepts and that are in need of revision have also been
strengthened. For example, when it was recognized that our students were consistently scoring low in nutritional aspects of nursing care, the School of Nursing Curriculum Committee reviewed lectures, courses, levels, and the entire
program and determined that the students needed more content and clinical
experience in the areas of nutrition and the disease process. The lower-division
nursing curriculum provided a general nutrition course that lacked specific theory necessary for nursing practice. Therefore, the faculty decided to require
students to take the course Nutrition in Disease. The clinical laboratory experience was structured to emphasize nutritional content necessary in the delivery
of care.

Darlene A. Franklin

Data from assessment may also be applied to teaching improvements in the
form of faculty development. At Virginia Polytechnic Institute and State University (publicly funded, Research I, 26,000 students), faculty members in the Department of Management have used assessment findings from a student case study
as the impetus to strengthen writing opportunities in the curriculum.

The results of the case analysis showed the need for greater emphasis on written and oral communication skills development. A workshop on integrating
writing into the curriculum, led by English department faculty, was subsequently held and attended by a majority of the faculty members in the Department of Management. Substantial changes in course syllabi to integrate more
effective writing exercises have been undertaken in conjunction with this workshop. Likewise, individual faculty have incorporated more oral communication
experiences into their respective courses. The overall evaluation has been used
to reexamine the entire curriculum in the department, and a thorough over-
haul of the undergraduate management major is currently underway.

Richard E. Wokutch, Larry D. Alexander, John A. Muffo

At Southern Illinois University at Edwardsville (public, Master's I, 11,300 students), Senior Assignments (SRAs) have been instituted as a means of assessing all
senior students in the forty degree-granting undergraduate programs at the institution. Each SRA is designed to allow baccalaureate candidates to demonstrate
the extent to which they meet the general and departmental expectations for graduation. Even though SRAs have only been in existence for a short period, their
influence on improving the teaching and learning environment is evident.

The most visible consequences of SRAs so far are not for the students overall,
but for faculty members, who are beginning to see how they and their students
can benefit. For instance, one social science and two science departments invite

seniors to engage in research under a professor's direction. Students are assessed on a written paper and oral defense of a poster describing their research. Some poster sessions have the air of a departmental party; student-faculty conversations stimulated by the posters can range in depth from technical to speculative and cover the breadth from science to social impact. High-quality posters can go to regional and national meetings and result in publications shared by students and professors. Two of these three departments permit second- and third-year students to work with the seniors, thereby encouraging student mentoring and even collaboration. SRAs of this kind require much energy and commitment. In return they elicit excitement . . . and even publications [see Chapter Eleven, Case 3].

Douglas J. Eder

Faculty engaged in assessment outside their specific departments may also gain valuable information that they can incorporate into improvements in teaching. At Northeast Missouri State University (public, Master's I, 6,200 students), faculty gain in-depth information regarding the teaching and learning environment on campus through their involvement in reading senior portfolios. Faculty involved in this assessment activity not only assist in collecting important institutional data but are also able to inform their own teaching through reflecting on the ideas and themes from these portfolios.

Faculty members who read the portfolios note direct effects on their classroom strategies. From getting ideas for an assignment to making a commitment to enhance expectations for quantitative reasoning in their courses, participating faculty are the most likely to implement findings from the portfolio review as they revise their own courses. Furthermore, faculty other than those directly involved [in the portfolio assessment] can be influenced by discussion of the findings at meetings of governance councils and committees. Findings are also presented to colleagues in divisional meetings, disciplinary meetings, and informal gatherings in university offices and hallways [see Chapter Twelve, Case 30].

W. Jack Magruder, Candace Cartwright Young

Winthrop University, a public Master's I institution enrolling 5,100 students, exemplifies an institution that collects data, analyzes them, and most importantly, utilizes them in pursuit of continuous improvement. As one component of its institutional assessment program, Winthrop University conducts computer-assisted phone surveys of its graduates to gather, among other things, student self-reported data on learning and personal development.

The computer-assisted interviews have produced a wide variety of results pertaining to the university's curriculum in general education and major fields and

to career preparation and advising. They have also provided systematic infor
mation on the postgraduate activities of alumni. For example, although about
eight in ten alumni indicate that they would attend Winthrop again if they
were to start college over, about 20 percent state that they would choose a different major. Results point to the need for earlier and greater student access to
information about careers in various major fields and improved career services
and advising. Findings also indicate that higher percentages of undergraduates
are obtaining jobs related to their field of study than was previously believed by
faculty in some disciplines, and this emphasizes the importance of the role faculty play in preparing students for such employment or postgraduate studies.

Joseph S. Prus, Elnora W. Stuart

Finally, assessment information can be used for improvements not only inside
the classroom but also outside. Combining the creative resources of staff from a
number of academic and student service units, faculty and staff at Ball State University (public, Doctoral I, 20,700 students) have developed a first-year survey
called Making Achievement Possible (MAP). The MAP survey covers a number
of important institutionwide topics, such as retention, college involvement, and
academic and life goals. Results from the survey have been used to improve the
overall institutional environment in a number of ways.

Making Achievement Possible provides the basis for a discussion between students and their academic advisers during their initial meeting. In contrast,
residence hall directors use the information in less formal ways as a basis for
counseling students with respect to adjustment in the halls. The results of MAP
have also been used by residence hall directors for program planning. For example, some residence hall directors have set up study skills sessions for those
students who have indicated they may need additional assistance with study
skills.

Catherine Palomba, Trina Stout

Conclusion

Successful assessment is directed toward improvements. Those improvements may
occur in teaching, student learning, academic and support programs, or institutional effectiveness. The bottom line is that assessment information must be applied systematically toward improvements if it is to have a lasting impact on the
institution.

CHAPTER NINE

ACCOUNTABILITY:
THE TRAIN IS LEAVING THE STATION

Principle Nine

*T*hrough assessment, educators meet responsibilities to students and to the public. There is a compelling public stake in education. As educators, we have a responsibility to the publics that support or depend on us to provide information about the ways in which our students meet goals and expectations. But that responsibility goes beyond the reporting of such information; our deeper obligation—to ourselves, our students, and society—is to improve. Those to whom educators are accountable have a corresponding obligation to support such attempts at improvement (AAHE, 1992, p. 3).

The Principle in Context

This ninth principle is for many faculty members, administrators, and assessment specialists the most contentious. In the midst of higher education's penchant for reflection, self-study, and self-regulation, calls for public accountability seem to chafe at the very soul of the academic enterprise. It is curious that while educators and researchers have for years stressed the benefits of a college education for both the individual and society (Bowen, 1977; Leslie and Brinkman, 1988), efforts by the public to raise questions of accountability at the institutional level have often been met with disdain.

As Ewell (1994) notes, some of the movement toward greater accountability in higher education has in fact been championed by individuals within the academy. The influential report of the Study Group on the Conditions of Excellence in American Higher Education (1984), though focusing primarily on assessment for improvement, urges accrediting agencies to insist on accountability by holding institutions responsible for formulating clear statements of expectations for student learning, developing appropriate assessment programs to gauge progress in meeting the expectations, and ensuring "systematic efforts to improve learning as a result of those assessments" (p. 69). Calls for reform, then, are clearly coming from sources both internal and external to higher education.

As pressure from outside the academy has increased, institutions have felt it necessary to respond to accountability mandates from accrediting agencies and state governments. This pressure has been so strong that by late 1986, institutions reported being more compelled to undertake assessment activities in response to state government pressures than to engage in assessment activities to support curriculum reform initiatives (El-Khawas, 1987).

A large part of the increased accountability pressures on higher education stem from concern about the effective use of publicly invested funds (Ewell, 1991b). Legislators, students, parents, and others have been vocal about their perception of "value" in higher education. Like bargain hunters in a department store, parents and students, in particular, have been interested in finding the best product at the lowest cost. Likewise, employers are demanding that students graduate with skills that translate in beneficial ways into the job market.

Those within the academy have not, for the most part, been receptive to these intrusions. Many faculty disdain accountability pressures and argue that to maintain the integrity of higher education, public agencies must not become involved in the affairs of institutions. They contend that external pressures often force them to measure that which matters least and neglect the most essential traditions of higher education.

Unlike faculty who call for resistance to outside pressures, Ewell (1991a) suggests that if we educators stand on the sidelines during debates over accountability measures (for example, national education goals, student right-to-know legislation, and state postsecondary review entities), we "run the dangerous risk of being left out of the first truly national effort to shape education policy in decades, and the consequent danger at a later point of a far greater intrusion based on protocols we had no hand in shaping" (p. 17). It would appear, then, that the accountability train is leaving the station; we can either jump aboard and attempt to steer it, or stand on the tracks and be run over by it.

Evidence exists that assessment activities do in fact lead to improvements in educational programs on college and university campuses (Banta and Associates, 1993). At the same time, however, these assessment efforts, designed and implemented to demonstrate institutional accountability, have generated little information that external publics find helpful. A clear need exists, then, "for academics to address decision-makers' needs for accountability data if the provision of resources to support those improved programs is to continue in the future" (Banta and Borden, 1994, p. 96).

The Principle in Practice

Colleges and universities with a broad view of accountability recognize their responsibility to a number of publics. Kean College of New Jersey (public, Master's I, 11,900 students) communicates broadly with its external constituencies in order to help ensure the successful implementation of assessment.

> *External audiences* for outcomes assessment in higher education include employers, graduate and professional schools, business leaders, governmental agencies, prospective students and parents, high school counselors, alumni, and financial supporters. The primary goal of communicating with this diverse audience is to convey the message that the assessment process will enhance the quality of education at the institution, thus adding prestige and integrity to the school's degrees [see Chapter Sixteen, Case 82].
>
> Denise Gallaro, Gail Cooper Deutsch, Donald Lumsden, Michael E. Knight

Similarly, the University of Houston-Victoria, a Master's I public institution enrolling 1,200 students, understands the important role its various constituent groups play on campus. As one of the components of their strategic planning process, institutional leaders have decided to acknowledge more fully the priorities and needs of the school's many publics by focusing on institutional quality at all levels.

> The age of management wish lists and self-serving faculty demands has given way to a recognition that the university serves a prioritized set of customer groups, both internal and external. The university is now seen by all as responsible to each of these groups for turning out credible and reliable products in terms of its graduates, retraining and personal improvement services, efficiency in rendering procedural service, and applied research and other community services.
>
> Paul A. Wagner, Larry Robinson

One of the groups to which institutions are increasingly called to be accountable is made up of employers. At the State Technical Institute at Memphis, a public Associate of Arts technical college of 11,100 students, employer satisfaction receives a high priority, given the institution's mission to prepare students for employment.

When the mission of a college is to prepare workers for immediate employment in technical fields, the importance of employers' satisfaction with graduates and graduates' satisfaction with employment cannot be overstated. This approval is so important that the Technology Accreditation Commission of the Accreditation Board for Engineering and Technology makes assessing it a requirement for all programs seeking accreditation. . . . To measure employers' satisfaction with graduates and graduates' satisfaction with employment, the department chairperson of chemical engineering technology periodically conducts systematic mailed surveys. The survey that is sent to employers identifies the graduate who is employed and is directed to the graduate's immediate supervisor. Both the supervisor and graduates are asked to (1) describe the work being done by the graduate; (2) classify the level of work (skilled craftsperson, salesperson, engineering technologist, engineering technician, supervision or management, engineering, other); (3) express an opinion about whether the graduate's educational background qualifies him or her for the work he or she is doing; (4) express an opinion about the advancement potential within the company for the graduate; (5) indicate whether or not the supervisor would seek more employees with the same educational background; (6) express an opinion about the graduate's educational weaknesses in performing present assignments and in advancing in the organization; (7) express an opinion about whether or not the graduate is qualified to perform the work of an engineering technician; and (8) rank a list of ten program objectives [in terms of their] importance in performing work [see Chapter Eleven, Case 6].

Janice Van Dyke, George W. Williams

Likewise, accountability to employers is an important aspect of the assessment program for faculty in the social work program at Kean College of New Jersey. Information collected on students regarding their fieldwork experiences is used for both improvement and accountability purposes. There are many reasons why this particular assessment strategy is successful.

First, fieldwork evaluations are completed by agency-based field instructors who hold master of social work (M.S.W.) degrees and have completed at least two years of post-M.S.W. practice experience. As such, they are external to both the program and the college, lending credibility to this method of assessment. Second, field instructors are typical of the professionals who will be employing program graduates, and by using their assessments, it is possible to assure that concerns that might exist in the practice environment as well as the academic environment will be addressed. Third, the material covered by fieldwork evaluations includes all three components on which the program must be assessed: knowledge, values, and skills. To assess the ability of students to perform in a professional role, assessment has to reach beyond the confines of the classroom experience, and field experience is designed to do just that. Fourth, since all students are evaluated at four points during the field experience, it is possible to do time series measurement of the pattern of professional growth of students in the program to determine not only whether the required knowledge, values, and skills develop but also in what sequence. Fifth, this approach allows the social work program to develop a performance-based assessment using a criterion-based measurement process. The data gathered in the process are utilized to guide program evolution and growth [see Chapter Eleven, Case 21].

Carol J. Williams, Dorothy Marie Rizzo

The group for whom assessment strategies have been most beneficial is students. Successful assessment programs recognize the importance of measuring and improving student learning and, therefore, demonstrate accountability to students. To assess student learning in the core program at Fairleigh Dickinson University, a private Master's I institution of 11,000 students, students must write about the three most influential ideas they have encountered in the program. They are asked to respond in two ways: (1) the paradigmatic mode (similar to an essay) and (2) the narrative mode (similar to a personal account) (Bruner, 1990). Faculty believe that the narrative mode is particularly helpful for students as they try to make connections between college and their own lives.

Although college and university faculty and administrators, the general public, and state and federal legislators undoubtedly hope students will apply some of what they learn to their lives and act in ways that will improve individual and collective well-being, rarely do these hopes translate themselves into assessments that look at how students personally make sense of what they are learning and utilize that learning in their lives (that is, how they learn in the narrative mode). Thus, students' own perspectives on what they are learning and what they think is important are largely overlooked.

Mary H. Beaven

Not only is it important to consider the various groups to which institutions are accountable, it is also crucial to pay attention to the ways in which that accountability is communicated. Midlands Technical College (public, Associate of Arts, 9,100 students) uses a variety of communication tools and media to demonstrate its responsibilities to the larger community.

Two of the most important aspects of institutional effectiveness are using results of data collection to effect change and making constituencies aware of the college's commitment to accountability. At Midlands Technical College, assessment results are communicated through an array of published reports including an annual *Institutional Effectiveness Report Card,* a detailed update on progress toward annual objectives prepared for the board of trustees; and the *Community*

Report, the executive summary of the report card, with additional highlights that demonstrate the college's accountability to the public [see Chapter Sixteen, Case 79].

James L. Hudgins, Dorcas A. Kitchings, Starnell K. Williams

Conclusion

Accountability demands have arrived, whether higher education institutions like it or not. As the case excerpts in this chapter illustrate, effective assessment programs measure outcomes and then inform their many publics of the ways in which campus programs and services positively affect students, the community, and society. Assessment, then, is an important component in demonstrating institutional accountability.

CHAPTER TEN

PERHAPS THERE ARE TEN?

The nine principles of good practice for assessing student learning provide comprehensive and focused guidance on what works in assessment. However, several recurring themes in accounts of successful practice on a variety of college campuses suggest that the principles are somewhat incomplete. In their original conceptualization of the AAHE principles of good practice, the twelve authors clearly articulated the concept that "there is no one best way of conducting assessment . . . but effective practices *do* have features in common" (Hutchings, 1993, p. 6). We wholeheartedly concur. We therefore offer a tenth principle, one based on the experiences related by faculty members, assessment specialists, student affairs staff, and administrators in the case studies we examined.

Our tenth principle is a composite encompassing several distinct, straightforward characteristics of good practice. Collectively, however, the characteristics shape an assessment environment that is much more difficult to discuss and grasp than those individual characteristics. Principle 10 asserts: *Assessment is most effective when undertaken in an environment that is receptive, supportive, and enabling.* More specifically, successful assessment requires an environment characterized by effective leadership, administrative commitment, adequate resources (for example, clerical support and money), faculty and staff development opportunities, and time. Although many of these characteristics have been addressed briefly in our discussion of the nine principles, we feel they are sufficiently important to merit their own treatment in this chapter, given their combined effect in establishing an environment conducive to good practice in assessment.

The Principle in Context

Of the first nine principles, the eighth comes closest to capturing the essence of our tenth principle. However, whereas principle eight addresses the conditions under which assessment is used for decision making leading to improvement, principle ten highlights the broader context within which successful assessment must occur. In other words, principle ten is a foundational notion composed of identifiable characteristics. While it is difficult to define how the individual characteristics combine to create an institutional environment that is supportive of assessment, we suspect those engaged in assessment know it when they have achieved it.

It is quite clear from the case studies we reviewed for this book that effective administrative and faculty leadership is an essential condition if assessment is to succeed on campus. Effective leadership, as evidenced in the "success factors" described in the cases in Part Two, is a means to offset some of the institutional barriers to change. These barriers include (1) complexity of assessment; (2) professional sensitivity toward assessment (that is, the view that assessment is a threat to academic freedom and the appropriate exercise of faculty judgment); (3) political sensitivity toward assessment; and (4) the time necessary to implement assessment efforts (Miller, 1988).

Administrative leadership and support for assessment is important for another reason. As Astin (1976) notes: "Strong administrative backing serves at least two critical functions: it provides committee members with an incentive to move ahead with the project and to find policy-relevant recommendations in the data; and it maximizes the chances that the recommendations will be put into action" (p. 65). Assessment data and results that are not used toward the purpose of improving the teaching and learning environment on campus, nor incorporated into the overall institutional mission and goals, fall far short of their potential in terms of creating exciting, beneficial, and lasting change for institutions.

Assessment will not succeed without a supply of necessary resources including materials, clerical support, and faculty and staff development opportunities. Undertaking a new assessment program also requires at least some financial support, irrespective of the size of the program. Expenses may include release time for faculty, instrument purchase or development, mailings, and salaries for additional clerical and support staff, to name a few. Additionally, visible incentives and rewards to promote faculty and staff involvement may be necessary (Astin, 1985). At a minimum, faculty and staff development opportunities will be needed to help ensure that all participants are adequately prepared to implement assessment.

It is also quite clear from the case studies submitted to us that successful assessment takes time. Since assessment efforts strike to the heart of the institutional mission—teaching and learning—it should come as no surprise that the adoption of assessment on a particular campus requires a commitment over a period of time. This commitment reflects the process aspect of assessment—developing, introducing, modifying, institutionalizing, and continually improving strategies and programs (Miller, 1990). And this process takes patience and perseverance. As Terenzini (1993) states: "In the United States, the institutions we hold up as exemplars in the assessment business have been about their work for a decade or more. Let us not expect to make significant, substantive changes in quality assessment overnight" (p. 13). Fortunately, however, it is never too late to begin the process.

Assessment, then, is most effective when it occurs in a receptive, supportive, and enabling environment. The following excerpts highlight the many characteristics that this environment comprises.

The Principle in Practice

Leadership is crucial. Leadership in assessment may come from an individual or a group of individuals. It may also originate from the administration, the faculty, or the student development staff. At Indiana University Kokomo, a public Master's II institution of nearly 4,000 students, acknowledgment of the importance of public speaking and the introduction of a new approach to teaching public speaking have led to an effort to assess perceived learning outcomes from the course. A questionnaire has been designed to elicit student responses to perceptions of course content, learning, and expectations. The success of the program has been attributed to leadership from both faculty and administrators.

> The overall success of this assessment can be attributed to a range of factors. That an assessment program was undertaken at all is a reflection of the vice chancellor of academic affairs' commitment to use assessment as a means of upgrading instructional quality. The success of this particular assessment is a product of team effort among the speech communication faculty.
>
> Samuel G. Lawrence, Susan Sciame-Giesecke

Likewise, assessment efforts at Santa Clara University, a private Master's I university of 7,700 students, have been guided by administrative leadership and constituent support. The actual assessment strategy focuses on assessing the critical thinking disposition of new students. The success of this research program has been attributed to a number of factors, including:

> (1) Leadership from the dean, not just as a source of funding but as a coinvestigator, which conveys a sense of significance and priority to this research; (2) enthusiastic cooperation from the student development area, particularly those staff and students who organize freshman week; and (3) adequate funding to purchase instruments and have them scored.
>
> Peter A. Facione, Joanne Gainen, Noreen C. Facione

At Winthrop University (public, Master's I, 5,100 students), leadership for developing assessment in student writing originates with the faculty. The interdisciplinary Writing Assessment Committee formed by the faculty examines changes in student writing from entry to exit. Success for this strategy has been credited to a concerted effort by faculty to broaden the discussions about student writing through collaborative, interdisciplinary dialogue.

> In 1989, interest in and concern about student writing ability—the area of focus embodied in the first goal of the university's general education curriculum—led concerned faculty to establish the interdisciplinary Writing Assessment Committee. Since the time of its formation, the committee has been responsible for creating a multifaceted approach to writing assessment to complement data on student writing performance obtained from a commercially developed standardized test used at the university.
>
> Margaret Tebo-Messina, Joseph S. Prus

Administrative support is a necessary condition for successful assessment, but this support does not necessarily have to entail the creation of a large administrative structure. At the University of Richmond, a private Master's I institution of approximately 4,300 students, the institutional assessment model is intentionally designed to be decentralized and administratively lean. The assessment efforts receive guidance from the office of the vice president for planning and through the Institutional Advisory Assessment Group that comprises twenty faculty and staff.

> The "findings" of the assessment experience affirm the notion that effective institutional assessment in higher education can occur without the creation of a new and separate administrative structure that can be cumbersome, invasive to the academic program, and expensive. The University of Richmond chose to respond to the need for institutional assessment without building an "empire," and it is clear that this plan of action may be both effective and efficient for other colleges and universities. Building a model of assessment that is economical also permits the institution to direct its resources toward other and, perhaps more central, elements of the academic program. At a time when faculty, administrators, trustees, and the public at large are looking for ways to streamline administration without sacrificing function, the University of Richmond's approach may be worthy of consideration.
>
> John A. Roush

Faculty and staff development is an important aspect of assessment. The implementation of a comprehensive program requires faculty, staff, students, and administrators to change some of their notions about teaching, learning, and the uses of assessment data. Developmental activities are an important means for facilitating this change. The University of Montevallo, a small public Master's I institution of 3,300 students, has used faculty development workshops as an important way to familiarize faculty with assessment. Specifically, the art department has introduced developmental activities to alter faculty members' perceptions about portfolio reviews.

> The College of Fine Arts has been conducting workshops for faculty on assessment for three years, and faculty have had the opportunity to attend other workshops on campus and at nearby institutions. The dean of fine arts participated in an assessment workshop at Alverno College and provided leadership for our assessment efforts.
>
> Sandra J. Jordan, Julia S. Rogers

At Central Missouri State University, a public Master's I university of 11,200 students, faculty development in the English department occurs through retreats. To facilitate the process of developing goals and objectives for English majors, the faculty use retreats to provide the focused setting necessary to carry out their work. Assessment is viewed as a means not only for improving the English program on campus but also for bringing together the faculty to discuss teaching and learning issues.

> Retreats must be carefully organized in order to utilize time to the fullest. For instance, faculty have discussed the application and evaluation of goals, an entry/exit component to the major, and the use of portfolios in assessment in the major. A workshop format, facilitated by faculty members from the departments, has been used. To keep discussion focused, questions are provided on handouts, and worksheets are directed and specific. Faculty have discovered through the process that moving retreats away from campus provides a better use of time since participants are not tempted to come and go. This basic format has been adopted for other retreats throughout subsequent semesters. Not only have faculty learned how to construct productive retreats that best focus discussion on assessment issues but also other nontraditional gatherings (outside departmental and committee meetings) have become more frequent.
>
> Deborah Alfino Wilson, Melanie S. Thomas

Adequate resources are a necessary component of successful assessment strategies on many campuses. At Northeast Missouri State University (public, Master's I, 6,200 students), faculty members are compensated for their work in evaluating senior portfolios. The portfolios are used to review student work to assess a variety of learning outcomes, including gains in critical thinking, interdisciplinary synthesis, scientific reasoning, and aesthetic appreciation.

Twenty faculty members are paid $500 each to participate in reading portfolios the week after spring graduation. Faculty frequently hesitate when asked but, once in the process, find it very rewarding. Anytime you get twenty faculty members in a room to talk about student learning for an extended period of time, good things happen. For many faculty, the week provides them with a better picture of student learning and the university experience than any other university committee or activity in which they engage. Faculty are exposed to the range of assignments our students are asked to complete. A science faculty member has to grapple with the aesthetic sophistication of student-written poetry, and a literature professor has to evaluate student mathematical-reasoning ability. Faculty generally finish the week having a renewed appreciation for the university experience and also having a better developed sense of areas in need of improvement. The opportunity for faculty to engage in active learning is one of the best consequences of the effort [see Chapter Twelve, Case 30].

W. Jack Magruder, Candace Cartwright Young

Radford University, a state-supported Master's I university of 9,400 students, uses an institutionally sponsored grant program to encourage and support faculty development of multiple-assessment approaches. Faculty prepare and submit proposals for funding, which typically average less than $2,000.

Among the activities funded through these proposals are focus-group interviews of current students and alumni, mail surveys of employers and potential employers, use of external evaluations of program development, use of facilitators for departmental revision of outcomes, purchase of standardized test instruments, and travel for assessment-related conferences. The School of Nursing, for instance, has used the money to (1) sponsor a faculty development workshop to diagnose difficulties in its systematic evaluation process; (2) survey twenty-five employer-graduate dyads to obtain time-referenced, developmental feedback on knowledge and skills and to determine how both graduates and employers evaluate graduates' skills over time; and (3) survey clinical specialists in home health care nursing who have completed the M.S. program, to identify areas—from teaching strategies and practicum experiences to curricular issues—in which the program needs improvement.

Steven M. Culver

Resources may assume a variety of forms. At Virginia Commonwealth University, a public Research I institution of 21,800 students, a number of institutional resources have been brought to bear on the task of developing and implementing assessment in the Bachelor of Social Work (B.S.W.) program. The specific strategy focuses on the contributions of the B.S.W. program to the professional writing competence of its graduates. Success of the program is attributed to a number of factors including leadership, involvement, clerical assistance, and financial support.

> All B.S.W. faculty are involved. The director of the program assumes the leadership and provides appropriate clerical support. The office of assessment funds the training of the faculty in holistic scoring and provides small financial incentives for participation.
>
> Barbara S. Fuhrmann

Finally, lack of resources is cited as a reason for the failed implementation of an assessment strategy at the University of Missouri-Kansas City, a Doctoral I institution of 9,800 students. The university had attempted to implement an exam for graduating seniors to assess skills across a number of departments. The assessment of communication skills—the particular area of interest for the Department of Communications—was abandoned primarily because of a lack of resources.

> Several negative factors caused us to abandon our plans to introduce a departmental test. Those factors included (1) no faculty reward structure; (2) no release time; and (3) no financial commitment accompanying the project. As a result, there was no financial incentive to continue the extensive work of developing, administering, and analyzing the departmental test results.
>
> Joan E. Aitken

Conclusion

A supportive environment, characterized by effective leadership, administrative commitment, adequate resources, developmental opportunities, and time is important for effective assessment. These components, though indirectly mentioned in the nine AAHE principles of good practice, are important enough in their own right to deserve focused attention from faculty, administrators, and assessment specialists. For indeed, without a supportive environment, most assessment efforts will fail to take root and grow.

PART TWO

CAMPUS EXAMPLES OF EFFECTIVE ASSESSMENT PRACTICES

In Part One, we discussed the AAHE Assessment Forum's *Principles of Good Practice for Assessing Student Learning* (American Association for Higher Education, 1992), illustrating them with excerpts from some of the 165 campus cases collected for this book. In Part Two, we turn to the specific areas of assessment that concern campus leaders: student achievement in the major (Chapter Eleven) and in general education (Chapter Twelve), student cognitive and affective development (Chapter Thirteen), classroom assessment (Chapter Fourteen), faculty development for assessment (Chapter Fifteen), and overall institutional effectiveness (Chapter Sixteen). In each of these areas, we provide a variety of brief descriptions of effective assessment approaches, written by the individuals who have developed and implemented them. Each of the eighty-six descriptions, or cases, is organized according to a common format:

background and purpose of the approach, description of the method(s) used, findings or outcomes of the assessment, use of the findings, and usually, factors contributing to the success of the approach.

Each chapter in Part Two begins with a "Chapter Guide" and a narrative introduction, the "Chapter Overview," which serve as detailed tables of contents for the cases. We also describe our rationales for any special groupings of cases and for the sequence in which the cases are presented.

In introducing the two principal sections of Part Two, those dealing with assessment in the major (Chapter Eleven) and in general education (Chapter Twelve), we have called attention to especially well-developed components of each of the reports in the areas of purpose, methods, use of findings, and success factors. We have looked for such characteristics as these:

Purpose. The purpose for carrying out the assessment approach is clearly stated. Student expectations are explicit and shared with the students.

Method. Methods are selected or constructed by faculty, and attention is paid to establishing the reliability and validity of instruments.

Findings. Assessment findings are detailed and related to the purposes stated earlier.

Use. Those who have responsibility for the outcomes being assessed are involved in selecting methods and implementing assessment. Assessment findings are communicated to these stakeholders, who then make use of the findings to improve their practice.

Success factors. Assessment that works—that leads to real improvement—is most often characterized by these features: (1) strong leadership for assessment initiatives; (2) relationship to goals that are valued within the institution, such as the improvement of teaching and learning; and (3) an ongoing commitment to using assessment findings to improve practice.

The descriptions of campus practice included in Chapters Eleven through Sixteen were selected for their strength overall, but each has some particularly interesting features. These features are summarized in the "look for" paragraph that introduces each case.

CHAPTER ELEVEN

ASSESSING STUDENT ACHIEVEMENT IN THE MAJOR

Chapter Guide

The chapter guide lists the cases contained in this chapter by institution, by subject area, by assessment method, and by case strengths. Institutions are organized by Carnegie Classification. The location of each institution and its approximate enrollment follow the institution name. The relevant case numbers follow each entry.

Institutions

Subject Areas

Assessment Methods

Case Strengths

Chapter Overview

This chapter contains case studies that exemplify the experience of two-year and four-year institutions in assessing student achievement in the major. The studies include specific examples of assessment practice in the fine arts, humanities, social science, and natural science disciplines. While it was not possible to provide descriptions of assessment in every discipline available for study on the nation's campuses, educators will find a wide variety of methods characterized here and a large number that might be applied in any given discipline.

The discussion of assessing student achievement in the major begins with nine descriptions (Cases 1 through 5D) that have particularly strong *purpose* statements. The first case is a detailed description of the context for assessment in a department facing an external assessment mandate from an accrediting agency. A step-by-step process is delineated for achieving a sense of ownership of assessment among faculty. Case 2 contains eight explicit goals for student learning and a matrix that illustrates how student achievement of each goal is measured via one or more of six assessment methods employed in a senior capstone course.

Cases 3 and 4 depict the role of Senior Assignments (SRAs) in a campuswide assessment program that measures student achievement at entry, midpoint, and exit. The first of these related cases is a detailed description of the process used to encourage faculty in forty academic disciplines to design methods appropriate for assessing student achievement of desired educational outcomes. The second describes the SRA in the psychology major.

Cases 5, 5A, 5B, 5C, and 5D are also related. Case 5 describes the setting and purpose for each of four specific departmental projects at the same college. Cases 5A through 5D then tell how these departments use a Sophomore-Junior Diagnostic Project in the major as a midpoint assessment of clearly articulated collegewide generic skills, such as critical thinking, effective writing, and oral communication skills.

The second group of cases in this chapter (6 through 14) illustrates the variety of *methods* that disciplinary faculty across the country have developed for assessing student outcomes. Case 6, from a two-year institution, shows how consistent systematic use of surveys for graduates and their employers can help faculty keep their curricula current in terms of meeting employers' needs. Case 7 exemplifies the power of multiple measures—tests, surveys, capstone experiences, and portfolios—in convincing faculty of the need to undertake new efforts to promote student learning. Case 8 presents evidence that faculty can create multilevel scoring criteria for grading student work and thus gain access to a level of detail about student learning that clearly suggests where improvements in curricula and instruction are needed.

Cases 9 and 10 detail two different approaches to assessing student achievement in foreign languages. Case 9 focuses on reading and listening comprehension in a curriculum for students minoring in French. Case 10 includes a form for rating students' oral proficiency in Spanish.

Cases 11 and 12 illustrate the value of using external examiners as assessors of student work. In Case 11, teachers and principals serve as critics of professional portfolios prepared by senior education majors. In Case 12, members of a citizens' advisory committee assist in evaluating the portfolios of business technology students.

Case 13 comes from a research university where faculty have applied research methods to outcomes assessment. In a seminar setting, the faculty raised questions about their program, then used existing data from student records as well as new information derived from questionnaires, interviews, and focus groups to formulate responses.

The final entry in the methods series (Case 14) originated in a master's degree program. This illustration of student self-assessment takes place in an assessment colloquium in which students develop attitudes and skills in reflective practice. Faculty learned from this colloquium that they needed to make changes in curriculum, methods of instruction, and administrative processes.

Rich *use of findings* characterizes descriptions 15 through 23. The first in this series, Case 15, illustrates that simply calling the attention of students and faculty to scores on a national licensing exam can improve student performance on this highly visible measure of program quality. Case 16 shows how careful monitoring of licensing exam scores over more than a decade at one institution has produced changes in curriculum and classroom assessment and has contributed to attainment of the remarkable record of 100 percent pass rates for thirteen years.

A more coherent, integrated curriculum was a result of the group interviews of senior majors described in Case 17. Mathematics faculty discovered that students were very likely at the senior level to have forgotten basic concepts learned early in their program. Thus, faculty took steps to ensure that those concepts would be applied again in upper-division courses.

In response to written suggestions made at the time of exit testing, one department formed a psychology student advisory council (Case 18). The council is responsible for recommending a second research course, additional lab experiences, and extended discussions about ethics—all of which were approved and implemented by the faculty.

Noteworthy improvements in assessment methodology occurred in a business course (Case 19) following the involvement of employers as assessors of student plans for use of venture capital. Cases 20 and 21, respectively, illustrate how careful study of the results of evaluating student internship experiences in sociology and social work have led faculty to undertake important new directions in the sociology curriculum and the training of field supervisors in social work.

Feedback from alumni and employers produced the departmental changes described in Cases 22 and 23. In Case 22, a dairy science department made changes in its published curriculum description and in academic and career advising of students after faculty discovered that only one-third of their graduates were employed in dairying. In Case 23, civil engineering faculty undertook improvements in computing resources, laboratory facilities, and the teaching of writing and speaking after hearing reports from current students, summarized by alumni/employers.

Case 24 contains an impressive list of *success factors*. A fourteen-step plan for developing assessment strategies and using the findings has been developed and shared with faculty in a series of workshops, technical manuals, and newsletters.

Setting the Context for Assessment

Inga Baird Hill

CASE 1: BALL STATE UNIVERSITY

Look for: Detailed description of the context for assessment, especially the relationship between assessment and professional accreditation and that between behavioral goals for students and instructional practices. Careful planning of assessment called attention to inconsistencies in expected student outcomes and teaching strategies in multisection core courses; faculty have addressed these inconsistencies.

Background and Purpose

The accreditation process for colleges of business has changed significantly since 1990. The American Assembly of Collegiate Schools of Business (AACSB), under competitive pressure to make business schools accountable, has developed and implemented new accreditation standards. Under the previous system, topics required by the AACSB had to be covered, typically in a course dedicated to each topic. Evaluation visits by accreditation teams usually involved ensuring that sufficient time was devoted in the classroom to such subjects as accounting, production, international business, ethics, finance, and marketing. Other resources were also evaluated, such as number of courses taught by professors with doctorates, student credit hour teaching load, and adequacy of the library and physical facilities. In contrast, the new accreditation system is based on the establishment by each college of a unique mission and objectives statement, accompanied by an assessment program to show that the objectives are being met.

In anticipation of this change and the necessity to prepare for accreditation review in nine years, the dean of the College of Business at Ball State University asked the college's Curriculum Committee to develop a program that would function effectively despite the ambiguity of evolving accreditation standards. Although the final form of the standards was not known at the time the charge was given, it was clear that fundamental changes were under way.

As the first step in the process, the department chairs in business met with the dean to develop a mission statement. This statement reflects the applied nature of research expected of faculty as well as the emphasis on excellence in undergraduate teaching that is the distinguishing characteristic of Ball State University (BSU).

In a next step, the Curriculum Committee met with department chairs to brainstorm objectives in each of the content areas in the mission statement. The resulting list was circulated to participants, who rated the objectives as to their importance. The objectives were then condensed into a list of skills, knowledge, and values all College of Business graduates were expected to have. Emphasis was placed on behavioral objectives related to student performance rather than on teacher activities.

During the 1992–93 year, professors teaching each of the core courses were asked to describe the objectives they were trying to achieve in those courses. Forms were developed to help them identify behavioral goals and the instructional activities and media used to teach the goals. These goal statements were collected by the department chairs and reviewed by the Curriculum Committee. Then these professors met with members of the Curriculum Committee and the dean's staff to condense the goals and review the statements of current practice.

The evaluation of the goals to assure adequate coverage of AACSB standards and the BSU College of Business mission proceeded in the fall of 1993. The difficult task of looking at the nine courses in the College of Business core was tackled by the Curriculum Committee. Redundancies and gaps were identified, and the configuration of the core as a whole was examined.

Method

Several professors spent the summer of 1993 developing an assessment plan to present to the faculty to move their thinking forward into the evaluation of goal accomplishment. Nine assessment activities were suggested to faculty, ranging from senior, alumni, and employer surveys to standardized senior exams, use of common questions on multisection course exams, and videotapes of student case presentations. A time frame for developing and implementing the complete program was decided upon.

The faculty responsible for each course met during the fall of 1993 to plan the adoption and implementation of at least one assessment method during spring semester 1994. Experimentation was encouraged so that experience could be gained with a variety of techniques. Professors were also encouraged to consider revision of course goals if they felt objectives needed to be addressed that were not currently part of the course outline. Repeatedly, it was stressed that assessment was a dynamic, evolving process that could provide professors with information useful to them in enhancing their teaching.

Findings

Involvement of faculty in every step of the process has begun to build a comfort level with identifying goals, discussing assessment of progress toward the goals in a nonthreatening, nonpersonal manner, and identifying developmental needs. A significant inconsistency existed in the teaching activities and student outcomes in different sections of multisection core courses. The assessment process highlighted the seriousness of this problem and provided a framework within which it could be addressed without raising academic freedom issues.

Through grappling with identifying course goals, faculty gained a real understanding of how significantly the accreditation process has changed and how important it is that they coordinate their classroom efforts with their colleagues— in order to build a better program not only for their students but ultimately for themselves. Assessment moved from being a tool of the promotion and tenure process to a tool for curriculum review and development.

Yet the excitement of talking with other faculty about *teaching* was perhaps the best outcome. Faculty had concluded that doing research was the most effective way to succeed in the college. The process of explicitly focusing on teaching and creating a mechanism for discussing it, questioning ends and methods, and exchanging ideas about it sent clear messages to faculty that teaching was the important function of the college. The new mission defined under the broader AACSB standards emphasized undergraduate teaching and applied research, including research on and development of teaching methods. Rewards, both tangible and intangible, could now be earned through teaching.

Use of Findings

Assessment results have been used at the individual class, departmental, college, and university levels. At the individual level, some faculty have used initial results to fine-tune their classroom activities and assignments. At the course level, faculty have utilized the results to mobilize a group response to the gaps between student outcome goals and their achievement that cut across sections of a single course. At the departmental level, the assessment process has been used by a department chair to work with a problem faculty member on improving teaching techniques and adhering to class requirements. It has also been used to give new faculty a familiarity with course goals and subject matter.

Several new courses are being developed to address gaps between AACSB requirements and current course offerings that were identified during the assessment process. Through College of Business representation on the university's General Studies Assessment Committee, the techniques developed in the College of Business program have been communicated to representatives from other parts of the university and have been incorporated into the process used to assess courses in the general studies requirements, thus extending the effect of involvement in assessment from the college level to the university level.

Success Factors

The process of setting objectives and developing assessment procedures has not proceeded without problems. Individuals have resisted change in their previous ways of thinking about teaching and assessment. Internal leadership and political and organizational problems within departments had to be handled. Yet strong leadership from the dean, consultation with the department chairs, assistance and support from the Office of Academic Assessment, a dedicated and creative faculty core in the Curriculum Committee, and widespread faculty involvement created a situation in which everyone had a stake in making the process succeed. Faculty were visibly rewarded for participating in the curriculum review and development process. Over time, faculty took ownership of the program, viewing it as a way to improve themselves rather than as a chore that had to be done to satisfy AACSB. We knew we were succeeding when a faculty member stated in a departmental meeting, "We aren't doing this for AACSB. We're doing it for ourselves."

The Capstone Course as an Outcomes Test for Majors

Faye D. Julian

CASE 2: UNIVERSITY OF TENNESSEE, KNOXVILLE

Look for: Clearly articulated behavioral outcomes for students as the basis for assessment and a matrix showing type(s) of assessment for each of eight outcomes. Students as well as faculty thus understand what assessment methods are designed to accomplish. A capstone course uses multiple instructors as well as multiple methods to help ensure reliability of judgments based on assessment.

Background and Purpose

When faced with a steadily increasing number of majors, a newly revised curriculum, and institutional concerns about performance funding, the speech communication department at the University of Tennessee, Knoxville (UTK) determined to revise its senior assessment procedures. Earlier outcomes tests were primarily standard information-recall examinations administered near completion of a student's program of study. In spring semester 1992, a capstone course was used for the first time as an outcomes test for speech communication majors at UTK. We determined that we might expect to arrive at a more accurate evaluation of the acquisition of essential skills and learning of our majors by measuring their competencies in a capstone course.

Method

As an outcomes test for seniors, the capstone course was conducted primarily through assigned readings, group discussion, written reports, oral presentations, and critiques. Two team teachers were joined as lecturers by five other members of the department. Students' skills and knowledge were evaluated on written and oral assignments as well as class participation. The course was designed to assess departmental curriculum goals and objectives. We expect our students to be able to (1) write in a clear, organized, and effective manner; (2) speak effectively and intelligently; (3) work constructively in groups; (4) make reasoned decisions; (5) use the library effectively for research; (6) evaluate critically what they read and hear; (7) sketch the broad sweep of rhetorical history and theory; and (8) understand various theories and perspectives embodied in the discipline.

To measure our objectives, we used a number of graded assignments. To evaluate writing skills, we had students prepare abstracts of journal articles. Worth 10 percent of the total grade, this assignment assessed writing, research, and theory understanding. An annotated bibliography, worth 15 percent of the total grade, also assessed writing and research skills as well as critical evaluation ability. A documented final paper accounted for 20 percent of the total grade. It assessed writing, research, and reasoned decision making. The midterm essay examination and the final examination were worth 10 percent each and were used to assess understanding of theories and perspectives.

Delivery, analysis, and critical skills were assessed primarily by a symposium speech and an oral critique of another student's paper. For symposia, students were grouped according to their primary areas of interest (for example, organizational communication, conflict, or propaganda). Each group then presented the theories of its area to the class. This exercise, worth 15 percent of the total grade, evaluated group decision making, discussion, and oral presentations. As an exercise in diplomacy and deliberate speaking skills, each student critiqued another student's paper for 10 percent of the total grade. Attendance and participation accounted for the remaining 10 percent of the final grade (see Table 11.1).

Findings

Of the twenty-four students who took the course, fifteen scored above their overall GPAs, four scored below, and five had scores identical to their overall GPAs. The mean grade in the class (81.09) was higher than the average for majors in the department.

We assumed that since ours is a writing-emphasis department (a student is required to write at least 3,000 words per semester in most classes), students would be proficient writers by their senior year. Abstracts were assumed to be a relatively simple assignment, and with this assignment as well as with the annotated bibliography and final paper, we were satisfied with the general use of library resources and writing skills that students exhibited.

Although we had suspected an oral communication deficiency and had con-

TABLE 11.1. OBJECTIVES ASSESSED BY TYPE OF ASSIGNMENT.

Objectives	Type of Assessment					
	Symposium	Abstracts	Annotated Bibliography	Final Paper	Critique	Midterm/ Final
1. Write clearly, effectively		x	x	x		
2. Speak effectively, intelligently	x				x	
3. Work constructively in groups	x					
4. Make reasoned decisions	x			x	x	
5. Use library effectively	x		x	x		
6. Critically evaluate what is read	x		x		x	
7. Sketch rhetorical history and theories						x
8. Understand theories and perspectives	x	x			x	x

sidered for some time a required performance course, we were somewhat surprised at students' lack of polished speaking skills in their symposia speeches and critiques. Poor organization, inadequate transitions, and faulty delivery resulted in low grades for nearly half the students.

One of the most disturbing findings involved the poor performance of students in one of the symposia. In dealing with a particular subject area, students seemingly had no theoretical background. These students, who had studied with one instructor, tended to think in terms of prescriptive lists. It is the informed judgment of the persons who taught the course that students in this dimension of our program have only superficial knowledge and lack a theoretical base.

The midterm and final tests were intended to assess students' understanding of a number of theories. The midterm, an essay examination with six questions, was too long for students to complete. Consequently, this assignment did not allow for valid assessment. The final asked students to compile seven to ten axioms of the discipline. These were creative, imaginative, and overall the best performance of the term.

Use of Findings

As a result of our findings, we have taken steps to strengthen our program of study. Our new major offers more flexibility and aims to ensure our students' awareness of the history and major concepts of our discipline. This major includes a required performance course aimed at enhancing a student's delivery skills. A required rhetorical theory course will guarantee our goal of introducing students to the history and theory of rhetoric. The new major also includes a required quantitative course and the capstone course.

In the future, instructors of the capstone will determine at the beginning of the term in which areas students are deficient. This is not to suggest that the capstone become a remedial course, but an understanding of areas of weakness can help us identify trouble spots in teaching and can alleviate unrealistic expectations. However, the course will continue to be theoretically based and not an upper-division repeat of the introductory survey course. At the risk of having assessment viewed as a threat to faculty, information about the poorly prepared students in the one dimension of the program was discussed with the faculty member in question.

With the capstone course as a means of senior assessment, we are convinced that we are on the right track. A capstone course for evaluation is far less obtrusive than stand-alone examinations. Ewell (1991b) suggests that for a capstone course to produce usable assessment information, it must be truly comprehensive, involve the judgment of more than one rater, and have rating scales that contain sufficient dimensions that diagnostic information can be obtained. Our capstone course met these criteria. To ensure that the course covered as much of the curriculum as possible, we had faculty contribute information about what knowledge and skills they thought students had learned. We used two instructors as graders, to provide cross-grading, and we used multiple assignments for adequate diagnosis of the final grade rather than relying on a single score for a single assignment, for example, a grade on a senior thesis.

Our discipline is one that is difficult to assess because of its dynamic nature, but just as communication constantly changes, so must our methods of testing and assessment (Aitken and Neer, 1992). In the future, we might well consider an academic portfolio for assessment or an ongoing process of evaluation in which preprogram assessment, a cornerstone course, and postprogram assessment are all used. New techniques of assessment may well offer more insight into our teaching effectiveness and our students' learning, but for now, the capstone course appears to be a reliable assessment tool for us.

The Departmentally Owned Senior Assignment as an Assessment Mechanism

Douglas J. Eder

CASE 3: SOUTHERN ILLINOIS UNIVERSITY AT EDWARDSVILLE

Look for: An overall campus plan that includes assessment at entry, midpoint, and in the senior year. Departmental Senior Assignments (SRAs) must provide for demonstration

Note: A model for Senior Assignments required of all students has existed since 1947 at the College of Wooster (Ohio). The program is called Independent Study at that liberal arts college. SIUE's Senior Assignment plan used elements drawn from Wooster's model and substantially altered them for use at a comprehensive state university. The author of this case gratefully acknowledges Wooster's assistance.

of student achievement in general education as well as the major field. The process of involving faculty in thirty-three academic majors in the design of assessment methods matched to their stated educational outcomes for students is described.

Background and Purpose

In 1986, Southern Illinois University at Edwardsville (SIUE) began to explore assessment mechanisms as ways to document university strengths, needs, and outcomes. Reacting in 1987 to further nudges from the Illinois Board of Higher Education, the university president appointed the Assessment Planning Committee consisting of students, faculty, staff, and administrators. By 1989, the committee had produced the "Plan for Assessment of Undergraduate Education." The plan, which meets North Central Association expectations, focuses primarily on (1) assessment of entering students' skills; (2) assessment at midpoint by means of a rising junior paper drawn from normal coursework; and (3) final assessment through departmental Senior Assignments. This case outlines the development of SIUE's Senior Assignments.

Since 1989, a successor committee, the Committee on Assessment (COA), has supervised all phases of assessment implementation. This group is composed of students, faculty, staff, and administrators. A faculty director, whose position was established by the original plan, executes the reasoned will of COA. This director's office and budget are both located in the Office of the Provost and Vice President for Academic Affairs, but the position also reports to the faculty senate. Therefore, while assessment at SIUE is positioned in the administration visibly and strongly enough to be taken seriously, it nevertheless is owned by and identified with the needs of the faculty.

Method

All of SIUE's thirty-three degree-granting undergraduate programs have developed Senior Assignments. Each SRA must allow baccalaureate candidates to demonstrate the extent to which they meet both major and general education expectations. Completion of an approved SRA is required for graduation; therefore, senior assessment is a "high stakes" process (Baker, O'Neil, and Linn, 1993).

The role of COA has been to assist each department to (1) formulate a statement of student learning objectives and (2) approve only those SRA plans that can measure corresponding student achievement. Regarding the first part of its role, COA received departmental statements containing various mixes of university-wide and discipline-specific ideals. These statements reflect many exercises in thought, argument, and negotiation. A composite example might include these objectives:

1. Student should have baccalaureate-level knowledge of the major discipline.
2. Student should be able to examine independently the research literature and report on a topic within the major discipline.

3. Student should be able to explain orally, using speech free of jargon, a technical topic in the discipline to a lay audience.
4. Student should be able to explain new developments in the discipline in terms of their ethical impact on society.

Regarding the second part of its role, COA received SRA plans that ranged from reluctant to truly creative and even heroic. COA's main task was to help departments match their SRAs to the educational objectives they claimed for their students. Scattered departmental cynicism about assessment made this job difficult. For example, a department espousing the third objective could not use a written comprehensive exam as its single assessment tool and claim to have fulfilled its assessment duties. A written exam, no matter how comprehensive, does not measure the third objective. Thus, the three-year working relationship between COA and some departments got prickly. However, it never became adversarial. At least five conditions contributed to that circumstance: (1) COA's makeup snuffs out "top-down" edicts; (2) COA recognizes that faculty priorities do not begin with a rabid faith in the virtue of assessment; (3) the director is committed to keeping communication open; (4) the provost is committed to making things work; and (5) all parties display good humor (usually) and agreement (sometimes) that perfection is not expected as part of the plan. Eventually, all departments submitted SRA plans that matched stated educational objectives, and COA approved them.

The original planning committee realized that even a very dedicated faculty, when facing stagnant budgets and the increasing workloads of the 1990s, would not happily embrace the added assessment burden. Thus, partly to ensure faculty support and partly to guarantee student motivation, most assessment mechanisms were embedded transparently within regular university functions. For example, the midpoint assessment, or rising junior paper (RJP), was to be drawn from writing assignments undertaken by students within regular classes. Thus, the RJP would imply no extra workload in terms of student or faculty behavior; it would be a "low stakes" process (Baker, O'Neil, and Linn, 1993). This is not the case for Senior Assignments.

The planning committee envisioned that different departmental SRAs could assume such forms as presentations, compositions and performances in music or theatre, shows and hangings in art, lab and field research projects in the sciences, or theses—each appropriate to and under the control of the discipline involved. While pursuing knowledge and demonstrating competence within these idealized SRAs, students were expected to discover that education exists beyond the lecture hall and that faculty can be competent, caring mentors. In return, faculty would find that even average students are more than classroom stenographers and that, with guidance, they can become true partners in scholarship. The planning committee completed its work with the cheerful hope that assessment could induce a more exciting academic life and bring joy to everyone. It left for its successor committee to figure out the few details of just how such high pleasures in theory were actually to be attained in practice.

Findings

The planning committee's optimism appears to be justified. The most visible consequences of SRAs so far are not for the students overall, but for faculty members, who are beginning to see how they and their students can benefit. For instance, one social science and two science departments invite seniors to engage in research under a professor's direction. Students are assessed on a written paper and oral defense of a poster describing their research. Some poster sessions have a casual air; others are more serious. Student-faculty conversations stimulated by the posters can range from technical to speculative and cover both breadth and depth of a discipline. High-quality posters have gone to regional and national meetings and resulted in publications shared by students and professors. Some departments permit second- and third-year students to work with the seniors, thereby encouraging student mentoring and even collaboration. SRAs of this kind require much energy and commitment. In return they elicit excitement and even publications. All SRAs cause faculty members to reexamine the quality of their programs and to initiate improvements.

SRAs within the fine arts permit students to compose, display, direct, or perform their own creations to audiences drawn from the university and the general public. Faculty members exercise critical review by examining gallery or program notes and querying the students about such things as technique and cultural influence. SRAs in foreign languages take the form of a true senior thesis that is written and orally defended in the target language.

Students have responded to these challenges with vigor. For example, a biology student investigated the role of the chemical dopamine as a protector of the retina from the damaging effects of light. The resulting poster went to a national meeting. An art student undertook a photographic and historical survey of local homes used in the Underground Railroad. The project formed the basis for a finely illustrated book. Psychology students examined subtle forms of sexual harassment on campus and compared the findings with theoretical models. The results raised consciousness locally and will be presented at a regional meeting.

There are, of course, less complex formats. Students in several disciplines undertake library research and write a paper in a capstone course. The paper is read by multiple faculty members. Insofar as the capstone experience involves the entire department in assessing its own learning objectives, this familiar arrangement is satisfactory.

Use of Findings

A substantial unanticipated positive consequence of the SRAs appeared in the form of financial support from the university president. Because individual departments own the SRAs, some of them have responded to assessment with greater enthusiasm and more individualized instructional opportunity than others. On the one hand, this is understandable because having faculty rearrange a curriculum and establish rigorous SRAs costs both time and money. On the other hand, if departments throughout the university were to create truly individualized SRAs, SIUE's education would be highly unusual, maybe unique, for a comprehensive state university. Assessment-driven improvements could add excitement to SIUE's mission of promoting undergraduate excellence for all its students. It could develop good students into better ones and bring a sense of joy to the faculty. Sensing this, the president responded to an assessment initiative and shifted significant recurring resources into a Senior Assignment Fund within the provost's budget. The fund assists departments already implementing individualized SRAs and recruits those that had previously hesitated.

Early results are evident. For instance, three relatively unenthusiastic departments are redesigning their SRAs to create active investigative student-faculty partnerships. New computer equipment bought specifically for their SRAs brings into these partnerships the considerable resources of the Internet and, through electronic communication, permits discussion and even review of students' written ideas by faculty colleagues located elsewhere. Money for travel helps students visit archives and museums in order to study primary sources, a process they otherwise would not attempt. In short, assessment has begun to boost faculty enthusiasm, raise educational expectations, and provide ways to measure the attainment of those expectations.

Success Factors

Factors contributing to initial success include:

1. Faculty ownership of the assessment process
2. Flexibility; acceptance of multiple Senior Assignment designs
3. Open communication
4. Desire to make things work
5. Leadership without zealotry
6. Support of the president and the provost plus substantial financial backing

Fostering Student Scholarship in Psychology Through Senior Assignments

Susan L. Thomas

CASE 4: SOUTHERN ILLINOIS UNIVERSITY AT EDWARDSVILLE

Look for: Specific behavioral objectives for psychology majors, which serve as the basis for a performance-based Senior Assignment. Faculty and graduate students serve as intellectual mentors for undergraduates conducting research projects.

Background and Purpose

As part of a comprehensive assessment plan, the Committee on Assessment at Southern Illinois University at Edwardsville (SIUE) required all departments to develop a Senior Assignment (SRA) to be implemented beginning in the 1993–94 academic year. The purpose of the SRA was to assess how well major departments were succeeding in achieving their educational objectives by giving baccalaureate candidates the opportunity to demonstrate their mastery of both general education and major academic requirements. While the format of the SRA was left to the discretion of the individual departments, the Committee on Assessment stressed that all faculty members of the department must be involved in evaluating the SRA.

Method

Overall Design. In designing its SRA, the psychology department focused on fostering independent student scholarship in conjunction with faculty mentoring. The goal is to have students integrate and apply existing knowledge to create a new body of work. This goal is consistent with Boyer's belief (1987) that students should be inspired by an overall vision of a field and that assessment should be based upon performance, both inside and outside the classroom. This focus on performance is also consistent with the stance of Halpern and others (1993) that performance-based assessment is "uniquely appropriate for psychology given the discipline's history of behavioral research" (p. 35). To achieve the goal of fostering independent student scholarship, the department established a series of educational objectives to be met by the SRA. SRAs should allow students to (1) demonstrate skills in statistical analyses and interpretation of data including computer applications and the use and application of laboratory and/or field research techniques; (2) demonstrate the ability to collect, collate, and understand information of a psychological nature; and (3) demonstrate the ability to communicate effectively both orally and in writing. In addition, SRAs should be designed to (4) encourage active student participation in departmental and university research; (5) encourage student awareness of the cultural, social, historical, and ethical influences and aspects of the discipline; and (6) offer experiences that will strengthen applications to area graduate programs (for those students wishing to apply).

To meet these objectives, the psychology department offers two options for the SRA from which students may choose. To understand the impact of the discipline on society, students may write a five- to seven-page paper (in American Psychological Association style with appropriate references) in which they relate psychological knowledge and techniques to an issue of social, ethical, health, or political importance. To understand the complexities of research, students may elect to do a directed research project. The project may be done either in an upper-class course (which is open to all majors, but all majors do not elect to take it) or as independent research under the supervision of a faculty member. In either case, the students defend their work in a formal presentation or poster session, which is attended by other students and faculty of the department. The best posters from these classes, authored by students and faculty together, are submitted to professional and/or undergraduate research conferences.

In any given academic year, there are approximately 150 senior psychology majors at SIUE. Given the large number of majors and the labor-intensive nature of the SRA, the psychology department has implemented a program that combines the knowledge and abilities of both its faculty and its graduate students.

Role of the Faculty. In this program, the faculty serve as intellectual mentors. It is the responsibility of the faculty (1) to help the student clarify an idea; (2) to help the student refine the design of the study or an outline for the paper; (3) to oversee the implementation of the design/outline; and (4) to give final approval for the assignment to be submitted for departmental examination.

To ensure that each student receives this kind of mentoring, the supervising faculty member is required to sign a form attesting to the student's progress at each of the stages listed.

Role of the Graduate Assistants. To ensure that the assessment process runs smoothly and the students receive an enriching educational experience, two graduate assistants are assigned the following duties: (1) Conduct periodic meetings throughout the semester on topics relevant to the assessment process. These general information meetings provide all students with the same information about the assessment process. Topics for the meetings include how to select a topic faculty adviser, how to select the appropriate SRA option, how to submit forms to the Institutional Review Board (for research utilizing human subjects), and how to design a poster. (2) Assist the student in further establishing a mentoring relationship with a faculty member. The assistants make the initial contact with the faculty member, informing him or her that a student would like the faculty member to be the student's topic adviser. This initial contact helps eliminate the status barriers for the student—when the student approaches the faculty member, he or she already knows that the faculty member is interested in working on the project. (3) Hold extended office hours during the week. The assistants are available throughout the week to answer general information questions. By holding office hours, they are available for students who enter the process late and have missed the general information meetings. (4) Keep progress records on each of the students. The assistants make periodic contact with the students to make sure the students' needs are being met and that they are progressing at an appropriate pace.

Assessment Instruments. In addition to increased participation in conferences, learning is assessed through the use of an SRA evaluation form and a student evaluation form. The SRA evaluation form assesses the students' work in terms of content, integration of information/evidence of critical thinking, adherence to APA guidelines, and presentation/ability to answer questions (for presentation and poster sessions). All evaluations are made on seven-point Likert scales.

The student evaluation form assesses student satisfaction with the SRA and how well students thought the educational objectives of the department were met by the SRA. All evaluations are made on seven-point Likert scales.

Findings and Their Use

Behavioral observations and discussions with students make it clear that the assessment program is having a positive impact. Undergraduate students express much more enthusiasm for conducting research than was the case previously. The number of submissions to undergraduate and professional conferences has increased significantly. Moreover, there is spontaneous student interest in submitting proposals for these conferences; students value the opportunity not only to present their own work, but also to learn about the work of others. This interest in taking their work beyond the classroom has instilled a greater sense of confidence in the seniors. Because of their experiences in doing research, these students approach their other classes with renewed vigor. They are motivated to examine the work of others critically and not just accept the results at face value.

Success Factors

These initial success stories can be attributed to two major factors: faculty enthusiasm and tying the SRA to educational objectives. Both of these factors focus on a positive educational experience for the students; the department views the SRA as more than just an assessment process—it is a unique and valuable learning tool. It is clear from student perceptions that they view the program as more than an assessment process, too, and this is the major reason why the SRA is successful.

The Sophomore-Junior Diagnostic Project

Jean P. O'Brien, Stephanie L. Bressler, John F. Ennis, Mark Michael

CASE 5: KING'S COLLEGE

Look for: Midpoint assessment of clearly articulated collegewide generic skills, such as critical thinking, effective writing, oral communication skills. The assessment is carried out in the context of a required sophomore course in the major, providing faculty and individual students with valuable data on student progress. Remediation may be based on the findings.

Background and Purpose

The goal of departmental curricula at King's College is to produce cumulative learning in the major while building on previous learning and skills, such as critical thinking, effective writing, and oral communication, acquired in the college's general education program. As part of the comprehensive assessment program at King's, systematic ways to assess this learning have been developed to determine at regular intervals whether students are progressing satisfactorily in meeting faculty expectations and whether the curriculum is assisting students in achieving goals set for the major. The Sophomore-Junior Diagnostic Project, completed in a required course early in the major, provides an opportunity for both faculty and students to determine if the first and second years of the curriculum are helping students meet the goals of the major.

Our experience shows us that assessment is best and most easily accomplished when it is incorporated into an actual plan of learning rather than "added on" to the curriculum. The midpoint assessment is planned so that students perceive it not as a separate evaluation but as part of an ongoing plan to diagnose and support student learning. This approach provides students with regular feedback on how well they are achieving goals communicated to them. They can then use this feedback to determine how they may improve their learning.

So that students (and faculty) do not see assessment as something "extra" to do, assessment strategies are embedded in coursework. The diagnostic project is assigned in a required course, usually during the sophomore year. This diagnostic project serves as an important assignment in the required course and meets dual purposes of assessment and course evaluation. Because the project is completed as a course requirement and receives a grade, students are motivated to take the assessment seriously. They are advised that they will benefit from the assessment because it will lead them to determine, with the help of the instructor, the extent to which they are progressing satisfactorily through the major and general education competencies. The project is graded by the course instructor, who provides students with feedback regarding their demonstration of learning that is consistent with the goals of the curriculum. At this point, success can be affirmed for the student or deficiencies identified and plans developed for their remediation. A major assessment project early in students' progression through the major allows faculty to avoid dealing with these deficiencies later, perhaps in the senior year, when it is often too late. The results of the assessment may also be reviewed by all department faculty so that, if appropriate, they may consider changes in the content of individual courses or in the sequence of courses for the major.

For feedback to be useful to students, it must utilize specific criteria to evaluate performance. Department faculty decide what general knowledge and specific major knowledge as well as level of skills (such as writing, thinking, speaking, and so on) students should be able to demonstrate.

Criteria-based feedback allows faculty to identify learning needs of individual students and assists in identifying recurrent learning needs that are not met by the curriculum and current teaching-learning strategies.

In the cases that follow, descriptions of Sophomore-Junior Diagnostic Projects demonstrate the diversity of midpoint assessment projects implemented by the political science, English, mathematics, computer science, and human resources management departments at King's College.

CASE 5A: POLITICAL SCIENCE

Look for: Sophomore-Junior Diagnostic Project in political science, with written and oral communication skills assessed via a research paper incorporating an interview and participation in a panel discussion.

Method

The Sophomore-Junior Diagnostic Project in Political Science is assigned as a requirement in the course Public Administration. The project is talked about throughout the semester and guidelines are provided for each stage of the project. Students submit to the instructor a written analysis of the power of a professional group in government, based on both data collected during an interview and information obtained through library research. Students are assigned to teams to prepare to address questions about the analyses raised by faculty and other political science majors in a panel discussion. Both the written and oral components are evaluated by the instructor for a course grade.

Department faculty meet to discuss students' written submissions and panel participation. This work is compared to students' performance in other major courses in order to fairly assess demonstration of the critical thinking, effective writing and speaking, research skills, and comprehension of political science concepts considered appropriate at the end of the sophomore year. Department faculty compare this assessment to students' required self-assessments to reach conclusions regarding student learning.

The department chair affirms student achievement by sending individual letters that inform students that they are progressing satisfactorily through the major and are appropriately developing general education competencies. Students who demonstrate deficiencies are directed, again by letter from the chair, to meet with the course instructor or adviser to discuss feedback and an action plan to remedy deficiencies.

Findings

While students often express anxiety about being assessed by the entire faculty, they are assured by the course instructor that faculty intentions are either to affirm their progress or work with them to determine any deficiencies they have and plan to remedy those deficiencies. While the course instructor assumes primary responsibility for guiding students' participation in this project, all department faculty communicate a positive attitude toward the project. Faculty find that most students adopt a serious approach to undertaking this assessment and look forward to receiving feedback. In addition, the project serves many of these second-year students as an introduction to interaction with faculty outside the classroom, as they often seek help from faculty in planning their project interviews.

Students view the focus of the project, an interview with a professional in government, as an opportunity to test the theories and concepts taught in class with the experiences related by professionals. The interview also provides students with firsthand information regarding the career opportunities available in public service.

An interesting by-product of this project is student perception that the department faculty care about whether students are learning as well as what they are learning. Students respond well to feedback that they perceive as representing the concerns of the department, and they use this feedback to develop confidence in their skills and knowledge in political science. Students tell faculty that they appreciate hearing in a formal way whether they are progressing as expected as political science majors.

Students find the recently added self-assessment as a way to begin determining their own strengths and weaknesses in completing projects. Students are able to make more accurate assessments of their writing and critical thinking skills when provided with clear criteria they can apply. These findings confirm that the project can serve as both an assessment and a learning tool.

Use of Findings

Writing deficiencies are the most common problems identified through this assessment project. Students are referred to the campus Writing Center where problems are more specifically diagnosed and direction provided to improve writing. Where initial projects are unsatisfactorily written, students are asked to rewrite reports.

Department faculty meet again to discuss students' progress in overcoming deficiencies and continue to monitor student writing in major courses to ensure that writing skills are improved and maintained.

The Sophomore-Junior Diagnostic Project in political science has evolved over the past several years. It has served as a focal point for departmental discussion of what the major is intended to accomplish and consideration of indications for needed change in the major curriculum.

As faculty have become clearer about what second-year students majoring in political science should know and be able to demonstrate, the project has been refined to accommodate these changes. For example, the panel discussions have been added to further assess critical thinking and effective speaking skills and to reinforce the importance of developing team skills and sharing knowledge with the class.

This process of determining what the major is intended to accomplish and how that will be assessed has encouraged collective responsibility for goal achievement measured by student learning. The process has improved communication of goals among faculty members as well as between faculty and students. The department has used faculty and student feedback from this process both to refine the project and to improve the learning-teaching strategies in the major.

CASE 5B: ENGLISH

Look for: A Sophomore-Junior Diagnostic Project in English that uses a portfolio containing three selected papers and a reflective essay exploring the student's approach to writing and the writing process.

Method

The Sophomore-Junior Diagnostic Project in English seeks to determine the writing and thinking ability of English majors through the use of a portfolio of writings developed in a required course. Students in English 251: Advanced Writing select from six assigned papers three pieces for further revision and editing. In addition to these pieces, the portfolio also contains a reflective essay, a meta-text exploring the individual student's approach to writing and the writing process.

The writing done in the course develops further the writing process approach central to the freshman writing course, CORE 110: Effective Writing, the basis of the writing program at King's. In the advanced writing class, students choose a specific topic for the work of the semester and research the topic through various kinds of papers: informational, reportorial (developed mainly through interviews), critical, researched, and autobiographical. In addition, students submit an annotated bibliography and keep a writer's log. The last four weeks of the course are devoted to portfolio development and the writing of the reflective essay. When the portfolios are submitted, students present them to the class, explaining the plan of the portfolio and sharing one piece of writing from the portfolio with the class.

The evaluation of the portfolio is done by the faculty member who teaches the class, and this evaluation is shared not only with the student writer but also with other department members. The portfolio counts for 75 percent of the course credit, the other 25 percent going for the writer's log, class participation in discussions, and involvement in and commitment to the workshop classes.

Findings

Developing the portfolio has been a source of gratification for students. For many, it is the breakthrough to the art of revising. A familiar comment is, "This is really the first time that I seriously worked at revision in an organized way," or, "During this class I have come to appreciate the process and craft involved in writing." In addition, students realize that material developed for one paper can successfully be incorporated into other papers and that a piece of writing can utilize various rhetorical approaches to develop a thesis.

Using criteria-based evaluation has proven to be an aid for many students in helping them focus the revising process. Moreover, since the assessment is being done in a specific course, students see the use of criteria not as a hurdle but as an aid in shaping the writing.

Perhaps the most satisfying result of using a portfolio for students is that they own the project. Since they select materials and are free to incorporate materials from multiple sources, they see themselves as writers. Many labor over the formatting and presentation, developing and honing desktop publishing skills to produce a portfolio that demonstrates professional pride. These portfolios can be added to as students develop further materials and are useful in applying for graduate study or for business positions.

For the faculty, the portfolios give a clearer notion of the students' range of ability in developing specific kinds of papers. Since students select the materials for their portfolios, faculty feel that the selection process demonstrates the students' abilities to analyze and evaluate their own writing. Department faculty recognize that the portfolio places a heavy burden not only on the student writer but also on the instructor of the course. However, faculty members, while deeply concerned about the elements of time involved in evaluating portfolios, attest to the value both for the students and for the department. Overall, there is a wide degree of satisfaction with this approach as a means of evaluating the writing skills of English majors.

Use of Findings

The English department has used the results of the Sophomore-Junior Diagnostic Project to develop further faculty-student relations, to develop departmental consensus on what the department expects from our sophomore-level majors in writing, and to inform our student majors of how well they are meeting the goals and objectives of the department.

Since the advanced writing course relies heavily on collaborative learning strategies including faculty-student conferences, students must establish a working relationship with their instructor. Peer editing/response groups further break down the reluctance of many students to share their writing and to learn from others. These groups also develop students' sense of being part of a community of writers working together. Some students continue to express concern that papers are not graded during the semester. The instructors of the course now focus more on how to read and use editorial comments and writing suggestions, both in class and in individual conferences, to alleviate this apprehension. In addition, instructors have also used midterm evaluations as a means of dealing with issues of concern to the students.

The English department has used the results of the course and student evaluations to revise the course material and the types of assignments. For example, students indicated that asking for the researched paper at the end of the semester created problems because of heavy library use due to requirements for other courses. Instead, they asked that the autobiographical paper be the last assignment. The change was made, and an interesting benefit occurred. The autobiographical papers coming at the end of the semester, when levels of trust and an open working relationship had been developed, resulted in papers that dealt with deep personal issues written with an openness that would not have been possible at the beginning of the semester.

Student evaluations show continued satisfaction with a course that demands that the students see themselves as writers, a course that assesses their ability at a specific point in their careers to meet departmental criteria for majors.

CASE 5C: MATHEMATICS AND COMPUTER SCIENCE

Look for: A Sophomore-Junior Diagnostic Project in mathematics and in computer science that includes an expository paper also presented orally. Several faculty read and evaluate the paper; peers help the instructor evaluate the oral presentation.

Method

The Sophomore-Junior Diagnostic Project for both mathematics majors and computer science majors is a component of Discrete Mathematics, a sophomore-level course required for both majors. The project revolves around a substantial expository paper on a subject related to the course. Students submit two formal drafts and give an oral presentation in class. The small size of the class (about a dozen) allows for a great deal of individual attention. Conferences with each student are scheduled to orient the student to his or her topic, to discuss a rough outline and an annotated bibliography, and to discuss the first draft. Additional guidance is given via a trip to the library, handouts on mathematical writing, demonstrations of how to use an overhead projector, and details on the instructor's expectations and how the project is to be evaluated. All aspects of the student's performance are discussed at a final conference. The project grade (about one-fifth of the course grade) takes into consideration input from other math/CS faculty who read the final draft and from peer evaluations of the oral presentation.

The math/CS project is an intensive experience which opens students' eyes to the wide range of skills needed by a professional. While all the students have used the library, most have not used the CD-ROM facilities and the interlibrary loan process. While all have taken a speech course, none have used an overhead projector. While all have written essays and papers for other courses, many find technical writing to be a greater challenge than writing in general education courses.

A challenge for math/CS faculty was their initial insecurity about "playing the role of an English professor." To focus faculty in their critiquing of student papers, an evaluation form was designed with the help of the college's writing-across-the-curriculum coordinator; the form elicits open-ended comments by posing a number of questions, some of which are specific to mathematical writing (for example, regarding the conventions for mixing prose and mathematical symbols). A specialized evaluation form for the oral presentation was also designed after a failed attempt to use the form designed for the required general education speech class.

Findings

For most mathematics majors and computer science majors, their project is their first experience with extended technical writing. As might be expected, even bright students have difficulties with this. Often other professors can confirm that a particular student has problems writing; surprisingly, however, the project often uncovers weaknesses (in constructing coherent paragraphs, for example) that do not show up in the writing of mathematical proofs or scientific lab reports. The reason that those types of writing do not detect these weaknesses is that they are often of a relatively simple structure or must conform to a fairly explicit format.

The oral presentations of students vary in quality as much as the written reports. But speaking skills are not a simple reflection of writing skills. Often a "weak" student gives a surprisingly professional presentation. Both types of communication skills need to be developed and assessed.

When it comes to researching the literature, students differ in their natural creativity and stick-to-it-iveness. This project reveals that students also differ in their knowledge about information gathering. Virtually all of our students need to increase their investigative expertise.

Use of Findings

The principal use of results from the projects has been to convey to students, both orally and in writing, the extent to which their growth in various areas has met departmental expectations. In a few cases, faculty have judged a student's writing ability to require remediation. In such a case, the student is given a grade of Incomplete—even though the overall grade in the course is satisfactory—until the student works with the Writing Center and corrects the deficiencies to the instructor's satisfaction.

The results from the projects have also been used to modify the format of the project and the method of its evaluation, particularly in regard to oral presentations. The use of an overhead projector, at first an option, was made a requirement after it became clear that presentations utilizing an overhead projector appeared more professional than those that did not. Peer evaluations of oral presentations provide wonderful insight into how perceptions of a presentation can vary. Peers also detected more errors in speech mechanics than did the instructor, who must concentrate on technical accuracy (which students are less able to evaluate reliably); this prompted the instructor to videotape all presentations. Student comments also produced a change in the evaluation form used.

Finally, the results from the projects have influenced pedagogy. Since first learning from a student that our library had added CD-ROM material, the instructor has kept up to date on the information resources available to students and has conducted tours of the library during the first week of classes. While students have always been provided with written guidance as to the conventions of mathematical writing, student performance showed the need for clearer guides and verbal reinforcement in class. Students' oral presentations also showed the need for written guidance and demonstrations on how (not) to use an overhead projector.

Happily, all these changes have borne fruit.

CASE 5D: HUMAN RESOURCES MANAGEMENT

Look for: A Sophomore-Junior Diagnostic Project in human resources management involves an analysis of a case study and a written memo to the president of the company in the case explaining the human resources problems and suggesting solutions. The student, the course instructor, and a human resources professional all use the same criteria to evaluate the student's critical thinking and writing skills.

Method

The Sophomore-Junior Diagnostic Project in human resources management consists of an assignment designed to assess critical thinking and writing skills as students take their first course in the major, Introduction to Human Resources Management. The students are given a case study describing a business that has begun to experience serious problems with its employees. The students' task is to write a memorandum to the president and founder of the company identifying the human resources problems and suggesting resolutions.

At the time the assignment is announced, students are given criteria that will be used to evaluate their critical thinking and writing skills. Upon completion of the assignment, the students, the faculty member, and a human resources professional evaluate the students' work on the same criteria. Feedback to students is given in written form, and individual conferences are held with students to discuss their progress and needs on an individual basis as well as to consider similarities and differences among the three sets of ratings. It is significant that at this point students are better able to internalize the standards of effective thinking and writing by comparing their self-assessments to others' evaluations.

Findings

At the faculty level, it was important to have department faculty agree on what knowledge and abilities students should be able to demonstrate during the sophomore year. Agreeing on the assignment and the criteria used to judge students' performance often led to spirited discussions as to what to expect of students as they entered our major. After several attempts, the assignment and the criteria were agreed upon. We found that it was important to try something and then fix problems as they occurred.

On a practical note, it is important to assign the memorandum relatively early in the semester to have time available to provide the requisite feedback to students.

At the student level, the assignment revealed several areas of critical thinking and effective writing that needed further development in order for students to progress successfully through the major. Although most students were able to apply human resources principles to the case study, few were able to do so systematically. The writing assignment allowed the instructor to provide feedback to students regarding the importance of a logical and persuasive organization in their writing.

In addition to organization, the tone of the memorandum turned out to be an important and common source of feedback to students. Often, in their zeal to correct the problems of the business described in the case study, students neglected to write their memos in a tone reflecting that they were writing to the president and founder of "their" company.

Use of Findings

The primary use of results from this project is to provide individualized feedback to students on their writing and critical thinking skills in the major. Students are impressed by the level of faculty attention to skills necessary to their collegiate and professional success.

When students are deficient in the skills necessary for success in the major, we are fortunate to be able to advise students to take advantage of our Writing and/or Study Skills Centers.

Perhaps the most unique feature of the Sophomore-Junior Diagnostic Project in human resources management is that we have an external human resources professional evaluate the students' writing and critical thinking skills in the major. We have found that area professionals are eager to participate in the project and feel that their involvement enhances the development of the next generation of human resources management professionals. In fact, many professionals offer to meet with students individually to discuss their writing and analysis of the case. The supporting feedback from professionals facilitates the likelihood of students following up on faculty suggestions for improvement.

Success Factors

The Sophomore-Junior Diagnostic Project has been successful in meeting its objectives: to assess and foster the development of basic academic skills in the context of a particular discipline. In fact, a recent survey at the college revealed very high levels of faculty and student satisfaction with the projects. To our faculty, it was important that each department have the opportunity to design a course-embedded exercise precisely with its goals and criteria in mind. Faculty ownership of the program and the observed improvement in student performance certainly contribute to faculty satisfaction with it. But both faculty and students benefit by establishing better teaching and learning strategies.

Involving Graduates and Employers in Assessment of a Technology Program

Janice Van Dyke, George W. Williams

CASE 6: STATE TECHNICAL INSTITUTE AT MEMPHIS

Look for: An assessment effort begun in 1979 that uses systematic, periodically conducted mailed surveys for graduates and their employers. Chemical engineering technology instructors use the survey findings to keep their curriculum current.

Background and Purpose

When the mission of a college is to prepare workers for immediate employment in technical fields, the importance of employers' satisfaction with graduates and graduates' satisfaction with employment cannot be overstated. This approval is so important that the Technology Accreditation Commission (TAC) of the Accreditation Board for Engineering and Technology (ABET) makes assessing it a requirement for programs seeking accreditation. The criteria for the TAC of ABET state, "An accreditable program must demonstrate employer satisfaction with recent graduates, graduate satisfaction with employment, career mobility opportunities, appropriate starting salaries, and appropriate job titles."

Method

To measure employers' satisfaction with graduates and graduates' satisfaction with employment, the department chairperson of chemical engineering technology at the State Technical Institute at Memphis periodically conducts systematic mailed surveys. Two surveys are sent to graduates who may elect to forward one to their immediate supervisor. Both the supervisor and graduates are asked to (1) describe the work being done by the graduate; (2) classify the level of work (skilled craftsperson, salesperson, engineering technologist, engineering technician, supervision or management, engineering, other); (3) express an opinion about whether the graduate's educational background qualifies him or her for the work he or she is doing; (4) express an opinion about the advancement potential within the company for the graduate; (5) indicate whether or not the supervisor would seek more employees with the same educational background; (6) express an opinion about the graduate's educational weaknesses in performing present assignments and in advancing in the organization; (7) express an opinion about whether or not the graduate is qualified to perform the work of an engineering technician; and (8) rank a list of ten program objectives as follows: having "no importance in performing work," having "minor importance in performing work," or "essential in performing work."

Findings

On the most recent administration of the survey, the graduates indicated a somewhat reduced emphasis on traditional wet-method analyses as well as on the operation of bench or pilot-scale unit operations equipment. They indicated the largest increase in emphasis on tests and evaluations with report requirements as well as on performing limited design and/or performance computations on chemical engineering unit operations and unit processes equipment.

The employers showed the greatest decline in emphasis for mass and energy balances, operation of bench or pilot-scale unit operations equipment, and limited design and/or performance analysis computations on chemical engineering unit operations and unit processes equipment. The largest increases in emphasis came in the areas of application of chemical principles, performance of tests with report requirements, and instrumental analysis. They saw very little emphasis, on the average, for mass and energy balances and limited design and/or performance analysis computations on chemical engineering unit operations and unit processes equipment.

Use of Findings

The results of the periodic administrations of these surveys between 1979 and the present have indicated to department members in chemical engineering technology at State Technical Institute at Memphis the processes and procedures that practitioners in the field consider most important for chemical engineering technicians to know. Few dramatic or sweeping changes have been made to the program as a result of these surveys because the questionnaires confirm that the goals of the program are sound and should continue to be stressed without major modifications. One change indicated by the surveys in 1986, an upgrade that had been anticipated and was confirmed through other measures, was a need for increased exposure to computers and computer technology. The implementation of this change resulted in a decreased emphasis on it in subsequent surveys.

Success Factors

This activity works because it gives direct, specific feedback from employers of chemical engineering technicians to the persons who design the courses and curriculum for those technicians. Faculty make it a point to know the laboratory processes, procedures, and equipment used in the companies that employ their graduates. This information is used to keep the curriculum current so that graduates are immediately productive on the job.

The rate of return of surveys is important to this activity.

Triangulated Assessment of the Major

Candace Cartwright Young

CASE 7: NORTHEAST MISSOURI STATE UNIVERSITY

Look for: Use of multiple assessment methods, including nationally standardized exams, questionnaires for seniors, and culminating activities such as research reports and speeches in capstone courses in major fields. Assessment has produced major changes in curricula and has led to campuswide goals for increasing student involvement in behaviors demonstrated to be effective in enhancing student learning.

Background and Purpose

In 1973, Northeast Missouri State University President Charles McClain initiated the practice of using senior exams to assess student performance in the major. Students were invited and later were required to sit for nationally standardized examinations in their majors. Beginning in 1975, students were also asked to respond to a questionnaire regarding self-reported levels of learning and satisfaction with the major program, general education, faculty, and advising.

In the mid 1980s, faculty members began discussing ways to complement the standardized testing and survey assessments. In 1985, the faculty senate decided to require capstone experiences and soon thereafter adopted a university portfolio project. Initial discussion of the capstone described it as an integrative experience in the major. However, faculty soon realized its tremendous potential for assessing student performance. The university also set an expectation for its graduate school placement rate and monitored progress toward this goal.

Method

All seniors sit for a nationally normed examination. Faculty choose the examination they think best measures their graduates' learning. Students receive individual scores, and faculty receive individual score reports for all graduating seniors. Faculty also receive aggregate data on the percentage of students above the 50th percentile and the percentage of students above the 80th percentile. In many instances, testing companies also provide information about student performance in discipline subfields, and Northeast Missouri State University (NMSU) aggregates student performance, comparing it with that of students from other universities.

All seniors must complete a graduating student questionnaire regarding their satisfaction with resources, processes, and learning outcomes. Departmental results are reported in a comparative format with the university averages.

Each major program requires students to complete a capstone experience as part of the curriculum. Faculty in each major determine the content of the course, and a number of models have emerged. Students might take a seminar on classic works in the field, or they might write a thesis. Some majors require that students sit for a locally developed comprehensive exam, some require students to report research at an undergraduate research conference, some ask students to give a research presentation before an external examiner, and some require students to give a speech to an outside group.

Findings

This multiple measures format provides the university with an ongoing database that is used to promote continuous improvement. A typical pattern on the campus in the late 1970s and early 1980s was for the nationally normed test results to be ignored initially by faculty. The second stage was for faculty to criticize the tests as inappropriate for the university's curriculum. However, after a number of years of disappointing results from talented students, faculty began to sit for the same exams or to review the exams more carefully. The faculty usually concluded that while the tests were difficult, they were reasonably good tests of discipline content. Faculty believed students should have done better given the fact that the material on the exams was taught in the curriculum. Upon examination of student transcripts, however, faculty realized that many students did not choose to take courses critical to an overall understanding of the discipline. Similarly, nothing in the curriculum or in the university culture communicated solid expectations to students that their learning should be cumulative. Thus, faculty in most disciplines initiated curricular reforms that required students to take more of the courses central to the major and in a prescribed sequence.

University surveys provide opportunities to assess trends in student satisfaction with various elements of the university, time-on-task behaviors, and self-reports of cognitive and affective learning. Over the years, NMSU has found that trends in students' self-reports in proficiencies such as math, writing, and scientific reasoning closely parallel the trends in standardized test scores and portfolio entries for the same cognitive areas. Furthermore, as the university has set goals for increased student time-on-task, faculty-student interaction, and advising, the survey results allow continual monitoring of progress.

Capstone courses provide a direct faculty vehicle for creating local assessment instruments to complement student surveys and standardized test scores. Capstones give additional information about student proficiencies in the disciplines' content, but also provide important opportunities to assess student attitudes and skills in many areas such as writing, speaking, collaboration, and critical thinking. The effectiveness of this assessment method is that faculty themselves design the capstone experience and draw conclusions about the overall strengths and weaknesses of their programs. When faculty internalize these strengths and weaknesses, they are more likely to initiate improvement strategies in their classrooms and in the curriculum.

Use of Findings

Use of results is the key to a successful assessment program. When leaders at all levels of the university use data to define problems and to monitor the progress of initiatives, assessment merits the praise it receives. When not used by the campus community, assessment merely exists as a bureaucratic paper exercise. NMSU distributes data to faculty on senior test scores, which can then be compared to the students' GPA, entering test scores, and transcript listings of courses. Faculty for many majors also receive data on discipline subscores. Shortly after the academic year ends, faculty receive survey results comparing the responses of their majors with the university average. When multiple measures all identify a problem, the evidence gains legitimacy and is more likely to produce a coalition for change. However, faculty exposure to the data is essential. Workshops and faculty presentations at other functions provide good methods for enhancing use.

Success Factors

If the trends in an ongoing database are negative or worse than expected, faculty egos become involved. Faculty then turn to examples of successful reforms from other majors or develop new ideas for improvement.

Presidential and vice presidential support of the assessment effort and their extensive role-modeling of data use contribute enormously to a campuswide emphasis on student learning and development of a scholarly environment. Assessment at NMSU has always been presented as a means for the campus community to judge quality on the basis of more than just GPA and credit hours. Similarly, faculty have been assured that assessment will never be used punitively, and improvement plans to correct weaknesses have a good track record of receiving financial support.

Assessing Concept Attainment in Undergraduate Core Courses in Mathematics

John W. Emert, Charles R. Parish

CASE 8: BALL STATE UNIVERSITY

Look for: Locally developed assessment of conceptual attainment in core math courses for several types of math majors. The core was designed to address recommendations of national professional organizations. Multiple-level criteria were developed to assess supporting work as well as multiple-choice responses.

Background and Purpose

During the 1988–89 academic year, the departmental Critical Issues Task Force at Ball State University formulated a new common core program for majors in mathematics, statistics, mathematics education, and to a lesser degree, actuarial science. One major purpose of instituting the core was to update the programs to bring them more in line with national norms and recommendations of the several related professional organizations in mathematics.

Once the task force recommendation was discussed, refined, and ultimately approved by the tenure-line faculty of the department, ad hoc curricular groups were appointed to delineate new courses and revise existing courses to fit the core guidelines as approved by the faculty. These were then channeled through departmental standing committees and ultimately to the tenure-line faculty at large for final approval.

Courses included in the departmental common core are First-Year Calculus, Linear Algebra, Introduction to Algebraic Structures, Discrete Mathematics, and Statistical Methods. The core is intended to provide a proficiency in fundamental mathematical concepts that any mathematically literate person should possess. This is to be effected by a change in content emphasis, course overlap, and the introduction of contemporary mathematical topics, instructional technologies, and associated assessment procedures.

Method

The purpose of the assessment is to obtain measures of conceptual attainment in the core material. Since several faculty are involved in teaching these courses, items were selected to reflect independence of instruction. Some items require analysis and synthesis of knowledge from within a given content area. Items that cross specific subject areas were also included in an effort to measure students' ability to synthesize knowledge from different areas. All items were classified into two categories: standard items (S), which would typically appear on a course examination, and nonstandard items (N), which because of their form or content would typically not appear on a course examination.

Items from these categories were interspersed, but their categories were not identified on the instruments. These items, generated by the instrument authors, were organized in two prototype instruments, each intended to be 1.5 to 2 hours in length. They are designed to be administered at the sophomore level, reflecting the normal completion time of the common core.

Subject selection and instrument administration were assigned to individuals within the department other than the investigators. Subjects were students, usually sophomores and juniors, who had completed appropriate core components. They were encouraged by the department to participate on a voluntary basis, but only fifteen students were able to participate in the initial administration of the instruments. The instruments were administered in a group setting.

Even though many items were multiple-choice, the subjects were encouraged to submit supporting work to be considered in the evaluation process. It was hoped that this would provide additional insight into thought processes and thereby give additional evidence concerning students' development of concepts and mathematical maturity.

The prototype instruments will be compared with standardized instruments, such as those contained in the PRAXIS series from the Educational Testing Service. Since the latter utilize multiple-level criteria, analogous criteria were generated for use in this study, as depicted in Table 11.2.

Subject responses to instrument items were evaluated by the investigators independently, and differences in interpretation were resolved jointly through dis-

TABLE 11.2. ASSESSMENT CRITERIA.

Score	Criteria
3	Conceptual understanding apparent; consistent notation, with only an occasional error; logical formulation, complete or near-complete solution/response.
2	Conceptual understanding only adequate; careless mathematical errors present (algebra, arithmetic, for example); some logical steps lacking; incomplete solution/response.
1	Conceptual understanding not adequate; procedural errors; logical or relational steps missing; poor response or no response to the question posed.
0	Does not attempt problem or conceptual understanding totally lacking.

cussion and additional consideration of the responses. The present study, however, did not formally address the issue of inter-rater reliability due to the small sample size.

Findings

Score means and frequencies for the subject responses appear in Table 11.3. The reader will note that items have been classified by their principal content area and categorized into standard and nonstandard types.

While the number of subjects and sampling method did not support statistical analysis of the data, some trends and pertinent observations are presented. Mean scores can be misleading, as suggested by items S_{10}, S_{11}, n_9, and n_{10}. In each case, the mean did not reflect the extreme diversity of subject responses. On the other hand, some means, such those for items S_2 and S_3, indicated relatively low levels of student understanding but were the result of having a few very low scores averaged with mostly high scores.

Subjects appear to be most comfortable with standard material from functions, limits, and derivatives. Most nonstandard material is handled marginally

TABLE 11.3 ITEM-SUBJECT MEAN SCORES AND FREQUENCIES.

Principal Content	Standard Items							Nonstandard Items				
	Means	Frequencies						Means	Frequencies			
		0	1	2	3				0	1	2	3
Functions												
S_1	2.8	0	1	1	13		n_1	0.9	3	11	1	0
S_2	2.4	2	1	1	11		n_2	1.2	5	3	6	1
Limits												
S_3	2.5	0	4	0	11		n_3	1.6	1	7	4	3
S_4	2.0	0	7	1	7							
Derivatives												
S_5	1.9	0	7	3	5		n_4	1.4	4	4	4	3
Integrals												
S_6	1.1	8	2	1	4		n_5	1.3	3	7	2	3
S_7	0.8	9	2	2	2		n_6	1.4	2	9	0	4
S_8	1.3	6	2	3	4		n_7	1.2	2	10	1	2
Sequences and series												
S_9	0.9	8	4	0	3		n_8	1.5	3	4	6	2
S_{10}	1.7	6	1	0	8		n_9	1.1	6	3	5	1
S_{11}	1.0	10	0	0	5							
Vectors							n_{10}	1.2	6	2	5	2

better than standard material in the areas of integration and sequences and series. However, performance in these content areas and in the nonstandard forms of items in functions and limits is deficient.

By considering the frequencies associated with the items, a clearer picture of subject success emerges. Of the items attempted by the subjects, approximately 60 percent of the responses were at least acceptable, while 40 percent lacked adequate conceptual understanding needed to address the item. Further, two-thirds of those giving acceptable responses presented complete or near-complete responses. From this point of view, the data suggest that most errors are not careless but rather indicate a lack of adequate conceptualization.

Use of Findings

Based on these findings, we anticipate more focused efforts toward (1) continued restructuring of the calculus curriculum; (2) continued work to identify more productive and efficient teaching methods and assessment procedures; (3) identification of other ways that existing instruction and assessment resources can be more profitably utilized; and (4) using PRAXIS instruments in a comparative study with the prototype core instruments. Such a study could provide other perspectives on assessment.

From a broader perspective, we hope to streamline and more carefully focus our departmental core to address the identified goals. These actions should produce a stronger major program and ultimately a more highly qualified graduate who can deal effectively with contemporary issues.

Success Factors

Several factors combined to make this project a reality. Based on previous experience in assessment activities, the authors of this case study were encouraged by the department chair to focus on core evaluation. Financial assistance from the university Office of Academic Assessment supported the formulation of the prototype instrument.

This assessment activity was timely for several reasons. Initiatives in assessment receive strong support in our university at all levels. Additionally, the recent national focus on academic assessment by professional mathematics organizations suggests such periodic reviews. Furthermore, our curriculum had been on-line for a four-year period, and the department needed to determine its level of effectiveness. Moreover, the dynamics of the core courses and their instruction placed the department in a mode appropriate for such an analysis to be of value.

Assessing French Language Performance

Judith E. Brisbois

CASE 9: UNITED STATES AIR FORCE ACADEMY

Look for: Emphasis on careful design, review, and improvement of a performance test for students taking minors in French. The test, Survival Training in France, incorporates reading and listening comprehension and writing.

Background and Purpose

At the United States Air Force Academy, cadets in any major may minor in a foreign language. In order to earn a foreign language minor, cadets must complete four courses beyond the basic level and pass a comprehensive examination at the end of the fourth course.

A new French minors test was initiated as an improvement over a previous instrument. Consisting of multiple-choice and cloze items, the former minors test did not allow the cadets to demonstrate adequately their French proficiency because it did not require them to produce the language in response to an authentic task. Moreover, we sought a new minors test that would be in line overall with the French program's testing methods. Across the board, we are moving away from discrete-point items and toward authentic production tasks.

All members of the French Division were involved in the process of constructing the new exam. Cadet responses would allow instructors to assess what minors candidates could do with the language, rather than what linguistic facts they could recognize.

Method

We chose a theme, "survival training in France," that would integrate all parts of the exam (listening comprehension, reading comprehension, and writing). We knew the topic to be authentic because two of our instructors had experienced survival training in France as cadets when they participated in the semester-long exchange program we have with the French air force academy. Furthermore, all of the minors candidates had undergone survival training, either in the United States or as exchange cadets in France.

The listening comprehension section consisted of a telephone message recorded by a native speaker. The message explained where to meet and what to take along for survival training, and outlined some important changes in plans. Cadets were allowed to listen to the recording twice, then were asked to fill out a grid, in English, listing when and where each squadron was to meet and what supplies were needed.

The reading comprehension portion asked for a summary, in English, of a page-long authentic passage taken from the novel *Papillon* about the ordeal of a well-known French prisoner. This selection connects with the survival training theme because escape and evasion training, along with capture and time spent in a simulated prison camp, are part of the program.

In the writing section, the cadets were asked to write a letter, in French, to a friend who was about to undergo survival training. They were to give advice based on their experience.

Responses to the listening and reading items were in English because a large body of second-language research indicates that responses in the less fluent second language sometimes fail to reflect accurately what has been comprehended from a passage. Responses in the native language are far more likely to show exactly what the test taker has understood from a text.

Findings

According to a survey administered to all cadets tested, most preferred the new format to multiple-choice, largely because they perceived it to be a more accurate and authentic measure of their proficiency. Additionally, the students asked for a mandatory oral portion of the exam (we did it on a voluntary basis because oral proficiency evaluations are extremely time consuming to administer), and for a culture portion to include historical events and cultural differences that had been discussed in the minors program.

The French instructors also found this instrument superior to the one previously used for three reasons. First, we arrived at a better idea of what the cadets could do with the language because they were required to produce it. Second, by carefully examining cadet responses, we were better able to determine whether or not any "holes" existed in our curriculum. Third, we now have data illustrating what could reasonably be expected from last year's minors candidates and will be able to use those data to compare results from year to year as the French curriculum develops.

Use of Findings

Because this was the first time we had administered the new exam, we did not use it as a basis for granting or denying anyone a minor in French. We did, however, use the results to test the test and to examine our curriculum. In terms of testing the test, we looked carefully at cadet responses to items on both the test and the follow-up survey to decide whether or not the tasks were appropriate. Three major changes were made to the exam based on the cadets' test and survey responses. First, although they did not have a particularly difficult time with the listening task, they suggested we play the tape three times rather than twice. Because one can, in reality, listen to a taped telephone message as many times as is necessary for understanding, we now allow them to listen three times. Second, because they asked for a culture section, one was added. The cadets are now asked to respond, in English, to several short-answer questions about cultural differences between the French and Americans. Third, the cadets suggested that the required length of the writing portion was excessive. Upon reexamining the instrument, we found no reason why the task could not be completed adequately in one page rather than one and a half, and made the appropriate change. We are still considering the possibility of including a mandatory oral proficiency interview.

Additionally, the cadets' responses provided us with a window on course articulation. Did any "holes" exist in our curriculum? Was there anything that the cadets could not do that they should have been able to do in order to earn a minor in French? Were they meeting our course/program outcomes? Careful examination of the responses indicated no major curricular deficiencies. In the future, we will compare the results with those of upcoming classes to help us determine the degree to which any changes that may be made in the French curriculum lead to improvement in production skills. We have already used the data in an effort to reexamine and refine our French program outcomes.

Success Factors

The minors test, though not perfect, worked fairly well. First, the test was carefully thought out and constructed. In developing the test, we sought guidance from a visiting professor who is an expert in foreign language pedagogy and from other faculty in the department. Second, we all shared our expertise by working together in developing ideas for testing techniques and in writing the various parts of the test, with some instructors working on reading, some on listening, and some on writing. Third, we were able to use the results to improve the instrument, and to help us examine our curriculum.

Assessment of Foreign Language Competence Based on ACTFL Guidelines

Robert J. Chierico

CASE 10: CHICAGO STATE UNIVERSITY

Look for: An evaluation of students' listening and speaking skills in Spanish. An oral proficiency rating checklist accompanies this example.

Background and Purpose

The assessment in foreign languages at Chicago State University is part of a universitywide assessment plan mandated by the board of governors. This segment of the comprehensive plan focuses on assessment in the major for the purpose of strengthening programs.

Method

The comprehensive assessment plan in foreign languages encompasses the areas of language, literature, and culture/history. We have now completed the language phase, which is divided into three subareas: speaking/listening, reading, and writing. Although instruments have been developed in all three areas, I will focus this discussion on speaking/listening.

The subjects being evaluated are all Spanish majors at different levels in their language study. The instrument used is the Oral Proficiency Interview developed by the Educational Testing Service and based on the American Council on the Teaching of Foreign Languages (ACTFL) guidelines for oral proficiency. Two of my colleagues and I were trained as oral proficiency testers and I received ACTFL certification.

A rating sheet listing learning objectives for the various levels was developed and is used for each twenty-minute interview. The sheet points out specific areas in which weaknesses as well as strengths are assessed and includes a space for suggestions for improvement (see Exhibit 11.1).

Findings

Pilot testing carried out in February of 1993 brought the following results: of the initial group of eleven, five were at novice level; two at intermediate; three at advanced; and one at superior.

Use of Findings

Since each level is based on specific learning outcomes, it is fairly simple to determine how curriculum can be improved. After reviewing the results, it was determined that the five novice-level students needed help with creating with language, maintaining conversation, survival situations of daily life, and asking and answering questions. I think that the most important benefit is that students now have an accurate idea of where they are and what they have to do to improve. For example, based on these results, I determined that my Intermediate Spanish class should incorporate more role-playing and re-creating of real life situations. In addition, we found that oral proficiency might be increased by pairing a native speaker with an American in additional tutoring sessions.

Success Factors

The activity was successful because, first, faculty were well trained to accomplish the goal. All of our faculty attended weeklong workshops in which they learned

EXHIBIT 11.1. ORAL PROFICIENCY RATING CHECKLIST.

DLI Scale	ACTFL/ETS Scale	Functions	Yes/No	Situation Cards
4/5*	Superior	Tailors language to audience	_____	Grey
		Negotiates, persuades, counsels	_____	
		Represents point of view	_____	

*Native-like speech and extensive vocabulary are distinguishing features between both.

DLI Scale	ACTFL/ETS Scale	Functions	Yes/No	Situation Cards
3+	Superior	Does above functions sometimes but not consistently	_____	Grey
3	Superior	Supports opinions and argues logically a point of view	_____	Yellow
		Hypothesizes	_____	
		Discusses abstract and concrete topics	_____	
		Unpatterned errors only	_____	
		Can get into, through, and out of unfamiliar situation	_____	
2+	Advanced Plus	Can do above functions sometimes but not consistently	_____	Yellow
2	Advanced	Narrates and describes in present time	_____	Orange
		Narrates and describes in past time	_____	
		Narrates and describes in future time	_____	
		Able to circumlocute	_____	
		Can be understood by person not used to foreign speakers	_____	
		Can get into, through, and out of unfamiliar situation with a complication	_____	
1+	Intermediate High	Can do above functions sometimes but not consistently	_____	Orange
1	Intermediate Mid/Low	Creates with language	_____	Green
		Asks and answers questions on familiar topics	_____	
		Can get into, through, and out of simple survival situation	_____	
0+	Novice High	Can do above functions sometimes but not consistently	_____	Green
0	Novice Mid/ Novice High	No functional ability	_____	
		Limited to memorized material	_____	

Applicant: _____   Language: _____
S.S. #: _____   Date: _____
Examiner: _____   Overall Rating: _____
_____   Second Rating: _____

PLEASE NOTE PATTERNS OF ERROR ON BACK OF PAGE

Source: Adapted by Adela Weinstein from ETS Oral Proficiency Testing training instrument, 1984.

the techniques of oral proficiency testing. Additional help was provided by our professional organization, which made available preliminary guidelines for the testing of reading and writing proficiency. In terms of preparing faculty for rewards, since evaluation for promotion and tenure is based on the three areas of teaching, service, and professional activities, involvement in assessment enhances credentials in one or both of the latter categories.

Professional Portfolio Process

Jean Ann Box, Carol D. Dean

CASE 11: SAMFORD UNIVERSITY

Look for: Detailed description of the contents of a professional portfolio required of senior education majors. Teachers and principals serve as external reviewers of the portfolio. Use of professionals as reviewers has built stronger relationships between the School of Education and the community it serves.

Background and Purpose

In 1991, the faculty of the Orlean Bullard Beeson School of Education at Samford University recognized the need for a senior project to assess the teaching abilities and skills of the graduating students and their expertise in applying the school's knowledge base, "teacher as a reflective decision maker." Faculty also noted the intense competition for positions in the education profession and felt a need to give Samford students an edge in marketing themselves. The two concerns were merged into one strategy: the professional portfolio, a process through which students reflect upon and assess their own learning, are evaluated by university professors and outside educators, and create a tool through which they can effectively present themselves in a competitive job market.

Method

Each student creates a portfolio during his or her senior year. The type of display case and the criteria for the contents are specific, but presentation encourages creativity.

The case itself is a thirteen-by-sixteen-inch leather-like presentation case with a zipper, containing five to six plastic display/scrapbook-type pages in the center for holding photographs, résumé, and statement of philosophy. There is at least one pocket to hold three-dimensional items such as teaching units, folder games, and teaching videos.

The content criteria are divided into three sections: "Professional Information," "Curriculum Planning," and "Instructional Implementation." Each section contains artifacts, respectively demonstrating the intern's understanding of child development and his or her ability to make (1) appropriate decisions about his or her own professional development and basic philosophical positions; (2) sound curriculum decisions through the creation of unit plans; and (3) effective instructional decisions while implementing the unit plans designed.

Artifacts contained in the portfolio include the following:

- Current résumé suitable for use when seeking a teaching position and any awards or other evidence of teaching-related experience
- Evidence of membership in professional organizations
- A succinct but polished statement of the student's teaching philosophy and concept of the teaching process
- Teaching units developed in methods courses prior to student teaching
- Two bound teaching units developed and taught during the student teaching internship
- Model lesson plan developed and taught during the internship, with accompanying observation form filled out by the university professor upon observing the lesson
- Photographs, drawings, diagrams, or descriptions of classroom activities conducted during the internship, including at least one bulletin board designed and used
- Worksheets, activities, or games developed by the student as an intern
- Videotape of a lesson presented during the internship
- Journal of student teaching experience
- Summaries of conferences with cooperating teachers and university supervisor
- Evidence of monitoring and measurement of student outcomes upon completion of unit(s) taught in internship classrooms

During the semester prior to their student teaching, students attend a series of seminars in which they become familiar with the format of the portfolio and with specific criteria required. They are encouraged to develop their own personal overall design or theme, write or redefine and rewrite their philosophy of teaching, and develop their résumés.

During the professional semester, students put together the actual portfolio, showcasing their own unique personalities and teaching philosophies and styles. They modify their written philosophy, reflecting on their fourteen weeks of firsthand experiences. They take numerous photographs—of their students' original bulletin boards and learning centers and special activities. The portfolio materials are arranged to present the student's unique teaching experience attractively and to demonstrate the student's commitment to his or her philosophy. Students include a reflective journal chronicling the thoughts, feelings, successes, and frustrations that are a part of each student's journey as an emerging professional. This process encourages the student to consider and assess his or her growth during the student teaching experience.

The culmination of the portfolio process is an evaluation by a university professor and an external reviewer and an oral presentation given by the student. Professional educators from the community are asked to review and evaluate portfolios according to definitive criteria on instruments developed by the faculty. The students present their portfolios in a seminar to faculty, family, and peers, explaining their philosophies and how they were demonstrated during the student teaching experience.

Findings and Their Use

Over the three years that this procedure has been in place, faculty members have noted that the students seem more aware of the process of teaching. They are more thoughtful in planning and more conscious of outcomes, both short term and long range. Computer and other technological skills have been strengthened as students realize that their efforts must be displayed in a very concrete form. Several unexpected outcomes include increased collaboration among students and the building of relationships with professionals in the community as teachers and principals serve as external reviewers. The image of Samford's teacher education department has also been enhanced as the process is continually being refined. One of the most positive outcomes has been that closure has been brought to the student teaching experience in a unique way.

Success Factors

Factors involved in the success of the portfolio process consist of leadership of the faculty, personal contact with students, and clear criteria and guidelines well developed by the faculty prior to beginning the process.

The primary caution that should be considered is that students need to be prepared prior to their student teaching semester so that the process is not overwhelming and does not take a disproportionate amount of students' time. Portfolio seminars conducted the semester prior to student teaching are strongly recommended.

Portfolios: Useful Tools for Assessment in Business Technology

Leslie S. Smith, Elizabeth H. Crowther

CASE 12: RAPPAHANNOCK COMMUNITY COLLEGE

Look for: Use of a citizens' advisory committee in evaluation of students' portfolios. Students benefit from this practical perspective on their work, and faculty develop closer relationships with individuals who can help them stay current in meeting employers' needs.

Background and Purpose

Business faculty at Rappahannock Community College were concerned with the preparedness of the students who were graduating and the relevance of their education to the real world. Several strategies were discussed as possible choices for assessment of the business students. Testing was dismissed because of the different types of business majors that are taught. The faculty felt that there was not one test that would judge all majors fairly. The group then decided that a portfolio project would best assess the different business majors.

Method

Portfolio projects developed for assessing business technology students were implemented in spring 1992 and reemployed in spring 1993. Chosen as a tool to add substance to our multiple measures scheme, the portfolios have proved an excellent method for involving the Citizen's Advisory Committee, which returns direct and applicable comments on the professional quality of the students' projects. The Citizen's Advisory Committee has been in place for many years, but had not been used for individual student assessment. Students in business technology programs are instructed by faculty to prepare a portfolio which includes—along with program-specific culminating projects—a résumé, completed state application, and cover letter that is written to respond to a particular advertisement. The Citizen's Advisory Committee reviews these portfolios in April and May and completes a review sheet for each. Comments are returned to the students before they leave Rappahannock Community College (RCC) in May.

Findings

Citizen's Advisory Committee and RCC reviewers make comments indicating how students can improve the presentation of their résumés and cover letters. The advisory committee feels that many of the portfolios are well done but finds a few that could cause capable students to be screened out of an interview. Therefore, particularly for those few students, this exercise can dramatically improve their chances of being hired into a position. Unlike other measures, the portfolio project provides immediate feedback and immediate results for the student.

Use of Findings

The Citizen's Advisory Committee has become more active and interested in helping with assessment and curriculum development. Students have benefited through the real-life exercise of developing the portfolio and having it evaluated by a potential employer. The faculty and students have benefited because the closer ties with the business community help keep the courses and programs relevant for today's employment arena.

Rappahannock Community College plans to continue the portfolio projects. In addition, it plans to develop mock interviews and general employment tests with business representatives. Plans are also in the making to expand the portfolio projects into other curricula.

Success Factors

The portfolio project is a success at RCC because it (1) assists students in meshing skills and presenting themselves in writing, (2) gives students a sense of how to apply their knowledge, 3) assists students in compiling a professional and effective application package to increase their chances of appropriate and timely employment, (4) involves the members of the Citizen's Advisory Committee directly so that they have a chance to assess student skills and comment on related instructional areas, and (5) lets RCC instructors determine how well their students are synthesizing classroom learning.

Assessment for Program Improvement: Focus on an Academic Major

John R. Barker, John Folger

CASE 13: VANDERBILT UNIVERSITY

Look for: An assessment seminar involving a research-oriented faculty in discussing program goals, gathering data, and using findings to improve the program. Existing information about students was combined with new data collected via questionnaires, interviews, and focus groups.

Background and Purpose

Human and Organizational Development is an interdisciplinary major that began in fall 1982 at Vanderbilt University. (The major was initially named Human Development, but to more accurately represent the program's instruction on organizational issues was changed in 1992.) The curriculum is a liberal arts and sciences–based preparation for a wide range of human service occupations. H&OD students learn about individuals, small groups, organizations, and society in a developmental sequence of courses. The program culminates in a full-time internship experience, usually taken during a student's senior year. Faculty in

H&OD focus the core curriculum on building student skills across four primary areas: interpersonal communication, community service, written and spoken communication, and critical thinking/problem solving. The major goal of the program is to prepare students for careers that involve finding solutions to human problems in organizations and communities. To focus the program in a time of dramatic growth and provide guidance for program improvement, a new department chair instituted an assessment project in August 1990.

Method

The overall design for the assessment was loosely modeled after the Harvard Assessment Seminars (Light, 1992), with monthly meetings of faculty to discuss program goals, review assessment data from multiple sources, and plan data-based improvements. John Folger served as coordinator for the assessment, and with graduate assistant John Barker, organized presentations and discussion by faculty involved in the Assessment Seminar.

Assessment activities were designed to answer questions about student characteristics and motivation (program inputs) and programmatic strengths and weaknesses (organizational processes and environment), and to identify the level of competence of the graduates (program outputs). This general assessment strategy corresponded roughly to Astin's Input-Environment-Output Model (Astin, 1991). The assessment process was open ended and oriented toward finding ways to improve the program. Although there was no a priori "grand design" for data collection, the H&OD assessment was guided by the belief that answering assessment questions required multiple sources of information. This "multiple lines of evidence" approach (Lipsey, Cordray, and Berger, 1981, p. 283) was supported by the department chair and other faculty members.

Like most universities, Vanderbilt systematically collects information about the aptitudes and characteristics of entering students, student grades, student ratings of instruction, and student course-taking. For the assessment of H&OD, those kinds of data were brought together with other information collected from students, faculty, program graduates, and employers to form a program database that was used for answering assessment questions. Original data collection activities included the administration of locally designed questionnaires, interviews, and focus groups. Tests and survey instruments developed elsewhere were also used as necessary.

The existing university records generally were satisfactory for providing information about program inputs. Previous academic performance, test scores, and extracurricular activities of students were available from student records provided by the college registrar. Information on program inputs was supplemented through the use of instruments like the Motivated Strategies for Learning Questionnaire (Pintrich, Smith, Garcia, and McKeachie, 1991) and the College Student Experiences Questionnaire (Pace, 1990).

Focus groups, surveys, and interviews provided the means for assessing the environment of H&OD. Focus groups addressed questions about student culture. Surveys and interviews were used to evaluate various components of the faculty culture. Transcript analyses and syllabi reviews were also used to investigate different environmental components of the H&OD curriculum.

To measure program outcomes, several methods were used. Two surveys of program graduates asked for their evaluation of the strengths and weaknesses of the H&OD major, as well as their suggestions about ways H&OD could be improved. Data were also gathered about graduates' jobs and career plans.

Commercial instruments were also used for outcomes assessment. The Assessment of Reasoning and Communicating (ARC), developed by the American College Testing program, was one instrument used to assess student learning in the areas of problem analysis and written and spoken communication. Using a matched-sample cross-sectional design comparing freshmen and second-semester juniors, an estimate of student gains in problem analysis and communication skills was made. The use of the ARC also allowed for comparison with scores of students at other institutions that had used the ARC.

Another measure of program output was obtained from a series of focus groups with several Nashville-area internship supervisors and employers of graduates. Although potentially biased toward the concerns of Nashville employers, the focus groups provided a rich source of data on program outcomes. Employers and internship supervisors discussed students' preparation for their jobs, the strengths and weaknesses of students' job skills, and how H&OD students compared with other college graduates the employers and supervisors had hired or used as interns.

Findings

Students who enter H&OD have impressive academic backgrounds, are primarily extrinsically motivated, and see the major as a way to gain knowledge and skills for today's job market. Most H&OD students also enter Vanderbilt with a substantial record of community service.

The environment of the program is characterized by a sense of innovation. Reports of "free riders" (that is, the academically unengaged) from students, however, substantiated faculty claims of having students who abused teaching innovations such as group projects and peer learning activities. The investigation of students' course-taking patterns found several students abusing their freedom to assemble courses for a content area specialization within the major.

The assessment of program outputs provided both positive and negative findings. Graduates of the program were generally very positive about their collegiate experience, although they had suggestions for program improvement: (1) develop specific content areas for the program, (2) provide a clearer image for the interdisciplinary program, and (3) make the program more challenging. Employers were also quite positive about H&OD graduates' knowledge and skills, although some would like graduates to have more specific knowledge related to their particular jobs.

The results of the ARC were not as positive. Both freshmen and juniors scored about average on writing and reasoning, and above average on speaking. When test results were adjusted for differences in aptitude test scores of H&OD students and the students in other institutions that had used the test, H&OD students were slightly below average, and were about average in gain from freshman to junior level. Apparently many students needed to develop their skills in critical thinking, problem solving, and written communication.

Use of Findings

The data generated by the Assessment Seminar facilitated faculty discussion and provided evidence for the department chair to use in making programmatic requests of the dean. The faculty used assessment data from syllabi review, graduate surveys, and focus groups as the basis for proposing that the name of the program be changed from Human Development to Human and Organizational Development, to acknowledge organizational behavior and development as a substantial component of the major's content.

The primary use of assessment data was to guide substantial revisions in the curriculum. Three areas of specialization are being planned to give the major more content focus and a greater level of specificity and challenge. A specific emphasis on critical thinking skills across the curriculum was investigated, with some classes implemented on a pilot basis. In other areas of the curriculum, some courses were resequenced. Other courses were restructured to standardize content across the various sections of each course.

In the most direct link of assessment information with the purpose of student improvement, data from program graduates and employers were shared with enrolled students to provide guidance as they planned their careers. Using the database as a resource, several students were able to contact graduates and get helpful advice on specific internship and career decisions.

Success Factors

Assessment in H&OD was successful in effecting program improvement because it focused on questions the department chair, the H&OD program director, and faculty determined to be important. The multiple lines of evidence approach provided information that was helpful in answering those questions. Persistence by the department leaders kept the faculty engaged in the planning and implementation of the curriculum changes. Acceptance and involvement of the faculty were critical. The use of sound research methodology and appropriate instrumentation was important because the faculty participating in the Assessment Seminar were trained to reject inadequate or inappropriate work. Acceptance of the assessment process was facilitated by the faculty culture, one of openness to change and improvement. The assessment initiated a substantial change in the curriculum, which is still being implemented. It is too early to say how much impact these changes will have on student learning.

It may take some time for faculty to grow comfortable with engaging in the public discussions that are required for the assessment seminar approach to assessment. In pursuing multiple lines of evidence, it is also important to manage information efficiently and disseminate research results appropriately. Developing an assessment program takes a substantial amount of time and effort, with the role of consistent leadership crucial to success.

Vanderbilt did not make an initial commitment to develop and continue an assessment process that would provide ongoing information to guide change. Recent changes in departmental and college leadership make the future of assessment of the H&OD program unclear. The initial focus on curriculum change has led some faculty to conclude that since the curriculum has changed, further assessment is not needed. Some faculty think the assessment should have put more emphasis on helping individual faculty improve their instruction. The priority for continuing efforts to measure student outcomes is not very high among faculty, since the H&OD program is successful in attracting good students and graduating successful alumni.

Assessment Colloquium: Master of Arts Program

Catherine Marienau, Morris Fiddler

CASE 14: DEPAUL UNIVERSITY, SCHOOL FOR NEW LEARNING

Look for: An assessment colloquium that assists students in the Master of Arts in Integrated Professional Studies program to develop self- and peer-assessment skills. Faculty agree that information from the colloquium has influenced major changes in content and sequencing of the curriculum and in administrative procedures.

Background and Purpose

The program for the Master of Arts in Integrated Professional Studies at the DePaul University School for New Learning is designed to integrate (1) workplace with classroom learning; (2) liberal learning skills with technical/professional expertise; and (3) theoretical concepts with practical application. Begun in 1985, the program serves experienced practitioners who develop personalized programs linking workplace learning and academic study. The Assessment Colloquium was built into the first-year Liberal Learning Curriculum to punctuate the link between work and learning.

The participants in the Assessment Colloquium are approximately fifteen students per cluster, who proceed together through the Liberal Learning Curriculum portion of the program, and a member of the college faculty who serves as an overall adviser for each student's curriculum.

The Assessment Colloquium creates a forum for students to develop attitudes and skills of reflective practice in order to inform their own learning, improve performance by integrating liberal learning skills with professional development, and engage in collaborative learning through feedback from student peers regarding individual development. Program objectives of the colloquium include promoting assessment as part of the learning process, obtaining feedback and evidence on the extent to which the learning/learner objectives are being met, and gathering information needed for interventions and/or program improvements.

Method

The Assessment Colloquium meets quarterly during the students' first year for three or more hours each session. Preceding each meeting, the faculty adviser poses guiding questions for the students to respond to in writing or in preparation for group discussion. The guiding questions differ for each session as the Assessment Colloquium shifts emphasis. The titles of the sessions are:

Session 1: Awareness Building [of liberal learning skills]

Session 2: Practice/"Technical" Development [of assessment skills and procedures]

Session 3: Self-Assessment and Its Intentional Application

Session 4: Integration or "Ownership" [of liberal learning and professional practice]

More specifically, Session 1 follows directly after the first course in which students have developed detailed working drafts of a learning plan for their professional focus areas. They have also begun to address development of liberal learning skills, captured in the following criteria: (1) capacity to engage in self-assessment and self-managed learning; (2) ability to engage in critical, synthetic, and creative thinking; (3) ability to apply moral reasoning to issues of values and ethics; (4) facility in verbal communication modes; and (5) facility in interpersonal skills. The first session of the Assessment Colloquium enhances awareness of the meaning of each of these liberal learning skills and engages the learners in self-assessment of these skills at their present point in their programs. An additional objective is to anticipate upcoming courses through examination of personal learning goals and current levels of knowledge regarding the subject matter.

Session 2 is attended by the students, the faculty adviser, and the students' professional advisers, who serve as key resources to the refinement and execution of the learning plans. The session addresses criteria for assessing students' work with respect to graduate-level expectations, college procedures for assessment of learning, and the liberal learning skills as they are being developed and applied in professional contexts.

Session 3 explicitly focuses on self-assessment. Students examine what self-assessment means to them and how they apply it and with what degree of intentionality, and they reflect on their experience to date. Students also learn to use the tools of self-assessment to provide feedback to peers for mutual development of their individualized programs.

The theme of Session 4 is integration. Students provide evidence that they are integrating liberal learning skills with information from the Liberal Learning Curriculum and with their professional development activities. An underlying theme of the session is ongoing development of professional identity and its alignment with the learning and goals of each student's program. Finally, feedback among peers and to the program provides a third dimension of this session.

Taken as a whole, then, the four sessions of the Assessment Colloquium are intended to help students move from the development of awareness through technical development of liberal learning skills to integration/ownership of professional and liberal learning abilities and practices.

Findings and Use of Findings

The most salient outcomes of the Assessment Colloquium as reported by students are that they (1) become intentional and facile in their use of self-assessment in their professional practice; (2) seek feedback from multiple sources more frequently and mediate that feedback more effectively than prior to their engagement in the M.A. program; (3) perform more effectively in their professional contexts (this is evidenced through promotions and increased responsibilities); and (4) take increasing charge of setting directions in both their work and personal lives.

The most significant outcomes for the program are the recognition that (1) students need guidance and instruction in doing meaningful self-assessment; (2) intentional self-assessment efforts tend to affect the whole person rather than just his or her professional dimensions; (3) feedback from students has influenced major curricular revisions, for example, content and sequencing of the Liberal Learning Curriculum, as well as of the goals and content of the Assessment Colloquium itself; (4) administrative procedures can impede students' academic progress and need continual monitoring and improvement; and (5) the Assessment Colloquium can function as a tool for increased retention by helping students to focus on and assume responsibility for their academic progress.

Success Factors

We believe the Assessment Colloquium has been a successful innovation for several reasons: (1) it is an intentional locus of assessment built into a program structure that already includes roles and responsibilities of the faculty and administration, thus creating expectations to "make it work"; (2) its aims are congruent with the curricular aims of the program and the philosophy of the college, (that is, improvement through reflection on practice; faculty and administration ask the same things of themselves as they ask of students in this regard); (3) the program's director served as both the advocate for self-assessment and the person who held faculty accountable for the goals of the colloquium (she participated in each session of each colloquium until faculty assumed a commitment to and ownership of colloquium success and development); (4) experience with the colloquium has led to an increasingly defined curriculum for it; and (5) faculty find the Assessment Colloquium a gratifying segment of the overall curriculum.

There are, however, some cautions we have recognized as the Assessment Colloquium has evolved. It has been important to monitor student workload demanded by the colloquium so that self-assessment is not perceived as a burdensome chore. It has also been important to maintain a policy that no single session of the Assessment Colloquium is graded. An evaluation of student performance in the colloquium is built into a broader-based evaluation of student progress in a mid program review that examines participation in the Assessment Colloquium as part of a larger set of activities.

Improving Professional Student Performance on National Board Examinations Through Effective Administrative Intervention

Arthur Van Stewart

CASE 15: UNIVERSITY OF LOUISVILLE

Look for: Improvement in National Board Examinations scores for students enrolled in a professional school as a result of calling the attention of faculty and students to disappointingly low scores. Motivating students to perform conscientiously can raise performance levels.

Background and Purpose

The outcomes assessment instrument most commonly used to evaluate the quality and overall effectiveness of doctoral programs in American dental colleges is the set of National Board Examinations administered in cooperation with the American Dental Association. Indeed, the National Boards-Part I (given at the end of two years of training) and National Boards-Part II (given in the fourth year of training) are the only measures of academic performance in dentistry that allow for both inter-institutional comparisons and long-term intra-institutional outcomes assessment based on a nationally standardized testing system. Because students from all American dental schools take the National Boards, the "boards" are considered very important outcome measures by faculty, administrators, and accreditation review teams. The National Boards, when coupled with a nationally administered preadmissions aptitude and skill measurement test (Dental Admissions Test, or DAT), also can be used to determine relative increases in student performance that can be attributed to the effectiveness of the educational program offered by the dental college.

When a new assistant dean for academic affairs was appointed at the University of Louisville School of Dentistry, one of his first undertakings was to examine the school's relative success on these examinations. A second step was to determine the degree of faculty and administrator awareness of their students' performance on these nationally administered tests. The natural desire to have respectable scores on the National Boards was amplified by (1) in-state competition with other health professions schools for very limited higher education funds, (2) a professional accreditation review that was scheduled to take place within the next few years, and (3) the announced need for the school to move from a parochial to a more national and international perspective in order to fulfill its role as an outstanding dental college and a national leader in dental education.

Method

The Office of Academic Affairs first collected summary data on the students' most recent performance on parts I and II of the national exams and also data for the previous ten years. In addition, the educational program coordinators (Curriculum Committee members) and department chairmen were canvassed to determine to what degree they were aware of the school's past and current performance profiles on the National Board Examinations. Finally, students and recent alumni were interviewed to determine how they perceived their own performance on National Board tests and the importance, if any, of the test results. After these early surveying steps were completed, the issue of performance on National Boards was judged by the dental school's administration to be of high priority because (1) scores on both part I and part II of the National Board Examinations were found to be lower than expected, (2) a majority of faculty did not realize how low the scores had fallen in the last three years, and (3) students and alumni were found to exhibit general ignorance and a pervasive apathy toward the school's performance on this important series of national tests.

Findings

The assistant dean for academic affairs prepared a summary of National Boards performance data for a ten-year time span. His analysis revealed three important phenomena: (1) individual student scores were seldom above national averages, even among demonstrably superior students; (2) the scores on some specific parts of the examination were declining and were significantly lower than they had been in previous years (in spite of a 25 percent growth in full-time faculty and a gradually improving dental school applicant profile); and (3) although the dental school prided itself on "clinical" training, the students' National Board performance on clinical subjects was not significantly better than it was on sections of the board examinations that tested the natural (nonclinical) sciences. There also appeared to be some very serious misperceptions of dental student performance by department chairmen, teaching faculty, and students (all three groups consistently reported that they believed that the school ranked "very high in comparison with most other dental colleges in the U.S. and Canada," when, in fact, scores were largely below the national average).

Use of Findings

Based on the recommendations of the assistant dean for academic affairs, an up-to-date and accurate profile of the students' performance on National Board Examinations was prepared and shared with members of the assistant dean's staff, the Department Chairmen's Council, and members of the Curriculum Committee. After looking at the data, all groups agreed that the scores were inappropriately, artificially, and unacceptably low. Efforts were made to convince students of the value (to them and to the school) of their taking the examinations more seriously. This goal was met by having meetings with each dental class several weeks before the National Board Examinations were given. In addition the dean and the assistant dean for academic affairs (plus any faculty who wanted to attend) participated in class meetings after the results were officially reported to the school. During these two class meetings, the composite part I and part II scores were compared with those of previous classes and with national norms.

To underscore the long-term importance of National Board scores to the student and to the school, scores on National Boards were entered into a newly created section on each student's permanent academic record. The academic dean also began sending congratulatory letters to the individual students who did well on the examinations as well as to the individual faculty who taught them or served as faculty advisers to the successful classes. The format for the dental school's departmental annual reports was revised so that department chairmen would be required to include summary reports on National Board performance in the disciplines taught by their department faculty. And finally, faculty and students were encouraged to see National Boards as an opportunity to demonstrate personal and institutional achievement and accomplishment that could offset the traditionally low DAT scores for entering students.

The results of the administrative intervention were striking. Within two years of the implementation of the new initiatives, student performance on National Boards-Part I rose to a level above the national average. Performance on National Boards-Part II rose even higher. In less than four years, the school's scores were raised until they ranked in the top 15 percent of all U.S. and Canadian dental colleges. When the National Board scores were compared with entering student DAT scores, the results were even more striking, demonstrating a highly desirable upward trend from DAT to part I, and on upward even further on the part II scores.

Success Factors

1. The person in charge of the Office of Academic Affairs had an excellent background in dental education and exerted leadership and administrative responsibility for identifying the problem, for focusing faculty and administrative attention on the issue of boards, and for leading the administrative effort to eliminate the problem.

2. When the nature of the scores was adequately documented and clearly summarized in briefing reports, almost all faculty and the majority of students felt keenly that the scores were underreporting the true capabilities of the students and the actual strength of the academic program. This created a high level of support for the new administrative efforts, which were expected to lead to improvement in National Board performance.

3. The interventions adopted by the administration were universally positive in nature. Neither faculty nor students were ever threatened or embarrassed. The system was designed to be positive in philosophy and emphasized gain in scores, achievement, and success.

4. The process included the dean and assistant dean for academic affairs, the Curriculum Committee, the Department Chairmen's Council, students, and alumni as an integrated and coordinated issue-focused workgroup.

5. Initial movement toward higher scores was publicly reported and institutionally applauded; specific disciplines (and faculty serving as course directors in the disciplines) were cited for their outstanding success.

6. Once the scores reached the desired levels, the improved scores began to be reported to the Office of the Vice President and to the university president and the state higher education authority as externally validated examples of the quality of the dental school program. This enhanced the reputation of the dean and of the school in general.

7. Finally, the school did not overreact by establishing harsh (punitive) policies or by finding fault with the existing instructional efforts, educational program design, faculty skill, student potential, or the National Board Examinations themselves. Instead, the process assumed that all of these were largely

satisfactory and that the actual performance deficit was tied to misperceptions and poor attitudes held by faculty and students.

Efforts to Continually Improve a Nursing Program

Karen A. Bowyer

CASE 16: DYERSBURG STATE COMMUNITY COLLEGE

Look for: Improvements in curriculum coverage and classroom testing techniques undertaken to address faculty concerns about student performance on a national licensing exam. These continuous improvement efforts have helped to produce licensing exam pass rates of 100 percent for thirteen years.

Background and Purpose

Faculty at Dyersburg State Community College take seriously the continuing need to improve the associate's degree nursing curriculum to ensure that all nursing graduates pass the NCLEX-RN (the state board exam).

Method

At the end of each semester, nursing students are given a National League for Nursing (NLN) Achievement Test over the subject matter studied during the semester. The NLN Achievement Test on Nursing Care of Adults is given in late November of the second year. An item analysis is reviewed by the nursing faculty in January.

Findings

NLN Achievement Test scores indicated that the nursing curriculum did not provide students with sufficient information on the endocrine system or peripheral vascular disease.

Students asked that the faculty-made tests given during the semester be prepared in the same format as the NLN achievement tests.

Use of Findings

The curriculum was changed to increase the amount of information students receive about diabetes and the endocrine system. A section on peripheral vascular disease also was added to the curriculum.

Items on these topics were added to the faculty-designed unit tests. Faculty attended a workshop to improve their skills in writing multiple-choice items and began to write their unit tests in the same format as the NLN Achievement Tests.

Students are now performing better on these two topics on the NLN Achievement Test on Nursing Care of Adults and they are better prepared for the NCLEX-RN.

Success Factors

The pass rate for nursing graduates is a very visible indicator of the quality of the program. Our pass rate has been 100 percent for the past thirteen years. Faculty have great pride in the success of this program, and they are constantly looking for ways to improve it.

Exit Interviews in Mathematics

R. Dean Riess, John A. Muffo

CASE 17: VIRGINIA POLYTECHNIC INSTITUTE AND STATE UNIVERSITY

Look for: Group interviews of senior mathematics majors to test analytical and oral presentation skills and knowledge of basic math principles as well as to gather opinions about student experiences. The finding that basic concepts learned early were most likely to be lost by the senior year led to changes in upper-division courses designed to reinforce earlier learning.

Background and Purpose

Mathematics majors at Virginia Polytechnic Institute and State University are interviewed in groups of five during the senior year in order to test academic achievement as well as to gather opinions about their experiences in the department and at the university. The primary purpose of the interviews is to identify specific strengths and weaknesses of the department's undergraduate program. A special interest is to judge intellectual growth among the graduating seniors. The faculty have found that interviews can enable a more refined assessment to take place than any other technique used to date.

The interviewing of individual senior mathematics majors had taken place for a number of years; the department traditionally has been interested in the opinions and achievements of its students. A more regular and formal process came about as part of the state-mandated outcomes assessment program, which places a heavy emphasis on departmental self-studies at Virginia Tech. The intention behind the interviewing of seniors has been to determine how well they have absorbed and can use basic mathematical principles upon graduation.

Method

National standardized examinations were reviewed in the past to determine how well they might measure the ability levels of graduating seniors in mathematics. The ones considered were not entirely satisfactory to the faculty, however, because the tests covered only a small amount of material beyond calculus. Of the four courses required of all majors at the junior level, only one area was covered by the standardized tests. No senior-level course content was tested by the examinations that were reviewed. The Major Field Achievement Test produced by the Educational Testing Service (ETS) is considered appropriate only for the minority of seniors planning further graduate study in mathematics. In addition, the faculty could not think of a way to ensure that students would invest their best efforts in taking written examinations of any type unless the exams were required for a class grade or graduation, a requirement that was perceived to be undesirable.

The department chose to conduct interviews with ten randomly selected graduating seniors during the 1990–91 academic year. The assistant department head conducted each interview along with a faculty member from the student's area of emphasis in mathematics, so that questions could be adjusted to individual student backgrounds. A set of thirty-one written questions was presented to the students, but they were discouraged from preparing for the session in any way. The questions were specific ones, requiring basic knowledge of mathematical principles and theorems. The students were asked to respond to the questions orally and in writing, using the blackboard available in the room where they were interviewed. The faculty involved felt that such a face-to-face approach allowed for observation of both analytical and oral presentation skills in an environment where the students were motivated to do well.

More recently, interviews have taken place in groups of five, rather than individually, because the faculty have found the students less inhibited in the small groups and responding more freely. Although the interviews are voluntary now, the department would like to make participation mandatory; students would not be penalized in any way for poor performance, however. A concern is that self-selection may be operating when only volunteers participate in the interviews, that is, that the weaker students are avoiding the process.

Even employing small groups, discussion can be tailored to individuals, not unlike the recently announced computerized testing developed by ETS. The approach taken for both the interviews and the ETS examinations is to ask more difficult questions in an area when one is answered correctly and a less difficult question when the answer is incorrect. This permits a more precise assessment of student learning than more traditional approaches.

Findings

The principal finding has been that students tend to do well with concepts and procedures taught in the later courses in the program (that is, at junior and senior level) but that some of the basic concepts taught at the lower levels are a bit un-clear near graduation due to lack of reinforcement in upper-division courses. This outcome was somewhat unexpected in that these students had proven themselves competent in mastering the basic concepts earlier in their collegiate careers.

Use of Findings

Adjustments have been made in the upper-division mathematics courses taken by majors to reinforce basic concepts taught earlier. The faculty in the department feel that such concepts are so important that graduating seniors should demon-strate a high level of mastery. The best way of guaranteeing this is to assure that the concepts are used beyond their introduction, in ways that are not duplicative of earlier experiences.

Success Factors

The faculty have a long history of caring about the performance of mathemat-ics graduates. The state-mandated outcomes assessment process provided an op-portunity to attempt some evaluation approaches that differed from those used in the past. The interview process permits the faculty present to tailor the inter-view to the background of the individual student, something that would be quite difficult by other means, even if a local written examination were developed.

The department faculty feel that the interviews are successful because they allow a broader yet more precise coverage of the six learning goals identified by the Committee on the Undergraduate Program in Mathematics of the Mathe-matical Association of America (MAA). The goals identified by the MAA include:

1. Develop mathematical reasoning skills.
2. Expand personal potential.
3. Understand the nature of mathematics with respect to various careers.
4. Develop the ability to derive a quantitative analysis of natural or social phe-nomena (called "mathematical modeling").
5. Develop technical communication skills.
6. Acquire fundamental knowledge of several types of mathematics. (Did the student take the right courses, and how much was learned in and retained from those courses?)

Standardized tests tend to measure only the sixth goal, and that one not as well as the faculty would like.

Listening to Your Students

Irene M. Staik, Julia S. Rogers

CASE 18: UNIVERSITY OF MONTEVALLO

Look for: Use of a student advisory council in psychology. Students meet on their own and make periodic reports. Several of their suggestions have produced changes in curriculum, instruction, and ethical behavior expectations for psychology majors.

Background and Purpose

In an effort to improve its effectiveness, the psychology program at the University of Montevallo has had its seniors, along with taking the ETS Major Field Achievement Test, respond to five open-ended questions. The purpose is to gather information from the students about the good and weak parts of the program and what they feel needs to be changed. One of the findings is that the students want to have a definite and consistent voice about what goes on in the program. They want to give input along the way and not just answer a few questions when they are ready to graduate.

Method

In the fall of 1992, the psychology faculty acted on this suggestion and established the Psychology Student Advisory Council. Eleven students, including freshmen through seniors, were chosen by the faculty to serve on this council. Formal invitations were issued to the selected students, and they were asked to write a letter of acceptance. The program head convened the first meeting and outlined the council's purpose and operating guidelines. The council was to meet at least once per term and to give a written statement at the end of each term pulling everything together that council members had done. The students took this task seriously and were self-motivated. No faculty attended their later meetings. They met; they talked; they reported in a timely fashion. The council's task was to make recommendations for program improvement, including a statement of expected ethical behaviors of psychology students in the classroom.

In fall of 1993, new students were added to the council to replace those who had graduated and a permanent position for an adult returning student was added. The program head met with the new council, went over again the purpose and operating guidelines, and gave members copies of the reports from the council of the previous year. The charge for the 1993–94 council was to continue program recommendations and to define more specifically expected student behaviors in the ethical statement.

Findings

One of the recommendations of the 1992–93 Psychology Student Advisory Council was that three hours of supervised research be added to the one three-hour course then available. Most students engaged in research were actually spending at least a year working on their research projects. These students typically go on to graduate school, and they wanted to be able to show research credit that more accurately reflected their efforts.

Students also indicated that they wanted some lab experiences. One student said, "Even an aquarium would be nice!" The school had never had an animal lab for psychology research, and the only lab equipment available was obsolete. Research projects typically have been surveys and other types of field research, not laboratory projects, and certainly not ones involving animals other than humans. In fact, the program had lacked any emphasis on cross-species comparative research and any direct experience with animal research. This has been evidenced by the relatively weaker (albeit respectable) showing of students on the comparative section of the Major Field Achievement Test in Psychology.

A third concern of students was lack of computers for their use in the program. Essentially, the only computers available were in faculty offices and a writing lab that had mainframe connections for word processing. Use of these computers for statistical analysis purposes was limited.

In the spring term of 1993, the students gave a report on ethical behaviors of students, and also included some concerns they had about ethical behaviors of faculty, such as keeping enough office hours. One said, "If a teacher doesn't want you to cheat on something like a take-home assignment, the teacher had better tell you not to!" The statements were good, but they were very broad, and thus open to misinterpretation by faculty and students. As a result, the 1993–94 council was asked to provide more specific ethical guidelines.

Use of Findings

In the spring of 1993, a second research course was added to the curriculum, so that students may now take Research I and Research II.

The addition of a faculty member with background in laboratory research has made it possible, with the assistance of grants he obtained from the campus Research and Special Projects Committee, to begin construction of a small lab for research with snakes. This faculty member is also raising other animals—chickens, quail, ducks—at his home for use in simple learning experiments such as imprinting. This adds both laboratory research and more direct experience with comparative psychology to the curriculum. Another faculty member received a grant for the purchase of computer software that can be used by students for laboratory research in cognition and perception.

The psychology faculty had influential direct input into the establishment of additional PC laboratories on campus, and have recently obtained five mainframe terminals for the psychology statistics lab, so that students can access statistical packages directly from the classroom for their three-course sequence in statistics, research methods, and experimental psychology.

One of the side benefits of the addition of supervised research hours has been the improvement of students' writing and oral presentation skills. They have taken pride in learning to express their work in professional writing, and have presented over forty-five papers at professional meetings and undergraduate research conferences over the past few years, which is an amazing accomplishment for a small school and program. The program also has an excellent track record for placing its graduates directly into Ph.D. programs, at least in part because of their research and writing experience. Former students report that the primary factor in their being accepted into graduate programs, as well as their success thereafter, was the extensive research experience they had as undergraduates.

Two faculty members from the psychology program prepared and presented a paper at a national meeting about the extensive participation of undergraduate students in research in this program. The paper was well received and is currently being prepared for publication in a journal.

The students feel that the continuing advisory council project relating to ethical concerns in the classroom should be published in the handbook for majors. More importantly, it should be read and discussed in more than one class in the curriculum: for example, in the statistics, research, experimental, and testing courses (all required of majors). It needs to be gone over again and again until it becomes part of the students' expectations of what they should be like within the program. One ethical requirement already in place is that all student research must be approved by the Human Subjects Research Committee (known at some higher education institutions as the Institutional Review Board), something that is not required of routine undergraduate research conducted as part of classes at many institutions. This requirement gives the students a much greater familiarity with the ethics involved in research than they would otherwise have.

Success Factors

From the beginning, in all areas of assessment from the taking of the Major Field Achievement Test (MFAT) to the Psychology Student Advisory Council, the psychology program has had excellent response from its students. One reason is that faculty believe assessment is important and pay attention to the MFAT results and to what students say. In the student handbook, there is a paragraph that explains all about accreditation, why it is important, why assessment is important, what the program gets out of it, how it is used in the program, and why faculty want students to do their best so that accurate assessment of program goals can be obtained. Students take the assessments seriously. They take the MFAT as if their graduation depended on it, although it does not even affect a course grade. They write extensive comments on the open-ended questions. They really appreciate the opportunity to improve the program.

For students, one of the rewards is being selected by the faculty to participate in the advisory council and being issued that very special invitation. This is seen as quite an honor, and students take their responsibilities seriously. Another obvious reward for students is to see their ideas incorporated in the program, to see that they make a difference.

For faculty, the rewards include making program changes that truly benefit students and seeing their students accepted and succeeding in graduate school. One of the cautions for faculty is that implementing some of these changes requires time and effort and may involve overloads for faculty that are not recognized or compensated.

New Venture Creation—The Ultimate Business Course Assessment

Donald F. Kuratko

CASE 19: BALL STATE UNIVERSITY

Look for: Business capstone experience involving evaluation by outside professionals of students' individual plans for new business ventures. Outcomes of this assessment process over its twelve-year history include development of a new course, several workshops, and numerous guest appearances in classes by the outside professionals involved in the evaluation. Development of students' communication skills is also emphasized throughout the curriculum with more intensity and purpose than heretofore.

Background and Purpose

A capstone course entitled New Venture Creation for seniors in business at Ball State University was initiated for two reasons.

1. Student evaluation: to evaluate the senior-level student's overall knowledge and ability in entrepreneurship gained through the program as well as to present an ultimate challenge in the student's preparation for the business world.
2. Program evaluation: to provide a continual (annual) evaluation of the business curriculum by soliciting feedback from the students regarding strengths, weaknesses, and the like.

Method

New Venture Creation is a carefully developed capstone course designed as the intersection of experimental and cognitive strategies to teach entrepreneurship. Early in the term, the class sessions simulate workshops to understand and analyze business plans. A new-venture creation manual (that is, a business plan preparation guide) is used to develop an appreciation for functional analyses. In the latter part of the term, each student works to develop his or her own business plan for a venture that will have solid potential. The student recognizes that he or she must submit this plan to a board of professionals. The student should examine each section of the business plan for its thoroughness in describing or developing a business to exist in the state of Indiana. This simulation of actual business development should reflect what the student has learned through the sequence of courses devoted to specific entrepreneurial skills and through the facilitating abilities of the professor.

The course culminates with the review and critique of the business proposals by a board of professional consultants, investment bankers, entrepreneurs, and venture capitalists. Each student presents the highlights of his or her plan for sixty minutes and the board reviews the proposals and evaluates them for their actual feasibility rather than as purely academic exercises.

The students are also evaluated for the completeness of their efforts. If a plan is judged as an acceptable venture capable of being financed and launched, the student receives an A. If a plan is rejected by the board, the student receives an F. In this manner, students learn the challenge and fear that confront contemporary entrepreneurs. In other words, entrepreneurs must put it all on the line. Therefore, with graduation only one week away (and with this course being a requirement for the major), students feel the tangibility of their need to put it all on the line also. Graduation results from students' efforts on their business plans, a true culmination of their college education. A student cannot repeat this course at Ball State University until one year has passed because it is offered only in the spring.

Findings

Two principal outcomes have resulted from this course. First, there is the holistic development of the student from two perspectives: as a person and as a potential businessperson. Students realize their own limitations as well as potential in pushing themselves through this challenge. It truly illustrates to the student who participates that self-reliance and self-motivation are key components in his or her development. The importance of good communication skills—both written and oral—is intensified in this ultimate presentation. As a future businessperson, each student grasps the complete picture of a business—start-up problems, financial challenges, operational concerns, and environmental risks—rather then having only a narrow functional perspective of business.

Second, the entire entrepreneurship program has benefitted in a continuous improvement process. Each year, the professional evaluators review and assess the students' strengths and weaknesses. Their input covers an evaluation of the business plans, a review of student communication abilities, and a critique of the overall program. These business professionals are a sample of the eventual market for our students, and thus, their assessment is critical in keeping our program viable and effective for our students.

Unanticipated outcomes were the direct and immediate benefits to the students. Over the years, several students have received actual investments (or recommendation to financial sources) from the evaluation board to start their businesses. Also many of the graduates have received immediate offers for employment from professionals on the evaluation board due to their demonstrated abilities in this course.

Also unanticipated was the national notoriety that this course initiated. National publications such as the *New York Times, Success* magazine, *Entrepreneur* magazine, and *Business Week* have devoted articles to our program because of the final do-or-die challenge. This has enhanced the program's status and resulted in greater pride on the part of the students.

Use of Findings

As a direct result of this course, continuous improvement has been applied to the course itself as well as within the overall business major. During the last ten years, the following changes have been introduced as a direct result of this course: (1) a new course, Creative Financing for Emerging Ventures, was developed and is now taught by one of the board members (who is a noted investment banker) in order to enhance students' financial understanding. This course is now offered each fall semester. (2) The accounting firm of Ernst & Young, which has three representatives on the evaluation board, volunteered two workshops for the students to help them prepare their financial statements. These are now conducted every year. (3) A number of board members now serve as either mentors or speakers for the class, depending upon their expertise. The board members volunteered their talents in order to assist the students. (4) The makeup of each evaluation team has been improved to include a successful graduate of the entrepreneurship program. This ensures the quality of the review process since there is a veteran who represents the student's position. (5) Communication skills of the students are stressed more now than in earlier years. This is a direct result of the evaluation process's uncovering a weakness.

These improvements were all initiated to help students. However, beyond this, students have benefitted directly from the interaction with these professionals in other ways. The professional board remains a networking opportunity for successful graduates. Students are invited to utilize this board of professionals for career reasons, either to seek start-up investment for a venture or to pursue other career opportunities.

Success Factors

Leadership and support from the dean of the College of Business has been instrumental in the development of this program. Due to its nontraditional nature, New Venture Creation could cause concern with some traditional administrators. Therefore, there must be a dean who understands the value of such an experience.

In addition, there must be a faculty member willing to build a solid evaluation board in which he or she can place trust. And the board must understand and believe in the faculty member in order to work closely together. This is an unusual experiment in business education; therefore, without a committed faculty member, a highly skilled and respected evaluation board, and a supportive dean, this type of course would never happen.

The Impact of Academic Learning on Work Experiences

Rosalyn Lindner

CASE 20: STATE UNIVERSITY OF NEW YORK COLLEGE AT BUFFALO

Look for: Important curricular changes undertaken in response to findings derived from evaluation of students' internship experiences. Methods for encouraging faculty and student involvement in assessment also are discussed.

Background and Purpose

The State University of New York (SUNY) requires that every campus conduct assessment of its major programs. To meet this mandate, the sociology faculty and students at SUNY-Buffalo met regularly for one year to discuss the mission, goals, and objectives of the sociology program. These discussions, while long and sometimes tedious, eventually resulted in agreed-upon mission and goals statements. When consensus was also reached on objectives, several assessment strategies were developed, one of which is described here. This activity was designed to measure a departmental objective focusing on students' abilities to apply sociological knowledge to a work or a real-world situation.

This specific objective and the resultant assessment activity were also chosen because the link between student learning outcomes and marketable job skills was frequently cited in a survey of recent graduates conducted by the department. Recent graduates had been asked about the impact of what they learned in sociology on their current jobs. As a result of this survey, the faculty were anxious to pursue this area in more depth.

Method

Several issues needed to be addressed before an assessment plan could be fully developed. Since Buffalo State is a public institution with primarily a commuter student population, our primary concern was that any assessment activity would be part of the "normal" educational experience. The student base at Buffalo State consists of people of all ages, who attend classes and hold down part- or full-time jobs and many of whom have family obligations. Adding additional time requirements, additional exercises or tests, and the like for assessment purposes only would meet great resistance.

The sociology faculty were also concerned that this assessment activity target different stages in student progress. Because most of the 350 sociology majors transfer into the department at the end of their sophomore year, it was very important to differentiate between juniors and seniors.

All of these considerations led to our choosing an assessment project that was centered around the department's internship program. As part of the requirements for the B.S. degree, each student must complete two internships in two different agencies, offices, or businesses. Aside from classes, each intern is required to complete a journal which details her or his responsibilities and observations. Interns meet several times during the semester to discuss their situations and progress. At the end of the internship semester, they are required to submit a ten- to fifteen-page paper on a sociological topic specific to their internship experiences and learning.

Everyone on the sociology faculty agreed to mentor a few students through their internships and to engage in "blind" evaluation of all of the final internship papers, in light of the program objective that targets application of learned sociological concepts and skills to the work environment. Also, student papers were reviewed to assess the writing skills of students. While writing skills were not a specific sociological objective, they were recognized as needed general skills that could be promoted within the program.

Findings

Some of the findings of this activity confirmed what the faculty believed from their informal observations. Seniors exhibited more sophistication than juniors in their ability to apply sociological concepts. Students completing their second internship experience showed markedly more skill in understanding the relationship between academic learning and the real world.

Other findings were surprising in that they contradicted conventional wisdom. While students rather consistently complained about the difficulty of mastering the required research and statistics courses, they exhibited more understanding in these areas than in other required areas, such as social theory, about which few if any complaints were ever lodged. So while the department constantly struggled over the research and statistics requirements, theory received little if any attention.

Use of Findings

As a direct result of this one assessment activity, two curricular changes are currently being addressed. First, course sequencing is being examined in light of the results. Currently, students are advised that they must begin taking the research/statistics sequence in their junior year, but there is no similar directive regarding theory. Also, there is currently no sequencing of theory courses with the internships. It is thought that some of the deficiencies that were noticed especially in the area of theoretical understanding were due to a lack of course sequencing. If students are to make the most of their internship experiences, perhaps a tighter sequencing of courses is necessary.

Second, a possible restructuring of the internship program is being considered. Various options are being investigated, such as requiring several written activities throughout the semester rather than one single paper at the end. This would result in better feedback on writing skills as well as sociological applications. Also, ordering the first and second internships so that the learning experiences build on each other in a more concrete sequence is being considered.

Success Factors

The chairperson of the department assumed leadership for assessment. It was essential that she had the support and expertise of the American Sociological Association. This put assessment into the realm of professionalism rather than of administrative ploy. All faculty members and a limited number of students were willing to struggle through the long process of achieving consensus on program goals and objectives because they came to believe that it might result in a better program.

At the beginning of the assessment semester, the chairperson and the students enrolled in internships had a lengthy discussion about assessment, its goals, and the proposed assessment activity. It was essential that the students understand that this activity was separate and removed from their course grades. They also needed to be aware of how their work would be used and be comfortable with the process. While some questions were raised throughout the semester, all the students willingly participated.

Performance-Based Assessment of the Bachelor of Social Work Program

Carol J. Williams, Dorothy Marie Rizzo

CASE 21: KEAN COLLEGE OF NEW JERSEY

Look for: Assessment using existing evaluation data (supervisors' evaluations of social work students' field experiences) resulting in improvement of the evaluation form and a new method to train field supervisors to teach concepts in which the data analyses identify areas for continuing program growth.

Background and Purpose

This assessment activity was initiated as part of the Collegewide Outcomes Assessment Program at Kean College. Social work was one of eight programs selected to participate in the first wave of campuswide assessment.

Method

In beginning its assessment, the social work program had at its disposal a wealth of data from evaluations of students' field experiences. An evaluation of each student is completed each semester for a four-semester sequence. Since these data were available, no effort had to be expended in data collection. Also, there were no problems in obtaining cooperation from students and field instructors, since the fieldwork evaluation is a required component of each of the four fieldwork courses. Thus, the data that were already available were utilized for a secondary purpose: program assessment.

There were other reasons for selecting this particular assessment strategy. First, fieldwork evaluations are completed by agency-based field instructors who hold master of social work (M.S.W.) degrees and have completed at least two years of post-M.S.W. practice experience. As such, they are external to both the program and the college, lending credibility to this method of assessment. Second, field instructors are typical of the professionals who will be employing program graduates, and by using their assessments, it is possible to assure that concerns that might exist in the practice environment as well as the academic environment will be addressed. Third, the material covered by fieldwork evaluations includes all three components on which the program must be assessed: knowledge, values, and skills. To assess the ability of students to perform in a professional role, assessment has to reach beyond the confines of the classroom experience, and field experience is designed to do just that. Fourth, since all students are evaluated at four points during the field experience, it is possible to do time series measurement of the pattern of professional growth of students in the program to determine not only whether the required knowledge, values, and skills develop but also in what sequence. Fifth, this approach allowed the social work program to develop a performance-based assessment using a criterion-based measurement process. The data gathered in the process are utilized to guide program evolution and growth. Finally, employment of program graduates in entry-level practice positions is the primary goal of our B.S.W. program.

Faculty were involved in the process by means of a modified Delphi process (Linstone and Turoff, 1975) through which a program model, including educational needs, goals, objectives, related program components, and behavioral outcomes were specified. This dialogue was expanded to include students, alumni, and field instructors through the forum of the Assessment Committee, which was formed during the early stages of the process. Faculty other than the principal investigators were not required to participate in data gathering or analysis. They were and are, however, actively involved in utilizing the outcomes of the assessment.

The first version of the data collection form developed to code and analyze this largely open-ended qualitative data set was created by using content analysis techniques, as described by Holsti (1969). This initial form was compared to the program model developed by faculty using the modified Delphi process described above. There was a high degree of consensus between the two, and any item found in one but not in the other was subsequently included in both. The resultant model expanded, over several iterations of the modified Delphi process, to become a one-hundred-page document, and the data collection form grew to sixty pages in length to assure that all relevant items were covered accurately and completely.

Findings

Students performed well in terms of the knowledge, values, and skills required of a professional social worker. They began fieldwork with high levels of knowledge and values. The initial level of performance in terms of skills was lower, but students showed continual growth in level of skills, until in their final semester, almost all were rated "high."

The content analyses revealed that field instructors were placing most of their efforts on the teaching of "micro" assignments (work with individuals and groups) and less on "macro" assignments (work with organizations, communities, research, statistics, and policy). Both micro- and macro-learning are required by the Council on Social Work Education, the accrediting body, since graduates are to be trained for generalist social work practice.

Use of Findings

In its most recent visit to our campus, the Council on Social Work Education had stressed the importance of integrating research and statistics into every aspect of our program. Assessment showed that field instructors were not teaching macro practice or not mentioning it in their evaluations of students, and research and statistics are two of the areas included in this designation. Since content analysis was used for the assessment, it was not known if such assignments were being omitted in field instruction or were being given and not recorded. The assessment liaison, who teaches macro-practice courses, began to work with those individual field instructors that she supervised to determine whether or not macro-issues were being addressed in the field by this group. She discovered that, in many cases, they were not. In other cases, macro-assignments were given, such as involvement in staff meetings or agency committees, but the field instructor did not focus on this as part of the student's fieldwork assignment when conferencing with the student or when writing the student's evaluation.

In response to this finding, we have initiated training for field instructors regarding generalist practice, its definition, micro- and macro-assignments that can be developed in the agency, and the agency's role in this important aspect of social work education. Field instructors received the initial training session with great enthusiasm and have been willing to experiment this semester with creative mechanisms for integrating macro-practice into their teaching. Several individual field instructors who have been particularly successful in their efforts have been asked to participate in a second round of training. Each of these field instructors will make a presentation at a workshop discussing the various techniques that they have employed to develop macro-assignments, pointing out both successes and pitfalls.

The assessment has also demonstrated to us the difficulty in achieving consistent standards of performance when each semester's fieldwork evaluation form is different from the other three in both form and content. The faculty will consider revision of the four fieldwork evaluation forms, with the intent of assuring that key elements identified in the assessment are included in each of the revised forms. Since the forms are used to evaluate student performance in the field, this will be another way of assuring that the desired material is being covered in the field as well as in the classroom, and that field instructors mention each key point in their open-ended narrative evaluation of program students. Inclusion of key elements on the form will also encourage field instructors to discuss these issues with their students in their weekly supervisory conferences. This discussion will further help students to understand and integrate the relevant learning and to link their learning in the classroom and the field more closely.

Success Factors

Assessment at Kean College was supported actively by the college administration from its inception. Release time, as well as recognition, were among the rewards provided. Faculty adopted assessment as their own activity. This allowed academic programs to experiment freely with methods of data collection and analysis for the purposes of internal program growth. Active leadership of this endeavor was provided by the college's assessment office, directed by Michael Knight. Faculty were given opportunities to engage in dialogue internally and to participate in regional and national conferences to enrich their knowledge and skills in assessment.

The findings of the social work program assessment prompted development of a performance-based approach to assessment, which captured a wide range of indicators of professional growth and development. Faculty became more aware of the linkages among program components and have attempted to share these discoveries with students, thus helping them to develop their own holistic models of generalist practice. Faculty were able to identify and address the issue of incorporating macro-practice material into the fieldwork program. Most importantly, the opportunity for dialogue among faculty, students, field instructors, and alumni regarding program objectives, components, and desired outcomes was strengthened and given a forum through the Assessment Committee. This discussion is continuing in all areas of program operation.

Dairy Science and the Core Curriculum

W. E. Vinson, John A. Muffo

CASE 22: VIRGINIA POLYTECHNIC INSTITUTE AND STATE UNIVERSITY

Look for: Changes in published descriptions of the curriculum and in academic and career advising of students in response to the finding derived from alumni and employer surveys that only one-third of the dairy science graduates were employed in dairying.

Background

The Department of Dairy Science is a relatively small department in the College of Agriculture at Virginia Polytechnic Institute and State University, a land-grant university that is the largest institution of postsecondary education in the state. Approximately fifteen students graduate from the bachelor's degree program annually. Some features of the program that make it unique among those at Virginia Tech include the following: (1) class sizes are small, allowing for a family atmosphere. (2) Students spend a lot of time in dairy barns on the campus. Their concept of hands-on experience is quite literal. (3) Some students participate in one of two animal-judging teams that involve competitions off-campus. The teams have won many judging awards. (4) The Dairy Club serves roughly seventy-five students annually, including all majors and fifteen to twenty others from other departments and colleges. It has about twenty-five activities per year, all of which are student organized and run, thus providing leadership, organizational, and interpersonal skills development opportunities. Participation in regional and national competitions sponsored by the American Dairy Science Association have led to the club's being named the outstanding dairy club in the nation in eleven of the past fifteen years. (It was second in the other four years.) (4) Employment opportunities have been quite good.

Method

During the 1991–92 academic year, as part of a state-mandated outcomes assessment program, the department conducted a survey of alumni. It was the fourth such survey done in the tenure of the current department head. The survey instrument used was quite specific to the profession but was not unusual in other ways.

In the same year, a survey of employers was conducted. While the number of employers participating was somewhat small (nineteen employers of eighty graduates), such a survey had not been done in the same manner previously.

Findings

It had been known for some time that approximately half of the graduating seniors are not employed in production agriculture; this information has been available via student exit interviews with the department head and a written form that is completed prior to graduation. For instance, some graduates have gone on to medical or veterinary school or even law school, and some are employed in a business unrelated to the dairy industry. This pattern is one of the primary reasons why the department has attempted in the past to maintain a curriculum that is as flexible as possible, allowing numerous elective hours, despite the focused nature of the discipline and close ties to the dairy industry.

A somewhat surprising result from the recent alumni survey was that only 30 to 35 percent of the respondents are currently involved in production agriculture. Despite the possibility of response bias in the survey, this information, along with the knowledge of the decreasing number of dairy farms, has led the faculty to consider the results as significant and to conclude that, while about half of all graduates will enter production agriculture initially, only a third are likely to be working in the industry later on.

When asked in which areas alumni felt a need for additional training, the responses were quite similar to those provided by current students, with the three most popular responses not being specific to the dairy industry: (1) general business management; (2) computer applications; (3) oral and written communication; (4) dairy enterprise management; and (5) applied dairy nutrition.

Perhaps the most interesting and useful result from the employer survey was the fact that the results were so similar to those gathered from alumni. This was especially true with respect to writing skills: both employers and alumni reported feeling "good" about the writing abilities of the graduates, but "less good" than they did about abilities in other areas.

Use of Findings

One of the most important results of the survey and the internal discussion that followed it is that the faculty in the department now see their role a bit differently than before. While they still consider their primary role as educating graduates to enter the dairy and related industries, they also recognize that approximately two thirds eventually will not be employed on dairy farms. In light of this reality, there is now an even stronger concern for students to acquire basic analytical and communication skills, which are transferable to other environments.

A tangible way in which this knowledge is used is in student academic and career advising. For production-oriented students in particular, the likelihood of career change is emphasized. All students are encouraged to develop broader knowledge and skills than those normally thought by some to be of value in managing a farm.

The broader description of the department's goals for its bachelor's degree graduates may best be seen from the introduction to its 1992 outcomes assessment report.

> The goal of the undergraduate academic program in Dairy Science is to provide students with an opportunity to acquire the level of general education, technical expertise, interpersonal ability, and communication skill needed for fulfilling personal lives and success in a variety of life sciences and business related careers. Approximately half of our graduates enter the production segment of the dairy industry. The remainder choose from a wide variety of careers which rely heavily on academic training in either business, economic, and financial principles, technical areas of the life sciences, or both. The substantial variation in careers of our graduates requires a flexible curriculum and places a premium on informed and timely academic and career advising.

Success Factors

Active faculty involvement in the assessment process, including the construction of the surveys and analysis of the results, ensured that the findings would be taken seriously by the department and acted upon. Prior knowledge of employment patterns of new graduates and trends in the dairy industry generally enabled the faculty to place the new information into a broader context.

Revision of the core curriculum and the writing-across-the-curriculum initiative at the university level also have provided support from outside the department for considering the broader educational issues involved in curricular planning.

Alumni Involvement in Civil Engineering

Richard D. Walker, John A. Muffo

CASE 23: VIRGINIA POLYTECHNIC INSTITUTE AND STATE UNIVERSITY

Look for: Changes in computing resources, laboratory facilities, and the teaching of writing and speaking as the result of assessment. Alumni advisory board members hosted a dinner for current student representatives during which a candid, structured discussion of the civil engineering major took place. The alumni summarized results of the discussion for the faculty.

Background and Purpose

The Department of Civil Engineering at Virginia Tech is one of the largest in the College of Engineering, which itself is among the largest in the United States. The department graduates approximately 150 to 200 students at the bachelor's degree level annually.

The Department of Civil Engineering, like most of the departments in the college, has an external advisory board or committee. In the case of the civil engineering department, the advisory board is made up entirely of alumni. One of the challenges for the department has been to find substantive ways to involve alumni in ongoing departmental operations.

Method

As part of a state-mandated assessment process, the department asked members of the alumni advisory board to assist the faculty in two specific ways during the 1993–94 academic year. First, they were asked to meet over dinner with a group of thirteen juniors and seniors, as well as two graduate students. In order to encourage open discussion, no faculty members were present. Three of the alumni summarized the results of the dinner meeting for the department. Topics included in the discussion were the environmental engineering option, use of computers, availability of faculty, advising and advisers, the mentor program, the cooperative education program, space and facilities, and the computer laboratory in the department.

In addition to the dinner discussion with current students, nine current or former members of the alumni advisory board responded to an employer survey aimed at assessing the strengths and weaknesses of graduates from the program. (Not all members of the alumni advisory board have been in positions where they were responsible for hiring civil engineering graduates.)

Findings

The results of the interviews revealed a number of issues on the minds of current students. Among the most important were these: (1) Opinions differed about the environmental engineering option. Some thought that it led to specialization too early, providing less of an overall perspective. Others liked the opportunity to study in that area of specialization as soon as possible. (2) At the freshman level, there was some dissatisfaction with the software and programming languages taught in the courses provided to all engineering students. (Students are not separated by major in freshman Engineering Fundamentals classes.) (3) At the junior and senior levels, where more classes in civil engineering are taken, not enough computer applications were integrated into existing classes or, alternatively, not enough classes were available with a primary focus on computing in the field. In addition, nonengineering applications such as spreadsheets were not available at all, leaving students to learn them entirely on their own. (4) The cooperative education program, where students alternate semesters of class attendance and full-time employment, was considered to be very desirable. One concern was that students with a grade point average below 2.5 were not permitted to participate in the program, thus penalizing those getting a "slow start" in college-level academic pursuits. (5) Space limitations have led to overcrowding, with the situation being the worst in the soils laboratory.

The results of the employer surveys may best be summarized by a quote from one of the alumni-employers. "Students are well prepared technically and are very computer literate. Communication skills and ability to work with groups of other technically trained people have improved since I was in school, but there is still room for improvement."

Use of Findings

The department has taken several significant steps either as a result of the study or because of reinforcement by it.

In the case of computer use in the classroom, the department has developed a computer laboratory with twenty-five stations and room to seat approximately fifty students. This, in turn, has encouraged civil engineering faculty to reserve the lab for one or more of their classes, in order to demonstrate the latest software. The students are then able to enter the lab at their leisure to use the software as part of their classroom assignments.

To respond to the criticism received about the soil mechanics laboratory, the department has completed a $100,000 renovation, including the addition of more space. Future students should now receive an improved and valuable laboratory experience as the result of feedback from past students.

The communication issue has been a concern of faculty for some time. More written and oral communication opportunities have been provided in existing classes. The department is participating with several others in engineering and the physical sciences in an externally funded interdisciplinary effort aimed at improving student writing through curricular innovation. In addition, the department is preparing to submit classes for review as "writing-intensive" classes in the university's writing-across-the-curriculum initiative, which will require all students, regardless of major, to take a specific number of writing-intensive classes in order to graduate.

Success Factors

A dedicated group of alumni was willing to assist the department by conducting student interviews over dinner and responding to employer surveys. Their knowledge of the civil engineering profession and of the department at Virginia Tech makes them an invaluable resource.

Faculty encouraged open discussion among students and alumni and were willing to listen and to operate on concerns resulting from that discussion and the results of the employer surveys.

America's Challenge—Assessing the Present, Preparing for the Future

Viola Gray Ellison, Michelle Henry Heard

CASE 24: UNIVERSITY OF ARKANSAS AT PINE BLUFF

Look for: Success factors associated with a campus assessment program of comprehensive testing in the major for all graduates. The program, which enjoys strong support from faculty, students, and administrators, is guided by a fourteen-stage process design communicated in faculty development experiences.

Background and Purpose

The University of Arkansas at Pine Bluff (UAPB), a historically black university located in southeast Arkansas's lower Mississippi delta, initiated a first for Arkansas: comprehensive examinations in major fields for all seniors. UAPB recognizes its mission as providing educational opportunities for a maximum number of individuals as well as a disproportionate number of students who are culturally, economically, and socially disadvantaged. Although we maintain an open admissions policy, the administration at UAPB believes that the graduate from each program in this institution should receive an education comparable to that available to those who graduate from other universities throughout the United States. A comprehensive examination in each major was approved and instituted for the purpose of strengthening the capabilities of the university's graduates and measuring their effectiveness for the jobs for which they are preparing.

One of the major goals of the comprehensive exam is to produce students who are critical thinkers and lifelong learners and who will leave the university with marketable skills in their discipline that promote intellectual self-reliance and moral sensibility. The emphasis is directly related to competencies where instruction and assessment are linked to the intended outcomes. The plan for comprehensive assessment is presented in five stages: (1) planning and design, (2) initial development, (3) prototype testing, (4) initial operation, and (5) sustained operation.

The program design includes fourteen specific procedures for carrying out an assessment plan:

1. Specify assumptions
2. Identify instructional objectives
3. Delineate outcomes
4. Cluster and order objectives
5. Cluster and delineate outcomes
6. Design test questions
7. Develop assessment modes
8. Organize management systems
9. Prototype test
10. Develop instructional system
11. Provide remediation and/or other intervention
12. Retest
13. Evaluate program
14. Refine program

The first stage in assessment involved an explicit statement of assumptions that provided a basis for discussion and program development. This stage included such questions as: "What do we believe about outcomes assessment at UAPB?" "What roles do administrators, faculty, and staff members play in developing an outcomes assessment program?" Once our beliefs were relatively clear, we began to identify sets of instructional objectives for each major (Stage 2), and from them, more specific learning outcomes were delineated (Stage 3). Such outcomes provided the basis for instruction.

Three separate but interrelated stages for objectives delineation exist. The first is Stage 4 of the design plan, in which the assessment of competencies is specified. The basic question is, "How do you know when a student has demonstrated competence?" Stages 5, 6, and 7 are parallel to, though not contingent upon, Stage 4. They focus on design of the test questions. Objectives and outcomes are clustered into instructionally cohesive sets, then ordered. Test questions designed to evaluate students are then projected.

Stage 8 is parallel to Stages 4, 5, 6, and 7 and is designed to develop the management system for the new program. In the planning process, one task force can focus on management at the same time that a second designs test questions and a third develops assessment systems. But their separate efforts, when coordinated, tend to support each other. In Stages 9 and 10, the program prototype is tested, and the instructional system evaluated (Stage 11). At this point, if mastery is attained, the student leaves the program. However, if mastery is not attained, the student is assigned an intervention model and is retested (Stage 12). In practice, evaluation and refinement (Stages 13 and 14) occur regularly. With each additional stage, new insights about the academic program are gained, leading to continual revision of previous stages.

Method

The two major approaches to learning—deductive and inductive—are used in designing criterion-referenced tests in all degree areas. The tests are designed in each major field to assess students' mastery of concepts, principles, and knowledge characteristically expected upon completion of an undergraduate major in a given subject. In addition to measuring factual knowledge, the tests are constructed to evaluate students' abilities to apply, analyze, synthesize, make sound judgments, and interpret material. Items on the tests are linked directly to specific instructional objectives and outcomes and, therefore, facilitate the writing of objectives and outcomes by faculty members. Seniors are required to take the comprehensive examination in their degree area during the semester in which they graduate. To accommodate institutional and departmental calendars, tests are administered twice every semester and upon request during the summer sessions.

Findings

One of the most significant changes that has occurred on our campus is that faculty members can talk more freely about the instruction and learning process because they have the data necessary to initiate the discussion. Administrators and faculty use a wide range of material to make decisions about the quality of the program they offer—the standards of the discipline, the texts available, the equipment and other resources available to students, and the actual enrollment in the course. The assessment process is an ongoing integral part of the university's efforts to strengthen and improve instruction, academic programs, and learning opportunities for students.

Use of Findings

Departments were able to examine the performance of groups of students on various elements of the curriculum. Results indicated that in some degree areas there were significant differences among student subgroups and class sections. Faculty members discussed and implemented common syllabi and were able to revamp their tests to reflect more accurately their curricula and to assess areas or subareas specific to institutional or departmental goals.

Success Factors

Besides being an instrumental factor in improving undergraduate education by bringing together faculty from throughout the university, this assessment activity also enhanced faculty communication and encouraged collaboration among faculty as they sought to bring about change in curricula and lifelong learning. The following key elements were essential in effective implementation:

- Federal funding for implementation
- Support from administration, faculty and staff, students, and alumni
- Faculty development workshops
- Documents (technical standards manual, procedures manual, supervisors' manual, faculty and student handbooks)
- Newsletters
- Professional presentation of activities at local, state, and national conferences

CHAPTER TWELVE

ASSESSING STUDENT ACHIEVEMENT IN GENERAL EDUCATION

Chapter Guide

The chapter guide lists the cases contained in this chapter by institution, by program area, by assessment method, and by case strengths. Institutions are organized by Carnegie Classification. The location of each institution and its approximate enrollment follow the institution name. The relevant case numbers follow each entry.

Institutions

Research I
  Public
    University of Wisconsin-Madison (41,000 students)   45
  Private
    Tufts University; Medford, Massachusetts (8,000 students)   46
Research II
  Public
    University of South Carolina; Columbia (26,700 students)   36
    Washington State University; Pullman (18,900 students)   41
Doctoral I
  Public
    University of Memphis; Tennessee (20,300 students)   33
    Ball State University; Muncie, Indiana (20,700 students)   40, 48

Program Areas

Chapter Overview

Development of students' generic knowledge and skills is of interest to faculty in all disciplines. Knowledge of basic concepts in the fine arts, humanities, social sciences and natural sciences is fundamental to a deeper understanding of any field. Similarly, one cannot move to an advanced level in a discipline without mastering at some level the skills of reading, writing, listening, speaking, calculating, computing, analyzing, synthesizing, applying, and evaluating. The campus examples in this chapter illustrate the variety of methods that faculty use to assess student achievement of appropriate levels of generic knowledge and skills.

Most of the case studies included in the first part of this chapter (Cases 25 through 36) depict campuswide, across-the-curriculum general education assessment programs that emphasize the importance of having explicit objectives for the levels of knowledge and skills students will develop as a result of their experiences in general education. Methods described include cognitive tests for freshmen (Cases 25 and 29), sophomores (Cases 28 and 29), and seniors (Cases 25, 26, 29, 33, 34, and 35); portfolios (Cases 27 and 30); senior projects (Cases 27, 32); transcript analysis (Case 35); surveys (Cases 25, 26, 28, 29, and 35); interviews (Cases 31 and 35); review of course syllabi (Cases 25 and 35); and comprehensive program reviews (Case 25). Two of these cases (33 and 34) suggest approaches for encouraging seniors to take seriously mandatory standardized tests. Case 36 contains the description of a multicampus faculty development project aimed at improving teaching as well as assessment in general education.

Assessment of generic skills in community college settings is the subject of the second set of cases (37 through 39) in this chapter. Testing for development of basic knowledge in introductory courses in economics, psychology, sociology, history, English, and speech is one approach (Case 37). Another approach is to evaluate the effectiveness of remedial or developmental courses in raising student achievement levels (Cases 38 and 39).

Increased and informed concern about students' writing skills is an almost universal outcome of the assessment initiatives that have been undertaken on campuses across the country. The third part of this section contains five examples of assessment of writing (Cases 40 through 44). Cases 40 and 41 describe attempts to improve the process of assessing students for placement in appropriate levels of introductory writing courses. Longitudinal development of writing skills is the topic of Cases 42 and 43. In the final example (Case 44), English composition faculty have based a common final exam for first-semester composition students on six specific skills they believe all students should develop in a first writing course.

Development of appropriate levels of quantitative skills is also a matter given considerable attention by faculty concerned about general education. Cases 45 and 46 focus on the study of students' math skills as they are manifested in courses in various disciplines that require a basic foundation in mathematics or statistics. Methods for assessing library skills (Case 47) and personal fitness (Case 48) round out this chapter on assessment in general education.

Faculty-Led Assessment

Fred D. Hinson, Judith M. Stillion

CASE 25: WESTERN CAROLINA UNIVERSITY

Look for: Clear enunciation of the eleven components of a core curriculum for general education, an internal program review process that uses multiple methods to evaluate courses in each of the eleven components periodically, and concrete illustrations of the uses made of assessment findings.

Background and Purpose

General education at Western Carolina University was revised in 1983 to reflect a thematic, rather than a discipline-based, approach to the core curriculum. The curriculum is divided into two major areas: foundations and perspectives. Written communication; mathematics; computer literacy; leisure and fitness; and thinking, reasoning, and expression courses are classified as foundations courses. Within the perspectives area are courses in social sciences and contemporary institutions, physical and biological sciences, the humanities, fine and performing arts, comparative cultures, and the human past. In addition, all general education courses are required to incorporate instruction and/or practice in seven skills defined in detail by the faculty. The skills are use of written communication, oral communication, critical thinking, logical reasoning, references and resources, the scientific method, and the process of valuing. The General Education Committee, reporting to the Council on Instruction and Curriculum of the faculty senate, is charged to monitor and assess the general education curriculum. A director of general education was appointed in 1990 and chairs the General Education Committee. In 1989, focus groups were formed to discuss commonalities between courses in each thematic area and to develop educational goals and methods of assessing them for each of the eleven areas of general education. Focus groups report to the General Education Committee and are composed of faculty teaching the courses in specific foundation or perspective categories. The assessment methods use multiple measures and are connected to an ongoing process of program review.

Method

The General Education Committee has established a process of program review that leads to systematic evaluation of each area of general education across a three-year time span. The program review process uses the results of multiple methods of assessment to evaluate courses in each of the eleven areas of study and to give feedback both to the focus groups and to the departments offering courses within the area. Components of the review process include (1) review of the educational objectives established for the area; (2) review of summative assessment data measuring student attainment of those objectives; (3) review of student responses to survey questions designed to determine if students perceive that the educational objectives and the seven basic skills of general education are incorporated into the curriculum; and (4) review of syllabi and samples of learning to determine if the educational objectives are built into syllabi and measured as a part of the ongoing testing in the course. The program review is carried out by the director of general education with support from the coordinator of undergraduate assessment. A draft of the results of the review is prepared and given to the focus group. After discussion by focus-group members, who have the opportunity to respond in writing, the results of the review are shared with the General Education Committee. The director of general education then holds a group meeting with the department heads involved to discuss the results. Questions are raised with each group of departmental faculty and written responses are requested.

In addition to program review, assessment of general education is carried out using two other approaches. First, growth in three of the seven general education skills is assessed by securing a sample of the abilities of entering students, using the Assessment of Reasoning and Communicating of the ACT College Outcome Measures Program (ACT-COMP) test. Four years later, seniors from that sample are again tested using the same instrument. Second, freshmen complete a self-assessment of skills and perspectives when they enter the university and a second self-assessment just prior to commencement, and alumni and employer surveys contain the same items, permitting self-assessment and employer assessment of general education skills and perspectives across time.

Findings

When the process began, the faculty were not very interested in taking the responsibility to assess student learning. There was confusion about the meaning of the seven skills. The members of the General Education Committee defined these skills and stated the minimum levels of instruction and practice in each skill expected to be incorporated in general education courses. In addition, a program review cycle and process were established. The focus group for the thinking, reasoning, and expression courses could not agree on common educational goals for the current courses. As they examined the students' needs, they recommended that this foundation area be changed to oral communication; the change will be effective in 1995. This was the first change made in the curriculum since 1984, and it is evidence that the review process is effective, since the faculty members making the recommendations were, in effect, abolishing their own courses.

Use of Findings

Many changes have occurred as a result of incorporating assessment into a faculty-owned model of continuous improvement and program review. Some of the most important changes are in perceptions and process. For example, faculty are now becoming convinced that they have a responsibility to assess learning in the general education program and are becoming more data oriented as they review student accomplishments on assessment instruments and students' perceptions of the courses. They are also beginning to understand that intermittent evaluations need to be replaced by continuous improvement processes in order to assure the best education for the students.

A second type of change that has occurred is the development of more specific information about the general education program, for faculty and students alike. For example, the specific definitions for each of the seven skills areas have been accepted by the faculty senate and the chancellor. These definitions not only permit us to evaluate the extent to which the skills are being taught and/or practiced but give us a common vision for student attainment. The definitions are being incorporated into general education manuals for faculty and for students.

A third type of change that has occurred as a result of assessment was a surprise. We found, through the work of the focus groups, that there was less coherence in the curriculum than we had anticipated. For example, the thinking, reasoning, and expression foundation courses included courses in psychology, philosophy, biology, physics, economics, communication, political science, law, and astronomy that had little or nothing in common. In recommending that this area be changed to one of oral communication, the members of the focus group recognized that thinking and reasoning were being taught across the curriculum but that faculty were not as successful in teaching and/or providing practice and feedback in the oral skills needed by our students. Other focus groups are still struggling with issues of coherence and common core goals.

Success Factors

This process worked because of several factors. First, the appointment of a director of general education was made at the request of the faculty. The director, who has taught in general education for many years, is respected by his peers and understands the curriculum, the students, and the pressures on faculty. Second, a representative committee of faculty meets almost weekly to monitor the evaluation process. This General Education Committee is a hardworking body that takes seriously its responsibilities for providing a general base for all majors. Third, focus groups, composed of the faculty delivering the instruction in the general education courses, created both the educational goals and the ways of assessing them. Therefore, faculty own the system. Finally, there is support and cooperation among four offices that are responsible for implementing the assessment and program review processes. These include the Office for Academic Affairs (through the associate vice chancellor), the assessment office, the Office of Institutional Studies and Planning, and the general education office.

Pilot Assessment of Learning Outcomes in a General Education Core Curriculum

Joanne Gainen, Peter A. Facione

CASE 26: SANTA CLARA UNIVERSITY

Look for: Detailed description of methods for getting started in general education assessment including defining the role of administrators, establishing task forces, and encouraging collegiality. Examples of assessment methods in six areas of a core curriculum are given.

Background and Purpose

On the theory that an understanding of assessment emerges from doing assessment, Dean Peter Facione of the College of Arts and Sciences at Santa Clara University established an Assessment Task Force on the Core Curriculum, chaired by then-Associate Dean Joanne Gainen. The university's core curriculum is defined by broadly stated goals in each of ten areas; each goal is translated into specific course requirements. Because the core curriculum is undergoing revision, and because core courses are offered within the College of Arts and Sciences, assessment of core learning outcomes offered an unusual opportunity to strengthen understanding and use of program-level assessment in the college. Thus, the primary purpose of the project was to foster a "culture of evidence" within the college, focused on learning outcomes.

The specific charge of the task force was to develop, in consultation with other faculty members, statements of specific high-level learning outcomes for each of six core goals; obtain preliminary descriptive data on actual learning outcomes; and present results to arts and sciences faculty in a series of colloquia and brief written reports. We specifically asked task force members to refrain from offering curriculum or policy recommendations. Instead, overlapping membership on the Arts and Sciences Task Force and the newly formed University Core Curriculum Committee (UCCC) was built into the plan so that the pilot assessment program would contribute to development of the new core curriculum.

Method

With help from department chairs in the college, we identified faculty members to serve on one of six distinct task force subgroups, each of which was asked to plan and implement a pilot assessment project for a single core goal. Each group consisted of four or five faculty, three or four from the department(s) most directly involved in supporting the requirement, and one from another department. For the first year of the project, we selected critical writing, ethics, ethnic/women's studies, mathematics, religious studies, and the Western culture sequence. In all communications about the project, we emphasized that its purpose was not program evaluation but inquiry and dialogue about curricular goals and learning outcomes.

Task force members attended a three-hour training session to discuss the project, learn procedures for goal clarification, and develop a plan to consult other faculty about the goals. At a second meeting, subgroups compiled the results of their inquiry, learned about assessment methodologies, then worked out preliminary plans for their projects. In follow-up meetings with the associate dean, each subgroup developed instruments, planned specific data collection methods, discussed results, and prepared its colloquium presentation.

The project time line was intentionally kept brief: task force members were selected and oriented in the fall; data collection and analysis took place during winter and early spring quarters. Results were presented in six noon-hour colloquia in late spring. Colloquia were attended by the dean (who also assisted in developing several of the projects), the chair and members of the UCCC, and the associate vice president for academic affairs. Draft reports were prepared by the associate dean in June, circulated for feedback, and completed in September.

Identifying and Clarifying Outcomes. Five of the six groups consulted with and/or surveyed faculty to clarify outcomes the current core curriculum is intended to achieve with respect to the subgroup's assigned goal. The Western culture group worked from criteria drafted by the classics department in 1992. Outcome statements included knowledge, skills, and "sensitivities" in varying degrees. For example, the mathematics subgroup identified skills in logical reasoning and translation of mathematical ideas as well as an appreciation of the uses of mathematics. The ethics subgroup identified four outcomes but focused only on moral reasoning. The ethnic/women's studies subgroup identified recognition of and sensitivity to diverse experiences as well as responsibility to promote an inclusive society. The writing subgroup identified both "crafting skills" (mechanics and word choice) and the ability to articulate and develop an original thesis.

Instruments and Methods. Measures used included essays rated on scoring criteria developed for this project (writing and ethnic/women's studies), a questionnaire and short skills examination (mathematics), an audiotaped class discussion of freedom and equality (Western culture), an audiotaped focus group on the religious dimensions of students' SCU education (religious studies), and an abbreviated version of the Defining Issues Test (DIT) (Rest, 1990) to assess moral reasoning (ethics).

The ethics group administered the DIT in six courses chosen to yield a distribution of majors and class levels (freshman through senior). The Western culture group devised a question on freedom and equality in premodern and modern times, which was discussed by a class of seniors majoring in political science. For the two projects involving essays, the subgroup identified an appropriate assignment in a core course and, with the professors' help, obtained students' written permission to use the essays anonymously. For religious studies and mathematics, we mailed invitations to representative samples of one hundred freshmen and one hundred seniors, stating that we were "engaged in a series of studies about learning achieved by students in the Core," and offering a $10 bookstore certificate for participation. Only twenty-five students responded in math, and eight in religious studies. In the case of religious studies, Dean Facione eventually audio-taped a discussion of the focus-group questions with the fifteen students in his senior capstone seminar.

Findings

In each case, the majority of the students' responses gave evidence of the learning outcomes identified by the faculty. However, sample sizes were small, and circumstances for the assessments were less than ideal, so participants were understandably reluctant to draw conclusions from these pilot studies.

Still, the twenty-six faculty on the task force became quite engaged in planning and implementing their pilot studies. Discussion in the colloquia was lively and well grounded in evidence. Participants were least receptive to the ethics study, although it had the largest sample size (119) and used a validated instrument (the DIT).

Use of Findings

The project's focus on description of learning outcomes generated useful discussion among task force members and the many faculty they interviewed to help them clarify curricular goals. Project initiators and participants also relearned some familiar lessons of the assessment movement. First, we learned that faculty become quite engaged in serious inquiry about learning outcomes; the most productive conversations occurred in the context of developing outcome statements and devising and applying criteria for evaluating essays. Second, we reaffirmed that assessment requires a great deal of work! Technical and clerical support from the dean's office was essential for timely completion of these projects. We also learned that few students are tempted by mailed invitations even when generous incentives and flexible scheduling are offered. (A methodology we plan to try in the future is to offer chances for a drawing to win a more substantial prize.) We obtained much better results using course-embedded methodologies: asking faculty to administer questionnaires in class (ethics); using assignments already planned by faculty (writing and ethnic/women's studies). And we found that developing our own measures and criteria yields far greater engagement in the process and interest in the results than choosing existing measures for convenience.

This project has had several very positive results for the college and university. It stimulated extensive discussion of student learning outcomes and successfully introduced influential faculty members to a range of assessment methods. The colloquia were attended by key academic administrators and faculty. Finally, members of the University Core Curriculum Committee reported that the work of the task force helped them formulate outcomes for courses in the new core.

Success Factors

The project seems to have benefitted from the initiative, support, and facilitation of the dean and associate dean; cooperation and support of the chair of the UCCC; and the curiosity, goodwill, and contributed efforts of participating faculty. The pilot study model allowed faculty to experiment freely with unfamiliar methods and to obtain some baseline data. Selection of an "outside" person for each subgroup was crucial, as these individuals brought interest, perspective, and expertise that enriched the planning process. Our emphasis on description of learning outcomes rather than judgment of program merits reduced (but did not eliminate) concerns about the project. During the instrument design phase, our participation helped to maintain focus on learning outcomes (as opposed to more familiar methods based on students' or faculty's perceptions of or satisfaction with those outcomes). At the same time, our facilitative stance enabled each subgroup to develop its own distinctive approach to assessment, reflected in the variety of projects described above.

The core assessment project continued in 1994–95, with four new subgroups addressing curricular goals in the arts, social sciences, and modern languages. The UCCC plans to adapt materials and methods from several of the pilot projects for assessment of the new core curriculum.

Demonstrating Student Achievement in an Honors Program

Steven M. Culver, Earl B. Brown, Jr.

CASE 27: RADFORD UNIVERSITY

Look for: Objectives for student achievement in honors courses that suggest assessment strategies that can be implemented in disciplines across the curriculum. The assessment process has resulted in the development of three new courses, a senior colloquy, and required objectives for every honors course.

Background and Purpose

The Radford University honors program, like many others, had relied on GPA and course requirements as measures of student achievement. To graduate from the program, students needed to do no more than maintain a certain GPA and complete a prescribed number of hours of honors work. These hours were required to ensure that students had several sorts of educational experiences, such as interdisciplinary seminars, independent studies, theses, service learning, and discussion-oriented courses, based on the notion that these experiences, in and of themselves, would ensure that our students had realized some unstated objectives.

New assessment procedures now ensure that students who graduate from the RU honors program can demonstrate competence in several qualitative areas, that is, the objectives of the honors program.

Method

A subcommittee of the Honors Council (composed of five faculty and two students), which assists the program director with the administration of the program, now requires students to submit with their final project proposal a portfolio of work accumulated over their career at RU. This work is accompanied by a cover letter that is crucial to the portfolio, for in it, a student argues that what she or he includes demonstrates that she or he has met all the objectives. How each student chooses to meet each objective is up to the student. The Honors Council encourages video- and audiotapes, musical scores, original research, proposals for honors credit work (students in the honors program may convert a nonhonors course into an honors course by proposing to change course requirements), or anything that the student believes would help her or him demonstrate that she or he has met all the honors program objectives.

The honors program wanted to ensure that its graduates demonstrate the ability to communicate effectively through writing, including the ability to do research. This objective could be met by submitting a paper or two written for any course taken at RU, whether honors or not. One of the papers submitted must demonstrate the ability to use research.

Demonstrating the ability to communicate effectively orally requires that a student make an oral presentation at a conference, during honors week, in a class, during the exit interview, or at the final banquet to honor the graduates. The ability to analyze and synthesize a broad range of material can be demonstrated through a researched paper, a creative performance or exhibit, or laboratory or other experiments.

Students need to demonstrate the ability to formulate a problem, develop a plan of action, and prove or disprove an hypothesis; to create and produce an original work; or to set up a thesis and test it. The Honors Council had such difficulty formulating this objective that members agreed to allow as wide a latitude as possible for students to demonstrate their ability. Thus, the council felt that students from all disciplines could find a way to meet this objective.

The final objective asked students to demonstrate the ability to take greater responsibility for their own learning (demonstrate curiosity, motivation, risk-taking characteristics, and the ability to bring knowledge and logic to bear on the issue being discussed). Again, the Honors Council wished to allow as much latitude to the students as possible to demonstrate this objective. The council suggested the following as possible ways of doing so: a proposal for honors credit, a final project, or a presentation at an honors conference.

Findings

The Honors Council found that graduating students chose a wide variety of ways in which to demonstrate these competencies. Only a few students have had to rewrite their cover letters, and one student revised a writing sample. Otherwise, we have been extremely pleased with this assessment measure. Through this approach, we have evidence that our students are able to do what we say they can.

Use of Findings

Honors Council members felt sure that assessment results would allow us to demonstrate that students who graduated from the honors program met our objectives. But we were surprised at the broader implications of what we had done. After thinking about the objectives developed for honors, the Honors Council decided that every honors course should list course objectives and discuss how the instructor intended to have students reach those objectives. We provided faculty proposing honors courses with our list of objectives and were pleased that many faculty incorporated our objectives into their course proposals.

The objectives that faculty proposed for their honors courses made us realize that many faculty expected students taking honors courses to possess certain skills prior to taking the course. Their proposals listed these and detailed how they expected students to demonstrate them but provided no course instruction in them. The honors program, recognizing this as a problem, approved three courses to provide students with some of these skills: a course in learning how to learn, a course in service learning, and a course in cultural learning. Each of these courses helps our students develop the skills necessary to meet honors program objectives as well as objectives established by faculty for their courses.

Individual courses can now be more clearly defined to meet honor program competencies, and student expectations are more explicit to faculty and to students. For instance, in a senior honors seminar, we provided students with a list of course objectives and suggested ways in which to meet them. We asked students to tell us early in the semester how they intended to meet these objectives. The result was, on the whole, quite positive. These students took greater responsibility for their learning, engaged in risk-taking behavior, and were able to determine their own strengths and weaknesses in deciding how to meet these objectives.

A final outcome of setting the objectives was the creation of a senior-level colloquy for students working on final projects, to provide them with the opportunity to learn from each other and to help each other while doing essentially individual projects. Because of this colloquy and because of the meaningful nature of the program objectives, more students over the past two years have graduated from the honors program than ever before.

Success Factors

What made this activity effective was the realization by both faculty and students that grades and courses no longer were adequate measures of competence. Students on the Honors Council and the Student Executive Board played a major role in creating the honors objectives. Their commitment to the objectives and their realization that this form of assessment would document their skills and help them present themselves to employers made the institution of the new requirements easier.

An Assessment of a Core Curriculum

Richard A. Schalinske, Robert A. Patterson, Gary L. Smith

CASE 28: CAPITAL UNIVERSITY

Look for: Competence statements for a core curriculum and a faculty-developed multiple-choice test designed to assess student achievement in core areas at the sophomore level. Sophomores' mastery of content and satisfaction with coursework were highest for the area of global awareness and lowest for that of science and technology.

Background and Purpose

In 1989, Capital University established a competency-based core curriculum to provide students in a variety of academic and professional programs with a singular context of liberal arts learning. Competencies, involving language skills, lifetime health, religious and ethical systems, fine arts, global awareness, and disciplines of the liberal arts, were clearly identified and organized into twelve multidisciplinary courses administered by separate core committees and a core curriculum director. Students were expected to demonstrate competency in each of the twelve by (1) achieving a passing grade in the core course; (2) achieving a passing grade on an assessment procedure for the core area as determined by the core committee; (3) obtaining a waiver or core course credit through the evaluation of an experiential learning portfolio by the University Competency Assessment Panel; (4) equating credits obtained at other accredited institutions with the learning outcomes of the core area; or (5) completing an academic major in which the required coursework provided learning in one or more of the core areas.

Over the next few years, the core curriculum was refined by validating many of the core committee assessment procedures and encouraging individual classroom assessment. However, aside from periodic surveys of student satisfaction with each course, there was no institutional measure of the core curriculum competencies. In other words, a procedure was needed to determine whether students had actually learned what the university said they would learn after taking the required core courses. Questions still remained about the levels of competency an entire class of students had attained and about possible inconsistencies in instruction or learning between the adult and traditional programs. But more importantly, there were very few objective procedures to indicate the practical strengths and weaknesses of the core curriculum courses so that each course could be reviewed and improved on a continual basis.

Method

While a multiple-measure procedure was envisioned for ultimately assessing the core curriculum, the Assessment Center decided initially to develop a relatively simple instrument that could not only measure student proficiency levels in the core competencies but also provide a general model for the development of more sophisticated and comprehensive measures. However, as a fundamental part of that model, the instrument would have to yield data that could be used practically at the macro, or institutional, level and also at the micro, or classroom, level. To reduce the time and effort involved in scoring, it was also decided to use a multiple-choice rather than an essay question format. Accordingly, each core course committee was asked to contribute five to ten multiple-choice questions that committee members felt would be representative of the competencies their students were required to learn. Questions that actually appeared on final exams or on assessment procedures used by the core committees were particularly encouraged.

Due to time constraints and, in at least one case, a reluctance on the part of a committee to assess learning in this manner, the final instrument was composed of thirty questions from four committees: global awareness, lifetime health, science and technology, and quantitative reasoning. However, these committees did represent a general cross-section of the competencies that were required throughout the core curriculum. There was also an almost equal distribution between content-oriented questions and those that required an application of one or more competencies.

The resulting Core Assessment Measure was administered to all traditional sophomore students as part of a mandatory university assessment testing policy. Results from a total of 222 sophomores, or approximately 75 percent of the entire class, were then analyzed by course and item, controlling for students who had actually taken the core course.

Findings

An analysis of the Core Assessment Measure revealed that students who had taken two of the core courses did reasonably well on the related items. While it was difficult to interpret the results without the benefit of previous administrations, the average correct response rates of 68 percent for global awareness items and 59 percent for lifetime health items were seen as probably reflecting realistic levels of mastery and retention; especially for those who took the course an entire year before. However the analysis also revealed an average correct response rate of 33 percent for science and technology items and 37 percent for quantitative-reasoning items. Since it was likely that these courses were taken after the other two core courses, the response rates raised serious questions about mastery and/or retention. Mean satisfaction ratings on the Sophomore Survey for the four courses mirrored the results of the Core Assessment Measure, with the ratings for global awareness being the highest and those for science and technology being the lowest.

Use of Findings

The first administration of the Core Assessment Measure was always considered a preliminary step in the development of a broader core curriculum assessment procedure. Thus, the results were expected to be used in many different ways and have a practical impact over a period of time. Initially, the results were used to help focus faculty attention on both classroom teaching/learning interactions and the types of procedures that could truly measure proficiencies in core curriculum courses. Such attention later led to an active inquiry into classroom assessment and learning outcomes by the entire faculty, culminating in a fall faculty retreat on the topic of assessment. The results were also used to illustrate the manner in which core proficiency levels could be compared between class sections and between the traditional and adult degree programs in terms of both general learning and specific content areas. A result from a very practical standpoint was that the data from the Core Assessment Measure were entered into a database for use in the statistical analyses of future pre- and/or posttest administrations. In this way, the measure can continue to be used to enhance the effectiveness of the core curriculum and produce a more refined institutional assessment procedure.

Success Factors

While the plans for an institutional core curriculum assessment were initiated by the Assessment Center, the procedure worked because the faculty were concerned about whether students were learning what the institution said they should be learning. This concern was already evident in faculty support for a competency-based core curriculum and a mandatory assessment testing policy. However, it was again quite prominent in their ready acceptance of the need to conduct such an assessment, even though there were varying opinions on how that could be accomplished. Equally important was that faculty were involved in all aspects of the activity and could take ownership of the procedure as well as the subsequent results. Because the results were not limited to the macro, or institutional, level of assessment, but could be fed back into the teaching-learning loop at the micro, or classroom, level, the procedure was able to generate initial and, more importantly, continued faculty support and involvement.

Value-Added Talent Development in General Education

W. Jack Magruder, Candace Cartwright Young

CASE 29: NORTHEAST MISSOURI STATE UNIVERSITY

Look for: Significant curriculum change as a result of careful review over two decades of student gain scores on a standardized exam in general education, supplemented with data from student surveys and portfolios. Strong advocacy by campus administrators, continual communication about findings and ways to improve, and commitment of faculty have sustained this institution as a leader in assessment. (First in a series of three cases from Northeast Missouri State University.)

Background and Purpose

Every student at Northeast Missouri State University (NMSU) participates in value-added assessment. It is our plan that students will use their entry data to identify weaknesses, and that they, along with their advisers, will make curricular choices to enhance their strengths and to correct their deficiencies. Encouraging students to set goals for their posttest is another responsibility of advisers.

Method

The intent of the value-added-assessment portion of the university's assessment program is to assess growth relative to stated general education objectives for knowledge and skills. These objectives include development in the basic skills of reading, writing, and math, but also include gains in values clarification, problem-solving, and critical thinking abilities and in knowledge of the liberal arts. The university requires all students to sit for a pretest during freshman week. Students are then retested using the same exam at the end of the sophomore year. Since the mid 1970s, the university has used a number of standardized instruments for this purpose, including the ACT Assessment Exam, ACT-COMP exam, and the Collegiate Assessment of Academic Proficiency (CAAP).

The university complements the information gained through standardized testing with feedback obtained in a series of student surveys, a locally developed sophomore student writing assessment, and the university portfolio project.

Findings

The use of standardized tests has the advantage of providing the university with an external reference point for student achievement. NMSU students perform very well relative to national norms. However, a principal area of focus has been on sophomore student change scores. (The change score is the difference between a student's entering freshman score and the sophomore score.) Perhaps most dramatic are the results that indicate problems. These red flags attract attention and proposals for change, especially if they are corroborated by data from our other assessment instruments. When student change scores in math actually went down, this unanticipated finding promoted change in the math curriculum. While student surveys and faculty classroom experiences had suggested weaker levels of student learning in mathematics than desired, seeing that students' sophomore scores were on average lower than freshman scores provided the catalyst for change.

Use of Findings

Negative findings regarding student learning in math caused the faculty to discuss desired outcomes for student math skills. Assessment data also indicated that the students who had negative change scores in mathematics tended to fall into two categories: those who took a noncalculation math course to meet the general education requirement and those who had not yet taken any college math.

The faculty senate changed the mathematics general education requirement to include a minimum of college algebra and trigonometry. Previously, students had been able to take a course that discussed math in a contemporary society but did not actually require students to perform mathematical calculations or to engage in mathematical reasoning. As students followed the new curriculum, math change scores improved dramatically. Improved results on the standardized exams were paralleled by increased student satisfaction with their ability to understand and apply math and to understand and interpret graphic information (as self-reported on a survey all students complete prior to graduation).

The change scores in science were also lower than desired. Here, the decision was made to require students to take two laboratory-based sciences (choosing from among biology, chemistry, and physics) and to eliminate as general education options science courses that focused on discussions of science issues in society. It was believed that students should be exposed to what it is like to think like a scientist. Again, student change scores in science increased significantly, and student satisfaction in the understanding of science as reported on student surveys went up.

Success Factors

One of the advantages of standardized test scores is that they appear so conclusive. In addition, faculty classroom experiences and student survey data reinforced the negative data from student test scores. The vice president for academic affairs (VPAA) regularly monitored assessment data, and his leadership on these curricular issues in general education was in large part the reason for placing the math and science questions on the agenda for discussion. Having the curricular changes validated by ongoing collection of data was also important.

The role of faculty-administration conversations grounded in the data has been vital to developing assessment-based improvement at NMSU. The curricular reforms noted above were in part the result of the VPAA presenting the data to several campus groups and encouraging discussion of the implications for the existing math and science curriculum requirements. Of equal importance is NMSU's continuing commitment to using multiple assessment measures. Building cultural expectations for multiple measures makes it less likely that inappropriate reliance on a single standardized test score will occur. Similarly, emphasizing that assessment is to be used for improvement and giving assurances that data will not be used punitively are important to obtaining faculty support for assessment.

Portfolios: Assessment of Liberal Arts Goals

W. Jack Magruder, Candace Cartwright Young

CASE 30: NORTHEAST MISSOURI STATE UNIVERSITY

Look for: Portfolios as an addition to an established general education assessment program utilizing standardized tests and student satisfaction surveys. Students learn about the portfolio requirement as freshmen, hear more about it periodically, and develop the portfolio as seniors. The faculty who read the portfolios learn much about their own teaching. (Second in a series of three cases from Northeast Missouri State University.)

Background and Purpose

Portfolio assessment at Northeast Missouri State University (NMSU) grew out of a decision to develop a local instrument to assess the liberal arts and sciences core curriculum. The local assessment was to serve as a complement to standardized tests and student satisfaction surveys already in use on the campus.

Each year a faculty committee writes the specifications for senior portfolios, which are collected in senior seminars and sent to the University Portfolio Committee for review by faculty the week following graduation. The portfolio gives us an opportunity to collect and review actual student work in our efforts to assess such learning objectives as critical thinking, interdisciplinary synthesis, scientific and mathematical reasoning, aesthetic appreciation, and co-curricular learning.

Method

Students are introduced to the idea of keeping their work during their first week at the university. Faculty are also encouraged to identify an assignment or project from each course that would be ideal to maintain in the portfolio. Advisers and faculty working with the sophomore writing experience discuss and may review the portfolio with students. However, the most formal aspect of the portfolio project currently takes place during a student's senior year.

By the beginning of each academic year, the University Portfolio Committee identifies the items to be included in student portfolios. Students are asked to prepare a portfolio according to the specifications and then to make a copy of the portfolio, at university expense. Faculty who teach senior seminars implement the distribution of specifications and the collection of portfolios. Senior seminar faculty in some cases conduct their own portfolio review at the course or discipline level prior to turning the university copy of the portfolios over to the University Portfolio Committee. The original portfolio is returned to the student as a formal collection of his or her college work.

Twenty faculty members are paid $500 each to participate in reading portfolios the week after spring graduation. Faculty frequently hesitate when asked, but once in the process, find it very rewarding. Anytime you can get twenty faculty members in a room to talk about student learning for an extended period of time, good things happen. For many faculty, the week provides them with a better picture of student learning and the university experience than any other university committee or activity in which they engage. Faculty are exposed to the range of assignments our students are asked to complete. A science faculty member has to grapple with the aesthetic sophistication of student-written poetry, and a literature professor has to evaluate student mathematical-reasoning ability. Faculty generally finish the week having renewed appreciation for the university experience and also having a better developed sense of areas in need of improvement. The opportunity for faculty to engage in active learning is one of the best consequences of the effort.

A final characteristic of Northeast's portfolio project is its requirement for student self-assessment. Each item submitted requires a brief self-analysis by students. For the portfolio as a whole, each student also submits a cover letter describing what he or she learned from reviewing four years of college work.

Findings

Faculty who participate in the reading of portfolios find the experience to be quite revealing about the type of work students are asked to do and about the numerous modes of thinking in which students are asked to be proficient. The range of modes of inquiry is a stretch for many professors who spend most of their time in matters related to their disciplines. Furthermore, there are distinctive modes of inquiry for different majors. How students respond to the request for submission of an interdisciplinary work varies from major to major, as do entries submitted to demonstrate growth in critical thinking.

For the last three years, the portfolio committee has been assessing the ability of students to make interdisciplinary connections. The university's core curriculum is based on disciplines. As faculty seek to identify the most effective means to develop students' inclination and ability to synthesize their various course materials, the portfolio provides evidence of existing practice. Three years of portfolio review of interdisciplinarity indicates that most students engage in interdisciplinary thinking but that some majors seem to offer students fewer opportunities (or expectations) to engage in these connections. Furthermore, committee members have decided that the concept of interdisciplinary synthesis is much more complicated than they previously thought. Some topics, such as environmental issues, demand interdisciplinary information by the very nature of the problem itself because they cross many disciplinary boundaries. However, other student submissions of interdisciplinary work demonstrate much more initiative on the students' part to synthesize theories, models, and information in creative ways. If it is the latter type of interdisciplinary thinking we are most interested in encouraging, how do we enhance student opportunities to synthesize elements of disparate subjects? Requiring that students take a course on an inherently interdisciplinary topic will probably not be as useful as carefully worded prompts and problem-solving exercises that encourage students to develop interdisciplinary connections.

Use of Findings

The university is currently reviewing the existing core curriculum, and the portfolio committee has formally and informally conveyed its findings. In addition to insights gained relative to interdisciplinary and critical thinking, the committee expressed reservations about student proficiencies in mathematical reasoning. Assessment data from the portfolios and other assessment methods will also play a part in the campus discussion of proposals for revision of the core curriculum.

Faculty members who read the portfolios note direct effects on their classroom strategies. From getting ideas for an assignment to making a commitment to enhance expectations for quantitative reasoning in their courses, participating faculty are the most likely to implement findings from the portfolio review as they revise their own courses. Furthermore, faculty other than those directly involved can be influenced by discussion of the findings at meetings of governance councils and committees. Findings are also presented to colleagues in divisional meetings, disciplinary meetings, and informal gatherings in the university offices and hallways.

Success Factors

Faculty are directly involved in developing specifications for student portfolios, and thus, portfolios can be carefully designed to demonstrate student learning in areas specified by the university community. The mere process of determining what learning objectives to assess is beneficial. As committee members meet to write the specifications for portfolios, refinement of faculty understanding of university objectives occurs. Participating faculty members are particularly likely to reflect on their own teaching in light of their portfolio-reading experience. Thus, at least 5 percent of the faculty are significantly affected each year by the portfolio process through their involvement in self-reflection and analysis of student learning.

Junior Interview Project on Teaching and Learning

Candace Cartwright Young, W. Jack Magruder

CASE 31: NORTHEAST MISSOURI STATE UNIVERSITY

Look for: Faculty-student teams conducting interviews to learn which teaching/learning strategies students consider most effective. Students pronounce grading the worst learning experience and writing papers the most valuable. Findings are reported to all students, faculty, and staff. (Third in series of three cases from Northeast Missouri State University.)

Background and Purpose

Northeast Missouri State University has been conducting student satisfaction surveys since the mid 1970s. However, we wanted to develop an assessment strategy that would give us greater understanding of which teaching and learning strategies students found most effective. Our interview project allows the university to ask students several in-depth questions that go beyond the information we receive through surveys. A commitment to faculty involvement and to limiting the amount of time required to conduct the study were two important considerations in the design of the project.

Method

Since we were interested in understanding effective teaching strategies, we decided to interview a random sample of one hundred second-semester juniors (students with seventy-five to ninety credit hours.) Eleven faculty members teamed with eleven upper-level students to interview one hundred students over a five-week period. Members of the Faculty Advisory Committee on Assessment developed the five-question interview schedule and pretested it with several students. After the pretesting, we developed a list of anticipated coding categories, which were adapted as necessary during weekly lunch meetings throughout the project.

Every Thursday, eight faculty-student interview teams interviewed two students. The other three faculty-student interview teams interviewed students who could not attend the Thursday interview time. Thus, each week, we had the potential to interview twenty-two students, with the actual number depending on how many students kept their appointments. Approximately 60 percent of the students showed up for their interviews, and with call-backs to schedule a second appointment, we were able to achieve a 70 percent participation rate. Student workers called students to schedule interview appointments and to remind them of their appointments.

At the interview, the faculty-student team took notes, and at the end of the twenty- to twenty-five-minute interview, team members separately coded the responses. Then the student and faculty member checked to see if their codings were identical; when they were not, they negotiated the coding conclusion. For each code selected, the team provided the key phrase from the interviewed student that supported the coding choice. Within one hour, the team could interview two students and code the results. At the weekly lunch meetings, the eleven interview teams discussed any coding problems and reviewed what interviewed students were saying. These conversations were extremely helpful in internalizing the information that students were conveying. At the end of the five-week period, interviewers met to analyze the tabulated results that had been compiled by members of the Faculty Advisory Committee on Assessment and student workers.

In an attempt to involve undergraduate council and division heads, we arranged for each person to participate in at least one interview. Each person in the Office of the Vice President for Academic Affairs also participated in an interview.

Findings

More than seven of every ten students interviewed (71 percent) cited teacher or pedagogy as a main reason for a course's being most valuable to them in terms of their learning. Students mentioned a teacher's positive attitude, a teacher's ability to develop class discussion, and class format. Students often said that even though a course was difficult, the teacher structured it to require student discipline and encourage improvement through frequent assignments and feedback. Thus, enhancing student's involvement in their learning through increases in the number of student assignments and faculty feedback was confirmed as a very effective teaching/learning strategy. Many students told us that the course they valued most in terms of their learning was also the course they enjoyed most (62 percent).

Forty-two percent of the students in our sample told us that their best assignment or learning experience was a paper, 15 percent reported a practicum or lab experience, and 14 percent reported a presentation. Fifty-eight percent of the assignments/experiences cited were individual projects, while 33 percent were group projects (9 percent not ascertained.) For most students (54 percent), the assignment or experience was most beneficial because of its relevance, 19 percent valued the assignment because it allowed the student to express his or her opinion, and 13 percent complimented the assignment for the quality of feedback received.

Somewhat to our surprise, grading was the reason given by 43 percent of students for their worst learning experience. Students felt their worst assignment was "unfair," "unclear," or "too much work for the credit assigned." Often, students mentioned a lack of congruence between lecture or discussion material and test material. In other instances, teachers were accused of a political or gender bias. Thirty-four percent of students cited teachers' "bad explanations" as the reason for their worst classroom experience.

Use of Findings

In this study, faculty interviewers were the most directly affected group and, thus, the most likely to make changes in the way they taught their courses. In some ways, changes in classroom teaching are the hardest changes to measure but the most important to effect. Precisely because of the university's interest in faculty use of the data, faculty were chosen as the group to write the annual interview schedule and to conduct the interviews. Participating faculty have encouraged other faculty to join the project. Several faculty have instituted similar interview projects among their own majors, and faculty have identified several new kinds of questions for the next interview project. The project certainly reinforces the notion of developing assessment processes that facilitate active involvement by faculty.

Student interviewers benefitted in that they developed a better understanding of the assessment efforts on the campus. The student interviewers were also very helpful in analyzing the tabulated results from a student's perspective. As with many evaluation strategies, future students will benefit most from changes faculty make in the classroom.

To enhance the impact of the findings beyond participating faculty, the results were sent to all members of the university community. (The report included the aggregated totals for each question, followed by a running list of the codes for each student interviewed, along with the key phrase used to justify the code.) The data have also been reported at several university conferences and have been used in speeches by faculty and administrators and in the university's recent accreditation self-study.

Success Factors

Several factors contributed to the success of this project. Faculty-student involvement was critical to having faculty value the results. Perceived legitimacy is vital for the desired outcomes of faculty change in the classroom and improved student learning. Faculty are more likely to make change in the classroom if they are the ones who develop the questions to be asked, conduct the interviews, and aggregate the results. If the interviews had been done by graduate students, faculty would value the project less and understand the results less well. To read a report of someone else's project has far less impact than to talk to students, discuss student concerns, and analyze the data personally. Finally, the project was effective because of its low cost-to-benefits ratio. (Costs included five lunches for the interviewers and eighty hours of student work to help prepare aggregate data sheets and the report.) Faculty and students who participated commented that their time commitment of approximately fifteen hours was very rewarding and even "enjoyable."

Evaluation of the Senior Project

Ernie Oshiro

CASE 32: UNIVERSITY OF HAWAII-WEST OAHU

Look for: Analysis of fifteen years of individual senior projects to assess overall development of writing, critical thinking, and research skills. The findings have led to changes in the policy governing senior projects, in student services, and in instruction.

Background and Purpose

The University of Hawaii-West Oahu (UHWO) is located eight miles west of downtown Honolulu. It has 700 students and is the only upper-division college in the seven-campus system of the University of Hawaii. Since UHWO's inception in 1976, senior projects have been a requirement for graduation, but until 1991, the senior project had never been evaluated. The recent assessment movement prompted the college to look more closely at this requirement: What are its objectives? Is it achieving its purpose? Are expectations, student workload, paper quality, and grades consistent among all disciplines? Is there room for improvement?

Method

To answer these questions, a study commenced in fall 1991 with the establishment of a database on relevant variables. The objective was to analyze writing ability, critical thinking, and research skills. With only one reviewer, it was necessary to evaluate each senior project quickly, with two readings of 107 senior projects over one academic year.

The minimum level of writing ability was analyzed in a variety of ways. One was for the reviewer to rate the paper relative to a minimum writing competency standard with a pass/fail score. Also, a computer program was used to rate reading ease, writing style, difficult words used, and sentence length for a sample of papers from various disciplines (*Readability Program for the IMB PC,* 1988).

Critical thinking was measured through a modified scale using Bloom's taxonomy of educational objectives (1956). Research skill was measured by the number of references, the use of statistical concepts, and the use of theoretical concepts from the major field. Furthermore, a scale that provides an insight into both critical thinking and research skills measured the integration of ideas from various sources.

Findings

The findings were revealing. In fifteen years, the senior project had evolved into a different task for different disciplines, and sometimes for different instructors in the same discipline. The disciplines were guided by an explicitly stated collegewide objective that the senior project be a product of original or library research and that students assist each other and share with each other their efforts. Everyone implicitly agreed that, besides the stated objective, the collegewide objectives also included having a culminating experience, improving writing, utilizing critical thinking, and improving research skills through independent learning. However, the disciplines also added their own objectives, which were not explicitly stated. For example, psychology emphasized the research report style of a scientific journal, while sociology promoted surveying and interviewing skills. Business instituted the business plan as its capstone model. At times, these additions to the collegewide objectives seemed to arise out of instructor knowledge rather than well thought out goals for the majors.

One deviation that all disciplines made from the explicit and implicit collegewide objectives was to allow students to substitute a practicum for the senior project. The practicum gives credits for on-site experiences. The usual requirements are to make daily journal entries and to provide a short summary of the experience at the end. Even though this writing is not the same as the longer, researched, and integrative writing of a senior project, most disciplines accepted the substitute. Similarly, group efforts were accepted as individual projects, even though the contribution of each student was not clearly specified. These exceptions occurred because, over the years, the senior project objectives were never clarified.

Because of varying instructor expectations, it was difficult to compare expectations made of students and student workloads. Although the length of the papers did vary significantly by discipline, this was due to the different teaching and research styles employed and not necessarily a reflection of effort. (It sometimes takes more revisions to make a paper short and concise than it does to write a long paper.) The quality of most papers was good and did not differ by instructor or discipline. All the papers met the minimum writing competency standard. However, the papers differed markedly in the use of statistical methods: over half of them had no quantitative analysis and one-fifth used only descriptive statistics (usually simple frequency distributions). Despite the lack of quantitative methods, the study showed that about 33 percent of the papers were very well done, 50 percent were good and passable, and 17 percent were poorly done. These results differed only slightly from the actual distribution of grades for the projects, with 57 percent receiving A's, 27 percent B's, and 17 percent C's.

The grade distributions varied significantly by instructor but not by discipline. Also, the average senior project grade was slightly higher than the average for all courses. This was probably due to the inherent nature of the senior project as process oriented, that is, the student researches, writes a draft, receives feedback, rewrites, and so on, until the final product is obtained. Evaluation occurs at every stage, and the grade tends to be cumulatively higher as the paper moves to its final draft.

Use of Findings

This study resulted in several significant changes in the policy for senior projects. The old policy is being reworked to be more specific about the objectives for the college and the disciplines. The clarification of objectives is having important results. First, the senior project is now driven by the goals of the majors rather than instructor knowledge. Second, expectations and student workload are more consistent among disciplines. Third, practicums that do not meet the written objectives of the senior project are not substitutable. And finally, group work is no longer acceptable for individual projects.

In addition to general changes in policy, smaller spinoffs resulted. A meeting with instructors to discuss the senior project study uncovered problems with inflexible class hours, inadequate computer help, and concern about grading. These problems are being addressed. However, the meeting also generated solutions: a complaint by one instructor about a large number of no-shows for the final oral presentations received an observation by another instructor that he handled the same problem with taped presentations, a good idea that will be more widely used.

In summary, the evaluation of the senior project has yielded significant improvements at the University of Hawaii-West Oahu. A new policy on the senior project is being drafted, collegewide and disciplinary objectives have been clarified, past exceptions to the senior projects such as practicums and group work have been limited, and smaller problems have been resolved. Time will tell whether these changes will have resulted in significant effects on learning as well.

Student Motivation and Standardized Testing for Institutional Assessment

Daniel J. Poje

CASE 33: THE UNIVERSITY OF MEMPHIS

Look for: Methods for encouraging freshmen and seniors to participate in standardized testing as a means of assessing achievement in general education.

Background and Purpose

One assessment tool that causes great frustration is the standardized test. Some form of objective data may be mandated by a governing board or state agency, and data provided by testing are certainly considered appropriate as part of a multiple-measures approach to assessment of a program. In either case, one obstacle causes coordinators to shy away from standardized tests or to consider the results suspect: student motivation. The desire to perform well on admission tests such as the American College Test or the Graduate Record Examination is intrinsic, but there is usually no such motivator for students taking examinations for institutional assessment. It is infrequently that a college or university will or can tie a carrot (for example, admission to graduate school) or stick (for example, graduation delay) to a standardized test used for institutional assessment.

At the University of Memphis (formerly Memphis State University), where an instructional evaluation program was begun in 1979, in response to directives from the Tennessee Higher Education Commission and the state legislature, we test graduating seniors to measure the impact of the university's general education program and also the undergraduate major fields. Over the years, students have challenged the testing requirement and have appealed to the president, chancellor, and board of regents for a waiver; they have sabotaged their computer-coded answer sheets by giving the same answer to all questions, "christmas-treeing" responses, or writing obscene messages in the borders; on occasion, students have refused to show up for a test, arrived unprepared, left early, or slept through it. One very bright student decided to answer all the questions wrongly and nearly succeeded! Such behavior calls into question the validity of the institution's results and makes it difficult to trust inferences about them. Our attempts to overcome this lack of student motivation have evolved as we have adopted various approaches, gimmicks, or tactics to improve student attitudes.

During the early years of state-mandated general education testing at the University of Memphis, we struggled with using volunteers and various sampling techniques to get groups of students in for testing. We soon discovered that the small cadres of volunteers were highly motivated, but their motivation to volunteer obviously skewed results. Random sampling overcame this bias, and we tried that for about a year with 25 percent of our graduating seniors. But the expressions of anger from some of the students made us realize that motivation problems would only increase if we continued this approach. Finally, we bit the bullet and began to require all students to take part in what we now call senior testing.

Method

The early years were tough. Some students were outwardly hostile to a new and added-on requirement of testing for graduation, and their unhappiness set a bad example for the majority of other students who were willing, at least, to cooperate and give reasonable effort. We began to provide refreshments for students as they checked in for a test. Our aim was to mollify angry test takers, or at least keep their mouths full so they would not distract others with negative comments. Later, we added a student opinion questionnaire, which we asked test takers to complete while waiting for a test to begin. This seemed to establish a quiet, test-like atmosphere in the auditorium and kept students from wandering around and spreading their discontent to others.

We also found a secret weapon that disarmed many a disgruntled student: the first contact they had with university staff upon entering the test site was with two elderly ladies, who welcomed them and checked them off the roster. These women were typical of everyone's grandmother, complete with smiles, a nice attitude toward college kids, and a maternal grace that defies description. On one side of the doorway, students would be lined up, some cursing and complaining about the test they were to take. On the other side of the door, the same students would suddenly remember their manners, calm down, and refine their language.

As we look back on these tactics, we realize they were not so much designed to motivate students as they were to negate the lack of motivation. During the early phases of our assessment activities, we talked about paying students, having prizes, putting scores on transcripts, and requiring a minimum score for graduation. The debates went on for years about the legality of one approach, the ethics of another, and the possible effectiveness of any of them.

Findings and Their Use

Each year brought with it a new set of annual results and renewed questions about student motivation, but no ultimate motivator was agreed upon. Each year also brought refinements in our logistics and administrative practices: we revised our testing calendar to accommodate students; our methods of communicating to students improved; a prepared introduction was given at each administration by a university official; we developed a policy for exemptions; a notice regarding testing requirements was placed in the catalog and schedule of classes; graduation analysts, chairs, and deans in each college became more familiar with and supportive of our assessment program; we reevaluated the test we were giving to measure general education and selected another based on student feedback and faculty evaluation; and we learned how to discipline students who left early or gave less than adequate effort to the testing program (we now ask their college dean to require them to return for retesting on another scheduled test date). These were small improvements, small experiments. An evolution was occurring; order gradually emerged out of chaos.

Success Factors

Then one day (we cannot say exactly when), we noticed that the grumbling student was the rare exception and only occasionally did we receive a result from someone who obviously did not put effort into his or her test. Something had changed, and despite all our hard work and efforts, we are willing to credit time and unwavering commitment as the weightiest variables. We recalled what assessment pioneers were saying fifteen years ago, "Be patient; it takes time," and we understood what had happened. Our instructional evaluation program had become a part of the university's culture and senior testing a rite of passage. The evaluation program is now not something added on, an additional requirement, but an actual part of our students' educational program.

Although we continue to be cautious and watchful about student motivation, the frustrations and headaches of the early years seem well behind us. Today, we believe our test results are a fairly accurate reflection of our students' abilities in relation to students from similar colleges and universities. Standardized tests are an integral part of our assessment activities, one among several measures we use for evaluating the general education program and major fields at the University of Memphis. We have seen student motivation improve with patience and perseverance.

Solving Logistical Problems That Impede Assessment

Albert M. Katz

CASE 34: UNIVERSITY OF WISCONSIN-SUPERIOR

Look for: Provision of child care to ensure that all seniors will be able to participate in mandatory exit testing.

Background and Purpose

The assessment program at the University of Wisconsin-Superior was developed with student input and participation; students were, and are, on the oversight committee. We have always tried to accommodate student concerns in planning both the substance and the implementation of the program.

Method

When we first began doing senior assessment during the spring term each year, we tried to accommodate student class schedules by offering several sessions of each exam. We administered the ACT-COMP exam on a Wednesday and again on Thursday, assuming each student would be free on one or the other. We were about three-quarters right. We administered the requested examinations for the major fields (mostly Major Field Achievement Tests from the Educational Testing Service) on two different days as well. Same theory. Same results.

Students who had classes scheduled on both mornings or both afternoons were to be excused from classes to participate in the assessment. That worked pretty well. However, we had enough irritation from faculty members and enough anxiety from students that we created the Campus-Wide Activity and Assessment Day, set it for the third Wednesday in April, and made it part of our class calendar. We thought we had handled the problem. But we had not remembered the law of unintended consequences.

Once all students were free from classes on the scheduled assessment day, we stopped offering multiple administrations of the assessment exams. But we soon learned that students were not free of their other responsibilities. About 40 percent of our students are nontraditional, and many are parents of preschool children. Almost every one of these folks is juggling a job, school, and parenting; their schedules are very tight. Their budgets are even tighter. A number of students called to say that they would really like to take part in the assessment activity scheduled for them, but since they did not have classes on that morning (or afternoon), they were supposed to be taking care of their children. They had no child care provision for the block of hours we wanted from them. They had already tried parents, siblings, friends, and other extended-family resources. No one could help them out. What did we suggest? These calls tended to come in a few days before the exams. There was no time to arrange an orderly response. We made a variety of emergency arrangements where we could.

Now, as part of our testing plan, we provide a temporary day care center in the facilities of the early childhood education department, staffed by early childhood education majors. Students who have a conflict between child care responsibilities and assessment requirements are invited to bring their children to this facility, at no charge, while they go to their assessment activity.

Success Factors

This action solves a significant problem for some of our students. It brings us closer to full participation by all our seniors and allows those with children to participate with peace of mind and to devote all their attention to the activity.

In addition, the very act of doing this, and making sure that students know the service is there, sends a message to all of our students that we are serious about assessment in general, and about their well-being and their problems in particular. The feedback we have received has come from the complete range of our students and is overwhelmingly positive.

Looking Beneath Standardized Test Scores

Linda B. Rudolph

CASE 35: AUSTIN PEAY STATE UNIVERSITY

Look for: Systematic, comprehensive evaluation of a general education program, including standardized testing, transcript analysis, a faculty survey, faculty interviews, and reviews of course syllabi. Personal communication of results to departments and continuing faculty development experiences have encouraged more faculty to accept responsibility for teaching generic skills.

Background and Purpose

Tennessee was one of the first states to mandate evaluation of programs, with rewards for excellence through performance funding. Austin Peay State University (APSU) chose to use this mandate to assess as a means for improving programs in a number of areas, particularly general education, since the institution is a liberal arts school.

APSU began an intensive research study of general education with the assistance of two grants from the Tennessee Undergraduate Excellence Program. The institution has a tradition of emphasizing general education, and with its designation as the liberal arts university for the state, there was increased interest in learning more about the effectiveness of the general education core.

Method

The vice president for academic affairs, John Butler, and the present author were responsible for the direction of the research. An APSU psychologist and statistician, Garland Blair, and a consultant from Northeast Missouri State University, Donald Kangas, developed the hypotheses and collected and analyzed the data.

One of the purposes of the study was to identify curricular experiences that had contributed to significant gain scores on the ACT-COMP assessment of general education. In addition to an extensive analysis of ACT-COMP scores as they related to student transcript data, a faculty survey of philosophy or attitudes toward teaching was administered. Written and personal interviews with faculty about the skills addressed in their classrooms were also conducted. Course syllabi were examined to determine if they reflected the general education goals and teaching philosophies of instructors.

Findings

Entering ACT scores appear to explain a large portion of the variation in the ACT-COMP scores of students. Only a small amount of variance was accounted for by one course or a combination of courses; however, this is not unexpected, since students complete approximately sixty courses for a degree. Student performance as measured by grades in general education courses, primarily in the natural sciences, social sciences, and math, also appears to be related to outcomes on the ACT-COMP exam.

The results of the faculty surveys of philosophies and teaching methods suggested that all faculty were not addressing the general education skills across the curriculum, particularly writing and math, and that attention should be given to teaching and testing on higher cognitive levels. Most faculty emphasized the skills of their discipline but did not see themselves as being responsible necessarily for promoting general skills such as writing, speaking, numerical ability, and critical thinking.

The examination of course syllabi revealed that there was inconsistency in syllabus structure and that few faculty members enumerated the general education goals addressed in their courses. Several "good" syllabi were identified based on subjective evaluations, and a model outline to guide syllabus development was distributed.

In the years since this original study was conducted, the results of the ACT-COMP exam have continued to reinforce several of the findings of this study. Students with strong backgrounds in math, natural science, and social science tend to do better on the test. There continues to be a need to emphasize communication and mathematical skills in the curriculum. A follow-up item analysis indicated specific areas of communication and mathematics to be addressed by instruction.

Use of Findings

The results of extensive analyses of assessment data on student learning outcomes have provided a clearer picture of student characteristics and helped both faculty and administration to understand more about teaching philosophies and practices and how they affect student learning. The indirect effects of the study have been as important as the direct results in that the data have stimulated discussion and introspection and have focused attention on effective teaching and curriculum development.

At the time the study described above was in process, a committee was studying the general education core in preparation for a move from the quarter to semester system. The study data were provided to the committee and were a part of the decisions relative to requirements of the new core. A new committee has been appointed to review the general education core once again, and these data, as well as updated information, will be provided to them also for their consideration.

The results of this study, in conjunction with other information and data, have provided topics for discussion in faculty development seminars. Each year, sessions have been held on teaching methods; on improving communication skills and critical thinking/problem solving; and on learning styles, cognitive levels, and other teaching/learning issues. The necessity for addressing these skills across the curriculum is also discussed with department faculty during annual visits by the associate vice president for planning and institutional effectiveness. Many faculty are beginning to accept responsibility for addressing general education skills such as writing and critical thinking in all classes—not just those that are discipline related.

A model syllabus has been placed in the faculty handbook, and all faculty have been asked by their college deans to describe in their syllabi the general education goals being addressed in their courses.

Success Factors

The leadership of APSU strongly supported the study of general education and facilitated the assessment process. The vice president for academic affairs continually encouraged the faculty to improve their courses and their skills, through verbal reinforcement and by providing the resources for learning. The associate vice president for planning and institutional effectiveness visits with each department annually and discusses outcomes assessment with the faculty, emphasizing areas of strength and weakness and encouraging faculty to address these areas. A booklet on using assessment outcomes for instructional improvement has been written and distributed to faculty. Faculty development seminars and special speakers continually reinforce these ideas. The activity was successful because of the continuing interest and support received from the university's leadership.

Multiple-Campus Assessment of General Education: A Course-Embedded Approach

Karen W. Carey, Frederic J. Medway

CASE 36: UNIVERSITY OF SOUTH CAROLINA

Look for: A general education assessment project on eight campuses of a state system (including two- and four-year institutions) that incorporates extensive faculty development. Faculty have developed modules for introductory courses in English, history, math, and biology that specify desired outcomes and indicate how student achievement will be assessed.

Background and Purpose

The USC system is made up of eight campuses: the main campus at Columbia and its five primarily two-year branch campuses, plus two separately accredited, primarily four-year campuses. With different missions and histories, admission criteria, and faculty and student bodies, the eight campuses have developed their general education programs somewhat differently. One important goal of the general education project was to address the need for course equivalency to facilitate transfer of credit, especially general education credit, between system campuses. Another goal was to improve or initiate communication between diverse faculty on the diverse campuses. In addition, the University was committed to strong programs of undergraduate education, and saw the project as an opportunity to educate faculty about assessment and accountability issues in a way that would involve them positively in improving student learning outcomes.

This project, supported by the Fund for the Improvement of Postsecondary Education (FIPSE) and the University of South Carolina (USC) provost's office, enabled university faculty to collaborate in reconceptualizing general education abilities and developing modules that embed assessment and make it an integral part of teaching general education courses. The initial courses for the project were selected because they satisfy the core curriculum requirements in the academic units on all eight campuses of USC. The project focused on introductory courses in four disciplines: English, history, mathematics, and biology. Faculty members applied to participate in the project, and a total of sixty were selected, based on their demonstrated interest in teaching and undergraduate education and recommendations from their deans and department chairs. Participants included at least one faculty member from each of the four disciplines on each of the campuses.

Before the project began, sixty faculty on the various campuses were surveyed regarding their understanding of the role, goals, and content of the introductory courses. In addition, they were asked about their perceptions of the work of faculty on campuses of a different type than their own, including how faculty members spend their time and their attitudes toward teaching. We also interviewed students who were then enrolled in the introductory courses on all the campuses, regarding their goals, expectations, and experiences in taking the courses.

Method

Faculty worked together for four weeks during the summer. During the first two summers of the project, an intensive three-day retreat was also held. Most of the four week-long summer workshop was spent in Columbia where part of a classroom building, including a computer lab to facilitate writing, were dedicated to the project.

The data collected from faculty and students, along with the university's newly proposed goals for general education, served as context for the intensive three-day retreat for the sixty faculty members chosen to participate in the project. Consultants from several other institutions set the stage and introduced faculty participants to this approach to assessment. During the retreat, faculty modeled the entire process they were to use during the summer workshop and gained some experience in collaborating, articulating desired outcomes, developing criteria, self-assessing, and integrating the assessment of general education abilities and skills with academic content.

For the remainder of the four-week summer workshop, these faculty worked together by discipline to redesign their courses in ways that specifically addressed general education abilities and goals and included explicit assessments of those abilities in the course context. Most of the disciplinary groups chose to incorporate assessment of written communication, oral communication, and either small-group communication or critical thinking into their courses. The use of collaborative learning was common to all of them. Consultants also met with the discipline-based groups.

This process included reading, research, and long and intense conversations about curriculum, teaching, and learning. After feeling frustrated and disoriented the first week, by the end of the four weeks, faculty were intellectually challenged and excited about the implications of assessment for profoundly changing their teaching. They left campus at the conclusion of the workshop with at least part of their courses redesigned and with the tools and confidence to incorporate assessment into their classes. And in fact, some faculty members had redesigned all their courses to incorporate assessment. At the end of the first two summers, workshop participants made a daylong presentation to deans, department chairs, the provost and associate provosts, faculty colleagues, and others. One purpose of this presentation was to provide practice in communicating the important concepts of assessment to others who had not been so deeply involved.

Faculty kept journals during the summer workshops and into the following year. We also collected other data from both faculty and students in the revised courses, including videotapes of some of the classes. The differences were obvious. The faculty group also met in February to exchange information about what was working and how, and what needed to be revised. Again, we tried to capture their ideas and reflections to improve our own processes. The following year, we repeated this process with another group of faculty. By the third year, all sixty faculty had been through a cycle of using the modules and practicing both assessment and collaborative learning.

Findings

Each of the four disciplinary groups has published its course modules in a format that can be easily adapted by others, both on campus and elsewhere. The biology group's modules are being published as a lab course manual. On each of the eight campuses, faculty who were involved in the project have done presentations for other faculty about assessing general education and about the work they did in the FIPSE project. Faculty using the modules reported that the first time around, class preparation and evaluation of students took longer but that students' attitudes and attendance improved, their anxiety lessened, and more students participated in the learning process.

Comparisons of classes using the new and old course formats showed that the new formats resulted in higher student grades, higher satisfaction for students and faculty, and better information about students' abilities to apply what they learned in other settings. In the calculus course, for example, faculty put much less emphasis on lecturing and multiple-choice testing and much more on interactive learning methods and written reports, so that students actually demonstrated their ability to communicate effectively in the context of mathematics. Faculty report and their syllabi show that they are now more concerned with depth and are sometimes willing to forego breadth of coverage to ensure student learning. Students are gaining experience in assessing their own learning using the criteria made explicit to them throughout the course.

Videotapes show students working in small groups, with faculty coaching and working with the groups; when lectures were used, the students felt sufficiently confident to ask questions, and others felt confident in providing answers for each other. Faculty who compared demonstrations of student learning, whether written or oral, in these courses with productions of students in their "before" courses found that their students' work was more thoughtful and more accurate and showed more depth of understanding. By applying theory to practice, talking with their colleagues on their own campus and other campuses, and listening to students, the FIPSE faculty developed a sense of what would work to improve both student learning and their own teaching.

The third summer of the project involved faculty from both previous years working together on modules that would be useful for others as well. We had been intentionally vague about what a module might be, because we knew their shape would emerge naturally through faculty discussions to conform to the needs of the courses and the rhythms of the faculty members' own teaching. As expected, the modules varied by discipline but were consistent within disciplines. The modules have been printed and they provide a model that others can adapt.

The most important results of the project are not the products on paper but the changes in faculty teaching and in the understanding of assessment as an important intellectual and educational activity. Like all good assessment, the FIPSE project was also an important form of faculty development. Those whose departments were not initially involved have requested to become involved in the next phase. Application of the model and processes used in this project is continuing with support from the provost's office and the university assessment committee.

Use of Findings

Faculty who participated in the project indicate that they now spend more time talking with colleagues about teaching and that they systematically self-assess their own teaching as well as integrate student feedback during the courses into their teaching. They also report that they have a new energy for teaching. A few reported concerns that students who are accustomed to passive learning in lecture situations find this approach to require too much work, and some of these students have transferred into traditional sections. This concern is expected to diminish as more and more faculty adopt the model. One department chair requested that we provide workshops for the entire math department, because those who had been in the FIPSE project were so far ahead of the rest of the group. Another dreaded teaching the part of the course for which there were no modules because both she and her students found it boring in comparison.

Another result of the project is the new respect faculty have for individuals on other types of campuses. This was an important goal of the project, the achievement of which has been verified by observation, self-reports of behavior, and changes in attitudes as measured on the Briarcliff scale. The fact that the regional campus faculty were and are full partners in this endeavor provides a springboard for future collaborative projects.

General Education Discipline Evaluation Process for the Community College

Sharon N. Robertson, Cathy A. Simpson

CASE 37: NORTHERN VIRGINIA COMMUNITY COLLEGE

Look for: Internal program review process to assess all aspects of the cross-disciplinary general education program, including student outcomes. Assessment methods include common final exams, student projects and assignments, portfolios, and videotapes. Review of findings has produced change in course objectives and content, methods of instruction, and library resources.

Background and Purpose

In Virginia, two-year institutions are required to assess student outcomes in programs and in general education. Collegewide assessments of students' general education, although useful in providing a very broad overview of performance, do not yield information sufficiently detailed to pinpoint areas of strength or weakness in specific disciplines that are part of the general education requirement in occupational/technical and transfer programs. Individual general education disciplines, such as biology, English, history, psychology, and foreign languages, are often not thoroughly assessed because they are not defined as programs or majors. Since the general education disciplines are seldom assessed, Northern Virginia Community College (NVCC) faculty and administrators developed the general education discipline evaluation process to assess student outcomes in these disciplines.

The general education discipline evaluation process helps faculty and administrators determine how each general education discipline contributes to students' achievement of the college's general education goals and objectives. Specifically, the process helps faculty understand the student population's goals, evaluate discipline effectiveness, guide discipline improvement, ensure institutional effectiveness, review the disciplines to assure that they meet state and college productivity requirements, and demonstrate the disciplines' commitment to the college's general education goals.

Method

Initially, to encourage faculty to participate in general education discipline evaluation, the coordinator of academic assessment and various administrators on the five campuses of NVCC identified faculty who were interested in exploring student learning and development, and invited them to serve on evaluation committees. Now that sharing the findings has generated sufficient interest in serving on evaluation committees, discipline faculty are elected by their peers and approved by each campus provost several months before the evaluation begins. Each committee includes discipline faculty from each campus, a faculty member from a different field, a division chair, a counselor, and Institutional Research and Learning Resource Center liaisons. Committee members must be respected leaders and willing to speak up and represent all constituencies within the discipline.

The coordinator of academic assessment conducts two orientations, one for the evaluation committee chairs in May and one for all committee members in August. This helps allay concerns and promotes a smooth operation. Each committee member receives a manual, written by faculty and administrators and approved by the college Curriculum Committee, that explains each step in the evaluation process.

A semester before the evaluation process begins, faculty develop or refine their discipline's goals and objectives. Developing these goals and objectives takes time because general education disciplines usually do not have disciplinewide goals. With the assessment coordinator's assistance, members of each committee evaluate a discipline's goals, student outcomes, curriculum, faculty and instruction, administration, productivity, facilities, and resources. They produce a report that includes a very important action plan. The action plan lists each recommendation, the rationale for it, a specific action or actions to be taken to implement the recommendation, the person(s) responsible, and a deadline. The evaluation process requires approximately two years. Disciplines are evaluated approximately once every seven to ten years.

The most challenging part of the discipline evaluation process is student outcomes assessment. Each evaluation committee designs and administers faculty and student surveys as indirect measures and designs at least one direct measure for assessing student outcomes. For example, economics faculty developed eight common macroeconomics and eight common microeconomics questions to be included on the final exams for the two introductory economics courses. Psychology faculty, with the assistance of a textbook publisher, developed a pre- and postsequence Field Test of Knowledge, which includes fifty multiple-choice questions and one essay. Sociology faculty created a set of common multiple-choice questions to test the level of basic knowledge and comprehension in the first-semester introductory course and collected a sample of student projects and assignments at the end of the sociology introductory course sequence. History faculty used selected questions from the NVCC Test of General Education as a pre- and postsequence measure of student gains in the American history and Western civilization course sequences. English faculty developed a pre- and postsequence writing sample for credit in developmental English courses and designed portfolio projects in developmental writing and reading courses. Speech faculty agreed to evaluate videotaped presentations made by their colleagues' students and to administer the Communication Competence Self-Assessment.

Findings

Findings derived from this systematic assessment process were varied and comprehensive, affecting numerous aspects of the disciplines. First, faculty developed the expertise to design indirect and direct indicators of student outcomes. Results of the student surveys indicated that most students took courses in the particular discipline surveyed to complete general education requirements; less than 5 percent said that they planned to major in that discipline. This helped discipline faculty realize that the majority of their students did not plan to major in their discipline and that the disciplines performed an important service function. Additionally, each committee identified the relationship between the students' goals, the discipline's goals and objectives, and the college's general education goals and objectives.

Most of the direct measures assessing student outcomes showed that student gains did occur over time, and some gains were more significant than others. For example, when the economics faculty administered the eight common macroeconomics and microeconomics final-exam questions, they learned that at least 70 percent of their students could answer almost every question. Developmental writing faculty administered a pre- and postsequence writing sample to ninety-nine students; 70 percent of those students received a posttest score that indicated the students had successfully met the course's goals and objectives.

Based on some of the findings of the direct measures, discipline faculty identified specific curricular changes needed to improve student outcomes, and provided an action plan with recommendations for implementing these changes. Some of the findings resulted in suggestions for further study into the effects of class size and teaching strategies, including the level of active participation involved. The nature of the process stimulated increased dialogue about teaching in the discipline among discipline faculty across the college. Several discipline evaluations emphasized the need for articulation among discipline faculty and faculty in programs requiring disciplinary courses. Similarly, several disciplines found that improved communications between counselors and discipline faculty was needed to enhance academic counseling effectiveness. Faculty identified personnel and equipment needs as well as Learning Resource Center needs to serve their disciplines.

Use of Findings

Several changes have already been made in response to the findings. Even before the evaluation was completed, faculty in some disciplines, such as history, redefined discipline goals and objectives. Geography and history faculty changed course offerings based on the committee's findings. In several disciplines, including English, faculty updated course content summaries to reflect more accurately what is being taught. Additionally, faculty in some disciplines have modified course content in response to the findings of several of the direct measures of student outcomes. For example, sociology faculty decided to increase the amount of writing required in some courses and to include more opportunities for direct application of the course content to problem solving. In contrast, the economics faculty felt that the test results validated their current course content.

The assessment process provided opportunities for professional development. To develop their expertise, faculty were given the results of an ERIC search for assessment measures in their disciplines. Some faculty on the committees presented papers about their findings at state, regional, and national conferences.

After each general education discipline evaluation report is reviewed by the college Curriculum Committee, which accepts, modifies, or rejects the report's recommendations, faculty and administrators make the suggested changes to improve the quality of instruction and student outcomes in the discipline. Additional faculty may be added in some of the disciplines that demonstrate a need for them. Equipment needs are met as funds become available. Resources will be added to the libraries to meet general education discipline needs. Finally, the assessment coordinator reports commonalities and differences among disciplines in a given area, such as the social sciences, to the faculty in that area and to the Curriculum Committee.

Success Factors

As faculty progressed through the general education discipline evaluation process, they realized how useful the findings were for identifying their disciplines' strengths and weaknesses. Faculty began to make curricular changes to improve students' achievement of each discipline's goals and objectives. The action plan provided in each report guaranteed that recommendations would be considered by the college Curriculum Committee. In addition, evaluation committee meetings provided a forum for dialogues about teaching and learning in the disciplines, and the evaluation process provided opportunities for professional development. Finally, administrative support was crucial to the success of the assessment process and reassured faculty of the importance of the evaluation.

Use of Assessment to Structure Remediation in Science Literacy

Sheryl Leverett Williams

CASE 38: GAINESVILLE COLLEGE

Look for: Details concerning the design and validation of (1) a test of entry-level science skills and (2) a remediation program to bring nonscience majors to a prerequisite level of understanding for success in physical science courses.

Background and Purpose

Gainesville College is a unit of the University System of Georgia and is committed to providing a meaningful educational experience to the nearly 3,000 students interested in either a terminal degree, two-year associate's degree, a transfer program, or certain programs of study affiliated with a nearby technical institution.

Gainesville College is virtually an open-door institution, committed to giving any student a chance at a college education, regardless of previous record or preparation. Entering students' preparations run the gamut from previous bachelor's degrees to virtually no college preparatory courses. For that reason, at least one remedial course, carrying no degree credit, in English, science, math, social science, or foreign language is required for two-thirds of all entering students.

The necessity for remediation in science is based on the number and types of high school science courses passed. However, the 74 percent of entering students who do not require remedial science show a great range of entry-level knowledge, particularly among nonscience majors in the physical sciences. The assessment program described here was developed to help determine the entry-level skills of these students and to initiate a remediation program to bring entering nonscience majors to a prerequisite level of understanding for success in physical science courses.

Gainesville College, in recognizing the special needs of its student population, has available to students an Academic Computing, Tutoring, and Testing center (ACTT), headed by master's degree–level staff members. The ACTT is designed to help instructors and students in a variety of ways, including maintaining teacher test files, administering makeup tests, tutoring students, and operating and maintaining computers for student use. The ACTT staff make this assessment-remediation program work.

Method

An important feature of the effort was the participation by both faculty and staff members in the construction and implementation of the assessment program. First, a group of faculty and ACTT staff members identified stumbling blocks to nonscience majors' achievement in the physical sciences, based on personal observation. This list was then pared to four areas for assessment: understanding and use of the metric system, use of scientific notation, construction and interpretation of graphs, and understanding of pH. Finally, a twenty-eight-question pretest was developed that included the construction of a graph from a data table.

The pretest may be administered the first day of class in any of the physical science courses designed for nonscience majors or, at the discretion of the instructor, in the ACTT during the first week of classes. The pretests are graded, and students are given a subscore in each of the four areas tested. This tabulated information is sent to instructors and to the ACTT. Any area in which the student did not demonstrate 70 percent mastery is highlighted. In those areas, the student must then remediate himself or herself through the resources available in the ACTT.

Remediation tools have been collected or written by faculty and ACTT staff and are on file in the ACTT. For instance, for students deficient in metrics, the ACTT "metrics" file contains a narrative written by one of the faculty members on the metric system, examples of conversions within the metric system, and practice tests with answers. A similar file exists for each of the other areas: scientific notation, pH, and graphing. ACTT staff are always available to answer students' questions as they work through these programs. When the student feels confident of mastering the material, he or she may request a retest from the ACTT staff. The retest is a short ten-question test taken in the ACTT and immediately scored by the ACTT personnel.

A record of student progress is maintained by the ACTT staff. If the student achieves 70 percent mastery on the retest, he or she has completed that section. If the retest reveals continued difficulty in mastering the material (that is, less than 70 percent mastery), the student is referred to the classroom instructor for personal tutoring. The instructor may then approve one last retest in the ACTT. In this manner, each student proceeds on a course of remediation tailored to his or her special needs as indicated by the pretest. A final posttest, quite similar to the pretest, is then administered. The posttest is an integral part of the course assessment, although each instructor has the leeway to vary the weight of the posttest in the overall course grade.

Findings

To date, 520 students have been administered the pretest, and 479 have completed the course of remediation, including the posttest. Twenty-three percent achieved 70 percent mastery overall on the pretest, while 85 percent have demonstrated mastery on the posttest. Ninety-five percent have shown improvement on the posttest over the pretest.

This assessment model offers several advantages for both instructors and students. From the students' standpoint, the model affords the best utilization of time, since the program is tailor-made for each student. Second, the student may work during the hours of his or her choice on the remediation, since the work is done primarily in the ACTT, which has extended hours of operation. Third, the student may set his or her own pace, knowing that help is always available.

Use of Findings

From the instructors' standpoint, the subscores may be used to indicate particular problems for classes as a whole, so that instruction can address those areas. Monitoring class performance can also reveal changes that need to be made in instruction. Most importantly, this assessment-remediation package has freed class time for pursuits other than giving the students skills that our faculty consider entry level.

The following faculty and staff at Gainesville College have been instrumental in developing and implementing this model: Linda Brown, Judy Forbes, Neva Latty, Barbara Williams, Julia Cromartie, Valerie Maxwell, Jane Lyons, Jason Ponders, and Lewis Rogers.

Assessment of Developmental Programs

Jeffrey A. Seybert, Donald F. Soltz

CASE 39: JOHNSON COUNTY COMMUNITY COLLEGE

Look for: Systematic evaluation of the effectiveness of developmental courses in reading, English, and math programs in terms of student achievement and progress, and an advising requirement instituted as a response to assessment findings.

Background and Purpose

Johnson County Community College (JCCC) has maintained an open-access admissions policy since its founding. This policy, shared by the vast majority of North

American public two-year community and junior colleges, allows any individual (generally eighteen years of age or older or a high school or GED graduate) to enroll in credit courses if certain conditions are met (for example, completion of an application for admission and, in most cases, of an entry-level assessment/placement test). A major result of this open-door policy has been enrollment of large numbers of students who are underprepared for college-level coursework.

Thus, most colleges have had to offer an increasing number of remedial, or developmental, courses, designed, theoretically, to bring these students to a point at which they can successfully complete college work. In fall 1991, JCCC offered 209 sections of below college-level reading, English, and mathematics courses. These courses enrolled 4,707 students, accounting for 13,666 credit hours, or 11.7 percent, of the college's credit offerings that semester.

Given that remedial/developmental education is a large and growing commitment on the part of the college, the decision was made in fall 1990 to assess systematically the effectiveness of the college's developmental offerings. Over the next eighteen months, the JCCC Office of Institutional Research undertook a series of research projects designed to evaluate the college's developmental reading, English, and mathematics programs in terms of student progress and achievement in those and subsequent college-level courses. The result of these studies generally indicated that students in these courses demonstrated significant gains on standardized tests upon completion of the courses, that passing rates ranged from less than 40 percent to more than 90 percent, that developmental students' GPAs typically dropped in the semester following their developmental coursework, and that although these students received passing grades in college-level courses related to their area of remediation, their grades and passing rates were lower than the norms for those classes.

In response to these findings, and as an attempt to improve developmental students' success in both remedial and college-level courses, the JCCC Underprepared Students Committee recommended implementation of a mandatory counseling process to help these students through their crucial first semester's work. At the same time, the committee strongly endorsed a research project to assess the outcomes of the counseling process. This case report describes the design of the counseling process, the results of its assessment, and the resulting actions taken by the college.

Method

A group of 269 students (151 male and 118 female) was randomly selected from students who entered the college in fall 1992 and were classified as underprepared on the basis of their low scores on the ACT ASSET reading or English subtests. These students were randomly assigned to one of three smaller groups. Group 1 comprised 88 students who were required to meet with a counselor once prior to fall 1992 registration to discuss appropriate courses, college resources for student assistance, potential difficulties they might encounter, and so forth. Group 2 comprised 90 students who were required to meet with a counselor five times during the semester, with the first meeting prior to registration to communicate the pre-registration information provided to Group 1. The four subsequent meetings were designed to monitor the group's progress and to provide support throughout the semester. Group 3 comprised 91 students who were designated as a control group and received no treatment per se; they were not required to see a counselor at any time during the semester but neither were they prohibited from doing so. A group of five counselors participated in the assessment project.

The impact of required counseling was measured in several ways. The GPAs, credit hours attempted, and credit hours earned by students in all three groups were compared. In addition, all students participating in the project received the Survey of Entering Students, following the fall 1992 semester. The survey elicited students' impressions of the college and their experiences during their first term. Included were items measuring students' judgments about their successes, their problems, and their instructors, as well as their perceptions of any counseling sessions they had attended.

Findings

Mean ASSET scores for the three groups were essentially equal at the beginning of the fall 1992 semester. Thus, at least based on this measure, the groups did not differ in ability level at the outset of the project.

Counseling Center records revealed that, on the average, the students in Group 1 (one required counseling meeting) visited a counselor 2.2 times during the semester. Those in Group 2 (five required meetings) made an average of 3 visits, and those in the control group, Group 3 (no required meetings), averaged 1.2 visits. These differences were statistically significant (that is, Group 2 > Group 1 > Group 3).

Following the end of the fall 1992 semester, academic records were located for 220 of the original 269 students in the study (82 percent). Thus, 18 percent (49) had either failed to register for the fall 1992 semester or withdrew prior to the deadline for doing so. Attrition rates for the three groups did not differ, and this overall attrition rate is only slightly higher than the college average (approximately 15 to 16 percent). Thus, approximately 70 students remained in each group.

On the average, students in the three groups attempted approximately the same number of credit hours during fall 1992 (7.7, 7.8, and 7.2 hours attempted, respectively, by Groups 1, 2, and 3). However, the two groups required to see a counselor earned significantly more credit hours during that semester than did the control group (6.8, 6.0, and 4.9, respectively), although the two experimental groups did not differ significantly. Since the two experimental groups did not differ in terms of semester GPA (2.2 and 1.8 respectively), they were combined, and the resultant GPA of 2.0 was found to be significantly higher than the 1.6 GPA earned by the control group. Thus, while all three groups attempted the same number of credit hours, the two groups required to see a counselor at some point in the semester earned more credit hours and achieved higher GPAs than did a control group that had no required counselor contact.

Survey responses indicated that more of the students in the required counseling groups than in the control group thought that their math skills, ability to fit into the college, and knowledge of how to get help had improved since they first entered JCCC. More students in the required counseling groups also indicated that they had made progress toward their goals.

Use of Findings

The results of this project to assess the impact of required counseling on underprepared students clearly reveal improved academic progress, academic achievement, and affective outcomes for those students. Based on these findings, the JCCC Underprepared Students Committee recommended that some form of required counseling experience be mandated for all entering underprepared students. This recommendation has been accepted by the college administration, and, as of the spring 1994 semester, all entering students whose ASSET reading and/or English scores place them in the underprepared category will be required to meet at least once with a counselor prior to their enrollment in courses at the college.

Success Factors

This assessment project and the resulting policy change were successful primarily due to the enthusiastic involvement and cooperation of individuals from several areas of the college and their shared commitment to improve underprepared student success. Faculty and staff on the Underprepared Students Committee and personnel from the Office of Institutional Research took the lead in designing and implementing the assessment project, in cooperation with the counseling staff and other student service personnel. And finally, considerable credit must also be given to upper-level administrative personnel for their willingness to listen and be persuaded by assessment results and then to commit the resources necessary to institute appropriate policy changes based on those results.

Placement for Success: The Writing Program Placement/Credit Portfolio

Linda K. Hanson

CASE 40: BALL STATE UNIVERSITY

Look for: Description of a program for placing beginning students in a writing course; multiple measures include standardized tests and portfolios.

Background and Purpose

Ball State University prides itself on being a premiere teaching institution. Consistent with that image are the time and resources invested to affirm the critical importance of writing skills for each Ball State student. General studies writing requirements span lower- and upper-division courses for all students. The Writing Program itself, housed in the Department of English, enjoys a reputation for responsible leadership in establishing writing instruction as a university priority. Program research and assessment results over the last decade have enabled the Writing Program to initiate successfully both major and minor changes in program structure, objectives, requirements, pedagogy, assessment tools, and faculty and student attitudes. Within that context, the Writing Program placement/credit portfolio was developed as an assessment tool to meet both the program need for consistent placement evaluation and the explicit university requirement for a credit-by-examination procedure for each general studies course.

The Writing Program philosophy assumes that each matriculating student is capable of completing the general studies writing requirements: six or seven credits in a two- or three-course sequence or the equivalent, with grades of C or above. Such an assumption demands that we place students for success, that, in other words, we attempt to predict their performance. We have depended upon an effective eight-step placement formula, refined through use, that relies upon a student's high school class rank and score on the Test of Standard Written English (TSWE), a subscore of the Scholastic Aptitude Test (SAT). The formula was initially developed in 1985 by using multiple regression analysis on data from 1,041 Ball State students enrolled in seventy-one sections of introductory writing courses, to determine what data could most closely predict their writing course grades. Investigators Forrest Houlette, Terry Schurr, and Arthur Ellen examined high school class rank; SAT verbal, SAT math, and TSWE scores; and Writing Program course grades. High school class rank contributed most to the model, with the TSWE a close second, so combinations of those two scores, roughly measuring motivation and achievement, made up the placement formula. Periodic review of the formula has examined contribution to the model by high school grade point average, high school English grade point average, and ACT scores. Increasing numbers of students entering the university with ACT scores enabled us, three years ago, to develop an alternate formula, replacing the TSWE with the ACT score. With the demise of the TSWE in March 1994, admissions asked us to provide SAT scores to replace the TSWE in the original formula.

The lack of a direct correspondence between SAT and TSWE scores makes this alternative highly unsatisfactory and exacerbates for a time the problem we originally sought to address with our placement/credit portfolio: not all students can or should be placed with our formula. Standardized entrance examinations have limitations, related in our experience to both gender and culture. Such limitations have shown up in conflicting TSWE and ACT scores (resolved by automatically applying the more favorable score), but even without both TSWE and ACT scores, irregularities or discrepancies may appear elsewhere in a student's record or in writing samples. Loss of the TSWE will reveal greater numbers of discrepancies because SAT verbal scores have proven less reliable predictors for our students than either the TSWE or the ACT. High school class rank has limited viability as a predictor as well for students who have delayed entering the university, who come from very small high schools, or who are unranked because their high school does not release such information. Finally, some students whose scores place them at the upper limit of a category may themselves want to challenge their placement because a successful challenge carries credit for the initial placement course and, if general studies writing requirements have not then been met, placement into the next course in sequence.

Placing students where they will be challenged and yet successful in meeting their general studies writing requirements demands that our placement system be responsive to students who fall in the gaps. The demise of the TSWE means that for the next two to three years, we must be more than usually attentive and responsive to students—and teachers—who question a student's placement. Fortunately, our placement/credit portfolio provides us that opportunity.

Paul Ranieri, director of the Writing Program from 1989 to 1992, inherited a credit-by-examination procedure that relied upon a single reader's review of a single impromptu essay and scores on a grammar and usage exam. To increase the reliability of our single reader's evaluation, we had to increase the number of papers read. Ranieri developed the guidelines for assembling the placement/credit-by-examination portfolios so that their content would reflect the goals and objectives of the Writing Program courses.

Method

Portfolios for Composition I and II require evidence of "cumulative accomplishment," "consistent achievement," and a range of writing tasks. Evidence of "cumulative accomplishment" includes not only an impromptu on-site essay but also a range of original essays "drawn from the best of [a student's] previous work." Criteria examined for "consistent achievement" are focus, development, organization, voice, sentence structure, and mechanics. At both levels, the range of writing tasks should demonstrate a student's "ability to respond to reading, to analyze texts, to produce research-based writing, and to write descriptive/expressive texts, problem-solution/expository texts, and persuasive/critical analysis texts." In addition to or clarifying those basic measurements, however, are course-specific portfolio criteria.

Course objectives distinguishing Composition I (published in a student manual entitled *The Writing Program 1993–94*) state that students should "develop a facility for the critical thinking and reading necessary for college work," "use evidence and inference effectively," and "understand and practice narrative, descriptive, expository, and argumentative forms of writing." For Composition I credit, six essays are submitted for review, one the impromptu essay written on-site in the Department of English and five drawn from the following types: review, information based, persuasive-argumentative, personal experience, narrative, descriptive, and process analysis. The portfolio must receive an overall grade of C to pass, or B if Composition I will be the student's last required Writing Program course. Two standardized multiple-choice examinations from the Educational Testing Service, the Descriptive Test of Language Skills (DTLS) in Conventions of Written English and in Sentence Structure, supplement the portfolio and require scores at the 70th percentile level. Students receiving credit must pass all three parts—the portfolio plus both tests.

Beyond the continuing development of skills identified for Composition I, the objectives distinguishing Composition II state that students should "develop an understanding of one or more of the literary genres" and "organize and write a formal research paper." For Composition II credit, five essays are submitted for review, one the impromptu (evaluative) essay written on-site, one an analysis essay, one a research paper or essay, and two drawn from the following types: comparison/contrast essay of two works of drama, fiction, or poetry; re-creation essay (rewriting of a literary text from a different point of view and often in a different genre than the original); narrative essay (fiction or nonfiction); reading/ writing autobiography; and personal reaction to a work of drama, fiction, or poetry. The portfolio must receive an overall grade of C to pass, or B if Composition II will be the student's last required Writing Program course. The standardized DTLS examination in Reading Comprehension and a series of library exercises evaluated by the instructional support librarians supplement the portfolio, both requiring scores at the 70th percentile level. Students receiving credit must pass all three parts—the portfolio, the DTLS exam, and the set of library exercises.

The demonstrable correlation between course objectives and portfolio requirements means we can assert with reasonable confidence that students who pass either the portfolio or the course could also pass the other. The procedure for evaluating the portfolio involves both a designated Writing Program faculty member and the program director. The faculty member reads and evaluates the portfolio on specific features of the texts ("consistent achievement in focus, development, organization, voice, sentence structure, and mechanics") and required writing tasks, then returns the portfolio with a letter detailing the evaluation and stating the credit/placement recommendation of pass or fail. The director of the Writing Program considers the portfolio recommendation in conjunction with the scores on the two exams before returning a decision to the student within the prescribed week.

Findings

The number of students so evaluated for credit and placement continues to remain small, although we anticipate it will rise over the next several years, particularly among honors students. To date, we have placed all such students accurately, meaning they earned C or above in the following class; no students have been awarded credit for Composition II as their last required Writing Program course.

Use of Findings

The Writing Program portfolio has been used to place nonformula students appropriately in Writing Program courses and to award them credit consistent with requirements for prerequisite courses. By extension, it has also replaced the credit-by-exam protocol of a single writing sample and grammar/mechanics exam, in order to provide us a more accurate evaluation of a student's ability to think critically, solve problems, analyze texts, communicate clearly to a specific audience, and use evidence and inference in persuasive and research-based writing.

Each student who submits a portfolio for evaluation receives from the director of the Writing Program both verbal and written feedback. Because we take seriously our responsibility to each student, that feedback details individual strengths and weaknesses that contributed to the placement and/or credit decision in the context of university and Writing Program expectations.

Information gained from students who have used this assessment procedure to challenge placement confirmed the accuracy of our original eight-step placement formula that automatically places 94 percent of the over 3,600 matriculating students into courses in the Writing Program sequence. Portfolios are crucial to our placement procedures for the other 6 percent who are predominantly nontraditional students (in the fullest sense), students with conflicting scores and grades, and students from very small or special high schools. Portfolios serve equally well for students who fall at the edges of our placement scales and would like to challenge placement.

Success Factors

The combination of portfolios with our placement formula provides us flexibility, consistency, and assurance that we are placing the greatest possible number of students for success while still challenging them. Students perceive that they gain as well, because a successful challenge saves them time and money while confirming the positive philosophy of the Writing Program.

Because both placement in a Writing Program course sequence and credit by examination are at issue, portfolio requirements that are evaluated in a timely manner and that correspond to course objectives are perceived as fair and appropriate. Successful use elsewhere, however, would require comparable correspondence between the types of writing included in the portfolio and the objectives for the course for which credit is being sought.

A Two-Tier Rating Procedure for Placement Essays

Richard H. Haswell, Susan Wyche-Smith

CASE 41: WASHINGTON STATE UNIVERSITY

Look for: Description of a two-tier procedure for scoring essays used in placing beginning students in a writing course. The procedure results in more accurate placements and saves faculty time and institutional resources.

Background and Purpose

In spring of 1991, we faced the task of implementing a new writing examination to place all entering freshmen at Washington State University. Not the least formidable was the problem of establishing a rating system. Each student would write two essays, one an argument and the other a self-evaluation. The size of examination sessions, taking place eleven times during the year, ranged from 50 to 1,500 students. There were five possible placement outcomes: basic writing, regular freshman composition, a tutorial taken in conjunction with regular composition, a series of ESL writing courses, and advanced credit. These placement results had to be made available for advising within twenty-four hours and, during the summer, within six hours. The placement operation had to sustain itself on a student examination fee, which limited the amount raters could be paid. And raters themselves had to be drawn from an ever-changing pool of more or less experienced teachers.

A further problem was that we were disillusioned with the standard procedural solution to these kinds of problems. Holistic rating allows for rapid, reliable, and cost-efficient placements by relatively novice readers, through standardized training sessions and quick, intuitive application of a simple criterion rubric and rating scale. But from experience, we knew that the holistic method, however sure it was in ranking written products, had difficulties in assessing impromptu essays in terms of writing potential, that is, in terms of best placement in a course. It also was poorly equipped to synthesize two distinct writing samples and to read through the specialized problems of ESL writers.

Method

Our solution, based on a design by Richard Haswell, emerged from two known facts: (1) high rater reliability occurs in the case of a majority of student essays because they are so unproblematic that they do not require a third or even second reading, and when read independently, typically they receive the same evaluation; (2) placements with the best validity are performed by readers who have the most experience and have long been teachers of the courses involved.

Our rating procedure divides readers into two groups. We call them tiers because they represent the two steps that an individual writing sample may undergo for a placement decision. A sample may be placed by only one first-tier reading, or it may be placed through multiple readings at the second tier. First-tier reading is very fast and essentially looks for only one decision, whether the student obviously belongs in regular freshman composition. Writing that presents to the first-tier reader any sign that the student might not belong in that course is turned over to the second tier. Second-tier reading is slow, scrutinizing, weighed, and usually multiple. Whereas the first-tier reader can place a student only in the regular course, second-tier readers can place a student anywhere, including into the advanced-credit category.

First-Tier Reading. Frequently only the start of the first, argumentative essay is read word for word; the rest is skimmed to size up organization and development of ideas—with the second, self-evaluative piece glanced at to see if it matches the general quality of the first. Either the sample is a clear-cut unproblematic placement into regular composition, in which case there is no other reader of the sample, or the sample goes to further reading at the second tier. The only decision to complicate this first-tier dichotomous decision is in the infrequent case that a writing sample is so exceptionally well written that it can be set aside for second-tier reading as a possible advanced-credit placement.

Second-Tier Reading. Samples that need a second reading can now be sorted into three piles. First separated out are students possibly in line for advanced-credit placements, then students who have declared English as a second language. The ESL writers are turned over to second-tier readers who teach the ESL sequence and are trained in the interpretation of second-language writing. The rest of the samples are read by administrators and longtime teachers of the implicated courses: basic writing, tutorial, and regular composition. Second-tier readers may make a placement decision on their own, if they feel sure of it, but they may ask others to read and then consult. Our corps of second-tier readers started three years ago with a small group of teachers and administrators possessing formal training in composition, especially writing assessment, but gradually we have been able to identify and promote readers from the first tier whose placements were consistent, accurate, and whose analyses of samples seemed especially keen.

Findings

Nearly every kind of outcome from this procedure has been so positive that we have continued to use and refine it, and even to adapt it to our universitywide junior-level portfolio examination. Distribution of placements across the courses has been acceptable. Fewer students are placing into the basic course, in part because, after second-tier discussion, teachers and administrators are more willing to put at-risk students into the tutorial joined with the regular course. (The tutorial consists of groups of five students who meet once weekly with a tutor to conduct peer-response sessions.) More ESL students are also being mainstreamed into the regular course.

Readers are happy with the procedure. They appreciate the removal of the psychological pressure that builds up through repeated blind ratings, the need to hold to preset standards, and efforts to make uneven and otherwise problematic essays fit a simplistic rubric. They like the quickness with which unproblematic readings are initially disposed of during tier one, and the open sharing of expertise during tier two. They also like the sense of possible advancement, with experience, from tier one to two.

In addition, they like the pay that the efficiency of the procedure allows. Tier-one readers are paid $20 an hour, tier two $40—all within the income from the $9 fee for the examination. The efficiency is owing to tier one. In 1991, of the samples produced by 3,755 students, 56 percent were placed in tier one—that is, read quickly by only one reader—at the rate of about one minute per essay. Of the 44 percent that proceeded to tier two, less than 3 percent needed two or more readings. We estimate that a typical reading costs, on average, about $2.50 per student. Income exceeding the per-student cost supports the administrative and clerical overhead, and leaves a small fund for research. Compared to a good holistic reading, where all folders are read independently by two readers and then folders with discrepant scores read a third time, our system requires about 40 percent fewer readings. Further, follow-up studies show that the first-tier readings, the origin of this cost efficiency, have good reliability and good validity. Recirculation of folders placed into regular composition with only one reading resulted in 97 percent of them being placed again in the same course. Students placed in regular composition with one reading achieved a success rate in the course higher than did other students there.

Use of Findings

The ability to deliver a cost-efficient yet accurate assessment with a short turnaround time has made possible a placement examination tailored to fit our local introductory writing program. The close match between assessment and curriculum—closer than could be achieved with national standardized tests or high school grade point averages—means that teachers now find fewer students enrolled in their courses who "don't belong." Follow-up studies tell us that fewer students fail, fewer withdraw, and fewer feel coerced into coursework that is below their level of expertise. In addition, the experience of regularly reading the sample writings of incoming freshmen gives us, the teachers and administrators, insights into the students who sit in our classes and the challenges that our curriculum may pose to them.

The two-tier system also has given us the confidence to implement a locally administered junior-level portfolio, an instrument of assessment formerly available only to colleges with small student populations. The savings on first-tier readings, and the speed with which all but the problematic pieces are evaluated, make feasible evaluating up to 3,500 portfolios each year. By adapting the concept of the two-tier system to faculty in other disciplines who teach upper-division courses, we have been able to recruit and train a group of first-tier readers to do the initial sorting of portfolios, leaving the more difficult decisions to experienced second-tier readers, drawn from the placement exam corps. Over time, the faculty from other disciplines will gradually take over responsibility for the second-tier readings; thus, the system integrates faculty development into the process of the reading itself.

Success Factors

The success of the two-tier method depends, in part, on a philosophical stance toward the limitations of any assessment to sort all students accurately. No assessment, of course, can do that; writing processes—not to mention writing courses—are too idiosyncratic. So if students are going to be misplaced occasionally because their work is read by only one reader, then the placement has to work in their psychological favor—they can only be placed too high, not too low. That is why our tier-one readers can only sign off on placement into the regular composition course, and why it takes two or more of the most knowledgeable and expert readers that our university has to place students anywhere else. It is also why we offer students given the lowermost placement into a basic writing course a chance to retest for free (very few take us up on this offer, but of those who do, over 75 percent have achieved a higher placement the second time around). We also reserve the right, based on teacher observation during the first two weeks of class, to move any student into a different course (again, this rarely occurs, but for those few cases, it is a useful option to have).

Finally, our approach works because we have built into it routine checks for accuracy. We want to know if students are succeeding in the courses we place them into, if teachers feel placements are accurate, and if our cost-efficient system maintains its cost efficiency (when problems crop up, as they inevitably do, we want to identify and solve them quickly). Being responsive to such concerns is critical, because a locally designed assessment must stay in step with the curriculum, with changes in student demographics, and with changes in assessment personnel. Fortunately, the dialogue required of second-tier readers on problematic essays provides ample opportunity to identify issues that must be regularly addressed to maintain a viable system.

Do Composition Courses Prepare Students for Upper-Division Writing?

Barbara M. Lawrence, Anne E. Mullin, Richard L. Sagness

CASE 42: IDAHO STATE UNIVERSITY

Look for: Composition teachers working with upper-division instructors in other disciplines to determine whether composition courses prepare students for the writing tasks expected in upper-division courses. Changes in objectives and methods of instruction have been made by the teachers involved, and more students are now referred to the writing lab for help.

Background and Purpose

Goal I of the Idaho State University (ISU) general education requirements states that students should be able "to express ideas in clear, logical and grammatically correct written English." To meet this goal, the university requires students to complete a two-course composition sequence (English 101: Composition, and English 201: Critical Reading and Writing) or demonstrate competence by written examination, advanced placement credit, or transfer credit. Students who fail to place into the regular English composition course must take English 51: Basic Writing, before beginning the Goal I required sequence. Assessing how well these composition courses prepare students for the writing tasks expected of them in upper-level courses became the charge of a task force consisting of eight faculty members, four from the Department of English and four representing the departments of history, health care administration, finance, and education. In addition to surveying faculty and students about writing assignments and perceived competence, pairs of task force members analyzed actual writing samples from students in upper-level courses.

Method

In each pair, an English department faculty member worked with a faculty member teaching an upper-level course in one of the other disciplines to design and implement an appropriate study of the writing done in that course. As an example, for a course required of senior secondary education majors prior to student teaching, the English and education professors wanted to see how well the writing of these senior education majors demonstrated mastery of the goals of the required composition courses taken at ISU. The writing sample for the analysis was in response to the course's traditional (and specific) assignment of a seven- to ten-page paper that "documents effective teaching practices for developing cognitive knowledge and skills, attitudes and psychomotor skills in junior high and/or high school level students for your subject major and/or minor. Effective practices must be supported by the research literature and referenced appropriately in your paper."

The team selected from among the published goals of English 101 and 201 (the University's required Goal I courses) seven criteria that met the education professor's stated criteria for evaluating his seniors' papers. They were (1) develop an effective thesis statement; (2) integrate appropriate primary and secondary textual materials to support the thesis; (3) organize the information to achieve coherence, emphasis, clarity, and specificity; (4) develop ideas through illustration, analysis, and consideration of multiple points of view; (5) use language to reflect senior-level mastery of the professional vocabulary and knowledge base; (6) develop paragraphs and transitions to enhance the reader's understanding of the relationships among ideas; and (7) avoid an excessive number of errors in spelling, word usage, and punctuation (including capitalization). Twenty-four seniors' papers were read and rated independently by the two professors, who gave a score of 1 for unsatisfactory, 2 for satisfactory, and 3 for superior for each of the first six criteria; the seventh was awarded a score of either 1 or 2. Agreement between the two raters ranged from 52 to 92 percent (judged statistically acceptable). There were no extreme disagreements; that is to say, in no case did one rater judge a paper superior and the other judge it unsatisfactory.

Findings

On the average, the students were judged satisfactory on all criteria but the seventh; about half the students were judged as deficient in avoiding an excessive number of errors in spelling, word usage, and punctuation. One student was rated unsatisfactory on all criteria by both raters; one was rated superior on all but one. Seven students received unsatisfactory ratings on four or more criteria, while six received superior ratings on four or more criteria. The findings of the English/ education team were paralleled by the other three pairs. Independently, the pairs judging the writing in the four courses concluded that approximately 70 percent of the student writers met the majority of criteria for Goal I writing courses at ISU, with about 50 percent failing to meet criteria involving grammar and usage.

Use of Findings

The finding of deficiencies in grammar and usage has not altered curricula in the required composition courses at ISU, which are grounded in prevailing composition pedagogical theory emphasizing process and acknowledging that direct teaching of grammar and usage does not improve writing. The finding has, however, stimulated more referrals to the university's Writing Lab which has developed special workshops in basic grammar skills and spelling.

Further, the assessment activity sparked interest in developing a writing-across-the-curriculum program, with informal discussions and exchanges of information about response to student writing and methods of incorporating prewriting and other such process activities into content courses. Also in the planning stage is a research study of the kinds of on-the-job writing required of graduates of the College of Education in teaching or administrative positions.

A striking outcome of the assessment activity was the realization by participants that while they agreed on the importance of writing skills in general and the published aims and goals of the required composition courses in particular, their writing assignments and terminology did not often reflect that agreement. By matching their vocabulary for thesis development, synthesis of source materials, consideration of audience and purpose, use of transitions and the like, composition teachers and those in the various disciplines now reinforce each other by reminding students of their shared concerns and evaluation criteria for effective academic writing.

A Longitudinal Study of the Development of Basic Writers

John M. Alexander

CASE 43: FERRIS STATE UNIVERSITY

Look for: Study of the development during the freshman year of students' knowledge, behaviors, and writing processes. The finding that exiting freshmen had not learned revision and editing skills produced an integrated sequence of required writing courses that take place throughout the four years of undergraduate education.

Background and Purpose

As an open-admission university, Ferris State University has a significant number of students who could be categorized as "basic writers." In order to assess change in writing processes over time, composition/rhetoric faculty conducted a study of the knowledge, behaviors, and writing processes of a large group of students as they progressed through the undergraduate curriculum. An earlier study of 750 students using criterion-referenced evaluations of pre- and post-sequence writing samples administered during a year-long freshman composition sequence identified twelve students who could be categorized as (1) basic writers, (2) individuals who demonstrated qualities of persistence and motivation as reflected by course completion and grades, and (3) individuals who demonstrated patterns of success in writing-intensive English and non-English courses beyond the freshman level.

The limitations of using writing samples for program assessment are well documented in the literature. Writing samples would not answer many of the questions we had concerning the performance of basic writers: How effective are writing-intensive courses in sustaining and improving writing performance beyond the freshman year? What changes in writing processes and behavior occur among a sample group of basic writers as they proceed through the undergraduate experience? Do basic writers become successful, mature revisers, and do they develop specific, task-oriented writing processes?

Method

In addition to the pre- and post-first-year writing samples administered to entering and to exiting freshmen, our selected students were asked to maintain process logs recording writing behaviors, use of time, prewriting activities, and attitudes toward undertaking writing-oriented tasks. From the final interviews and the analysis of the final documented paper, including its prewriting and rough drafts, a team of investigators drew conclusions about the writers' knowledge of writing processes, attitudes, and the ability to produce an effective, documented final draft of a researched project.

Findings

Writing as a Social Act. The greatest improvement among the subjects in our study appears to be centered in a category we call "writing context." We were surprised that despite all the attention paid in our freshman composition program to language (sentence structure, grammar and mechanics, and word choice) and form (organization, development, and logic), the areas of most improvement were in the rhetorical features labeled "context" (audience, purpose, and task). Four years later, the gain among the improvers in the freshman pre- and post-sequence writing sample group (those who also most likely persisted to graduation) was significant, indicating an increased awareness of process and social context of written communication. It would seem, based on these data alone, that as these basic writers continued through their undergraduate years, they became increasingly adept at comprehending the rhetorical and social functions of written communication.

Three years later, selected seniors offered evidence that social context remained both a conscious and an internalized feature of their knowledge of writing processes. Of the students interviewed, those who took course work requiring frequent term papers, written projects, and proposals expressed the importance of the role of audience in written communication.

Revision Strategies. A key factor indicating maturity in writing is the behavior accompanying the revision of text. Beginning writers do not share with experienced writers the same understanding of the revision process, nor do they share the same revising behaviors. Typically the beginning writer edits rather than revises, meaning that the beginning writer focuses on surface-level editing such as spelling and word changes. The experienced writer is concerned for the message that is being developed in the text. This writer will view the revision process as a process of discovering meaning within the text.

During the first interview, each participant was asked how he or she would go about revising the writing sample that had been written by the participant as a freshman. At that point during the research, we were encouraged by their responses. Most indicated that the writing needed massive revision, and most indicated that they would revise by conducting additional research on the topic, going to the library, getting facts, and looking up statistics.

However, our enthusiasm over the students' revision skills was significantly dampened by the close of our investigation. Their discussion of what they would do was radically different from their actual performance as measured by the analyses of the multiple drafts of their written projects. Even though it was obvious to the students that we were interested in their revisions (we collected drafts of their papers during each stage of composition), they did little revision. In fact, it could be said that only one participant revised at all. The majority of the students paid attention to surface errors only, changing the text in ways that did not affect the meaning. In other words, they still revised like inexperienced writers.

Confidence in Writing. One of the most solid, almost unquestioned, premises governing the teaching of beginning writing is the role of attitude and self-confidence in improving writing performance. Anxiety, writer's block, and writing apprehension are assumed to be negative variables in the writing process. Among the seniors we interviewed, most explicitly expressed confidence in their ability to handle written tasks. We are well aware that our sample population is not representative of seniors as a whole, for we likely recruited only students who have enough confidence to undergo the kind of scrutiny we administered.

Conclusion. This study developed with the understanding that no single, quantifiable measure of performance would be reliable enough to come close to measuring the progress of basic writers through an undergraduate curriculum. We have observed and recorded much of what the existing research already tells us, that basic writers will plan better and pay more attention to the role of audience and purpose if required to do so in courses within the major, that there appears to be a direct relationship between student writers' confidence and the number and variety of written tasks in an undergraduate education, that the time required to produce significant cognitive maturity in beginning writers goes far beyond the freshman writing course and, perhaps, even the four-year undergraduate experience.

Our interviews and direct observation of writing performance of a group of graduating seniors indicate that even with numerous writing and writing-intensive courses, revision and editing skills remain undeveloped, knowledge of writing processes lacks specificity, and written projects resemble, more often than not, rough drafts riddled with numerous surface errors. When talking about their own writing, basic writing students as seniors initially tend to dwell on those indicators of surface correctness at the sentence level that had mainly labeled them as basic writers prior to college-level instruction. Not trusting their own experience and perception as writers, our senior subjects tended to fall back on the prescriptive abstracts found in handbooks.

Of some encouragement, as these seniors spoke of their college writing experiences, was that they revealed a knowledge of the social role of discourse, of the context in which writing takes place, and of the all-important goals of audience and purpose. Evidence suggests that the freshman experience in written communication succeeds in increasing the basic writer's understanding of social context and sense of confidence in situations requiring communication skills. As basic writers continue to write in their chosen career areas, this knowledge of context and perception of confidence increases. We suspect that these attitudes will carry over into the careers of those successful basic writers who were the focus of our study.

Use of Findings

Based on the findings of our study, we were able to provide documentation for a revision of the written communication portion of our general education requirement. Beginning in the fall of 1993, the year-long freshman writing requirement was revised to include a laddered, vertically integrated sequence of writing courses throughout the four years of an undergraduate education. The development of writing-intensive courses was encouraged for all programs on campus. In the composition program itself, greater emphasis was placed on documented research writing, writing in the major, and revision strategies.

Assessing Writing Through Common Examinations and Student Portfolios

Booker T. Anthony

CASE 44: FAYETTEVILLE STATE UNIVERSITY

Look for: Assessment of critical thinking and writing skills using holistic scoring of essays written during a common final exam given to all first-semester composition students. Information from the common final as well as from student portfolios is also used to identify instructors' weaknesses.

Background and Purpose

In the spring of 1989, the Fayetteville State University College of Arts and Sciences developed an assessment program to review placement instruments and exit examinations for major academic disciplines in the college. The purpose was to assess academic programs in order to determine how to improve teaching effectiveness and student learning. The English department began using student portfolios in English composition classes as a measure of assessing the process of writing and of evaluating composition teachers who use common syllabi and administer the departmental common final examination.

Method

The Common Final Examination (CFE) is a forty-five minute writing test designed to assess the student's ability to write an organized, coherent, and effective essay that reflects critical thinking and writing. The department believes that after a semester of workshop writing, the student should be able to demonstrate—in a limited time period and in much the same way as a drama or music major is called upon to perform on demand—the ability to formulate a central idea, select an effective rhetorical strategy, develop ideas logically and coherently with adequate supporting details, use varied syntax and precise diction to present ideas clearly and efficiently, create a voice and tone appropriate to the audience and purpose, and observe the conventions of standard edited American English.

While the examination is the same for all students, the format differs from morning to afternoon each day of the examination. The department does a holistic reading of the essays in the last week of regularly scheduled classes—in timely fashion for student appeals and final grades. On a scale of one to six (with six being excellent and one being unacceptable), each essay is scored by two English faculty, but not by the student's instructor. A total of seven is considered passing. Some essays require a third reader.

While the student's writing portfolio can be used for screening students for advancement into major disciplines, assessing University College programs, evaluating teachers, or providing students with employment portraits, the English department requires the portfolio especially for students who have failed the CFE and who appeal. The departmental policy is that the student must pass both the course and the departmental examination.

A student who appeals the results of the CFE must show, through the writing portfolio, that the CFE performance was not representative of his or her total writing performance. A writing portfolio usually contains original and final drafts of major papers and the student's CFE. The departmental assessment committee then reviews the portfolio; next, the committee recommends that the instructor pass or retain the student who is appealing.

Prior to each scoring session, English faculty convene for practice grading of sample essays. Additionally, approximately four English faculty are involved throughout the year in professional scoring sessions in some capacity with the Educational Testing Service. These faculty are closely involved in training departmental colleagues in the process of holistic scoring.

Findings

The department began maintaining consistent statistics on the CFE in 1990. The passing rate is as follows: 70 percent in fall 1990, 76 percent in spring 1991, 86 percent in fall 1991, 87 percent in spring 1992, 86 percent in fall 1992, 89 percent in spring 1993, and 90 percent for fall 1993. In fall 1992, there were forty-three appeals (7 percent) out of 576 students who took the examination; the assessment committee approved twenty-five appeals and denied eighteen. In spring 1993, there were twenty-two appeals (4 percent) out of 521 students who took the examination; the assessment committee approved nine and denied thirteen.

Before requiring the writing portfolio and using the departmental examination, the department could not monitor carefully the academic integrity of grades as well as the degree to which effective teaching and student learning occurred. The argument has been that the professor is responsible for the course and has accessible knowledge of each student. Additionally, some critics contend that test results or grades are routinely used to reveal ineffective teaching or incompetent students. Our department is more concerned with the accountability we have to students, parents, and taxpayers who seek positive outcomes in higher education. How effectively can the student write at the end of the first-year writing experience? How well has the department prepared the student to do well on national writing examinations such as the National Teacher Examination? How effectively can our students write once in upper-division disciplines?

After examining portfolios of students who appealed, the department found that a few writing instructors were not following the departmental common syllabus. The content of portfolios showed, moreover, that a few instructors were not adhering to agreed-upon departmental objectives and grading standards for the writing program. Also, a few writing instructors thought the mechanics of writing to be insignificant in the regular grading process. (A student might receive an A on a paper replete with mechanical errors.)

A major disadvantage of the self-guided instructor in this type of program is that the student who fails the departmental examination can argue, and rightfully so, that he or she has not been prepared effectively to compete with other student writers. The majority of the students who appealed actually presented more professional format and content when the essays were untimed and when revision was feasible. Students who sought an audience before submitting papers to instructors presented an effective portfolio and did well on the CFE. Students who did not seek a peer audience before submitting papers, or who did not attend the Writing Center tutorials, did not present effective portfolios and did not perform well on the CFE. Many of the portfolios of students who appealed—meaning students who had failed the CFE—did not contain sufficient revisions of essays.

Use of Findings

Since we started assessment in composition, there has been more dialogue among faculty. In English Composition I, there has been an attempt to sequence writing assignments with the understanding that the student writer may gain a better understanding of himself or herself as a writer. In English Composition II, we concentrate more on shorter documented essays than on "the" research paper. When students know, too, that their writing will be evaluated beyond the immediate classroom, there is a tendency to present a better product, or professional portfolio; there is an aim of writing for an intended audience.

Success Factors

Co-workers in other disciplines can no longer have grounds for asking, "What are English teachers doing?" Individual English faculty are pleased when 90 percent of six hundred students can pass a departmental examination. Such measurements of learning also suggest that English faculty are willing to take the lead in showing accountability in higher education with the aim of improving teaching and learning.

Assessment of Students' Quantitative Needs and Proficiencies

William O. Martin

CASE 45: UNIVERSITY OF WISCONSIN-MADISON

Look for: Measures of student achievement in mathematics at the junior level developed by faculty teaching upper-division courses in disciplines other than mathematics. Dissemination of findings has produced changes in math prerequisites for some courses and the adoption of a campuswide quantitative literacy requirement.

Background and Purpose

During the 1980s, the governor of Wisconsin, the president of the University of Wisconsin (UW) System, and the board of regents called for UW system institutions to begin assessing the general education of their students. Specifically, each campus was directed to develop programs to assess the quantitative and verbal proficiencies of rising juniors and to have these programs operating by 1991–92. Several campuses chose to administer standardized, commercial tests to a sample or all of the junior class. At Madison, there was concern about the institutional and departmental utility and validity of such tests, considering juniors' diverse goals and their varied quantitative and verbal backgrounds; consequently, locally meaningful and valuable assessment programs were developed that also met the external requirements. Pilot verbal and quantitative assessment projects run by faculty in English, mathematics, and statistics began operation in 1990. The focus of this article is the quantitative component of the assessment initiative.

Method

The quantitative component is designed to assess whether students have the specific quantitative capabilities needed in their chosen upper-division courses. For example, engineering and physics juniors' capabilities in multivariate calculus and differential equations could be examined while social science students might be tested on their abilities to use formulas, tabular data, and graphs. Each semester, we have administered custom-designed tests in a sample of four to nine courses from across the campus. Participating courses have ranged from Principles of Advertising and Construction of Classroom Tests to Biophysical Chemistry. Courses are chosen to reflect the breadth of junior-level offerings across departments and colleges at the university. Faculty play a key role by ensuring that the tests we design examine what they want and need from students in their courses; the tests do not directly target the content of prerequisite mathematics or statistic courses.

Tests usually are given during a regularly scheduled class period in the second week of the term. Corrected test papers, along with solutions and references for review, are returned to students within a week. Mathematics graduate students correct the tests and record information about what students have done; they do this by coding yes or no responses to a series of statements about possible student solutions. The degree of success achieved by a student on each problem is also rated on a five-point scale. This scoring procedure allows us to return corrected, free-response tests to students quickly while retaining data about their performance for later analysis.

Findings

The quantitative assessment project generates two types of information: (1) the quantitative demands placed on students by instructors in other departments and (2) the quantitative capabilities of these students in relation to their instructors' expectations. On the departmental side, we have encountered three general levels of quantitative prerequisites for junior-level courses.

Level 1. These courses have no formal quantitative prerequisites. Students are expected to have basic skills in arithmetic, algebra, geometry, and statistics, including the ability to read and interpret graphs and tables.

Level 2. Prerequisites for Level-2 courses include one semester of calculus and sometimes one college statistics course.

Level 3. These technical courses, such as those in engineering and physical sciences, require three semesters of calculus.

Instructors generally expect student familiarity with basic, introductory materials studied in prerequisite courses; rarely do they ask for the full range of advanced technical capabilities covered in the mathematics curriculum. Commonly, instructors emphasize students' understanding of basic concepts over their ability to carry out specialized manipulations.

The primary focus of our assessment work is on the match between faculty expectations and student capabilities; from this perspective, there has been a range of outcomes for individual courses.

Tests sometimes revealed few, if any, problems. In some classes. most students correctly answered most or all of the test questions, so no further action seemed warranted.

Tests sometimes revealed technical competence mixed with conceptual difficulties. A more common outcome has been that most students did well on the test as a whole but many had difficulty with several problems. Often, students were quite adept at routine computational or manipulative tasks; they had less success applying their quantitative skills in nonroutine situations that required either interpretation of quantitative information or the use of mathematics to model physical situations.

Students in some Level-2 courses (requiring a semester of calculus) displayed good knowledge of basic statistics and algebra but little understanding of calculus.

Tests in some nontechnical courses revealed that students had serious difficulties with precollegiate quantitative material, such as the use of graphs and tables, routine arithmetic, or basic statistical skills.

Unfavorable test results do not necessarily imply there is a fault with existing curricula. We routinely compare student assessment test results with student grades in prior collegiate mathematics and statistics courses. At times, poor results on assessment tests corresponded either to low grades in prior courses or to a complete lack of quantitative course work. In other classes, little correspondence was evident between test results and quantitative course work.

Use of Findings

Our individualized, consultative approach has not led to many dramatic or highly visible curricular changes. Evidently, though, this assessment work has had an impact both at individual faculty and at the departmental and university levels: (1) individual faculty have changed their teaching plans, both during a semester and in subsequent semesters, because of assessment outcomes; (2) departments have reviewed courses because of assessment findings, and one department changed course prerequisites; and (3) a university curriculum committee recommended a quantitative baccalaureate degree requirement, citing findings of our committee. The faculty senate has since passed the recommendation.

Responding to the impending quantitative requirement, several mathematics and statistics faculty members, including several members of our assessment committee, are developing new quantitative course work. This was necessary because it became apparent, as we worked with instructors of Level-1 courses to develop tests, that existing mathematics and statistics courses did not meet the quantitative needs of their departments. Courses under development are aimed at students not interested in pursuing the traditional mathematics sequence through calculus. To develop better information about needs for basic quantitative skills, the quantitative assessment committee met with faculty in several large departments whose degree programs did not require college mathematics or statistics. At these meetings, the committee clarified the knowledge gained from earlier assessments.

A challenge of our collaborative approach is to bring less favorable findings to the broader attention of faculty in affected departments in a way that encourages reflection on the significance of the results and stimulates action, if warranted. We have had some success in promoting such reflection and responsive action by individual faculty members and departments.

One effective strategy has been to meet with faculty groups (for example, in curriculum committee or departmental meetings) after circulating a summary of assessment findings from one of their department's courses. Often, we find that faculty members who participated in assessment are our best spokespersons at such meetings. Having a departmental colleague speak about the results and their implications is certainly preferable to having an outsider suggest that a department might want to consider some action. This further supports our belief that the project's effectiveness is closely tied to faculty ownership of and involvement in the assessment process.

Our findings are reported to mathematics faculty in several ways: (1) copies of all our reports are sent to the chair of the mathematics department, (2) summaries of student performance on different types of problems were distributed to all faculty members, and (3) our committee has spoken at mathematics faculty and committee meetings about assessment findings. This reporting does not directly cause change, but awareness of problems shown by local data can influence faculty as they review the curriculum. Our findings have been mentioned by groups revising precalculus and calculus curricula, indicating that assessment has influenced mathematics faculty and courses.

The quantitative assessment project at Madison is developing very specific information about the quantitative capabilities of emerging juniors by asking faculty what they expect, then assessing whether students have that necessary knowledge. Initially, the greatest effect was on course instructors who participated in the assessment; recently, we have begun to see a broader impact. Assessment information has been used by university committees, faculty in other departments, and groups in the Department of Mathematics, leading to curricular changes at each level.

Success Factors

Close collaborations with faculty and a nonprescriptive approach may ultimately have a greater real impact on undergraduate instruction and learning exactly because assessment is not then seen as an externally imposed chore but as a useful exercise that clarifies faculty expectations and provides meaningful information about student quantitative proficiencies.

A Detailed, Multisite Evaluation of Curricular Software

Steve Cohen, Richard A. Chechile, George E. Smith

CASE 46: TUFTS UNIVERSITY

Look for: Evaluation of nine interactive computer programs designed to help students learn statistical concepts. Detailed assessment of conceptual gains coupled with tracing how students interact with the software suggests where their learning is deficient. This gives faculty detailed information that they can use to improve the effectiveness of their instruction in promoting student learning.

Background and Purpose

Virtually no introductory-level course in the college curriculum is taught with less success than statistics (see Hansen, McCann, and Meyers 1985; Greer and Semrau, 1984). All but a small fraction of students memorize their way through the material, achieving at best a limited grasp of a few concepts in descriptive statistics and virtually no grasp of concepts in inferential statistics. The Curricular Software Studio at Tufts University, in collaboration with Tufts faculty who teach introductory statistics, tried to address this problem by developing ConStatS, a set of nine interactive computer programs that requires students to experiment with statistical concepts. To learn whether ConStatS is effective at helping a much larger fraction of students gain a deeper understanding of an abstract subject matter like statistics, we undertook a detailed evaluation.

Method

To begin, we worked through each ConStatS program and determined the comprehension points we expected students to learn (Cohen and others, 1994). Each part of the program was assigned responsibility for conveying a specific comprehension point. This activity produced a database of over 1,000 comprehension points, clearly too many to test. However, many of the points were similar. Where possible, we combined comprehension points into a cluster and specified a unifying concept that defined the cluster. The effort yielded 103 clusters. For each cluster, we constructed a question to test conceptual understanding. The questions were reviewed by an inside evaluation team (four persons) and by two outside statistical consultants. The 103 questions were divided into three similar, but not identical, tests of conceptual understanding. In addition to testing conceptual understanding, we were interested in learning how students used the program. We developed and installed in ConStatS a facility for tracing just how the students interact with each part of the software. The traces offer a complete behavioral history of each student's interaction with ConStatS. A taxonomy was developed to classify each interaction as one of several types (an experiment, information retrieval, and the like) (Cohen, Tsai, and Chechile, 1995). The traces offer an opportunity to investigate a student's experimental style of learning.

The trace facility also verifies how different classes that participated in the evaluation used ConStatS. Sixteen different introductory statistics classes at Tufts and four classes at outside universities participated in the evaluation. Statistics courses from seven different disciplines—biology, child studies, education, economics, engineering, psychology, and sociology—were represented, with most students taking introductory statistics for psychology. Each course had a unique way of using ConStatS and incorporating it into an existing curriculum. Each part of ConStatS was used differently by each course. The traces informed us about which parts of the program were used substantially and which were hardly used at all.

Two other assessment instruments were also designed and employed. The first was a ten-question test of basic mathematical skills necessary to use the program. ConStatS has very little math, but does require a basic working knowledge of fractions, decimals, ratios, and variables. The second instrument, a survey of topics addressed in each course, was designed to assess which concepts were emphasized through books, lectures, and/or homework. To establish a reference point, three classes at Tufts were used as control groups. Two of the classes were taught by a member of the team that designed ConStatS. The control group classes used standard mainframe and microcomputer tool-based statistical software, but did not use ConStatS. In all, 662 students participated in the experimental group, and 77 in the control group.

Findings

Results of the comprehension test showed that students using ConStatS did better on 94 of 103 questions. The control group averaged 40 percent whereas the ConStatS group averaged 53 percent. Comprehension test results indicated that students had trouble with elementary concepts as well as advanced concepts. An item analysis showed that five of the six questions most highly correlated with success on the comprehension test involved probability. Taken at face value, this result stands contrary to the conventional wisdom that minimizes the role of probability in teaching statistics.

Many students did not score a perfect 10 on the test of basic mathematical skills. In all, 19 percent had trouble converting a decimal (.375) to a fraction, while nearly 34 percent had trouble with ratios. Table 12.1 shows the relationship between basic skills and conceptual understanding for both the control and ConStatS groups. Percentages in the table represent results on the comprehension test.

Use of Findings

We have used the results both to improve the ConStatS program and to inform teachers specifically what their students are not understanding. With 103 questions

TABLE 12.1. BASIC MATHEMATICS SKILLS SCORES.

	Score		
	8 or less	9	10
Control group	37%	41%	44%
ConStatS group	46%	54%	57%

mapped directly to parts of the program, we were in a good position to pinpoint which parts of the program were ineffective and why. We added fifteen new exercises to ConStatS and several new options to existing exercises. These additions were guided by the evaluation.

As we graded the comprehension tests, we looked for patterns in the errors to help us understand and identify persistent misconceptions. For each question, we identified the concept involved and the errors in common. In all, we found patterns of errors on 15 of the 103 questions. For instance, many students who misread histograms appeared to treat them as bivariate rather than univariate plots. We provided the teachers with a list of the misconceptions, and explained that when the concepts are introduced in class, it might be a valuable exercise to first dispel the misconceptions. Some teachers expect that students may only have difficulty learning advanced concepts (Webster, 1992), and some may be surprised to learn about the elementary misconceptions. This kind of feedback permits instructors to emphasize preliminary concepts on which the more advanced concepts rely.

Success Factors

Members of the evaluation design team were experts in the subject matter (introductory statistics) and the technology—ConStatS running under Windows. Detailed, technologically based assessment instruments, like the trace facility, might have been difficult to coordinate if specialists had not had a common understanding of the evaluation problem, the subject, and the technology. Each member of the design team also brought a unique expertise and point of view to the evaluation design. All members of the team were dedicated to establishing a benchmark for detailed assessment. Each wanted to move beyond global measures and attitude assessment to detailed, multivariate measures of comprehension.

The evaluation was funded by the Fund for Improvement of Postsecondary Education, and that support provided the resources necessary to do detailed and systematic work. Teachers both inside and outside of Tufts received small stipends for participating in the evaluation. Finally, treating the evaluation as a field test with several sites, each using the software its own way, helped us learn under what circumstances the program works best.

Assessment of Library Research Skills

Donna L. Sundre, Lynn Cameron

CASE 47: JAMES MADISON UNIVERSITY

Look for: Systematic means of assessing entering and developing library skills, and use of an assessment day to gather data from all students. Faculty are now making more assignments that promote student learning of library skills.

Background and Purpose

In the fall of 1989, James Madison University was experiencing a renaissance of interest in assessment activities. Having designed an institutional assessment day, the university was inviting faculty and staff to develop new instruments to learn how well the mission and goals of liberal education were being met. Toward this end, discussions and planning commenced with members of the Carrier Library faculty and the Office of Student Assessment. What has emerged from that beginning is a systematic means by which the entering and developing library skills of our students can be assessed throughout their academic career. We have collected information that has allowed us to make difficult decisions in financially constrained times with much more confidence. We have improved our services to students and faculty.

Method

In the fall of 1989, a small team gathered to create an instrument to assess the effectiveness of the university library's instructional efforts. The James Madison University Carrier Library is a highly service-oriented library that provides a great deal of instruction across the campus, and the university's recently inaugurated assessment day provides an ideal occasion and random samples of 300 to 400 students for data collection.

Two formal assessment days are scheduled each year. The first, which is designed solely for entering first-year students, occurs in the fall on the day before classes begin. The second occurs early in the spring semester, generally in late February. All undergraduate classes are canceled, and second-semester sophomores and first-semester juniors are assigned to rooms across campus for assessment purposes. The campuswide assessment day also provides a convenient time, free of room, time, and class conflicts, for the assessment of graduating seniors by their major departments and for faculty development workshops. We began by designing a fairly short assessment test that would focus on four general library skills areas: (1) basic library skills: encyclopedias, statistical sources, biographical references, government documents, citations, Library of Congress, and so on;

(2) Leonardo: proper use and knowledge of the types of materials contained in our on-line catalog system; (3) search strategies: search procedures and selection and evaluation of alternative reference and information sources and indexes; and 4) library services: familiarity with interlibrary loan, circulation, reserves, and reference services.

In addition, we included a few items requesting information about library attitudes, usage, and experiences. The information collected from this initial assessment effort was so useful, we decided to create an additional tier of library assessment by testing incoming freshmen. We felt that baseline data for entering students would make sophomore performance levels even more meaningful. Our entering-student library skills assessment test includes the same items reflected in the library skills objectives covered in the original sophomore test and also assesses the Virginia Standards of Learning Objectives for Library/Information Use.

The third and final tier of the library skills assessment program evolved naturally from our data collection and scrutiny of incoming-student and sophomore-level library skills performance. Most academic departments at the university expect students to develop advanced skills in library research; thus, the third tier of library assessment involves specialized library skills instruments. Designed by library and academic department faculty, these instruments assess research strategies and information sources specific to given majors.

Exiting seniors in a given department take the senior library skills assessment instrument as a part of the department's assessment design. All academic majors at James Madison have assessment designs and strategies in place. Most academic programs have been systematically collecting program and student assessment data for over five years; thus, a library skills test designed specifically for their majors is considered a supplement. The library faculty who serve as liaisons with the academic departments have developed several customized library skills assessments for inclusion in the major assessment instruments and have a strategic plan to cycle in all majors in five years. Majors currently participating include business, chemistry, English, health sciences, mass communication, psychology, Russian, sociology, and speech pathology.

Findings

Although our entering freshmen have shown a high level of performance on the library skills test, sophomores score a full standard deviation higher on the same test. This is significant, both statistically and educationally. The use of our systematic assessment days has allowed us to collect data on the same students over a two-year period; thus, we now know that there are significant gains, as measured by dependent t-tests, for our sophomores over their entering library skills test performance. Student attitudes toward electronic sources of information have consistently been very positive, and our assessment data indicate that all of our students prefer active instructional modalities. We also know that freshmen score very poorly on questions measuring the Virginia Standards of Learning for Library/Information Use, even though 98 percent of those who take the test have received library instruction in elementary or secondary school.

Our students in chemistry, mass communication, and psychology score very high on their library skills mastery tests. Although the *Library Skills Workbook* is required of all freshman English students, we found that over 25 percent of our sophomores had not completed it. This gave us information that we could use to work more closely with the English department faculty. We also know that 65 percent of our sophomores have never used government documents, indicating a significant underutilization of a valuable resource.

Use of Findings

Presentations and publications on our library skills assessment results have been provided nationally and at the state level. In addition, presentations have been given for the library faculty as a whole and for individual academic departments. This form of information sharing has been more successful and dynamic than the filing of reports from one office to another. We are beginning to reap the benefits of our labors. The following are some examples.

The English department has required students enrolled in English 101 and 102 to complete the *Library Skills Workbook* during the fall semester. This department is now requiring majors to take both a sophomore and an upper-level research course, to obtain more experience with the sources and strategies important to their field.

Results from our entering-student assessments have provided Virginia high schools with valuable articulation information. The library has strengthened its services, to more fully support those rated most effective through our assessment efforts, with increased course-related instruction, more reference librarians at the desk, handouts of major specific information, and a much greater investment in electronic access to information. The university has implemented a new on-line catalogue system, and our assessment results played an important role in identifying weaknesses in the old system. The liaison librarians have worked closely with academic departments on the assessment of library skills in the majors; as a result, faculty have become more aware of library resources and have asked for additional library instruction as an integral part of the courses.

Success Factors

As we look back over the last five years, we believe that there are characteristics of our institution that make success in assessment activities more likely. This university has developed a culture that invites inquiry. A climate of caring about student progress and development permeates the institution, and assessment activities are an integral part of this climate. The president of the university fully supports assessment activities. An institution that supports two formal assessment days each year for the systematic collection of data must consider that data valuable. The Carrier Library faculty is service oriented and proactive, and its enthusiasm and cooperation have been most effective in garnering the support and participation of academic departments. Finally, James Madison has a well organized and professional Office of Student Assessment that has provided support, both technical and emotional, to members of the library and academic faculty for all of their assessment inquiries.

Assessing Fitness/Wellness in General Studies

Gwen Robbins, Debbie Powers

CASE 48: BALL STATE UNIVERSITY

Look for: Systematic evaluation of the development of knowledge, attitudes, and behaviors promoted in a two-hour fitness/wellness course required as part of a general studies program. Several improvements were made in fitness assessment methods, and faculty in physical education were able to make significant contributions to the literature of their discipline as a result of this assessment project.

Background and Purpose

A general studies program (GSP) totaling forty-one semester hours is required of all undergraduates at Ball State University (BSU). This program is designed to help students develop knowledge, skill, and values that should be held in common by all graduates of the university. The two-hour course Physical Education Fitness/ Wellness (PEFWL), which combines physical fitness activities and integrated lecture topics related to wellness, is a component of this GSP.

The PEFWL requirement is a springboard toward a total university commitment to fitness and wellness. In fact, "we value wellness" is one of eight components of the mission of BSU. In addition to this course, the university offers wellness-oriented residence halls; the Institute for Wellness; wellness programming for faculty, staff, and students; and a multitude of opportunities to explore the six dimensions of wellness (spiritual, social, emotional, physical, occupational, and intellectual).

PEFWL uses a two-fold approach: a series of classroom lectures that covers a variety of wellness topics and laboratory activity sessions where progress is made toward achieving physical fitness through a specific aerobic activity. One fifty-minute class per week is spent in a large-group lecture (90 to 125 students).

Students enroll in PEFWL according to the desired aerobic activity in which they want to participate. Two times per week, the student attends this activity lab with twenty to thirty other students who selected the same aerobic activity. Selections include physical conditioning, fitness walking, jogging, swimnastics, bicycling, rhythmic aerobics, and fitness swimming. The General Studies Subcommittee assesses the total GSP every five years. The goal of this assessment is to ensure that the courses making up the program as a whole meet or exceed the standards established in the *General Studies Document.* The PEFWL program goals, as stated in this document are: (1) "These courses will provide the students with aerobic activities that enhance fitness and wellness"; and (2) "These courses should provide the student with an understanding of the need for physical fitness and life-long concern with wellness."

Physical education faculty teaching the seven PEFWL courses perceived that the courses were making a positive impact on students' lives. This hypothesis had never been tested however. During spring semester 1989, a project team was assembled to assess the PEFWL courses and address several questions: Are these courses having a positive effect on student lives? Are students acquiring fitness/wellness knowledge? Do cardiorespiratory endurance levels and flexibility improve? How are resting heart rates and blood pressure affected? Does body weight or body composition change? In short, are we doing what we say we are doing? A follow-up assessment was conducted in 1993.

Method

For the 1989 assessment, approximately 1,500 students were randomly computer selected from sections of the total PEFWL course offerings to take part in the mass program assessment. This was approximately one-third of all students enrolled in the program (that is, one-third of all fitness walking sections; one-third of all jogging sections, and so on). Attention was given to balancing selection of courses so that early, middle, and late class times were represented. The project team set out to assess four major elements: (1) knowledge gained during the course; (2) attitude toward the course; (3) current life-style; and (4) physical fitness changes. Knowledge and physical fitness tests were administered as both pre- and posttests. The knowledge test consisted of fifty multiple-choice questions. Current life-style was assessed through a sixteen-item life-style inventory called "Healthy Life-Style: A Self-Assessment," which is to include a five-year follow-up.

Findings and Their Use

The outcomes of the massive assessment have been valuable to both students and faculty:

1. Since significant improvement was made in a majority of the physical variables, college-age norms based on the posttesting results were developed for each fitness test. These norms are valuable in helping instructors assess student performance and guide students in personal goal setting.

2. Improvements, valuable to physical education teachers and students, were made on several commonly used fitness tests, including the following:

One-mile walking test. The norms developed for this test are now more realistic for college-age students. Norms for previously used walking tests focused on older adults.

Abdominal curl. Compared to the sit-up test, this test is a safer and more accurate measure of abdominal endurance. This one-minute timed test is performed by curling the upper body forward until the extended fingertips slide three inches along the floor.

Push-up. Women (in a modified position) and men perform this one-minute timed test by lowering the body until the elbows form a right angle and the upper arm is parallel to the floor. The elbow angle eliminates confusion of body positioning in relation to the floor.

500-yard water run test. One of the most exciting outcomes of the entire project is this original cardiorespiratory endurance fitness field test. Now nonswimming water exercisers can be fitness tested in the water. No longer must they climb out of the pool to perform the step-test, 1.5-mile run, or the 1-mile walk to assess aerobic fitness. This new test generated an extensive laboratory research project that confirmed its validity (Kaminsky and others, 1993). As a result, aquatic experts around the world now have a valuable cardiorespiratory activity-specific field test to use in their exercise programs.

3. The PEFWL program and assessment initiated the writing and publication of a college textbook, *A Wellness Way of Life,* now in its second edition and used internationally in fitness/wellness courses (Robbins, Powers, and Burgess, 1994).

4. The investigators of this assessment project became convinced that a course of this design, in which students focus on one specific aerobic activity per semester, is superior to fitness/wellness courses that offer a smorgasbord approach (that is, two weeks of one activity, followed by two weeks of another). Also, undoubtedly, having aerobic activity accompany lectures is superior to having only classroom lectures in a course. The PEFWL students develop an understanding of the "gain without pain" concept and discover that exercise can be enjoyable and social. They learn that aerobic exercise is a lifetime activity and, when intertwined with other wellness habits, can help them pursue their maximal potential.

5. The assessment demonstrated that students were improving fitness and acquiring basic fitness/wellness knowledge. Faculty are now assured that their efforts have a positive impact on the present and future lives of their students (see Table 12.2 and Exhibit 12.1).

TABLE 12.2. PRE- AND POSTTEST PHYSICAL ASSESSMENT AND KNOWLEDGE RESULTS.

Physical Variable	Pretest Mean	Posttest Mean	Significant Improvement (.05 Level)
Thigh (M)	12.80mm	13.63mm	No
Subscapula (M)	13.89mm	13.62mm	Yes
Body composition/ Sloan formula (M)	13.33%	13.50%	No
Tricep (F)	21.04mm	20.71mm	No
Suprailiac (F)	20.70mm	17.68mm	Yes
Body composition/ Sloan formula (F)	24.88%	23.66%	Yes
Resting pulse (M)	80.90 BPM	79.60 BPM	Yes
Resting pulse (F)	83.20 BPM	82.70 BPM	No
Blood pressure systolic (M)	115	114	Yes
Blood pressure systolic (F)	129	123	Yes
Blood pressure diastolic (M)	79	77	Yes
Blood pressure diastolic (F)	75	72	Yes
Weight (M)	170.70 lbs.	171.60 lbs.	No
Weight (F)	136.90 lbs.	137.20 lbs.	No
Abdominal curls (M)	65.23 in 1 min.	75.19 in 1 min.	Yes
Abdominal curls (F)	58.15 in 1 min.	69.05 in 1 min.	Yes
Push-ups (M)	36.56 in 1 min.	43.58 in 1 min.	Yes
Push-ups (F)	30.75 in 1 min.	37.63 in 1 min.	Yes
Sit and reach (M)	2.08 in.	2.46 in.	Yes
Sit and reach (F)	4.35 in.	5.14 in.	Yes
1.5-mile run (M)	11:51 min./sec.	11:19 min./sec.	Yes
1.5-mile run (F)	15:52 min./sec.	15:03 min./sec.	Yes
1-mile walk (M)	14:28 min./sec.	13:13 min./sec.	Yes
1-mile walk (F)	14:47 min./sec.	13:37 min./sec.	Yes
5-mile bicycle ride (M)	15:15 min./sec.	13:48 min./sec.	Yes
5-mile bicycle ride (F)	16:50 min./sec.	15:03 min./sec.	Yes
500-yard swim test (M)	10:39 min./sec.	8:32 min./sec.	Yes
500-yard swim test (F)	10:40 min./sec.	9:42 min./sec.	Yes
500-yard water run (M)	8:26 min./sec.	7:26 min./sec.	Yes
500-yard water run (F)	9:22 min./sec.	8:59 min./sec.	Yes
Knowledge of Wellness/Fitness	Pre 29.93	Post 34.4	Yes

Note: N = 1,114. M = male; F = female.

Table 12.2 is reprinted with permission from the *Journal of Physical Education, Recreation & Dance*, February, 1992, pp. 17–21. *JOPERD* is a publication of the American Alliance for Health, Physical Education, Recreation and Dance, 1900 Association Drive, Reston, VA 22091.

EXHIBIT 12.1. HEALTHY LIFE-STYLE: A SELF-ASSESSMENT.

1. I exercise aerobically (continuous, vigorous exercise for 20 to 30 minutes) _____ times per week.
   a. 5 or more (6.9)
   b. 3–4 (21.1)
   c. 2 (21.8)
   d. Less than 2 (50.2)

2. Whenever possible, I try to increase my activity level by walking or biking rather than driving, participating in leisure sports, taking the stairs rather than the elevator, and so on.
   a. Almost always (12.4)
   b. Frequently (36.1)
   c. Occasionally (42.0)
   d. Almost never (9.3)

3. I make sure my diet is varied and well-balanced each day (fruits, vegetables, lean meats, dairy products, and whole grains).
   a. Almost always (17.2)
   b. Frequently (33.8)
   c. Occasionally (37.4)
   d. Almost never (11.5)

4. I intentionally include fiber in my diet on a daily basis.
   a. Almost always (10.5)
   b. Frequently (18.6)
   c. Occasionally (39.4)
   d. Almost never (31.2)

5. I limit the amount of fat, saturated fat, and cholesterol I eat (including animal fats, eggs, butter, oils, shortenings, and fast foods).
   a. Almost always (13.7)
   b. Frequently (28.2)
   c. Occasionally (36.4)
   d. Almost never (21.4)

6. I smoke _____ packs of cigarettes per day.
   a. 0 (87.9)
   b. Less than 1 (8.0)
   c. 1–2 (3.9)
   d. More than 2 (.1)

7. I use other forms of tobacco products (smokeless, snuff, cigars, pipe) _____ times per day.
   a. 0 (95.0)
   b. 1–2 (2.2)
   c. 3–4 (1.2)
   d. 4 or more (1.5)

8. I wear a seat belt while riding in a car.
   a. Almost always (52.4)
   b. Frequently (18.9)
   c. Occasionally (16.7)
   d. Almost never (11.8)

9. I obey traffic rules and the speed limit when driving.
   a. Almost always (35.7)
   b. Frequently (40.1)
   c. Occasionally (19.5)
   d. Almost never (4.6)

10. I examine my breasts (females) or testes (males) on a monthly basis.
    a. Almost always (8.8)
    b. Frequently (13.1)
    c. Occasionally (32.5)
    d. Almost never (44.5)

11. I have healthy coping skills for the stress in my life.
    a. Almost always (16.3)
    b. Frequently (39.3)
    c. Occasionally (35.3)
    d. Almost never (9.1)

12. I include relaxation or "me" time as part of my daily routine.
    a. Almost always (26.7)
    b. Frequently (36.2)
    c. Occasionally (27.7)
    d. Almost never (9.3)

13. My consumption of alcoholic beverages can be approximated to be:
    a. 0 drinks per month (19.8)
    b. 1–7 drinks per month (34.2)
    c. 8–12 drinks per month (16.7)
    d. 13 or more drinks per month (29.1)

14. I schedule on a regular basis health/medical screenings: blood pressure and cholesterol checks, Pap tests (female), physical examinations, dental checkups, and so on.
    a. Almost always (20.1)
    b. Frequently (25.1)
    c. Occasionally (34.8)
    d. Almost never (19.5)

15. I would categorize my weight/body fat to be:
    a. Within 5 pounds of ideal (36.9)
    b. 6–15 pounds overweight/underweight (42.8)
    c. 16–25 pounds overweight/underweight (13.1)
    d. More than 25 pounds overweight/underweight (6.7)

16. I feel enthusiastic and happy about my life.
    a. Almost always (33.6)
    b. Frequently (50.4)
    c. Occasionally (13.7)
    d. Almost never (.5)

Note: The 1989 percentages of response for each item are given in parentheses.

CHAPTER THIRTEEN

ASSESSING STUDENT DEVELOPMENT AND PROGRESS

Chapter Guide

The chapter guide lists the cases contained in this chapter by institution, by student development area, and by assessment method. Institutions are organized by Carnegie Classification. The location of each institution and its approximate enrollment follow the institution name. The relevant case numbers follow each entry.

Institutions

Student Development Areas

Assessment Methods

Chapter Overview

Faculty and administrators are concerned not only about what happens to students during the 15 percent of their time that they spend in classes but also about the development that occurs during the 85 percent of their waking hours not spent in the classroom (Boyer, 1987). Colleges and universities include student development goals in their statements of mission, and design advising and other support systems to promote this development. However, such systems can only be effective if they are responsive to students' needs and preferences. Thus, faculty, student affairs personnel, and institutional research staff have designed assessment activities to track student progress and to ascertain students' interests, needs, and levels of satisfaction, in order to provide direction for planning, developing, implementing, and continuously improving student services.

Every institution is interested in retaining students and ensuring that they make progress toward their degrees. Advising systems that assist students in making steady progress are viewed as among the most important support services a college can provide. Most of the descriptions in this chapter incorporate the use of assessment to improve advising systems.

Although many four-year institutions have begun to conduct studies of students' progress based on analyses of their transcripts, this is an assessment technique that has been used particularly effectively at two-year institutions (Walleri and Seybert, 1993). The setting for Cases 49 to 51 is the community college campus. The first in the series (Case 49) concerns a study of underprepared students initiated in 1981. Transcript analysis revealed that too many students were not following the advice of advisers following placement testing and were enrolling in courses that required skills in which they needed remedial work. The faculty responded to these findings by initiating a mandatory testing and course-placement system.

The second example (Case 50) describes a transcript study that revealed that many students planning to transfer to a four-year institution were not completing specific lower-division general education course requirements in a logical sequence or in a timely manner and, thus, were accumulating many more credits than they needed for transfer. Initiating a more intrusive advising system has helped students become more efficient in selecting and completing just those courses that will be most helpful to them in completing their plans to transfer.

The approach to evaluating student advising in the large multicampus community college system that is the subject of Case 51 involved collecting data from advising center coordinators, faculty advisers, and students. Analysis of the findings suggested the need for a systemwide advising policy and more focused training for advisers.

Most of the remaining descriptions in this chapter characterize assessment activities underway at four-year institutions. As at two-year colleges, the principal emphasis is on improving student advising.

Cases 52 and 53 involve the use of standardized self-report instruments to identify student characteristics that may be related to early academic performance and subsequent persistence in college. In the first of the cases (52), students' reports of their learning and study strategies are used to improve their attitudes and approaches to academic work and to assist faculty and administrators in individualizing their advising approaches. In the second case (53), a required freshman seminar small enough (fifteen students in each section) to allow each instructor to be perceived as a mentor is the setting for administering an inventory that sheds light on students' academic and social motivation and receptivity to support services.

As Case 54 illustrates, freshman progress reports five weeks into the first semester can assist in identifying students in academic difficulty. This early warning system signals the need for intervention and arms faculty advisers with specific information they can use in helping new freshmen.

Freshman surveys are the assessment tools applied in Cases 55 and 56. In the first case (55), emphasis is placed on the systematic development of a survey—a process that includes studying current literature and existing national survey instruments. That survey can now be tried on other campuses. The institutional research staff responsible for the survey also used an experimental design to test the efficacy of a one-credit orientation course established to assist students identified as at risk by virtue of their survey responses.

The second freshman survey (Case 56) is a component of a larger Institutional Impact Study, initiated in 1981. One of the most significant actions undertaken by the institution in response to survey findings was to develop a training program for staff to prepare them to meet and assist students more effectively.

The Student Involvement Study in Case 57 is also a component of the impact study described in Case 56, which is now in its second decade. Research has shown that students' involvement in their studies and extracurricular activities can enhance their development in college. A questionnaire was designed to provide data for year-to-year monitoring of freshman involvement, longitudinal studies of the involvement of freshmen who stayed to be seniors, and evaluation of involvement intervention efforts. Tracking student involvement in learning outside the classroom is the purpose of the student development transcript described in Case 58. Recording students' participation in campus and community activities can furnish tangible evidence that an institution is using multiple approaches to promote students' intellectual growth, leadership abilities, aesthetic appreciation, and interpersonal skills.

Designing cross-disciplinary assessment activities at a large research university is a particularly daunting task. At one such institution (Case 59), a preliminary step in studying the learning experience of students has been an open-ended interview for freshmen. The interviews have helped faculty comprehend the importance of the campus climate in influencing student success.

The authors of Cases 60 and 61 have conducted student development research using multiple measures of students' opinions, attitudes, values, and experiences. In Case 60, findings from studies of students' progress in achieving a clear sense of identity during the college years are used to suggest types of courses and teaching strategies that faculty may use to promote identity formation. In Case 61, measuring students' personality characteristics and attitudes toward social issues at three points in their first two years of college has yielded findings that have encouraged faculty and staff to develop a freshman seminar and offer additional opportunities for students at all levels to apply their classroom learning.

Evaluation of all the student services provided by a community college is the subject of Case 62. Measurable effectiveness indicators derived from user surveys and audit instruments are used in setting goals for improvement and monitoring progress.

Alumni surveys constitute an important component of most comprehensive campus assessment programs. The Institutional Impact Study mentioned in Cases 56 and 57 includes a survey for graduates that consists of a common core of items, to which everyone responds, supplemented by questions developed by the faculty of eight undergraduate academic colleges (Case 63). The combination of items on which the responses of departmental samples may be compared with the campus average and items unique to a program has provided the kind of compelling evidence that has produced substantive changes in programs and services over the years since the survey was initiated in the early 1980s.

A Ten-Year Effort to Assist Underprepared Students

R. Dan Walleri

CASE 49: MT. HOOD COMMUNITY COLLEGE

Look for: A program begun in 1981 to enhance prospects for success for underprepared students. Transcript analysis and a survey to determine student intentions were used. Outcomes of assessment include initiation of mandatory assessment and course placements, more emphasis on applications in teaching math, and outreach to high schools to assist with their reform efforts.

Background and Purpose

In 1981, Mt. Hood Community College established the Student Success Task Force, which was to focus initially on the problem of student attrition. The task force was a response to growing national, state, and local concern that the open-door community college had become a "revolving door," and that the commonly held belief by administrators and faculty in a "student's right to fail" had become an accountability problem threatening public support. The task force was charged with reviewing all college programs and services, with the aim of identifying strategies to enhance the prospects for student success. The task force consisted of some forty members representing all areas and levels of the college.

Method

Of particular concern was the 50 to 60 percent of entering students that failed to score at the college level on the college's assessment/placement examination, Career Guidance Placement (CGP). Assessment and appropriate course placement was not mandatory, and although the vast majority of entering students was tested, there was no prohibition against concurrent enrollment—students enrolling in courses requiring the very skill levels they were attempting to remediate in developmental education. Other concerns included the lack of concrete criteria for successful exit from developmental education courses and the number of terms students could continue within developmental education.

A broader concern addressed by the task force was how to define student success. Since it could not be assumed that all students sought a degree, how was successful nondegree exit from the college to be differentiated from attrition?

Based on a review of these issues and related background information (transcript analysis of underprepared students), the task force recommended the establishment of a mandatory assessment/course-placement system (guided studies) and the collection of student intent data (to occur in 1983 and 1984). In addition, explicit criteria were put in place for successful exit from developmental education, controls were developed to prevent concurrent enrollment, and policies established to limit the number of terms that students could continue to enroll in developmental education courses.

At the same time, a student intentions data collection system was initiated as part of the student registration process (students were asked their educational goals, vocational goals, and the like).

Faculty involvement throughout the process has been critical. For example, the faculty reviewed all courses to determine which would be available for enrollment by guided studies students. Many faculty members were concerned that higher standards would negatively affect enrollment. Through experience, however, faculty learned that this fear was unfounded, and they gradually became supporters of the new program. In addition, a report was produced from the intentions data, providing a profile of each course. These reports were distributed at the beginning of each term, and faculty used them to adjust their instructional approaches and for program-marketing efforts.

Findings and Their Use

The mandatory assessment/placement program has now been in operation for over ten years. As result of our initial positive findings, both guided studies and the student intentions data collection system have become permanent features of the college. Over the last few years, the CGP test for entering students has been replaced by a series of tests for the particular areas of reading, writing, and mathematics. In the area of mathematics, a reform effort has been initiated to stress applications, along with the use of technology, to replace the traditional focus on learning through drill and practice. In the areas of both mathematics and composition, an outreach effort has been initiated to work with the high schools on Oregon's educational reform effort. In summary, the process begun in 1981 has transformed the organizational culture, with all activities now focused on student success and continuous improvement.

Success Factors

There were several key factors responsible for the success of the above initiatives. Primary was the vision and leadership of a key administrator, Paul E. Kreider, then vice president of Mt. Hood and now president. Another factor was the cohesiveness among the three deans, who were able to facilitate the process.

Yet another success factor was the role of institutional research, which documented the process and provided evidence that the initiatives were having their desired effect. The latter element was also an organizational factor in that openness and the use of relevant information became an institutional value. The primary lesson learned was the value of patience and persistence. "Staying the course" was critical to the overall success of the effort.

Course Efficiency

Jack Friedlander, Peter R. MacDougall

CASE 50: SANTA BARBARA CITY COLLEGE

Look for: Use of transcript analysis in an ongoing study of students' course-taking efficiency. Student time and institutional resources have been saved by intrusive advising procedures that encourage students to take only the courses they really need for transfer to a four-year institution.

Background and Purpose

A major goal of Santa Barbara City College (SBCC) is to have as many students as possible complete the associate's degree and the transfer requirements in as efficient a manner as possible. Our research revealed that a substantial number of students with a transfer objective were completing well in excess of the sixty units needed to transfer.

This led us to question whether students were taking the classes needed in a logical and timely sequence to complete their degree and transfer requirements. To address this concern, the decision was made to analyze student transcripts to gain insights into student course-taking patterns.

Method

A computer program was used to analyze student transcripts to identify which lower-division general education transfer requirements were completed in the first thirty to sixty units at the college. The program analyzed the classes students completed that fulfilled the lower-division general education requirements in areas such as natural science, English, and mathematics. In addition, the program identified those units that were nontransferable or in excess of the units required to meet a general education, major field, or elective requirement.

Findings

The analysis of student transcripts revealed that students planning to transfer from SBCC to a campus of the University of California (UC) or of the California State University (CSU) were not efficiently selecting the courses needed to satisfy the lower-division general education requirements at those institutions. Moreover, many students were taking more courses than were needed to satisfy lower-division general education, major field, and/or elective requirements in certain areas while not completing requirements in others. The inefficiencies in student course-taking behavior resulted in students spending more time than necessary to meet lower-division requirements.

By not completing all of the CSU and UC lower-division general education requirements at SBCC, students were subjected to completing the unique lower-division general education requirements in place at each UC and CSU campus. This resulted in students having to take additional courses at the transfer institution to satisfy requirements that could have been met at SBCC. Students' taking a longer time than needed to complete their lower-division requirements has resulted in increased costs to the students and the state. Furthermore, having students enroll in more courses than necessary compounded the college's problem of needing to serve more students but having steady-state or diminished resources.

Use of Findings

The findings of the study were reviewed by college faculty, counseling staff, and administrators and resulted in the following changes: (1) All students with a goal of degree, certificate, and/or transfer now are required to complete an educational plan. The plan identifies specific courses needed to meet college graduation, transfer institution, and lower-division requirements. (2) An early registration program was instituted for continuing students. To participate in this program, students are required to meet with a counselor or faculty adviser to review their progress toward meeting lower-division graduation and/or transfer requirements. (3) A student planning tool was developed for students to verify courses needed to meet transfer/graduation requirements. (4) A computer program was developed to identify students taking excessive units in transfer/graduation categories. These students are required to see a counselor to discuss their academic progress. (5) Procedures were instituted to replicate the course-taking-efficiency study every other year to assess the extent to which progress has been made toward increasing student course-taking efficiency.

As a result of the interventions implemented, the number of units completed by students that exceed transfer/graduation requirements in specific categories has declined dramatically. In addition, the percentage of students who complete lower-division general education requirements in a timely and logical sequence has increased. Reducing the number of excess classes in which students enroll has freed seats in those classes for other students, who otherwise might have had to wait an additional semester or two to gain access to those courses.

Success Factors

The approach to applying assessment results to improving college practices was effective because members of the counseling and student services staff were involved in the design and conduct of the study. They also were asked to provide the leadership in developing and implementing strategies for addressing the problems identified in the study. In addition, the project addressed needs felt to be essential by both students and the institution.

A primary factor in the success of this assessment project in effecting change was that the study was built into the college's ongoing procedures for assessing institutional effectiveness and, thus, was an institutional priority. Faculty and staff were provided with progress reports on the results of their intervention strategies to increase student course-taking efficiency. This added credibility to the value of the college's program of systematically assessing institutional effectiveness. The college faculty and staff were made aware of project findings and implications and, through existing governance committees, were asked to develop and implement strategies for addressing the problems identified in the assessment study.

This example of assessing the efficiency of student course-taking patterns illustrates the benefits of an ongoing and focused program for assessing the effectiveness of institutional practices. The findings and their subsequent application to changing institutional practices yielded savings in time and money to students, enabled the institution to educate a greater number of students, and saved the state money by not supporting courses in excess of those needed by students to achieve their educational objectives.

Assessing and Enhancing Academic Advising in a Multi-College Institution

Michael Rooney, Maria Harper-Marinick

CASE 51: MARICOPA COMMUNITY COLLEGES

Look for: A comprehensive formative evaluation of advising services undertaken across the ten campuses of the nation's second largest multicampus community college system. The assessment findings have produced a systemwide policy for advising, training modules for advisers, and redeployment of personnel to strengthen advising services.

Background and Purpose

The Maricopa County Community College District (MCCCD) in Phoenix, Arizona, serves a geographic area of about 9,226 square miles and a population of about two million people (60 percent of all Arizona residents). The purpose of its systemwide advising program is to ensure continual awareness of student needs and continuous improvement of the quality of advising services. The District Academic Advising Council (DAAC) was established to create a process to provide a framework and theoretical base for organizational change and to assess the needs indicated by advisers and students for improved advising and services. Its assessment report, accompanied by all levels of institutional support, heightened awareness and concern for consistent, quality academic advising throughout the district. The DAAC has identified goals and objectives for this program as well as appropriate resource materials, delivery methods, training, and technology. Program and process evaluations are both qualitative and quantitative.

The mission of the Maricopa Community Colleges is to create accessible, effective, and affordable environments for teaching and learning; to provide, throughout the curricula, the essential skills and knowledge students need in order to function in a changing world; and to increase access and success for students who are at risk of educational failure.

Maricopa Community Colleges award nearly 3,000 associate's degrees and more than 1,600 certificates of completion annually. Transfer programs are a strong component of the MCCCD offerings. Approximately 36 percent of the undergraduate enrollment and 48 percent of the upper-division enrollment at Arizona State University are transfer students from the Maricopa Community Colleges. It is critical that academic advising services be accurate and current within such an environment.

Method

As could be expected in a community college district this large, a significant disparity existed among types of individuals delivering advising services, and there was a lack of quality control measures to ensure continual awareness of customer needs and continuous improvement of the quality of the advising services provided. Therefore, a process was undertaken to provide a framework and theoretical base for organizational change. The purpose of this initiative was to provide a districtwide forum for emphasizing strengths and identifying challenges in the delivery of advising services throughout the institutions.

It was in order to formalize the process for creating a new framework and theoretical base for implementing organizational change, that the District Academic Advising Council, consisting of representatives from each MCCCD institution, was established. The DAAC includes program advisers, faculty advisers, counselors, and college and district administrators. The charge given to the council included the following objectives: (1) to assess the current status of advising at each of the colleges; (2) to make recommendations for the improvement of advising services; (3) to develop academic advising policy and related guidelines; and (4) to evaluate, on an ongoing basis, the effectiveness of advising services.

Before any important districtwide enhancements to academic advising could be accomplished, benchmark data needed to be established. Once this was done, subsequent evaluations would have reference points that would enhance the meaning of the data collected.

The first component of the benchmark-setting exercise was a survey of, and an oral report by, all the colleges' advising center coordinators. The questions, developed by the DAAC, were both quantitative and qualitative. A follow-up meeting was then held in which advising center coordinators discussed their responses with council members. A report was then written to summarize the status of advising programs throughout the district. This report was used in at least three important ways. First, it was shared with the Chancellor's Executive Council, composed of the vice chancellors and college presidents of the Maricopa colleges. Second, the results were used, and continue to be used, to gauge progress made in enhancing advising services at the ten colleges. Third, the report was used to raise the level of governing board and key administrator awareness and concern about the quality of academic advising in the district.

The second major component of establishing benchmark data was an academic advising audit. A modified and abbreviated version of the American College Testing Advising Audit was conducted at each institution in the Maricopa district to identify advisers' perceptions regarding the strengths and weaknesses of current advising practices. This information on the quality of advising services has become the blueprint for the work of the DAAC. The results clearly showed a need for districtwide advising policy and procedures and a need for a better system of adviser selection, training, and recognition.

The third component of the benchmark data was a faculty adviser needs assessment. Of those full-time faculty advisers who responded to a written survey, 96 percent stated that they not only wanted and needed better advising training but wanted training to be mandatory.

The fourth component of the benchmark data was a student evaluation of the advising services they received. Twenty thousand surveys were administered at the district colleges. They were administered over a twelve-month period in order to determine whether students perceived qualitative differences in the services at different points in the academic year.

Findings

The preliminary assessment initiatives made it clear that academic advising was, with a few notable exceptions, undervalued and underfunded at the district colleges. No overarching governing board policy gave direction to this important component of student success. Consequently, there were no common procedures guiding the delivery of the service.

Another major finding was that adviser training, when available, was fragmented and episodic. Moreover, there were no systematic means for recognizing or rewarding exemplary advisers or advising programs.

Use of Findings

As a result of the program evaluation and needs assessment efforts, the DAAC developed a policy on academic advising and detailed accompanying procedures. The DAAC also developed three modules for use at all of the colleges in training new and returning advisers.

A number of changes have occurred within the advising programs at the colleges. Several campuses have bolstered their advising staffs considerably; others have merged such services as advising centers and transfer centers in order to strengthen advising and informational services for students. Other colleges within the system have realigned their administrative structures in order to give more attention to, and support for, academic advising. Still others have improved the quality and use of the technology that supports academic advising in the district.

Success Factors

The evaluation plan to assess program effectiveness included the implementation of several instruments to collect quantitative and qualitative data from a variety of sources, including service providers and recipients. Once these evaluation efforts were successfully put in place, the individual institutions were able to replicate them from time to time on a smaller scale at the local level. This has become an ongoing quality assurance effort.

The advising assessment effort has worked because it was carefully planned and implemented. In an approach consistent with Continuous Quality Improvement and Total Quality Management principles, people were involved at every step of the way. Their input was sought, was valued, and was utilized to enhance a service critical to the ultimate success of the student.

One of the most satisfying things to happen recently helped verify that these efforts have begun to pay off. In 1993, the Maricopa Community Colleges won the Two-Year College Institutional Award for the work that has been done to assess and enhance its advising services.

Use of the Learning and Study Strategies Inventory (LASSI) in Assessing Student Personal Growth and Development

Martin Hope, M. Cristina Grabiel

CASE 52: WINTHROP UNIVERSITY

Look for: Use of a nationally normed self-report instrument to examine student characteristics that might affect student academic performance. Students' scores on the LASSI motivation scale proved to be a better predictor of freshman GPA than SAT scores or high school rank.

Background and Purpose

Winthrop University has developed a multimethod, comprehensive approach to the assessment of student personal growth and development (SPG&D). Use of the Learning and Study Strategies Inventory (LASSI) was selected as one method for examining student learning and development in order to improve our efforts in predicting, explaining, and enhancing student success. Involved in this study were SPG&D co-coordinators Martin Hope and Cristina Grabiel, assessment director Joe Prus, associate professor of psychology Larry Hatcher, instructors of the class sections used in the study, and the 950 freshmen who participated in the two-year administration of the instrument. The study's goals were to (1) give explicit feedback to students that would help them understand the strengths and weaknesses in their approaches to and attitudes toward academic work; (2) provide information concerning student learning strategies, to aid faculty in advising and administrators in recruitment and retention efforts; and (3) assess the predictive powers of the instrument's ten scales.

Method

LASSI is a self-report instrument developed to determine student strengths and weaknesses that potentially affect academic performance. It is divided into ten scales, which are rated and compared to a national norm, thus providing feedback on how each student compares to other students. In order to facilitate student feedback at Winthrop, a student guide to interpreting LASSI results was written and disseminated to each student completing the instrument.

In the first administration of the instrument, each of the freshmen was given the results and interpretive guide. It was recommended that students consult with individual academic advisers regarding the meaning of these results and their implications for academic work. In addition, students were invited to attend one of two sets of workshops designed to assist them in obtaining necessary skills and information in areas identified as problematic by the instrument. Advisers helped students further examine their results and determine the most appropriate workshop to attend. Workshops were offered in study skills and time management, motivation, career services/the meaning of education, and stress management. A total of eighty students attended these workshops.

Additional follow-up analyses were conducted the following semester to determine if LASSI results for entering students would be valid in predicting first-year academic success.

Findings

Data indicate that, as a whole, the members of Winthrop's freshman class are quite similar to freshmen across the nation in their learning and studying strategies. Not surprisingly, considerable variation across individual students was found.

Follow-up studies found that seven of ten LASSI scales correlated significantly with college freshman-year GPA. The motivation scale most strongly correlated with GPA, at almost the same level as SAT scores. This scale served as a more accurate predictor of academic success than either SAT scores or high school rank. (Since LASSI is a self-report instrument, some caution must be used when making predictions.) A further analysis of returning students the following fall revealed that four LASSI scales (motivation, time management, concentration, and self-testing) demonstrated significant correlations with retention.

Use of Findings

Findings have been shared with the student participants, faculty, and relevant administrators. Students gained a better understanding of their own academic strengths and weaknesses, faculty were aided in the advising process, and administrators were given useful information for their work in recruitment and retention.

Success Factors

The success of this activity was due largely to the careful planning undertaken by a number of individuals representing a variety of departments and disciplines. This concerted polyperceptual team effort helped develop an approach that was both more creative and more thorough than it would have been if implemented by a more limited number of planners. The open give-and-take of all participants proved essential to the activity's success.

Use of Formal and Informal Data in Assessing a Freshman Seminar Mentoring Program

Donna Prior Sullivan, Judy Jones Walker

CASE 53: LYNN UNIVERSITY

Look for: A holistic approach to advising implemented in a required two-credit Freshman Seminar. Longitudinal tracking via data from the College Student Inventory facilitates identification of factors related to academic success and persistence.

Background and Purpose

Lynn University has developed a unique mentoring program for freshmen, which includes formal and informal data collection. The goal is to develop a comprehensive network of information to assist in detecting difficulties in adjustment to the university environment. All freshmen are required to enroll in the two-credit-hour course entitled Freshman Seminar. Enrollment typically includes approximately three hundred students (fifteen per mentoring section).

Method

Formal data are collected via a nationally known instrument, the College Student Inventory (Strail, 1988). The inventory provides information in a variety of areas related to student adjustment, such as academic and social motivation, predicted academic difficulty, and receptivity to support services. Thus, this measure provides for the early identification of students at risk. The self-reported student inventory is administered and tabulated results are made available to mentors by the fourth week of the semester. Summarized information from the inventory is reviewed by mentors, interpreted to students, and shared, as appropriate, with various campus departments and individuals familiar with its purposes.

Informal data are collected as a part of required Freshman Seminar assignments. These assignments include journals, reflection papers, and a career exploration project. The assignments enable students to discuss experiences and express their feelings on such topics as residential life, personal development, interpersonal relationships, and health issues. Students also provide ongoing feedback to mentors regarding the relevance of the assignments, guest speakers and activities, and the value of these to their university experience. Methods used to obtain such process evaluations have included one-minute evaluation summaries, session rating forms, and postsession verbal reactions/discussions.

Three additional assessments are conducted during the course. They include a course evaluation, an evaluation of each mentor's performance, and a pre- and postseminar measure of change in students' self-perceptions across several motivational and skill areas.

Findings

The process yields both qualitative and quantitative information of value in identifying students' adjustment needs. This information permits mentors to assist in tethering students' needs to the resources available on campus. Our review of qualitative comments offered on the course evaluations shows that students recognize and appreciate the fact that there is an individual who is sensitive to their particular concerns. This holistic approach to the advisement process supports each student's sense that he or she is linked to the greater university community.

Use of Findings

Both formative and summative data are derived from the Freshman Seminar and mentoring process. In response to formative data, immediate adjustments can be made to ensure course relevance. The summative information creates a foundation for course revisions for future semesters, as needed.

The dean of freshmen provides faculty with a profile of the freshman class via the institutional summary of student inventories and anecdotal information derived from observations. This increases faculty sensitivity to the changes in the "traditional" college student. The student inventory also permits longitudinal tracking of individuals across multiple semesters. This will facilitate the identification of specific variables related to retention and academic success.

Success Factors

We believe the methods we have adopted are successful for our institution because the mentors are empowered with the necessary information to work effectively in meeting the unique needs of their students. Students benefit from the accessibility and sensitivity of their mentors and the support of the campus community. A critical variable to note is administrative commitment to the provision of resources necessary for student success, including the commitment to the Freshman Seminar program.

Freshman Progress Reports

David A. Wissmann, Fred Geer

CASE 54: AVILA COLLEGE

Look for: Use of freshman progress reports to detect academic problems as soon as possible, increase the effectiveness of academic advising, and thus promote the retention and success of beginning students.

Background and Purpose

Freshman progress reports were initiated at Avila College to strengthen adviser-advisee relationships, catch academic problems early in individual courses, increase the efficiency of academic advising, and increase the retention and success of freshmen. All faculty who teach and/or advise freshmen are involved in the assessment process. Freshman progress reports were designed to (1) diagnose problems and be a catalyst for possible solutions regarding course-specific problems and (2) provide additional (nonscheduled) contact between advisers and advisees.

Method

Step 1. All first-semester freshmen are assessed by the instructors of each course in which they are enrolled. Faculty receive a freshman progress report form five weeks after the semester has started. They are asked to assess each freshman's attendance, skills and academic performance. When appropriate, faculty suggest areas in which a student needs out-of-class assistance, such as tutoring or skill development. Finally, the faculty member indicates whether this assessment has been discussed with the student. If so, the faculty member is asked to indicate the outcome of the discussion (see Exhibit 13.1 for a sample report).

Step 2. All completed freshman progress reports are sent to the academic vice president's office, where they are distributed to the appropriate academic adviser. The adviser reviews the reports along with any other information about the advisee that is available. An appointment between the adviser and the advisee is then scheduled.

Step 3. During the scheduled appointment, the adviser and the advisee examine and discuss the information. In those instances where the advisee is progressing at an appropriate rate, the adviser provides encouragement and support. If, however, the information reflects areas of concern, the adviser and advisee engage in problem-solving activities.

Findings

A wide variety of outcomes of the five-week progress reports have been observed: (1) advising has been seen by the advisee as a resource, rather than just as a scheduling hurdle to overcome during registration; (2) closer relationships and improved communication between advisers and advisees have occurred; (3) academic and personal/social concerns have been identified in a timely manner, leading to more effective utilization of the Student Resource Center; (4) retention and success of freshmen both during the first semester and in subsequent semesters have been enhanced; and (5) the processing of the assessment tool by all parties (instructors,

EXHIBIT 13.1. SAMPLE FIRST-YEAR STUDENT PROGRESS REPORT.

Student Name:

Course:

Instructor:

Date:

PROGRESS REPORTS FOR CONTINUING STUDIES

The purpose of this *five-week report* is to inform the student of his or her present academic progress and to assist the adviser during the interview.

The purpose of academic advisement is to resolve the problems that students encounter in their first year of college, to improve their academic performance, and to reduce student attrition.

1. How do you assess the progress of this student?
   Above avg.   Avg.   Below avg.
2. Which of the following were used in your assessment? (Circle all that apply.)
   a. Quizzes   e. Homework
   b. Examinations   f. Attendance
   c. Papers   g. Other (specify)
   d. Classroom discussion
3. Circle student's attendance record:
   a. Is adequate   c. Does not attend at all
   b. Needs improving
4. Circle appropriate area, if student needs tutoring:
   a. Writing skills   d. Course content
   b. Reading skills   e. Analytical skills
   c. Mathematical skills   f. Interpretative skills
5. Circle appropriate description(s) of the student's performance:
   a. Works conscientiously and consistently
   b. Is improving
   c. Is doing adequate work but is capable of doing better
   d. Fails to realize *demands* of college work
   e. Should consult with the instructor
6. Have you discussed this assessment with the student?
   Yes   No
6a. If yes, what was the outcome?

Instructor signature:

---

academic vice president office staff, and advisers) has proceeded more smoothly than anticipated.

Use of Findings

The primary changes that have taken place as a result of the five-week freshman progress reports are in the areas of adviser-advisee relationships and the utilization of the Student Resource Center. Improvements include greater and earlier contact between advisers and advisees, a significant increase in the quality of adviser-advisee relationships, and a greater likelihood of students using the Student Resource Center. Students have benefitted from this assessment activity in several ways. They have received an increased amount of support from advisers, have become more aware of campus resources, and have made academic and personal/social changes that lead to greater retention and success.

Success Factors

Leadership from the academic vice president served as an impetus for the success of the five-week freshman progress reports. In addition, faculty awareness and interest in outcomes assessment led to support of this activity. Finally, the positive experiences of faculty during advising sessions with freshmen reinforced the importance of this activity.

Using a Freshman Survey to Identify At-Risk Freshmen

James W. Pickering, James A. Calliotte

CASE 55: OLD DOMINION UNIVERSITY

Look for: Careful developmental work on a freshman survey that predicts academic difficulty and attrition. A one-credit orientation course and additional advising have been initiated to assist students identified as at risk.

Background and Purpose

This assessment project began in the same way that many administrative projects begin: an administrative alarm was sounded, a committee was convened, data were gathered and analyzed, and recommendations were made. The key factor that differentiated this from other routine administrative projects was the interest of two researchers in finding a more effective way of identifying a group of at-risk students whom they felt could be helped to be successful. The alarm which was sounded in 1987 was that nearly 25 percent of the entering freshman class at Old Dominion University was in academic difficulty after the first semester. Questions that were raised included: (1) Were we admitting students who were not able to succeed? (2) Did we appropriately advise students? (3) Were we offering the necessary services, and were the students in need using them? (4) Could we identify these at-risk students prior to their experiencing academic problems?

A committee was convened and charged to answer these questions. The committee's first step was to verify whether the problem actually existed or whether the 1987 experience was an anomaly; the committee discovered that this rate of academic difficulty had been a pattern for several years. A second step involved reviewing all the data available about several recent freshman classes. High school GPA, race, and gender were found to be the best predictors of academic performance. But cognitive and demographic data still left much of the variance in performance unaccounted for. Finally, several years of Cooperative Institutional Research Program (CIRP) freshman survey data were reviewed (Astin, Green, and Korn, 1987). For our needs, the scope and purpose of the CIRP survey were too global, the item pool was too limited, and the time for scoring prohibited early intervention, which was considered essential.

The researchers then set about developing the Old Dominion University Freshman Survey (Pickering, Calliotte, and McAuliffe, 1992) to (Phase I) improve predictions of academic performance at the end of the freshman year and persistence into the second year over what was possible with existing cognitive and demographic data, and (Phase II) identify at entry a group of freshmen who exhibited a greater potential for academic difficulty and/or attrition, and design interventions for them based on this research. Phase III involved full incorporation of this research into the academic advising and assessment programs, and Phase IV involves norming our freshman survey on freshmen at other institutions and on subpopulations such as freshman athletes at Old Dominion University.

Method

A review of the literature on noncognitive variables associated with academic difficulty and attrition, as well as an examination of the types of variables from the CIRP survey that showed promise, led to the development of survey items and appropriate response formats. The original Freshman Survey (Calliotte and Pickering, 1988) has undergone several revisions and now includes the following sections: (1) "Reasons for Deciding to Attend College," (2) "Reasons for Choosing Old Dominion," (3) "High School Experiences," (4) "Self Estimates of Abilities and Traits," (5) "Self Descriptions," (6) "Predictions About Your Academic Success," and (7) "Predictions About Your Involvement with Old Dominion." The criterion measures used for validation of the 1988 Freshman Survey were first-year GPA collected at the end of the spring semester and attrition or retention collected at the end of the following fall semester.

The Freshman Survey was factor analyzed, and its factors were found to be better predictors of academic performance and persistence than either the traditional cognitive or demographic predictors. However, a scoring method was then developed that was found to be the most powerful noncognitive predictor of academic performance and persistence (Pickering, Calliotte, and McAuliffe, 1992). Probation and attrition scores were developed separately using X^2 analyses performed on each item with the dichotomous variables of either (1) academic difficulty (GPA < 2.0)/academic success (GPA ≥ 2.0) at the end of the spring semester or (2) attrition/retention at the end of the second fall semester. One point was assigned to any response to any item that was chosen by a disproportionate number of people in academic difficulty (probation score) or attrition (attrition score). These scores then represented a tally of the number of items that the student answered the same way as students in academic difficulty or attrition. Using discriminant analysis, the probation and attrition scores significantly improved the predictive ability of traditional cognitive and demographic factors. In addition, when probation and attrition scores were graphed, it was found that as the scores increased, students' chances of being in academic difficulty or attrition, respectively, also increased.

Findings

Phase II involved setting a cutoff for the probation score and using it to identify at-risk freshmen for additional intervention. One standard deviation above the mean (12) was chosen as a conservative figure. In the norming, students with scores of 12 or higher had a greater than 50 percent chance of academic difficulty. Using 12 as a cutoff score, 115 at-risk freshmen (about 12 percent of the freshman class) were identified using the 1990 Freshman Survey. These at-risk students self-selected or were placed into one of three treatment groups or a no-treatment comparison group. Group 1 students were enrolled in a one-credit orientation course and also received additional counseling. Group 2 received the orientation course only. Group 3 students were not enrolled in the course and, thus, received additional counseling only. Group 4 did not release their survey results to their advisers nor were they enrolled in the course, and thus, they became the no-treatment comparison group. There were statistically significant differences between the treatment groups combined and the comparison group, although not between the treatment groups individually. While 65 percent of the treatment-group students were academically successful at the end of the freshman year, only 35 percent of the comparison group achieved success. Additionally, 84 percent of the treatment-group students were retained, in comparison to only 60 percent of the no-treatment group.

While this investigation began as an effort to examine the existing database to find variables related to freshman academic difficulty and attrition, it resulted in the development of an instrument and a methodology for identifying and treating at-risk freshmen. The principal finding was that noncognitive factors significantly improve predictions about academic performance and persistence. While admissions criteria can be used to identify students who are admissible, their range is then restricted, and they are quite limited in their ability to make fine discriminations among admitted students. Clearly, noncognitive predictors are needed to assist in making these critical discriminations. The second major finding was that an instrument could be developed that could be used to assess noncognitive predictors. Through Phases I and II, the Freshman Survey was validated as an effective noncognitive measure for identifying freshmen at risk for academic difficulty and attrition. Finally, a methodology featuring early identification and early intervention was established. Phase III involved the full incorporation of the Freshman Survey into the assessment and academic advising programs, development of a profile form for presenting results to advisers and students, and establishment of a treatment program for freshmen identified as at risk. Phase IV involves exploration of additional populations and subpopulations with which the Freshman Survey may be used. For example, in a recent doctoral dissertation, Cunningham (1993) successfully normed the Freshman Survey for freshmen athletes.

Use of Findings

The results of this research have informed discussions of university admissions requirements and retention efforts, and have been particularly influential in the development of the freshman academic advising program. Use of the Freshman Survey after admission and prior to enrollment has enabled staff to identify at-risk students at a critical time, when traditional admissions predictors were ineffective. The primary beneficiaries are students who are identified and treated and perhaps prevented from needlessly experiencing academic difficulty or attrition.

Success Factors

Collaboration, knowledge, intuition/vision, hard work, and serendipity were the factors that led to the success of this project. Collaboration was the key, as the effort brought together two individuals with overlapping areas of expertise (student development and retention) as well as different areas of responsibility (academic advising and counseling on the one hand and assessment and research on the other). Importantly, this project also involved a collaboration between the areas of academic affairs and student affairs.

Assessment of Student Treatment

A. Michael Williford, Gary O. Moden

CASE 56: OHIO UNIVERSITY

Look for: A freshman satisfaction survey conducted since 1978 that has produced improvements in advising, registration, and staff training. Freshman-to-sophomore retention has increased by 20 percent since 1978. (First in a series of three cases about Ohio University.)

Background and Purpose

The Student Treatment Study is one of several studies in Ohio University's multidimensional Institutional Impact Project, which was developed in 1981 by a task force of Ohio University faculty and staff at the request of the university president. As the project name indicates, it is an ongoing program of assessment of institutional impact, outcomes, and continuous improvement. The Student Treatment Study is used to measure student satisfaction in all areas of campus life, collecting information on the attitudes and perceptions of new freshmen after one quarter of enrollment. It assesses how freshmen feel they are treated by the staff of various areas or offices, how they rate the quality of information they receive from these staff or offices, and their perceptions of and reactions to various processes they go through. The instrument was developed at the University of Missouri-Columbia and adapted for use at this university.

All departments with which freshmen come in contact are evaluated in this study. Benchmark data for each department were collected in 1978 to measure departmental progress in subsequent years. In addition, individual departmental results are compared to campuswide norms. This information is used in a process of continuous program improvement, where freshmen (clients) evaluate the services they receive. Where problems are identified, existing programs are reviewed and changed, or new programs are implemented.

Method

The Office of Institutional Research at Ohio University conducts the treatment study using a questionnaire that includes a semantic differential scale to measure freshman ratings on such things as accessibility, courtesy, and efficiency; it also solicits comments and suggestions about university offices and processes that freshmen experience. This study is done every three years, and changes in scores are plotted from one freshman class to another to identify trends. Now, the freshman study is being expanded to assess perceptions of treatment received by all Ohio University undergraduates, graduate students, and osteopathic medical students.

Findings

Individual profile reports are prepared for each academic department and college. Each academic unit receives a profile showing its students' perceptions of treatment by faculty and academic advisers, perceptions of information about and the process of academic advising, and perceptions about getting help with academic problems. Departments receive reports that compare their profiles over time to show their progress. Comparisons are also made between each department and universitywide norms. Departments receive only their own results and the universitywide results.

Most areas have improved between 1978 and 1993, but the greatest improvements are in academic areas: treatment by faculty, information about what to expect in the classroom, and information about getting help with academic problems and the process of getting that help. These improvements resulted from training programs for faculty advisers and new initiatives in student advising.

Use of Findings

Treatment study results are considered part of a campuswide continuous improvement effort. In 1978, freshmen reported that treatment from university personnel associated with the opening week of classes was lacking in terms of courtesy, accessibility, friendliness, and sympathy. As a result of these findings, the dean of students initiated a training program for all staff working with freshmen during this time. Subsequent treatment study results showed improvements in reactions to staff. Since then, the training program has been conducted on a permanent basis.

In response to similar survey findings, health center receptionists were trained in positive customer relations techniques and the student union front-desk staffing was reorganized to focus on improving student services. Treatment survey responses from minority freshmen led to the creation of two minority outreach programs.

Treatment study results showed that the process of advising undecided freshmen was unsatisfactory, frustrating, complicated, and inefficient. A faculty training program was developed, advising manuals were created, new advisers were recruited, and funds were provided for advisers and students to meet in informal luncheon gatherings.

Treatment study responses revealed that freshmen perceived the student registration process at Ohio University to be slow, inefficient, and frustrating to use. As a result, a new student registration system, featuring on-line Touch-Tone registration and degree audit reporting, was implemented.

Freshman retention at Ohio University has improved steadily since 1978. Then, 67 percent of entering freshmen returned to Ohio University as sophomores. Under open admissions, the retention rate increased to 78 percent by 1986. Even with selective admissions policies implemented recently, the 86 percent freshmen-to-sophomore persistence rate is higher than similar figures for peer institutions. One of the reasons for this improved retention is the continual feedback to faculty and staff who provide services to freshmen. Freshmen are especially sensitive to the campus services they receive. Improving the treatment, information, and processes has led to increased freshman satisfaction, involvement, and retention. By expanding the freshman project to a study of all undergraduates, graduate students, and medical students, opportunities for improving the quality of services will be extended to all Ohio University students.

Assessing Student Involvement

A. Michael Williford, Gary O. Moden

CASE 57: OHIO UNIVERSITY

Look for: A questionnaire assessing the involvement of freshmen in academic and social activities. Intervention strategies designed to increase involvement have helped to boost student retention. (Second in a series of three cases about Ohio University.)

Background and Purpose

The Student Involvement Study is another of the several studies in Ohio University's multidimensional Institutional Impact Project, which (as mentioned in the previous case) was developed in 1981 by a task force of Ohio University faculty and staff at the request of the university president. The involvement study first was conducted at Ohio University in 1979, as part of the University of Michigan's Project CHOICE (Center for Helping Organizations Improve Choice in Education). The original questionnaire was revised in 1982 and has been administered annually since then.

Research has shown that in comparison with peers, students who are more involved in activities related to their formal education grow more as individuals, are more satisfied with their education, persist in their education to graduation, and continue their learning after college. Colleges and universities should encourage student involvement on their campuses. One way to do this is to study the phenomenon.

By assessing student involvement, Ohio University identifies one aspect of the university's impact on its undergraduates. Experiences during the freshman year affect students' development and performance throughout college. Indeed, attrition occurs most frequently during the freshman year, and retention programs most often are directed toward freshmen. Involvement studies provide information that is important to retention programs and student development activities.

Method

The Office of Institutional Research, in cooperation with the Office of the Dean of Students, annually conducts the Student Involvement Study. A four-page questionnaire, given to all freshmen living in the residence halls during the spring quarter, collects information on students' academic involvement, social involvement and activities, and commitment to and satisfaction with Ohio University. Questionnaires are distributed and collected by residence hall staff, and the response rate is about 90 percent.

Analysis of questionnaire data has taken three forms: year-to-year analyses of freshman data; longitudinal studies of freshmen and seniors; and analyses of involvement intervention efforts. In the intervention involvement study, responses have been used to identify freshmen who were likely to leave Ohio University for reasons other than academic disqualifications. Various methods of intervention, usually implemented through contacts by residence life staff or faculty, have been developed to assist these students.

Findings

Studies of changes in each freshman class and longitudinal freshman-to-senior studies have shown increases in student involvement over the last decade. It is apparent that involvement is strongly related to the undergraduate educational experience and retention of students at Ohio University. Being involved in the life of the campus, both academically and socially, is important to these students. Most freshmen read a number of books outside of class, and most report using the library. Students take advantage of academic advising, both formally with the academic adviser and informally with other faculty, residence life staff, and other staff. Many freshmen demonstrate interest in faculty research or career-oriented programs.

Students' ratings of commitment to Ohio University have increased over the years of this study. These ratings are important because a positive relationship exists between freshman attitudes toward faculty and students' decisions to return to Ohio University as sophomores.

Freshmen are involved in and are committed to participating in a variety of events and activities that complement their academic programs. Students spend most of their weekends on the campus. They attend cultural events, and they socialize with their peers, both on- and off-campus. They participate in a variety of extracurricular activities, especially intramural athletics, Greek life, residence hall activities, and clubs. Students rate personal adjustment, relationships with other students, and perceptions of the campus environment as more important than getting involved in formal organizations and activities.

The longitudinal involvement study results have shown that positive changes in involvement occur from the freshman to the senior year. In the area of academic involvement, the incidence and frequency of academic contacts increases from the freshman to the senior year, especially contacts with faculty. The incidence and frequency of social contacts with faculty and advisers also increases from the freshman to the senior year. Social involvement increases in some areas but decreases in others. The number of parties attended decreases significantly from the freshman to the senior year, but the number of friends on campus increases. Participation in cultural events and extracurricular activities increases. The importance of graduating from Ohio University and satisfaction with making the right choice in attending Ohio University increases. Some patterns of involvement are established during the freshman year and do not change significantly by the senior year.

For example, study time, the number of social outings with friends, and the number of weekends spent on campus do not change.

Use of Findings

Results from the involvement intervention project reveal that students likely to drop out can be identified while they are still enrolled. In 1983, the provost's office, the dean of student's office, University College, and the Office of Institutional Research devised a plan to identify and intervene with freshmen who had more than a 2.0 GPA and were identified by the involvement study as being at risk.

Beginning in 1991–92, the intervention program for these students was expanded in two ways. In three academic colleges with relatively high female dropout rates, female freshmen with a GPA over 2.0 were asked to complete a brief involvement questionnaire after fall quarter. Then staff from residence life and advisers from the three colleges contacted these potential leavers. In addition, females with a GPA over 2.0 in those colleges identified as having low student academic and social involvement were placed on the intervention list. Findings demonstrate increasingly positive effects of the involvement intervention process. Significantly high numbers of those students identified as potential leavers actually returned the next fall. Early identified females had the highest return rate after three intervention contacts, two in winter quarter (residence life staff and academic advisers) and one in spring quarter.

In 1982, before the intervention program began, 19 percent of all freshmen with a GPA of 2.0 or higher dropped out by their sophomore year. This number was reduced to 9 percent in the 1992 class.

The importance of encouraging students to become involved in campus life has been recognized at Ohio University. We have demonstrated a strong positive relationship between student involvement and academic success. As Ohio University admits and enrolls more academically capable freshmen, academic and student affairs staff are developing new ways to involve and challenge these students.

The Student Development Transcript

R. Dale Bullard

CASE 58: UNIVERSITY OF SOUTH CAROLINA AT SUMTER

Look for: A student development transcript that provides a record of out-of-class experiences designed to promote communication skills; service to campus and community; critical thinking; leadership; and moral, physical, and social development.

Background and Purpose

A student development transcript (SDT) was developed by the student affairs division of the University of South Carolina at Sumter because of two basic beliefs. First, those of us on the student affairs staff believed that as much learning occurs outside the classroom as inside. Second, we believed there was a need for students to see a relationship between their participation in activities or events and their growth and development in important areas of life. We felt that students, in part, believed in the importance of classroom learning because the university maintained an academic transcript of their work. It then seemed logical that a transcript system for recording student growth and development in campus and community activities would also communicate to students the importance of these activities. The SDT system gave credibility to the efforts to engage students in growth experiences outside the classroom.

USC Sumter's mission statement includes these comments: "The University emphasizes the development of the whole person. The institution especially seeks to foster in students the disciplines essential to an educated citizenry. These include the ability to communicate through effective writing and articulate speech, as well as quantitative competence, creative and critical thinking, and the integration of knowledge. Classroom experiences, student activities, and physical education programs provide opportunities for cultural enrichment, leadership development, intellectual growth, and interpersonal relationships contributing to a sense of self-reliance and self-esteem." The SDT system is an effective instrument to document the efforts of the student affairs division to support both the USC Sumter mission statement and student affairs goals.

Additionally, the SDT system was developed to provide a more complete picture of a student's college experience. A student development transcript used in conjunction with an academic transcript can provide greater insight about the student and his or her interests, background, and potential. The SDT was believed to be a tool that would promote lifelong learning, serve as a good assessment tool, and be a valuable resource to students, employers, graduate school admissions officers, and scholarship committees. We also theorized that eventually the process of documenting student participation on a transcript would motivate students to become involved in campus and community life.

Method

The SDT system records student growth and development in nine areas: communication skills, community service, critical thinking, cultural/fine arts, leadership, moral development, physical development, social/interpersonal skills development, and volunteer service to the university. An SDT committee composed of representatives from all areas of student affairs and three student members categorized most of the traditional activities and events that occur both on campus and in the community into these nine growth areas. The committee meets every two weeks and constantly reviews new requests from students, faculty, and staff for inclusion in the SDT system. A brochure is mailed to all new students each semester, describing the SDT system and the activities that qualify for SDT credit. Information is also available at various locations on campus.

Depending on the type of event or activity, we use different methods to verify student participation. To maintain the integrity of the SDT system, USC Sumter does not allow self-reporting by students. The sponsor of an event, a club adviser, or a community organization officer must verify the student's participation on a SDT credit form. All data entry is done in the student records office. A personal computer database system is used instead of a mainframe because the backlog of mainframe programming projects that exists would have meant waiting several years for the project to come to fruition. Like academic transcripts, the SDT transcripts are printed on security paper. Semester SDT reports are mailed to students, and students have thirty days to report any errors.

Findings

The SDT system has received widespread approval from students, faculty, staff, community leaders, business leaders, board of trustee members, the dean of our campus, and the president of the university. One of the major findings is that the original vision for the potential and utilization of the system was too limited. Initially, the primary focus was on recording student participation, but new ideas for utilizing the system to improve the quality of life for students continue to develop. Communication increased between faculty members and student affairs as both groups sought to implement ideas related to the system. Having a system to record nonclassroom growth and developmental experiences caused the campus community in general to be more aware that learning takes place outside the classroom and that there is a relationship between participation and self-development.

Use of Findings

As the vision for the system grew, so did changes in how the information was utilized. First, the academic advisers, who are full-time paid staff, were linked to a read-only screen of the SDT transcript via our campus network system. Advisers now talk to students about both their academic progress in the classroom and what the students are doing or not doing outside the classroom. Looking at both the academic and SDT transcripts can provide advisers with valuable insights into academic, social, and personal situations faced by the student. Improved retention is one objective of linking the advisers to the SDT system. Advisers can also register students for membership in campus student organizations. The adviser sends the registration form to the student life department, which forwards the form to the appropriate student organization, which contacts the student. The process of having student organization information available in adviser offices has provided students with broader and easier access to involvement opportunities with those organizations.

Collection of data became more important as new ways to use the system were developed. Initially, we tracked only the number of users and activities utilized. Now, tracking is done on the number of activities available by term, the reasons for SDT transcript requests (for example, for employers, for oneself, for scholarship applications), and a semester-by-semester comparison of the number of participants for each activity offered. A review of the data after each semester helps the staff think about why participation was or was not adequate in the various categories. Currently, tracking has begun on participation by age, race, and gender. This will enable a determination of whether particular activities are appealing to specific categories of students.

The SDT system has also helped student affairs staff in planning and balancing the activities for students. Staff members request programming plans from all departments on campus. They then sort all planned activities into the nine developmental areas of the SDT. Adjustments and changes are then made to the programming plans of the student affairs division when either duplication or lack of developmental opportunities exists. By including and reviewing as much information as possible about future activities under the nine SDT categories, the student affairs division can plan a better balanced program of growth and developmental opportunities for students.

Success Factors

The SDT system worked because of three factors: need, concern, and positive action. The need, documentation of nonclassroom learning, represented an opportunity to help both the students and the institution. The students were helped because they received credit for the nonclassroom experiences and they learned to see relationships between participation and self-development. The university was helped because it gained an effective assessment instrument for student growth and development. The concern existed because, by their very nature, student affairs professionals care about students and their welfare. The positive action was a result of the decision to act on the idea in the first place. A great idea benefits students only if the initiative is taken to bring the concept to life.

"Worth Doing Badly": A Longitudinal Study of Student Experience

Anita Gandolfo, Russell K. Dean

CASE 59: WEST VIRGINIA UNIVERSITY

Look for: A faculty-designed interview process as part of a longitudinal study of 128 students at a research university. Through self-discovery, faculty learned the importance of a positive campus climate in promoting student development and that involving students in outcomes assessment can contribute to that climate.

Background and Purpose

This activity was principally informed by the West Virginia University (WVU) philosophy of outcomes assessment—and by inexperience. At WVU, our goal is for outcomes assessment to improve the learning of students rather than simply documenting achievement. It seemed logical to us as members of a task force charged with developing a comprehensive assessment plan for the institution to try to find out something about the learning experience of students as a preliminary step in that process. A longitudinal study was initiated as a type of preassessment activity by a group of naïve but well-meaning faculty members, none of whom had any experience with this type of project. It confirms the provocative twist on that old adage, "Anything worth doing is worth doing badly."

Method

Using a preliminary open-ended interview, we recruited 128 freshmen at new student orientation during the summer of 1991. We planned to track their academic development each year through analysis of institutional records and to conduct annual interviews with the students. Task force members were trained in the techniques of open-ended interviewing by an experienced colleague. Since we entered into this project precipitously, with no experience and limited knowledge, we made little attempt to get a representative group of students; we approached students as they completed their course registration and asked if they would speak to us. Serendipitously, our study group of 128 students correlated very closely in gender, race, residence, and high school GPA with the total group of entering students.

Now, we do the analysis of academic development from records each semester and plan our interviews for the second half of the second semester in each academic year. The interview protocol is developed by the task force (now the Assessment Council) and combines at least one open-ended question with questions that we believe will help us in our assessment efforts. For example, in the process of developing an assessment plan for the general education curriculum, we wanted to know whether students had any notion of a coordinated program with specific learning goals or saw only a list of "requirements." Thus, one of our questions in our freshman-year interviews became, "How do you feel about having to take courses outside your major?" Another question—"What has been the greatest help to you in meeting your goals this year?"—was designed to help us learn more about the student support structure. We also asked, "What has been the greatest hindrance to you in achieving your goals?"

Findings

We discovered in this process a rich array of information, some of which is institution-specific, and some of which correlates with national studies. For example, in our analysis of academic work, we confirmed the well-known fact that high school GPA is the strongest predictor of academic success, but we also learned that students from one specific out-of-state location were least successful academically at WVU. Further investigation revealed the fact that this group of students also had the highest rate of residence hall infractions and a high incidence of involvement in judicial matters.

Our interviews indicated that both the strongest support and greatest hindrance for students was the same—peer involvement. Interviewees credited their fellow students with helping them adjust to campus life and acquire effective learning strategies, often simply by confronting these problems together with the interviewees. Students also pointed out, however, that the strong social bonds forged often militated against success in college, as there was always someone who wanted to chat—or party—when a paper was due or an exam was imminent. And students stated that few freshmen have the self-discipline to resist the temptation to abandon the academic for the social. These responses highlighted for us the importance of the campus climate for student success, something we have just recently discovered is well documented in Astin's *What Matters in College?* (1993). The response to our question about required courses outside the major was surprising because, although it confirmed our suspicion that students generally had no concept of any overall purpose to those requirements, it also indicated that they were not unreceptive to the idea of more general learning.

All this was from the first year of our study. Subsequent analysis has given us more valuable information that is beyond the scope of this brief review, but it has shown us that such a study is of enormous benefit in highlighting the value of assessment in providing a knowledge base for policy decisions and for informing the entire assessment project at an institution.

Since our process is rather open ended, most of our outcomes have been unanticipated. Even when our information confirms the anecdotal, there is usually some unanticipated twist that provides valuable new information for us.

Use of Findings

Our first finding was immediately utilized, as we reorganized our recruitment efforts to place less emphasis on the location that was bringing us less able students and more emphasis on an alternative location. The academic profiles have also helped us target the at-risk student, and that information is currently informing retention efforts. Our interviews helped us develop an assessment plan for general education that focuses on improving delivery (by means of faculty development through classroom research) at the same time that it attempts to document student learning. Although the importance of the peer relationship has indicated a direction for our efforts in strengthening the campus climate for entering students, we have not yet developed any workable strategies to make use of that information. One of the greatest benefits of the interview process is that it has shown us the importance of involving students in the assessment process, and this will, we are convinced, foster a more positive campus climate for everyone.

Success Factors

We believe this is a successful activity because it is simple and provides information almost immediately, thus offering the good feedback that all learners appreciate. It certainly takes leadership (someone who is task oriented with good organizational skills), but does not require exceptional talent. It is relatively easy to administer, even in a large school such as ours. Another important aspect of our assessment effort is that it is principally faculty directed, and we believe that was especially significant in this activity. Faculty members have a great deal of unverified information about students, and that background was very useful in structuring this study and analyzing its results.

Exploring Educational Factors That Promote Identity Formation

John F. Van Wicklin

CASE 60: HOUGHTON COLLEGE

Look for: Use of students' identity development, assessed via James Marcia's identity status interview, to alert faculty to the need to identify programs and instructional techniques that promote student exploration of beliefs and goals in the process of making ideological commitments.

Background and Purpose

A study was initiated to explore educational factors associated with identity development in a representative sample of college seniors at Houghton College. Identity formation is a major developmental task of young adulthood, and the college experience can and should assist this process. The goal is to explore educational factors that distinguish students who make progress in identity development from those who do not. As factors are identified, educators can focus attention upon them. Depending upon circumstances and related to educational factors under consideration, this may mean adding new program components or modifying existing ones.

Method

A representative sample of ninety-five seniors (40 percent of the eligible population) at Houghton College was given James Marcia's identity status interview (Marcia, 1980) as well as measures of a number of educational variables, including faculty mentoring, cognitive and learning styles, involvement in student activities, and cross-cultural experience. Most instruments were locally crafted surveys, with the exception of the identity interview and a measure of cognitive and learning styles (Griffith and Chapman, 1982). Although seniors are used in this study, I have conducted other studies on first-year students to establish baselines.

At Houghton College, our work with the identity interview focuses on precrisis and postcrisis identities. Students whose beliefs and goals are either weakly held or not based on a process of personal exploration are precrisis ("identity diffused" or "foreclosed" in Marcia's terms). Students who are engaged in a process of exploration of beliefs and goals or who have ideological commitments based on personal exploration are postcrisis (that is, "identity achieved").

Findings

The major finding is that almost 40 percent of the seniors studied are in a precrisis identity status, suggesting that four years of liberal arts education has done little to assist the process of identity formation. This is compatible with findings cited by Pascarella and Terenzini (1991). They claim that there is modest evidence to suggest that between two-fifths and two-thirds of freshmen enter college and leave four years later with their identities relatively unexamined.

Educational factors significantly associated with precrisis seniors include their having fewer faculty mentors and less involvement in peer discussions than postcrisis seniors, a cognitive style characterized by dualism or multiplicity, a learning style that favors factual classes and multiple-choice tests, and limited cross-cultural experience. Factors related to postcrisis identity include relationships with faculty mentors who help students overcome personal difficulties and challenge them to rethink their position on issues; greater involvement in peer discussions than precrisis students; a cognitive style characterized by relativism or contextualized commitment; a learning style that favors theoretical, issue-oriented courses; a learning style that favors essay tests permitting integration of ideas; and greater cross-cultural experience than precrisis students.

Use of Findings

Using identity development as an outcome measure helps college educators identify programs and techniques that have psychosocial impact. For example, if certain kinds of classroom techniques, faculty mentoring, peer discussions, and cross-cultural experiences are associated with advanced identity development, then these factors warrant careful study. Once specific changes are implemented, one can conduct follow-up assessments of identity development in order to explore institutional progress.

This research is personally exciting because it generates ideas for modifying the educational environment in ways that promote identity development. Here, by way of illustration, are four plausible ideas:

Freshman seminar. Many of our colleges need a credit-bearing course that introduces first-year students to the mission of liberal arts education. In the context of a specific course, faculty can begin to implement objectives that could eventually be extended to the general education curriculum as a whole. The freshman seminar can be a place for active and cooperative learning techniques, faculty mentoring, peer discussions, and the practical application of liberal arts disciplines to real-world issues.

Cross-cultural experience. Perhaps nowhere in a college curriculum can one become as immersed in the critical exploration of diversity as in a course where one lives with native people in different cross-cultural or subcultural settings. College educators should give serious consideration to making this a general education requirement where it does not already exist.

Active and cooperative learning techniques. Educational techniques that encourage students actively to explore different goals and beliefs and that promote engaging discussions of ideas and issues with supportive peers and faculty mentors will promote identity development.

Image papers. As students actively explore alterative goals and beliefs, they are likely to acquire broader images of self and society. Perhaps some students do not improve their images while in college because the process of imagination is not sufficiently conscious and deliberate. The exploration process could be enhanced by having students identify and articulate the images they apprehend, through a sequence of course-embedded activities and exercises. For example, I ask students to write image papers in one of the following four categories, based upon several classes and the associated readings: image development, image refinement, image reversal, or image "busting."

Image papers can be growth-producing not only for students but for faculty as well in that these papers will provide feedback about the images actually reaching students at their levels of understanding. Student papers will refine and improve the professor's images of self and world as well. It would be interesting to determine whether most professors know what images of self and world they convey through a given discipline or through specific courses.

In summary, liberal arts programs of high quality promote identity formation. If large percentages of seniors still possess precrisis (or unexamined) identities, there is plenty of room to improve the educational process. As we successfully identify techniques and experiences that promote identity development, we will in turn be enhancing the quality of our educational programs.

Impact of the University Experience on Students' Values, Attitudes, and Self-Perceptions

Roger C. Loeb

CASE 61: UNIVERSITY OF MICHIGAN-DEARBORN

Look for: A study that monitors a variety of attitudinal and personality variables during students' first two years in college. Results have convinced faculty and student services professionals to offer new multicultural experiences, to increase opportunities for internships and community service, and to improve advising by adding a freshman seminar.

Background and Purpose

Assessment in higher education has focused primarily on the accumulation of academic knowledge and secondarily on measuring the means or process of such accumulation. However, in an era of declining social influence for such cultural institutions as the extended family and the church, it can be argued that much of the responsibility for socialization is being shifted to educational institutions. The contemporary college or university thus may be expected to foster adult development, to nurture mature moral values, to encourage social and political attitudes befitting world community citizens, and to promote aesthetic appreciation and expression. The function of the college is to foster such growth without necessarily determining its direction. But there is little evidence to show whether higher education is meeting the challenge. At the University of Michigan-Dearborn, we decided to select a representative group of new students and to assess a variety of attitudinal and personality variables over time.

Method

Assessment participants were 160 new college students attending a commuter campus. Nearly 90 percent (141) took part in the second phase of the study and approximately 60 percent (95) completed all three phases. The final sample consisted of predominantly (95 percent) full-time students, most of whom (69 percent) were employed at least part-time. Fifteen percent had minority status.

A five-part survey was administered in all three phases. Initially, it was given to all 160 participants in their first two days of classes. They provided personal background information, then answered questions concerning their degree of concern about twenty-three social issues such as AIDS, crime, and mental illness. Next, the students were asked to describe themselves on fifty-three personality traits, using a seven-point Likert scale, and then to describe how they thought their peers (high school peers in phase one, college peers in phases two and three) would rate them on the same traits. Students then assessed the quality of their lives and predicted the quality five years in the future on a "ladder of life" measure. Finally, they described their attitudes toward members of fourteen ethnic, religious, or socially stigmatized groups on seven-point Bogardus social distance scales. Phase two was conducted near the end of the students' first college semester; phase three utilized a mailing to all of the students still attending the university, midway through the second semester of their second year. Telephone follow-ups encouraged participation.

Findings

Students demonstrated substantial drops in reported social distance (less prejudicial views) over time toward most of the groups examined, such as Arab Americans, individuals in wheelchairs, and mentally ill or developmentally disabled persons.

Much of this change occurred within the first semester, but the pattern continued over the two-year span of the study. Changes in attitudes concerning social problems were less widespread and took place more slowly. Greater concern about environmental and political/governmental issues emerged during the two years examined.

The students' descriptions of personality characteristics were more resistant to change. There was a pattern, however, in which certain positive traits (energetic, friendly, important, reliable, and trusting) dropped after one semester, only to return to original levels by late in the students' second year. We had not anticipated the apparent drop in self-esteem or self-confidence that occurred during the first semester of college, but it provided the stimulus for reviewing the program and services offered to new students.

Use of Findings

Although students demonstrated a desirable decrease in prejudicial attitudes, faculty do not consider their role in this area as complete. Multicultural experiences are being developed and expanded throughout the university. A section on diversity has been added to freshman orientation. A conscious effort is made to reflect diversity, including such perspectives as sexual preference and disabilities, in all cultural activities. Ethnic organizations for Native Americans, Hispanics, African Americans, Arab Americans, and Asian Americans are actively supported.

Encouragement for the emerging social concerns is provided through such programs as environmental studies (supported by the Dearborn Naturalist Association); political internships (including ones in Washington, D. C., and Ottawa, Canada); and other internship and cooperative educational opportunities in mental hospitals, probation departments, hospices, and child abuse programs. On

Martin Luther King Day, classes are canceled and students are provided with a wide range of one-day volunteer opportunities. Two other programs developed recently are Students Against Violence to the Environment and the Student Coalition Against Hunger and Homelessness.

To help new students with the adjustment to college, our advising efforts are focusing on freshmen. A freshman seminar has been developed to help new students learn their way around the university and to develop academic skills. A volunteer experience is a component of this program. We are currently working on a midterm progress report that will enable faculty to give students early warning and guidance for potential academic difficulties. Finally, the Program of Academic Support is provided for students with weaker academic preparation.

Measuring Effectiveness in Student Development Services

Jo Ellen Cantrell

CASE 62: SPARTANBURG TECHNICAL COLLEGE

Look for: Use of thirty-five effectiveness indicators that permit every department in student development services to assess its effectiveness, track quality, and make improvements. The indicators assess effectiveness of operations as well as student satisfaction.

Background and Purpose

Accountability has been a major movement in higher education in this country and also in the technical college system in South Carolina. In 1989, the student services division at Spartanburg Technical College began pursuing quality in its efforts to become a model student development program. As the division began discussing quality in student development services, questions began to surface. How do we define quality? How do we know we are being effective in providing services to students and prospective students? What are our specific goals for improvement? How do we know when we improve?

Method

In the student services division, thirty-five effectiveness indicators are used to determine the quality of services provided to prospective students, enrolled students, and graduates. Indicators measure quality in admissions, counseling, student support services, the women's center, financial aid, job placement, student activities, and career planning services.

Each department in student development services defined specific measurable indicators of effectiveness to use as benchmarks for tracking quality and making improvements in services offered. Developing a set of measurable effectiveness indicators was a lengthy process (a minimum of nine months), in part because the measures had to be ones that we could implement efficiently and accurately. Each department chose several indicators that would measure the effectiveness of internal operations as well as customer satisfaction.

Each effectiveness indicator had to be measurable, with a description of the measurement method, results of measurement recorded periodically and reported annually, a goal established for improvement, and an annual evaluation with improvement opportunities developed where appropriate. The goals for improvement were included in the division's annual planning process.

Examples of indicators developed include the following:

Counseling Department. *Indicator.* The number of customers seen by counselors who felt that services received were effective or not effective, as a percent of the number of customers surveyed.

Description of measurement used. The Counselors' Evaluation Form was given to applicants who scheduled an appointment for test interpretation and/or career counseling. A monthly summary report was submitted to the dean of students. Data are compared to results from the previous year.

Measurement of results. Statistical data show results of the research completed. Students' responses revealed a need for improvement in the way employment opportunities are explained to prospective students.

Goal for improvement. The goal is to increase the percentage of strong agreement for the characteristic "explained employment opportunities."

Evaluation and implications of measurement results. For 1991–92, the level of strong agreement for "explained employment opportunities" was 58.5 percent. For 1992–93, the level increased to 70.1 percent. Counselors participated in in-service training on labor market trends presented by the Employment Services Commission. The training appears to have been effective, since customer satisfaction increased more than 10 percent the following year.

Financial Aid Department. *Indicator.* Number of errors made in student financial aid records as a percent of the files audited each term.

Description of measurement used. An audit instrument was developed based on the audit requirements of the Department of Education. Two audits were completed in the 1990–91 and 1991–92 award years. These files comprised a 10 percent sample of the active files for two quarters each year.

Measurement results.

Error rate in 1990–91 files: 19 percent

Error rate in 1991–92 files: 5.4 percent

Error rate in 1992–93 files: 5.9 percent

Goal or target for improvement. The goal is an error rate of less than 5 percent for the audits conducted in 1993–94.

Evaluation and implications of measurement results. The errors discovered in each year were reviewed by type and frequency. Training was conducted for financial aid staff on specific ways to correct previous errors. This training resulted in almost a 20 percent reduction in errors the first year. The error rate increased slightly with new regulations and turnover in personnel. More training was scheduled to decrease errors to the goal rate of less than 5 percent.

Findings

Two years of measuring results of effectiveness indicators in student services has benefited the division by (1) providing objective measures of quality that reflect the health of each department; (2) giving obvious warning signals when results are below goals set or previous performance; and (3) assisting the department in developing prescriptive remedies to improve performance.

Since this was their first real effort to measure quality in an objective manner, student services staff were unsure what the results would reflect. The first-year indicators provided numbers and percentages that were to be benchmarks for future comparison and did not hold any significance by themselves. Some departments were surprised that the error rate was higher or the participation rate lower than anticipated. Customer satisfaction survey results were extremely positive and confirmed that student services' staff were customer oriented. Overall, student services departments see effectiveness indicators as built-in thermometers that can be used to measure the quality of their performance consistently.

Use of Findings

Every department in student services has been able to make improvements or to confirm the quality of services provided as the result of implementing measurable performance indicators. The admissions department has improved the process of giving the skills assessment to applicants for student admission; counseling staff have improved the quality of career information provided; job placement services are undergoing major surgery to improve services; and student activities have been redesigned based on customer guidance.

As shown in the previous two examples of quality indicators, the financial aid and counseling departments were able to provide training for staff to improve performance and reduce errors. Objective measurement using an audit and input from customers enabled staff to identify problem areas. If these two departments had not measured the quality of their efforts, errors might have continued, with staff holding a false sense of their ability to provide accurate and effective service.

Being able to measure effectiveness in student services has given the division great pride in its job performance. If anyone asks, "How do you know your department is effective?" student services staff at Spartanburg Technical College can show him or her!

Success Factors

Developing effectiveness indicators and measuring results are successes in student services at Spartanburg Technical College because the staff are focused on quality improvement and have a genuine concern for student success. The staff in this student services division are risk takers and are willing to try innovative strategies if they benefit the students.

Applying Alumni Assessment Research to Academic Decision Making

Gary O. Moden, A. Michael Williford

CASE 63: OHIO UNIVERSITY

Look for: A general alumni survey with questions added by individual colleges that has produced improvements in the colleges. Sustained attention to survey results by trustees, the president, and deans has ensured that the data will be used to make improvements. (Third in a series of three cases about Ohio University.)

Background and Purpose

Ohio University has made an institutional commitment to use alumni research in program review, curriculum planning, academic program planning, and student assessment. This is part of a commitment at Ohio University to assess the institution's impact on its students. An institutional impact task force of faculty and staff was appointed in 1981 to develop a coherent, systematic, and ongoing assessment program. The primary goal of the assessment was to enable the university, in five to ten years, to describe systematically what was happening in its life as an educational institution.

Method

Earlier efforts in collecting alumni information had not been successful because different academic colleges and departments used different instruments. While information collected from such surveys could be used within departments, the surveys did not allow for interdepartmental comparisons. To counter this problem, a new instrument was designed to study graduates after they had been away from the university for at least five years. The questionnaire was divided into three major sections.

The first section asks about such traditional outcomes as type of job, employment status, salary, employment satisfaction, relevance of educational experience to employment, and problems in seeking employment. Another group of questions inquires about various competencies needed for success. These questions ask respondents to evaluate fourteen different competencies in terms of whether they are needed and the extent to which each was developed at the university. The competencies include such items as the ability to think analytically, apply knowledge from the major field to new problems, acquire new skills and understanding, write well, and communicate orally.

The second section asks about programs of study and about satisfaction with undergraduate programs at Ohio University. Alumni are asked to rate undergraduate major programs on such items as academic advising, level of rigor and scholarship, interaction with faculty, quality of instruction, and career planning and placement associated with their majors.

Staff from the institutional research office worked with each of the eight academic undergraduate colleges of the University College in designing the third section of the questionnaire, which contains college-specific questions. The section for the College of Arts and Sciences includes items on student services and non-major course requirements. The College of Business Administration has developed items on teaching and advising and asks about participation in student organizations. The College of Education asks thirty-seven questions about needed competencies. The College of Engineering asks about academic programs, availability and quality of equipment, and nonmajor course requirements. The College of Fine Arts uses items on employment opportunities and career preparation in the arts. The College of Health and Human Services poses questions about continuing education after graduation, participation in professional organizations, use of microcomputers, and contacts with prospective students. The University College (general education) section asks questions about requirements, student services, and evaluation of the degree in general studies.

Findings and Their Use

Reports on alumni research are presented to the dean's council on a regular basis, and information from these reports is incorporated into decision making. In addition, each college receives its own personalized report, designed to meet specific information needs.

The academic colleges have used the survey results to develop a number of programs and evaluate different curricular options. For example, College of Arts and Sciences faculty were concerned about student perceptions of the college's numerous course requirements that are in addition to general education requirements. Responses from alumni led to the conclusion that this required coursework was important to the arts and sciences curriculum and was quite relevant to graduates' careers.

The College of Arts and Sciences also used the survey findings to develop a new awards program. Because information from the open-ended questions led to the conclusion that particular faculty had been extremely influential in graduates' personal development, the college instituted an awards program for faculty. Part of the information used for awards selection comes directly from the open-ended questions.

The College of Business reviewed the alumni data in the aggregate for the college, and in certain particulars for each academic department within the college, to identify specific strengths and weaknesses of each academic unit. Alumni reported that they had not had enough contact with business executives while they were in their undergraduate programs. In response, the college developed the Executives on Campus Program, through which active business executives regularly visit the college and take an active role in undergraduate instruction.

Business graduates also reported a need to sharpen their writing skills. As a consequence, the college emphasized writing skills by changing courses to incorporate more written assignments, papers, and essays. In addition, multiple-choice tests were replaced, whenever possible, by essay examinations.

Information about the recruitment process is used heavily by the College of Communication. Because most communication majors are first-generation academics in the field, they and their families lack understanding about the career paths of communication graduates. For example, parents of entering students often ask, "What types of jobs can a person get with a degree in communication?" Alumni research is used extensively in planning recruitment programs for new students and precollege orientation programs for parents and students that describe career paths, salaries, and examples of professional success of graduates of the College of Communication.

Application of alumni research in the College of Engineering assisted the dean and external advisory board in developing a college plan for the 1990s. This process required an extensive scan of both the internal and external environments. The alumni data collected by the institutional research office became an important part of that study by providing information about the strengths of graduates in a volatile market for engineers.

Involvement of alumni stemming from the alumni research project led directly to a change in the curriculum of the College of Engineering. A member of Ohio University's national alumni board who was also an engineering graduate became involved with the college after reading the annual report on alumni generated by the institutional research office. The board member noted that while engineering graduates had given very high evaluations to the engineering program, they had also reported a lack of training in broad interpersonal communication in their undergraduate major. As a result of this finding, the board member met with the engineering dean to discuss ways to incorporate more training in interpersonal communication in the engineering curriculum.

In the College of Health and Human Services, alumni research is used in program review to document the strengths and needs of academic programs. This documentation is crucial since all university academic programs are reviewed every five years. Each department in the college develops profiles of its graduates to document their success, the quality of their preparation, and their ratings of the department's academic program.

Success Factors

Alumni research collects both general and program-specific information, often simultaneously. The key to using these data successfully is flexibility in meeting and melding a variety of information needs. Through careful coordination with many campus constituencies, this information has been applied to a variety of programs. The colleges, planning groups, individual departments, and university trustees have come to rely on information provided in the alumni research program and use it in both near-term and long-term planning and decision making at Ohio University.

CHAPTER FOURTEEN

ASSESSMENT AT THE CLASSROOM LEVEL

Chapter Guide

The chapter guide lists the cases contained in this chapter by institution, by subject area, and by assessment method. Institutions are organized by Carnegie Classification. The location of each institution and its approximate enrollment follow the institution name. The relevant case numbers follow each entry.

Institutions

Subject Areas

Assessment Methods

Chapter Overview

As the preface to this book makes abundantly clear, federal and state officials, members of coordinating and governing boards, and accreditors are asking for evidence that institutions of higher education are accountable for their use of resources. Decision makers in these sectors would be most satisfied—and relieved—if colleges and universities could answer questions about accountability with reports containing a few numbers based on objective measures that everyone could agree are both appropriate and reliable.

Administrators and faculty, in contrast, point with pride to the diversity in American higher education as one of the institution's greatest strengths, and argue that the complexity of student learning and other outcomes cannot and should not be reduced to a few numbers. Moreover, they say that decisions regarding levels of quality and directions for improvement must be based not on a few so-called objective measures but on a rich array of qualitative as well as quantitative data collected and applied locally.

Both sides can agree that student learning begins in the classroom. Improvement in the most important outcome of higher education—student performance—cannot take place if there is no change in the teaching or amount of learning that takes place in individual classrooms across the country.

This chapter contains examples of assessment practice that can be used to improve teaching and learning in individual classes. The first example (Case 64) illustrates how Primary Trait Scoring, a technique developed to score the student essays collected as part of the National Assessment of Educational Progress, can be used to make classroom grading more explicit and systematic and thus more comparable from one class to another and more meaningful to external publics.

The second example (Case 65) offers methods for encouraging students to engage in self-assessment as they make selections of materials for inclusion in a portfolio. Case 66 suggests how students' reflections on portfolio materials can help them relate coursework to their career objectives.

The fast-feedback forms created by the authors of Case 67 enable students to assess an instructor's teaching style and other factors that facilitate or impede learning. The forms, which may be used at the end of each day, week, or topic, enable instructors to make immediate adjustments in teaching that may increase student learning. Case 68 also suggests a simple technique that any teacher might use to help students improve their learning in a given class: ask students to provide answers to the question, "What can I do to improve my performance in this course?"

Case 69 illustrates the use of quality-improvement strategies in the classroom. Students form teams and provide formative evaluation of teaching and learning that the instructor can use to make immediate improvements.

Making Traditional Graded Tests and Assignments Serve Contemporary Needs for Assessment

Barbara E. Walvoord, Virginia Johnson Anderson, John R. Breihan, Lucille Parkinson McCarthy, Susan Miller Robison, A. Kimbrough Sherman

CASE 64: UNIVERSITY OF CINCINNATI AND MORE THAN 200 NORTH AMERICAN COLLEGES AND UNIVERSITIES

Look for: Application of a national assessment procedure, primary trait scoring, to make traditional classroom graded work serve outcomes assessment purposes. Expected student outcomes and the criteria for outcome assessment are thus more public and more comparable across classrooms.

Background and Purpose

The authors have adapted national scoring procedures to make traditional classroom graded work serve modern assessment needs. By making grading criteria and procedures more explicit and systematic and more informed by current research and practice in assessment, we hope to make outcomes and the criteria for their assessment more public and more comparable from one classroom to another.

Method

To give classroom graded work the characteristics just described, the authors have used a national assessment technique, primary trait scoring (PTS), for their own classroom tests and assignments and have taught PTS in workshops to faculty at other institutions. PTS was developed to score the essays of the National Assessment of Educational Progress (Lloyd-Jones, 1977).

In PTS, the teacher, using past student papers if available, first identifies the "traits" necessary for success in a particular assignment. For instance, for a biology assignment in which her students designed, carried out, and wrote up their own scientific experiments, Anderson identified as important these traits: title, introduction, scientific format, methods and materials section, handling of nonexperimental information, design of the experiment, operational definitions, control of variables, collection of data and communication of results, and interpretation of data. Under each trait, the teacher composes a three- to five-point rating scale. For example, under "methods and materials," Anderson defined a 5 (the highest score) in this way: "Contains effectively, quantifiably, concisely organized information that allows the experiment to be replicated; is written so that all information inherent to the document can be related back to this section; identifies sources of all data to be collected; identifies sequential information in an appropriate chronology; does not use unnecessary, wordy descriptions of procedures." A score of 1 is defined this way: "Describes the experiment so poorly or in such a nonscientific way that it cannot be replicated."

The intermediate scores are also defined. The student can then be awarded a score under each trait and a composite score with the traits weighted. A teacher who develops such a scale has made traditional grading very explicit and systematic.

To expand the benefits, we recommend that PTS be taught in workshops, where faculty state their course objectives, make sure their major graded tests and assignments are likely both to teach and to test those objectives, and then construct PTS scales for those tests and assignments, constantly sharing their work with each other and, thus, opening graded work to the influence of current research and of colleague feedback. The authors have led such workshops for faculty across the country.

Findings and Their Use

The power of PTS lies not only in making assessment more explicit, systematic, informed, and public but also in informing the entire teaching and learning process, as documented in our study *Thinking and Writing in College: A Naturalistic Study of Students in Four Disciplines* (Walvoord and others, 1991). For example, Breihan gives his history students a checksheet for their argumentative essays that is derived from PTS but simplified. A grade of A is defined in this way: "The paper adequately states and defends an argument and answers all counterarguments and counterexamples suggested by lecture, reading assignments (specific arguments and authors are mentioned by name), and common sense." Knowing specifically what he values most, Breihan now can plan instruction to help his students learn these skills. Further, students know what is expected and can take responsibility for their own progress.

A teacher can also use PTS as a classroom research instrument to compare the performance of students in one class with that of students in another, as Anderson did in our 1991 study, to investigate whether students performed better after she had made pedagogical changes.

Even when teachers are introduced to PTS during a two- to three-day workshop, where they do not have the time or the samples of student work to construct an entire scale, many faculty can make their assessment process more systematic, criteria more explicit, and teaching more helpful to students. These outcomes are documented by teacher reports and supporting examples of assessment instruments from eleven faculty from Whitworth College in Spokane after their participation in Walvoord's workshop (Hunt, 1992.)

Further, PTS has wider applications only beginning to be realized. First, assessment skills—stating desired outcomes and criteria in very explicit terms—developed in individual classrooms can also be applied to assessment programs in an entire department, program, or college. Second, comparisons can be made among various courses. For example, after examining faculty PTS scoring scales for papers in general education courses, an institution could say to its publics, "X percent of our general education courses award students a passing grade when the students can define a problem, analyze causes of the problem, weigh various solutions, and present a rationale for the one they recommend."

In addition to permitting "bottom-line" assurances such as the preceding, PTS scales, with their designation of levels of performance, would allow an institution to publicize the percentage of its students who achieved at various levels on such problem-solving assignments. Such a system would facilitate tracking student performance over time and allow at least rough comparisons among the standards for students in various settings.

An advantage of PTS for such public uses is that results can be expressed only as descriptions of the skills being required, not as single, context-free numerical scores that can too easily be used beyond their limits for high-stakes decisions. More research is needed on how to make such descriptive results most understandable to the public.

Assessment for Learner Empowerment: The Meta-Cognitive Map

Gary M. Shulman, David L. Luechauer, Carol Shulman

CASE 65: MIAMI UNIVERSITY AND BUTLER UNIVERSITY

Look for: A meta-cognitive map that faculty can use to show students what they will learn in a course at what level of cognitive complexity. When coupled with a student portfolio, the map enables students to demonstrate how they have fulfilled faculty expectations. This technique is being implemented in communications courses at Miami University.

Background and Purpose

We believe that excellence in teaching and learning occurs when both faculty and students are cooperatively engaged and actively involved in the educational process. In this context, "empowerment" refers to the sharing of control in the teaching-learning process. Empowering faculty develop or use methods that facilitate student ownership of learning, commitment, independence, creativity, excitement, and intrinsic motivation. Empowered learners feel (1) that they are "pulled" by the course content, rather than "pushed" by faculty or grades, and (2) that their learning performance is primarily in their own hands.

Combining a meta-cognitive map with a student portfolio assignment involves the learner in self-assessment while it simultaneously contributes to an empowered teaching-learning environment. Students are thus empowered to be responsible for creating evidence of their learning and assessing the type of learning taking place. Accountability is demonstrated by the supporting materials, or learning manifestations, included in the portfolio. In addition to course content, students learn about how they learn by taking ownership of the process. By assessing the meta-cognitive maps of peers, students learn about different learning styles and how to give constructive feedback. Thus, the maps serve as guides for assessing the students' portfolios.

Method

Central to our empowerment strategy is the meta-cognitive map. It is prepared in advance of the course by faculty and completed throughout the term by students. Faculty outline course content by listing general learning objectives and specific learning outcomes in the first two columns (see Exhibit 14.1, an abbreviated version of the map that would be used for an actual course). For example, identifying strategies for gaining attention in the introduction of a speech might be a general learning objective for a public speaking course. That objective would be

EXHIBIT 14.1. META-COGNITIVE MAP.

Learner: _____ **Course:** _____

Shaded area below indicates expected classification for each learning outcome

General Learning Objectives	Specific Learning Outcomes	Learning Classification			
		Recall	Understand	Apply	Evaluate
Fill-in by Instructor	*Fill-in by Instructor*				

Source: Adapted from workshop materials prepared by David P. Langford and Myron Tribus.

listed in the first column. Several specific outcomes for that objective (for example, including a quotation, startling statistic, anecdote, and humor) might be listed in the second column. Adapting Bloom's taxonomy (1956), faculty then indicate the target level of learning (that is, recall, understand, apply, or evaluate) for each outcome by lightly shading in the corresponding cells on the map. Students are given the map, which provides a content overview of the course and learning expectations, at the beginning of the term. Although faculty determine what is to be learned, students share control over how learning is to be demonstrated.

The choice of performance examples to include in the portfolio is the means by which the student documents personal learning. The student decides how to demonstrate the expected level of learning in the portfolio by choosing documentation examples that support each of the specific outcomes listed on the map.

Students aim for learning target levels represented by the shaded cells on the map. Using a portfolio entry cover sheet (see Exhibit 14.2), students sequentially number each of the products (for example, tests, journal entries, papers, projects, faculty or peer performance critiques) of their learning that will be included in the portfolio. They also provide on the cover sheet a brief description of each portfolio document and an explanation specifying the type of learning they achieved for the learning outcome(s) represented by the entry. The cover sheet entry number is referenced on the corresponding cells of the map, thus visually linking the learning classification (recall, understand, apply, evaluate) and specific learning outcomes to portfolio exhibits or documentation.

To illustrate, a speech might demonstrate learning at various levels for several different specific learning outcomes. A cover sheet attached to the speech outline would describe which specific outcomes and corresponding levels of learning are represented by each portfolio entry. The corresponding entry number derived from the cover sheet would be written on the appropriate cell of the meta-cognitive map by the student. If the student used a joke to begin the speech, she or he would write the entry number for the outline under the "apply" column next to the specific learning outcome "humor" on the map. Other cells representing different elements of the speech (for example, the conclusion or the use of supporting material) are also linked to appropriate levels of learning, using the same entry number. This process provides a convenient cross-reference system for assessing course learning and takes into account that multiple-learning outcomes might be derived from a given performance. Consequently, documents in the portfolio

EXHIBIT 14.2. PORTFOLIO ENTRY COVER SHEET.

Learner: _____ **Date:** _____ **Entry #:** __

Entry description/Overview

Specific Learning Outcome(s)	Learning Classification Target	Explanation
Identified from Map Above	*Self-Assessed by Student*	

Peer assessor: _____ **Date:** _____

Peer feedback: (To what extent does this entry meet learning classification target expectations? [Shaded area on map.])

appear more logical because they are placed in a broader learning framework. The map facilitates communication between faculty and students by guiding and prompting a learning rationale for items included in the portfolio.

Findings

Once students become aware of what we mean by types of learning, we ask them to think about these as they apply to class performance. The meta-cognitive map reinforces the idea that ultimately the student must take responsibility for his or her learning. The first step in taking responsibility is to assess one's own behavior. We are trying to reduce the student's dependence on the faculty for rewards (grades) and have the student develop the ability to reward himself or herself. Students also realize that they have the opportunity to influence the facilitator's evaluation of their performance. By giving students this opportunity, we believe that we are encouraging them to judge the quality of their learning. The underlying assumption is that the success or failure of one's life is largely dependent on one's willingness to evaluate the quality of one's performance. Students can resolve to improve their performance if they find it deficient.

Students are typically amazed that they are trusted to make self- and peer assessments. We find that they rise to the occasion once there is alignment between faculty and student goals. The notion of having concrete evidence of learning (the portfolio) that can be readily communicated via the meta-cognitive map to others, such as parents and potential employers, encourages serious involvement in the process. Students also take ownership for their class behavior because they are involved in the assessment process. Because they monitor their own behavior regularly, students can see when they need to work on process improvements to effect changes in their learning.

This approach supports the creation of challenging and stimulating classes that increase student feelings of ownership, self-efficacy, and motivation. The combining of the meta-cognitive map and the portfolio entry cover sheet with the student portfolio assignment allows students to own their learning of the expected course outcome and encourages a substantial majority of them to perform high-quality work. We believe that this approach can be used by other faculty to involve students actively in managing their learning.

Use of Findings

Teaching should be evaluated in the context of learning. Therefore, we recommend that the student learning portfolio be used to complement the faculty teaching portfolio. Assessment of the teacher's portfolio for what was taught can be enhanced with a perspective that takes into account the student's portfolio of what was learned. The documented degree of congruence between teacher learning goals and student learning performance provides powerful subjective and objective feedback for continuously improving the teaching-learning process.

Success Factors

This activity works because it encourages students to become learning oriented rather than grade oriented. The meta-cognitive map allows students to manage their own learning and easily keep track of their progress. The process encourages them to make a habit of self-assessment. The structure of the map provides flexibility and creativity by allowing students to justify how various entries might fulfill course learning expectations. By promoting personal meaningfulness and commitment to learning, this activity aligns student and faculty goals for each course.

The Portfolio as a Course Assessment Tool

Carolee G. Jones

CASE 66: BALL STATE UNIVERSITY

Look for: A detailed explanation of the introduction of a portfolio, with a reflective essay as a key component, as an assessment tool in a single course. A simple portfolio evaluation tool is included.

Background and Purpose

An assessment portfolio is an organized, systematic presentation of evidence used by the teacher and student to monitor the growth of the student's knowledge of content, use of strategies, and attitudes toward the accomplishment of goals. I decided to include a portfolio in a sophomore business communications class, as one of my tools for assessing student development of communication skills. The purpose was to provide an opportunity for students to begin to assess their own communication development, to make them aware of the need for communication skills in the work world, and to help them identify a plan for improving their ability to communicate.

Method

The portfolio assignment was introduced at the beginning of the semester, and as activities were executed in class, the possibility of their inclusion in the portfolio was discussed. About three weeks later, a more extensive discussion was conducted about potential content and ways to organize the material. Then students were assigned the task of preparing an outline of expected content. Options included developing a portfolio that focused only on work prepared for the current course or a portfolio that included previous communication activities so that progress over a longer period of time could be reviewed.

Regardless of the choice made, a key component of the portfolio was a reflective essay. The essay began with a brief introduction identifying its purpose and any or all facets of communication that would be discussed. In the body of the essay, students reflected on their strengths in each of the identified areas and reported on the activities and circumstances that were responsible for development. The summary also included conclusions they drew about the relation of their communication skill to their anticipated career choice.

The preferred method of organization was placing the reflective essay first, followed by an appendix that documented and supported statements made in the essay. Examples of previous work were displayed to demonstrate the expected format and content. Here is one excerpt from a student's essay about communication skill development in the class:

> One of the skills I have developed in the business communications class is the ability to work with people. We were introduced to concepts of group communication and asked to use these concepts in different kinds of group situations. On page 5 of the appendix, I have included a journal of the types of activities conducted and my reactions to the events. Included also are some of the problems I encountered and the ways in which I dealt with them. For instance, our group included an individual who was very shy. I found this to be a frustrating experience at first; however, I worked diligently at seeking ways to make her comfortable. As a result, she gradually began to contribute.

Since the purpose of the reflective essay is to provide an opportunity for students to determine what the course means to them individually, it is important to promote the idea of multiple options for reporting. But an important factor in selecting the method of portfolio presentation is deciding which method will be easiest for the reader (in this case the teacher) to understand. For example, students discussed the possibility of including videotapes and decided that a summary of the tape with a note that it was available could be included.

Evaluation of the portfolio was discussed to alert students to assessment criteria. Determining benchmarks for evaluation was a primary concern. This was an excellent opportunity to use advisory committee members or other knowledgeable members of the business community to set the standards. Doing so provided an opportunity to get realistic, practical input. Another suggestion is to use team evaluation, capitalizing on the strengths of department members.

Regardless of the method or members used for assessment purposes, clearly defined criteria are critical and must be identified. Based on feedback from previous students, I decided to use the format shown in Exhibit 14.3 in the business communications class.

Findings

Student resistance to an unfamiliar activity was anticipated. During midsemester evaluation time, when students provide feedback to the instructor about how the course is developing, this assignment was identified as a source of frustra-

EXHIBIT 14.3. CRITERIA FOR PORTFOLIO EVALUATION.

PORTFOLIO EVALUATION

Your portfolio can earn a potential 50 points. These 50 points are allocated as follows:

Organization (15 points)
Presentation is logical	1 2 3 4 5
Appendix and introductory statement are coordinated	1 2 3 4 5
Coherence is apparent	1 2 3 4 5
Total	_____

Content (15 points)
Selection of items included is appropriate	1 2 3 4 5
Examples demonstrate overall communication ability	1 2 3 4 5
Examples effectively support specific ability identified	1 2 3 4 5
Total	_____

Presentation (10 points)
Items are mechanically correct	1 2 3 4 5
Appearance is professional	1 2 3 4 5
Total	_____

Overall Effect (10 points)
Impact on the evaluator	1 2 3 4 5
Total	_____

Total Points Earned _____

By Linda Annis and Carolee Jones, Chapter Fifteen, p. 188, in Seldin and Associates, *Improving College Teaching,* Bolton, MA: Anker Publishing, 1995. Reprinted by permission.

tion. In class discussion, students recognized that their inability to relate the assignment to any similar previous experience was the basis for their concern. Once they understood the process that would be used to lead them through the reflective essay, they felt more comfortable about the assignment.

At the end of the semester, the portfolio assignment was described as a gratifying experience for the students, as reflected in one student's comments that "this class provided an opportunity for me to think about an important skill required in my career. For the first time in my life, I began to see the value of my assignments and how they connected to my future. I wish more teachers would require portfolios."

Use of Findings

From the instructor's point of view, planning for classroom activities in relationship to the real world was the most obvious enhancement. Discussions of the worth of these activities elicited personal experiences from students and thereby expanded the potential for a smooth school-to-work transition. The benefits to students from this emphasis on bridging the school-to-work gap were significant as students were continually confronted with the connection between what they were learning and how they would apply this learning to their respective career choices.

Success Factors

Planning an activity of this type requires a great deal of preliminary reading and thinking. Anticipating problems and questions provided a solid framework for this developing model. The key factor in the success of this assignment, however, was carefully introducing the concept to students in stages and guiding students through the process in a systematic way. The more students saw the relationship between their coursework and their career objective, the more enthusiastic they became about the portfolio. Assigning a portfolio without a careful step-by-step process of explaining it throughout the semester can lead to extreme frustration.

As in all plans for assessment, more than one tool should be used to determine a student's level of success. However, the power of the portfolio for encouraging students to interact with and interpret their own growth process, as well as for improving instruction, makes it a very significant contribution to education.

Fast Feedback Permits Students to Assess Faculty Performance

David L. Luechauer, Gary M. Shulman

CASE 67: BUTLER UNIVERSITY AND MIAMI UNIVERSITY

Look for: A fast-feedback form that permits students to assess instructor performance continually. Use of the form produces suggestions for immediate improvements in instruction.

Background and Purpose

We had a colleague who was disappointed to find out that only two of eighteen students could solve a "creativity" problem on his exam less than a week after he delivered three inspired lectures on the theory, needs, methods, and importance of creativity. Another was disappointed in the quality of the final exam essays she received, even though she gave only multiple-choice tests during the semester. The irony is that both of these people spoke at length about how their "assessments" indicated significant deficiencies in students' creative problem solving and writing skills. Thus, a virtual paradox was created for the students. Faculty espoused a need and desire to see one set of behaviors yet they modeled and enacted another set. It should have come as no surprise that the students responded to the behavior which was modeled rather than that which was espoused.

Method

We have developed a method that forces faculty to ask and answer the question, "Am I doing what is necessary to prepare my students to perform the behaviors upon which the institution, department, or I will later assess them?" This method empowers students to challenge both the insights and the methods presented by dominant orthodoxies and breaks the essentially competitive or hierarchical results-oriented dynamic that is built into the traditional classroom experience.

We have created "fast-feedback" forms that can be distributed to and filled out by students at the end of each day, week, or topic (see Exhibit 14.4, a sample of a fast-feedback form for an organizational behavior class). The form may be completed in the last five minutes of class or taken home and turned in at the next

EXHIBIT 14.4. FAST-FEEDBACK FORM.

The following is designed to help shed some light on processes that may help or hinder our understanding of the concepts we study. Please be honest in your answers—they are in no way related to your grade. Feel free to write on the back if necessary.

	Strongly Disagree					Strongly Agree
Personal Evaluation							
I did all my readings prior to class.	1	2	3	4	5	6	7
I wrote questions/comments I had about the readings before class.	1	2	3	4	5	6	7
I actively participated in class exercises and discussions.	1	2	3	4	5	6	7
I thought about how the readings applied to my life/job/ and so on.	1	2	3	4	5	6	7

Comments about the readings for this topic:

Session Evaluation

The stimuli (for example, exercise/film/and so on) were linked well to the readings.	1	2	3	4	5	6	7
The stimuli were well prepared, organized, and easy to follow.	1	2	3	4	5	6	7
It was clear to me why we were engaging in the stimuli.	1	2	3	4	5	6	7
The stimuli helped me understand the topic better.	1	2	3	4	5	6	7
I had "fun" while learning about this topic.	1	2	3	4	5	6	7
There was a good balance between theory and application of this topic.	1	2	3	4	5	6	7

Any comments, ideas, or suggestions for how to improve the coverage of this topic:

Facilitator

David seemed genuinely concerned about how the class performed.	1	2	3	4	5	6	7
David encouraged us to ask questions and answered them well.	1	2	3	4	5	6	7
David seemed knowledgeable about the material.	1	2	3	4	5	6	7
David is approachable and easy to talk to.	1	2	3	4	5	6	7

Final comments, questions, or suggestions regarding class that you would like to tell David:

class session. We created the forms to assess our instructional style and other factors that might facilitate or impede student learning of the concepts we cover in our classes. The forms focus on the topic's approachability, the instructor's encouraging questions and concern for student performance, the applicability of the content to real life issues, and the suitability of the experiential learning activities we use. Additionally, they assess student levels of preparation and factors that may influence student efforts. Finally, we leave space for students to write questions, comments, or suggestions. In short, the forms provide fast and continual feedback regarding how well we are doing to create the empowering and learning-focused climate we hope to attain. They allow us to explore whether students are engaging in passive acceptance and regurgitation of the subject matter or are actively involved in creating and processing experiences from which to learn. We believe that this approach essentially changes the traditional hierarchical relationship between students and faculty and allows our students to see that we are all co-participants in the process of knowledge creation.

We tabulate the responses after the forms have been completed and present the results in three to five minutes during the next class meeting. Typically, we compare our current performance to past performances, answer any questions, and address issues or concerns that were raised by the students. We might use the results to encourage further class discussion or link them to theories we are currently exploring. Finally, we post the results and comments at the front of the class for students to review.

Findings and Their Use

Bureaucratic control causes people to feel helpless, out of control, and vulnerable. We have found that this feedback activity drastically reduces such feelings in our students. These feelings are reduced even further when we act upon student suggestions and respond, when possible, to student needs. When such action is not possible, we take the time to present honest and compelling reasons. For example, some students suggested that we meet in various other locations due to the discomfort associated with the room in which class was held. However, due to class conflicts and transportation problems, many of the locations they suggested were not acceptable. When this issue was presented in class and explained in full, we agreed to meet in the regular room but made efforts to improve the climate (for example, some brought rugs, pillows, posters, and the like).

Other changes we have made as a result of engaging in continual student assessment of our performance have included (1) changing paper, exam, and other due dates; (2) inviting guest speakers who discussed practical applications of the principles we were exploring (for example, the father of one student worked in a firm competing for the Baldrige award); (3) adding supplemental class sessions or extending coverage of a topic that students were struggling to grasp; (4) reducing time spent on topics that students grasped more easily than expected;

(5) modifying experiential learning activities to make them more salient; (6) changing readings and other supports to make them more salient; (7) finding new and creative places to hold class [for example, going to a local museum); and (8) discovering more about the personal and learning needs of our students. The fast-feedback process allowed us to make corrections to both class content and process during the term in which students experienced those phenomena, rather than discovering students' feelings at the end of the term when it was too late to make any changes.

The assessment process has increased our rapport with our students, maintained the mutual level of trust we need to run our classes, and been positively noted in our teacher rating forms at the end of the semester. More importantly, it has provided significant and useful feedback on the learning process.

Success Factors

Three words describe why we have had success with this approach to faculty assessment: trust, authenticity, and responsiveness. We have succeeded in attaining these ends by allowing students to complete forms without signing their names, by encouraging critical feedback, by separating this activity from any grade-related evaluation, and by sharing the results in a timely fashion. Finally, because we act upon students' ideas where and when possible, students feel a sense of responsiveness they have rarely experienced in higher education. The assessment practice has helped us create a climate in which students honestly express their likes, dislikes, needs, and suggestions. This climate facilitates the kind of learning and educational partnership we believe most faculty who really care about assessment are seeking.

Using a Midcourse Correction to Improve Learning in Mathematics

Janice Van Dyke

CASE 68: STATE TECHNICAL INSTITUTE AT MEMPHIS

Look for: A midcourse correction technique in which students are asked after the second test what they can do to improve their performance in the course. Responses have assisted the instructor in several ways. Homework is now graded, and a listing of errors has been compiled and described.

Background and Purpose

Some college students, especially those at open-access institutions who are taking precollege courses, are not fully aware of the correlation between their study habits and grades. Consequently, at State Technical Institute at Memphis, time was spent during the first day of a developmental mathematics class emphasizing this connection. Various campus resources that could provide assistance with studying were described and discussed. A classroom assessment activity was conducted later in the term to help students recognize and internalize their own accountability for learning.

Method

After the second test of the term, on which grades had dropped slightly from the first test, students were asked to respond to the statement, "What I can do to improve my performance in this course." The last five minutes of class were used for this activity, the replies were tabulated by category overnight, and the results were described and discussed during the next class period.

Findings

The activity cited most often by students to improve their performance in the course was working more problems. Other activities cited were reviewing videotapes of lectures in the learning lab, asking about homework problems that could not be worked, taking notes, reading the chapter, finding a study partner, speaking up when the teacher is talking too fast, keeping one's mind from wandering during class, copying problems on paper while the instructor is working them at the chalkboard, and doing homework at home instead of immediately before class.

Use of Findings

As a result of this assessment activity, the instructor has begun assigning more homework problems and covering more examples in class. In addition, homework assignments are scored, and a list of mistakes that students made most often is compiled and discussed during the next class period.

Success Factors

This activity worked because it was entirely student focused. It concerned a matter of high priority to students, and it involved them in the solutions to the problem. The open classroom discussion of students' responses reminded them of habits and activities that could help them succeed.

Using LEARN Teams in Course Evaluation

Kathryn H. Baugher

CASE 69: BELMONT UNIVERSITY

Look for: A LEARN training manual that prepares faculty and student teams to undertake formative evaluation of individual classes. Students build teamwork skills while learning quality-improvement strategies. They collect and analyze data from classmates, then suggest improvements to the instructor.

Background and Purpose

The LEARN process is a type of formative assessment, designed to enable a team of students working with the instructor to improve classroom teaching and learning. Belmont University's involvement with LEARN began as a pilot study during the fall semester of 1992 with twelve volunteer faculty participants. The university undertook the study because the provost saw the LEARN program as an opportunity to improve teaching and learning during a course rather than at the end of the semester. As an instructor himself, he knew both the faculty and administrator frustrations experienced with the traditional end-of-course evaluation system.

Our involvement with LEARN continues on a voluntary basis. Faculty across the institution have participated. The purpose of the project is to offer faculty and students a way to be involved in the formative assessment and improvement of their own teaching and learning.

Method

Belmont offers the program each term through an introductory meeting for interested faculty members during which limited training and materials are provided. Occasional meetings are held later in the term to troubleshoot and give encouragement.

The LEARN process begins with selecting the course in which it is to be applied, enlisting a team of students (usually three to five) to assist in evaluating the class, and working with the team through the improvement process outlined in the LEARN manual (Baugher, 1992). The team brainstorms; surveys the class; uses cause-and-effect diagrams to determine root causes of issues identified by the class; and suggests, implements, and monitors improvements. The team cycles through this process three or four times during the course.

While LEARN is designed for use in a single classroom, it has been used throughout a school of nursing, a school of pharmacy, in administrative settings, in remedial courses, and across multiple courses. The reports of LEARN teams are intended for the use of a particular class and professor; however, the provost at Belmont has allowed faculty members to submit LEARN team results in lieu of course evaluations if a faculty member wishes to do so. Faculty members and students are supportive of this idea, and many have selected this option.

Findings

Each LEARN team uncovers opportunities for improvement that are unique to the team's particular class. Improvement issues selected by teams have included improving class preparation, developing study partners, evaluating class progress by using a class mission statement, reorganizing homework assignments to improve learning, training class members to work in teams, and many others. Surveys by LEARN teams at the end of their courses strongly indicate that students believe the improvements undertaken by the teams have positively affected their learning.

One highly positive result of LEARN team activity is the realization on the part of students that they play an active role in the teaching/learning process. Students have become much more involved with their own learning as an outcome of their experience with a LEARN team in the classroom. Students have also encouraged other faculty members to use LEARN in their classrooms.

Use of Findings

As stated earlier, the results are intended to improve learning within a particular class; however, we are finding that professors use what they learn to improve other classes. LEARN teams also uncover improvements that would be beneficial to an entire system—such as a need to train students to work in teams or a need for the computer center to train student lab assistants in particular ways. We have begun work on a feedback mechanism that LEARN teams will use to report improvement issues and suggestions to our vice president for quality and professional development; this will enable the entire campus to benefit from the work of classroom quality teams.

Secondly, we have seen an interest among the students in learning more about Continuous Quality Improvement and have begun to develop a certification program. This program is still in the early stages, but ultimately, it will allow students, regardless of major, to learn the basic ideas and tools of continuous improvement and apply them. We believe that this will help our students enter their lives after college better prepared to deal with the issues of quality and continuous improvement.

Success Factors

This activity works with faculty members and students because it is formative assessment. For too long, the end-of-course evaluations used most often have been too late to be effective. Many students and faculty are ready for a change.

LEARN teams have been successful at Belmont across the institution because of the leadership of the provost and other senior leaders, who have been willing to spend time encouraging instructors and providing the resources they need. The LEARN program is a time-consuming process. It takes real commitment on the part of the faculty members, students, and administrators involved.

The reward has been improved learning and an increased sense that students and faculty work together to produce learning. We feel that the commitments we have made of time, energy, and money have been well rewarded.

CHAPTER FIFTEEN

FACULTY DEVELOPMENT TO PROMOTE ASSESSMENT

Chapter Guide

The chapter guide lists the cases contained in this chapter by institution, by focus of faculty development, and by subject areas. Institutions are organized by Carnegie Classification. The location of each institution and its approximate enrollment follow the institution name. The relevant case numbers follow each entry.

Institutions

Baccalaureate I
>   Private
>> Manhattanville College; Purchase, New York (1,600 students)   73

Focus of Faculty Development

> Classroom assessment   74
> Clinical skills assessment   75
> Faculty grants   70, 71
> General education assessment   73, 74
> Portfolio use   72, 73
> Student development   73
> Student writing   72, 76

Subject Areas

> Communications   74
> Dental hygiene   75
> English   70
> General education   74
> Mathematics   70
> Multiple disciplines   70, 71, 73, 74, 76
> Nursing   70
> Oral communication skills   74
> Political science   74
> Sciences   70
> Sociology   74
> Theatre   74
> Writing   72, 76

Chapter Overview

While faculty routinely assess the achievement of individual students for the purpose of assigning grades and giving students information about their personal strengths and weaknesses, most have had little formal training in measurement or evaluation that would prepare them for these assessment responsibilities. Moreover, the concept of looking at student performance in the aggregate for information about the effectiveness of courses or entire programs of study in promoting student learning is a relatively new one, for which very few academics have specific preparation. Thus, faculty development activities designed to convey specific evaluation skills should be an important component of a campus assessment initiative.

This chapter begins with three examples of faculty development *planned to promote expertise in assessment* (Cases 70, 71, and 72). The first example (Case 70) describes the launching of a campuswide assessment program with the following faculty development components: attendance at national conferences on assessment, campus seminars, and a faculty grant program. The second example (Case 71) depicts a competitive summer grant program that has enabled faculty individually and in groups to learn, through experience, techniques for developing cognitive tests, portfolios, and surveys. The third example (Case 72) illustrates a simple but effective faculty development strategy: administering a survey to faculty then reporting the results in a colloquium.

In a second set of examples (Cases 73, 74, and 75), faculty development is not the result of a centrally planned initiative but rather *occurs naturally* as faculty come together to consider and improve student assessment in general education or the major. In the first of these examples (Case 73), eight faculty representing the major divisions of science and math, language and literature, the social sciences, and the performing arts are elected for terms of three years to read student portfolios in the major. They meet regularly throughout the year to discuss readings in assessment and the methods they will apply to the portfolios. Their reports to individual students and to their respective faculties concerning the student strengths and weaknesses they have observed in the portfolios have produced improvements in teaching and learning over the two-decade history of portfolio assessment on their campus.

The next example (Case 74) began as an effort to employ classroom assessment to further student attainment of general education goals. The project quickly evolved into a rich faculty development seminar that begins with training in classroom assessment techniques, then continues with regular meetings throughout the year, and culminates in an annual report from each participant on assessment methods used, findings, and changes undertaken in response to the findings.

The third case in this trio (Case 75) began as an effort to improve assessment of students' clinical performance. It continued in an ongoing series of faculty discussions focused on discrete aspects of providing patient care. Faculty became much more self-conscious about their own knowledge in each area of focus and consequently were able to increase their collective consistency in evaluating student performance.

The chapter concludes with a case in which a faculty development initiative was undertaken *in response to assessment findings* (Case 76). Five years of departmental program reviews revealed nearly universal disappointment with the writing performance of seniors. The institution's response was to develop writing-across-the-curriculum requirements and to prepare faculty to teach and assess student writing in writing-intensive upper-division courses.

Using Grants to Initiate Assessment Activities

Ruth G. Gold, Rosalie Hewitt

CASE 70: NORTHERN ILLINOIS UNIVERSITY

Look for: Campuswide assessment initiative involving a series of seminars, some with recognized assessment leaders; sponsored faculty attendance at national conferences on assessment; and a faculty grant program. Faculty grants in several departments have led to revised curricula and improved instructional strategies.

Background and Purpose

In September 1986, the Illinois Board of Higher Education (IBHE) recommended that "each college and university shall assess individual student progress in meeting the objectives of general education and the development of baccalaureate-level skills and incorporate the results of assessment into the reviews of these areas" (Illinois Board of Higher Education, 1986). Although Northern Illinois University (NIU) has been dedicated to maintaining the quality of its programs and the preparation of its graduates since its inception, the IBHE document was the first to label this process as "assessment," focusing on objectives of general education, achievement of baccalaureate-level skills, resources committed to these components of the undergraduate curriculum, progress of cohorts of students, comparisons of student achievement among cohorts, and identification of curricular strengths and weaknesses. This date in 1986 marked the beginning of a strong assessment movement at NIU.

During fall semester 1987, an NIU faculty task force on assessment was formed to become educated on the topic of assessment, identify current assessment practice, explore ways of obtaining new assessment data, and plan with appropriate faculty bodies the implementation of improved assessment methodologies. Along with other Illinois public universities, NIU received $100,000 in additional state funding for assessment activities in fiscal year 1990, and the university's new Assessment Steering Committee provided direction for its allocation. With this financial support, an assessment coordinator was engaged to initiate departmental projects, organize campuswide activities, and institute a program of faculty grants to implement innovative assessment strategies. With the guidance of the associate provost and the Assessment Steering Committee, the assessment coordinator began planning and conducting universitywide studies of undergraduates, graduating seniors, students who withdraw from NIU, alumni, and employers of NIU alumni. Also, plans were drawn up to establish a longitudinal student database for research purposes, and steps were taken to develop a university plan for assessment.

During the next two years, the composition of the Assessment Steering

Committee was expanded to ensure faculty representation from all the undergraduate degree-granting colleges as well as from faculty committees that might be involved in student outcomes assessment. The committee's name was changed to the Assessment Subcommittee of the Undergraduate Coordinating Council (the faculty committee with oversight for all aspects of undergraduate education). Additional faculty grants were awarded, several members of the faculty attended national conferences on assessment, recognized speakers on assessment were brought to campus, and a series of on-campus assessment seminars was initiated. Assessment activities at this point, while not involving everyone on campus, were campuswide. Faculty from all six undergraduate degree-granting colleges were involved in discussing and implementing assessments in their disciplines, cooperative assessments were begun between academic and student support units, and the administration gave its full support to the efforts.

Method

One of the early initiatives, the assessment grant projects, proved to be successful for three reasons: (1) in most cases, findings were used to promote curricular change and strengthen programs within disciplines; (2) the small amount of support provided by the grants and their subsequent success encouraged other, less assessment-oriented faculty to become involved; and (3) the recipients of grants became supporters of the assessment movement and have acted as resource persons within their disciplines and individual colleges. Grant-supported projects have shown that assessment of student outcomes is an integral part of curricular design and revision, and the findings of these projects have been used to modify existing programs. Some of the projects have focused on individual degree programs, while others have been in the area of general education, or on issues of interest to a wider audience, such as the types of communications skills desired by members of the business community as they recruit NIU graduates.

Each year a call has gone out from the associate provost, inviting faculty to submit proposals for projects to be funded in the subsequent fiscal year. Historically, the call has gone out around the end of November; proposals are submitted early in March; the Assessment Subcommittee reviews the proposals by early April; and notice of funding is received by faculty shortly thereafter. Funding awarded in April is then available to faculty on or after July 1. Approximately $40,000 has been distributed annually to support four to six proposals per year.

Faculty wishing to submit proposals are instructed that "the purpose of the grant proposals should be directly related to determining the extent to which students are reaching the goals of the baccalaureate degree, both in their major programs and in general education. Funds may be used to plan, develop, and administer a pilot program or to continue an established assessment program. Proposals may be directly linked to departmental assessment plans developed in preparation for the North Central Association visit or they may be interdisciplinary or mutually supported by a group of departments."

In reviewing proposals the Assessment Subcommittee applies six criteria. Proposals are favored that (1) seek to identify students' strengths and weaknesses as a means to strengthen the existing baccalaureate experience; (2) show the applicability of the results to the overall task of refining and implementing the university assessment program; (3) relate directly to departmental or unit assessment plans; (4) give evidence that the department is willing to help support the proposal with its own resources; (5) come from departments proposing to continue the assessment of students over time; and (6) come from departments preparing for program reviews or accreditation reviews within the next two academic years.

Each grant recipient is expected to file a written report describing the activity, the results, how the results will be used to improve the baccalaureate experience, and plans for future assessment activity based on results of the project. In addition, a description of the discipline-specific educational outcomes and baccalaureate skills assessment data is reported by each department in the seven-year review of comparable programs mandated by the state board of higher education. This provides a basis for continued program revision and development.

Findings and Their Use

An example of a grant-supported project that continues to have an impact on the undergraduate curriculum is the Assessment of Writing in Freshman Rhetoric and Composition, supervised by Robert Self in the Department of English. This four-year project first examined the exit criteria used to evaluate the reading and writing skills in the freshman English program. These criteria were used to evaluate performance on the English Core Competency Examination, which placed incoming freshmen in appropriate courses. The criteria also influenced what was taught in the freshman English courses. Since the existing exit criteria were found to be inadequate measures and there was inconsistency in the curriculum as it was being delivered, the first two years of the project resulted in the development of new criteria for the assessment of student writing. These new criteria, in turn, guided faculty in the revision of curricular goals and methods for teaching students. During the third year, the evaluation criteria and process were further refined, and faculty were asked to revise their pedagogy. The fourth year of the project was used to assess whether the new criteria and revised curriculum actually resulted in better writing in the freshman English courses. The result of this project, which initially sought to validate existing criteria for evaluating freshman writing, led to changes in how students were placed in freshman English courses and how they were taught to write once placed in those classes.

In the School of Nursing, Elaine Graf is currently examining the writing skills of upper-level nursing students, utilizing the criteria established in the English department. The skills of the nursing students were evaluated over time as the writing skills established in the English courses were reinforced in the nursing program. The six-point writing-criteria scale developed by the English department was found to be very usable within a professional degree program and was significantly correlated with paper grades assigned by the faculty, although there was higher inter-rater reliability among the research team members than among the nursing faculty. A significant improvement in writing skills occurred when the criteria were applied to writing samples from upper-level nursing students. These students will be tracked to determine if the writing ability is sustained or continues to grow as they complete the nursing program, and faculty will have the opportunity to review their analyses and grading of nursing papers, perhaps with the goal of integrating the articulated English criteria into nursing faculty grading philosophy.

In 1990, a joint project was conducted in the College of Liberal Arts and Sciences through the Department of Mathematical Sciences and five science departments to assist those departments in preparing for program reviews. The departments developed an alumni questionnaire, asking graduates about their general educational experiences, their extradepartmental requirements, and discipline-specific questions. The questionnaire was sent to all alumni who had graduated between 1983 and 1989 and who had current mailing addresses. Respondents were generally satisfied with their experiences at Northern Illinois University; however, many graduates felt more writing courses should be required and more emphasis should be put on academic advisement. As a result, departments in these areas were prompted to include more writing in their curricula and to better inform students about the availability of academic advisement. This survey, although simply designed, had a longer lasting impact than originally planned. It had been conceived to demonstrate to the governing board that graduates were satisfied with the program in the math and science departments, but it concluded with specific changes in the way the departments delivered instruction and services.

A final example of assessment grant projects promoting curriculum development was in the School of Nursing, where two faculty engaged in a project designed to contribute to their National League of Nursing accreditation review. One facet of the project was to select and use an instrument that could evaluate the critical thinking skills of nursing students. In researching the available alternatives, it was decided than none of the current standard critical skills assessment "tests" were appropriate for the nursing definition of critical thinking. In order to determine whether nursing students develop an ability to evaluate a situation and make life-saving decisions in moments of great stress, the nursing faculty decided to develop their own assessment methodology. This method will help the School of Nursing determine whether its students are developing the appropriate skills, and whether the curriculum, as currently structured, provides the intended instruction. The methodology developed in nursing, although narrow in scope, may have implications for application in other areas of health care.

In addition, those same faculty were also interested in a broader definition of critical thinking, one that is generalizable to a wide range of real-life experiences. These faculty have designed an interdisciplinary course to develop broad critical thinking skills in students across the major programs; this new course will be piloted in the honors program. The results of this pilot project could provide guidance for faculty who are reviewing NIU's general education program, and the new critical thinking course has the potential to fill a gap within the general education curriculum.

Success Factors

The advancement of assessment at Northern Illinois University has been a slow developmental task, and its acceptance as an integral component of the academic process continues to evolve. A critical element in that advancement and acceptance has been the willingness of faculty to become involved and their demonstration to others that assessment can include useful, rewarding, and sometimes exciting activities that actually do lead to improvements in what is taught and what is learned. The use of small assessment grants provided the motivation for interested faculty to establish new ways of gathering indicators of student outcomes and student success. These data answered questions about the strengths and weaknesses of programs and, thus, allowed faculty to channel their efforts and resources to the areas most central to the university's mission. Without the involvement of faculty, the advancement of assessment would not have occurred; without the grant initiative, the involvement of faculty would have proceeded much more slowly. The results clearly show the impact that the assessment grant initiative has had upon curricular development and revision across the university.

Summer Assessment Grant Program for Faculty

Catherine Palomba, Deborah Moore

CASE 71: BALL STATE UNIVERSITY

Look for: A program of awarding summer stipends to faculty who submit winning proposals for assessment projects. Faculty have developed pre- and posttests and portfolios to assess student learning, and survey instruments to assess satisfaction of constituent groups. Curricula, instruction, and assessment have been improved as a result of this faculty development initiative.

Background and Purpose

Assessment at Ball State University is carried out through a combination of universitywide and college- and department-level activities. In addition to other projects, the Office of Academic Assessment has responsibility for conducting freshman, senior, and alumni surveys and for standardized testing. The office also acts as consultant to colleges and departments as they undertake assessment projects. One of the ways the office helps support assessment in the colleges and departments is through the Summer Grant Program. Faculty assume substantial responsibilities as they carry out assessment projects; the purpose of the grant program is to provide recognition of these efforts.

Method

The Office of Academic Assessment has a pool of summer money that is awarded to faculty, on a competitive basis, as summer stipends. Faculty who are interested in completing assessment projects submit proposals to the office. The proposals are reviewed by a committee consisting of one faculty member from each of the six colleges. The committee is chaired by the assistant director of the Office of Academic Assessment. The committee's recommendations are advisory to the director. The director also negotiates with college deans and department chairs to establish summer projects.

Faculty members applying for grants are asked to submit proposals describing the purpose of their projects, the assessment goals and activities of their departments, how the proposed projects fit into departmental assessment plans, and how their departments will use the information generated through the proposed activities. Each proposal also must include a description of specific project goals and methodology, a time line, and a budget outline if funds are being requested for project expenses. The required cover sheet for the proposal includes a statement of support from the department chair and approval signatures from the chair and dean. Proposals are submitted in January and reviewed in February, and decisions are announced in March. Faculty stipends awarded through the competitive process have generally been around $1,800. In some cases, the stipend has been split between two or three faculty for a jointly submitted project.

In addition to the awards given through the competitive process, some awards are also given in response to specific requests from colleges and departments. This has occurred when a college or department has identified a particular need. In these cases, one or more faculty members are invited to complete the project.

Grant recipients are asked to submit a brief written report at the conclusion of the project. An outline is provided for this purpose. In addition to asking the grant recipient(s) to describe the project's objectives, activities, and results, the outline asks recipients to indicate how and when the results will be used. It also asks them to describe how the assessment project has influenced the department. Plans for future activities and hints and/or reflections for future assessment practitioners are also requested.

Findings

We have found that a great deal of interest and effort can be stimulated with respect to assessment, even with a modest summer grant program. In summer 1992, thirty-five faculty from twenty-five departments participated in the program. The following year, fifty-five faculty from thirty-seven departments took part.

The projects supported by the grant program have varied greatly. Grant recipients have developed standardized tests, introduced portfolios, and created survey instruments. Many of the recipients have been involved in the general studies course evaluation, which requires each department to demonstrate that its general studies courses are meeting the goals of the general studies program. In summer 1993, a committee of eight individuals from the College of Sciences and Humanities reviewed and prepared a critique of each department's assessment plan. A narrative describing a model for assessment planning and a matrix outlining assessment activities in the college's twenty-four departments were also developed. At the conclusion of the project, the dean or associate dean visited each department in the college to share the committee's evaluation of that department's plan. As a result, many departments are rethinking and revising their assessment plans. Overall, the Summer Grant Program has greatly increased assessment activities on the campus.

Use of Findings

The assessment techniques and instruments developed by faculty participating in the program have affected students in a variety of ways. Faculty teaching a broad array of courses have developed pre- and posttests to demonstrate cognitive learning. Survey information has resulted in programmatic changes in several departments. Assessment information developed through summer projects has also been used in accreditation reviews.

Success Factors

In fall 1991, the provost and vice president for academic affairs at Ball State University issued a statement about academic assessment. The statement set forth the expectation that each college, department, and school would undertake assessment activities. The general studies subcommittee of the faculty senate requires assessment of general studies courses. The Summer Grant Program has helped facilitate this assessment mandate. Although the stipends have not been large, a real effort has been made to distribute funds as broadly as possible. As a result, nearly every department and every college has participated in the grant program.

We offer the following cautions. While faculty are generally aware of the increased need to undertake assessment, they are not always sure of what constitutes an "assessment project." Occasionally, faculty need some guidance in proposing appropriate projects. In addition, a competitive program will not always produce proposals that address a department's most pressing assessment needs. The positive impact of our grant program on assessment has been increased by consulting with faculty, chairs, and deans about possible projects before grant proposals are submitted.

Stimulating Faculty Interest in Portfolio Assessment

Pat Huyett

CASE 72: UNIVERSITY OF MISSOURI-KANSAS CITY

Look for: An easy-to-use strategy for engaging faculty in improving their assessment skills: design a faculty survey and schedule a meeting to discuss the findings. The experience reported here stimulated faculty interest in using portfolios in assessing student outcomes.

Background and Purpose

After using proficiency testing for more than twenty years, the faculty at the University of Missouri-Kansas City (UMKC) decided to explore the possibility of using portfolios as alternative assessment tools. The campus coordinator of writing assessment worked with the director of composition and eventually with the entire composition staff to develop a strategy for encouraging faculty to share ideas and methods.

Method

First, faculty were surveyed to find out who was using portfolios. We learned that slightly less than half were doing so. We also asked those who were experienced in using portfolios and those who were not what they would like to know about them. Portfolios for classroom use were defined as sets of papers students produce during the semester. Most often, students submit revised papers representing their best work in a portfolio or folder at the end of the term. Usually, the students prepare a cover letter that describes the collection of materials and provides some self-reflection upon the contents.

From faculty responses to the initial survey, a second questionnaire was developed. The following questions were administered in a subsequent campus mailing.

1. For which courses have you used portfolios?
2. Who determines what papers go into the portfolio?
3. When you grade the portfolio at the end of the semester, do you give each paper a grade, or do you give one grade for the portfolio?
4. How do you assess students throughout the term? Do you give a midterm grade? Do you tell students if they are doing below average work so they can drop the course?
5. If you reserve grades for midterm or semester's end, what sorts of things do you look for when you go over student papers? Generally, how do you mark papers?

6. Do you combine student conferences with written comments? How often do you schedule student conferences during the semester?
7. What differences in your teaching or student responses have you noticed in using portfolios as opposed to grading/returning/averaging student papers?
8. Have you had some problems with portfolios? Have you found them less useful in some classes than others?
9. Briefly describe what you see as the advantages and disadvantages of portfolio assessment.

Questionnaire responses were compiled, edited, and distributed to faculty along with an article from the current literature on portfolio assessment. We scheduled a colloquium and asked five instructors experienced in portfolio use to serve on a panel to share their knowledge and to answer questions.

Findings and Their Use

Faculty reaction was enthusiastic. Many remarked that this was one of the most substantive faculty development meetings they could remember. We discovered how portfolio use varied from teacher to teacher, and this proved of interest to those who were experienced portfolio teachers as well as to those who had never used them. Many who participated reached the conclusion that portfolios are more pedagogically sound than teaching writing in the old way—by reading, grading, and averaging. Portfolio development emphasizes writing as a process and impresses upon students the importance of revision.

Several months after the initial activity, we conducted a third survey. We discovered that greater percentages of faculty are using portfolios and are enthusiastic about doing so.

This faculty development activity reflects the philosophy that teachers can best teach other teachers. We feel that using portfolios is better for students and puts faculty in the role of teacher-as-coach or nurturer, rather than teacher-as-judge or critic.

This is also a major first step in getting faculty to consider the use of portfolios in programwide assessment. Now we hope to explore further the possibility of programwide assessment.

Success Factors

Having our staff share with each other their strategies for making the portfolio useful gave them a sense of empowerment and a sense that what they do in their classrooms matters to others. This activity helped to take away the mystery as well as the anxiety for those who had wanted to use portfolios, but had been afraid to try. This locally-initiated-and-designed strategy was a far more productive way of encouraging faculty to use portfolios than simply declaring their use by administrative fiat. We are now in a stronger position to discuss with our teachers ways to institute programwide portfolio assessment as an option to proficiency testing.

The Portfolio: A Crucial Link Between Student and Faculty Development

Catherine R. Myers

CASE 73: MANHATTANVILLE COLLEGE

Look for: A campuswide portfolio assessment program that involves a cross-disciplinary team of faculty in evaluating students' portfolios, communicating with individual students concerning their work, and reporting to faculty on collective student strengths and weaknesses. The portfolio committee meets regularly throughout the year for reading and discussion.

Background and Purpose

Manhattanville College instituted a portfolio system in 1971, with help from the National Endowment for the Humanities. The process of developing the format for the system took three years. The system addressed the need to assess students' ability to perform certain tasks that the faculty deemed important competencies for a graduate of Manhattanville. These abilities were not effectively measured by good grades on a transcript. The ability to undertake and complete research projects successfully, to do critical analysis in a long essay, to assemble a good bibliography through work with different kinds of sources, to complete quantitative analyses and laboratory work in the sciences, and to explore the relationship between the major and other areas of coursework—these were the first competencies that students were asked to demonstrate in their portfolios. Over two decades, the statement of the desired competencies has changed, but the essential format of the portfolio has remained, as has the means by which portfolios are evaluated.

Method

In the portfolio goes the evidence of the student's developing competencies: study plans, study plan rationales, annual evaluations of the student's achievements, and essays and reports on research that the student and faculty adviser believe meet the competency requirements. The portfolios demand the space of ten five-drawer files in the dean for studies' office. In an age of computer transcripts and machine-scored tests, the worn brown file seems anachronistic. However, its presence demonstrates the complex and sometimes untidy accumulations that are part of the process of self-education.

Behind the conception of the portfolio is a definition of the relationship between students and their degree work that many faculty find desirable. The portfolio is designed to encourage reflective learning. Students are asked to evaluate their progress each year. They are asked to provide a rationale for their choice of major and their other courses.

Students are also asked to develop a statement about the academic work that has been most significant for them. In addition, they are asked in their first year to read through the college catalog and plan their program for four years. The program first proposed can be and is frequently changed. However, from the first year, students are encouraged to design the entire four years of their degree program.

The portfolio system also strengthens bonds between faculty and students. A faculty adviser is provided for each student to help him or her complete portfolio requirements, and the adviser must sign all submissions for the student's portfolio. Some faculty are more effective as advisers than others. However, the requirement for advisers' signatures dramatizes for students the importance of one-on-one dialogue with a faculty member and shows students that faculty are concerned about each student's whole program, not just his or her accomplishments in that faculty member's course or discipline.

What often seems to outsiders or critics to be the most impractical aspect of portfolios is the task of reading them. At Manhattanville, this task is undertaken by a committee of eight faculty who are elected by the faculty for three-year terms. The faculty represent major divisions in the disciplines: science and math, language and literature, the social sciences, and the performing arts. At each reading period, depending on the size of the particular undergraduate class being reviewed, there are about 250 portfolios to be read. Each is read by at least two readers, whose evaluation is recorded on a checksheet that enumerates the competencies and allows room for written comments. When readers disagree, the whole committee reads the portfolio in question. The process is usually completed in seven or eight days of reading at the end of the spring semester. The first submission of the portfolio is made in the sophomore year, and a full submission is made at the end of the junior year. Students who wish to apply for honors resubmit their portfolios in the senior year.

Findings and Their Use

The information gained from the portfolio readings is used in several ways. Each student receives a letter informing him or her that the portfolio has been read. Significant faculty comments on the portfolio are relayed to the student by this means. If the portfolio has deficiencies, the student is asked to address the defects and resubmit it. Sometimes, because of deficiencies or changes in program, students make several submissions. Some of these portfolios are read during the regular semester in order to make a speedy response to the student. (The portfolio committee meets regularly during the school year for reading and discussion.) Students who fail to achieve a successful portfolio have to postpone graduation. However, most students manage to submit their portfolios in time to graduate. The best portfolio receives a special reward at the annual honors dinner.

The portfolio committee makes a report to the faculty on the reading of portfolios. The report notes significant trends in students' programs, new and ongoing problems students have in responding to requirements, and the committee's sense of the academic strengths and weaknesses that portfolios have revealed. This report has always been made to the faculty rather than to the administration. Although the readings may reveal deficiencies in particular major programs, the departments involved are not taken to task by any of the academic deans. Instead, the problems are addressed informally by the faculty members who are concerned with the issues. The informality of these exchanges has probably helped to ensure the vitality of the portfolio. Although a more formal challenge to the deficient departments might appear more efficient in protecting quality, the informal exchanges help to keep the portfolio process from becoming embroiled in faculty politics.

In reading the portfolios, faculty can see how the structure of the curriculum affects students—the requirements that are meaningless to them and those that enable them to develop a new perspective on their learning. The goals of individual courses and the major programs are continually under review in the course of the reading. Faculty can compare by means of student submissions the meaning of a grade of A or C across the curriculum.

The portfolio requirements are intended to encourage reflective learning and students' initiative in planning their studies. Many students initially understand very little about these goals. Improvement in the thoughtfulness of the first annual evaluation has been accomplished by having students write it in the last weeks of their year-long required freshman seminar. Students are taught criteria for evaluating their own academic development. And faculty learn that they must teach students how to articulate their understanding of the ways in which a particular course contributes to their total plan for their liberal arts degree program.

Success Factors

The system has worked because faculty get useful feedback from the review process. Faculty can see how students relate their work in a particular course to their whole degree program. Faculty can compare their own work with students to that of other faculty. The system has endured as a resource for faculty as well as students, a resource that motivated faculty find valuable as an ongoing evaluation of students' success in meeting the goals of the college's degree program, the different disciplines, and the individual courses.

Learning Research: An Interdisciplinary Faculty Approach to General Education Assessment

Margaret Tebo-Messina, Marilyn Sarow

CASE 74: WINTHROP UNIVERSITY

Look for: A faculty training seminar, regular meetings, and participation on interdisciplinary teams charged with assessing seven general education outcomes. All of these activities are designed to help faculty collect data in their own classes and respond appropriately to the findings. Participants must make an annual report on the methods they have used, their findings, and ways they have responded to what they have learned.

Background and Purpose

The gap between assessment data and curricular reform is an ongoing concern of higher education, particularly in an area as diverse and challenging as general education. The Winthrop University Learning Research Project, initiated in 1989 by the Office of Assessment, assesses the university's general education program (centered around seven broad goals, each of which includes a set of generic objectives) and closes this gap instantly. It accomplishes this by enlisting and training faculty to collect data in their classes, to respond appropriately to their findings and to work in interdisciplinary teams devising program level assessment tools. The project is multidisciplinary: every major academic unit and more than twenty disciplines are represented.

Method

The Learning Research Project involves faculty in the articulation of course-specific general education objectives, and the use of classroom assessment techniques to determine if these objectives have been attained. In addition, it involves faculty in interdisciplinary teams that create university-specific assessment tools.

The project assumes that the best way to promote campuswide concern about the quality of the general education curriculum is to engage faculty in its assessment at the classroom level. Consequently, new participants who join the project receive materials and training in goals clarification and the use of classroom assessment techniques, and join goal-specific interdisciplinary teams engaged in the creation of program level assessment tools. To date, more than 10 percent of Winthrop faculty have become "learning researchers."

Findings

The project benefits Winthrop's general education curriculum in several ways: it increases faculty awareness of, and sense of responsibility for, education goals that transcend disciplinary boundaries; it closes the gap between the collection and use of data at the classroom level, thereby increasing the potential for quality outcomes; it creates positive attitudes about the benefits of assessment; and it provides a venue for the interdisciplinary creation of new assessment tools.

In their annual reports faculty detail the information their assessment efforts yield and the changes in the curriculum or presentation made in response to their findings. In many cases, participants create course-specific, unique assessment measures to gather relevant data. As for the faculty teams, they too create unique instruments. The Quantitative Team, for example, devised attitude and skills assessment tools that have been piloted in a variety of courses and have already altered the handling of subject matter.

Similarly, the Aesthetics Team, composed of faculty from the departments of art and design, English, mass communication, music, social work, speech, and theatre and dance, is exploring how metaphor can be used to assess general education goal number six, the understanding of "the creative process, and the interconnectedness of the literary, visual, and performing arts throughout the history of civilization." Consequently, they have selected readings and exercises and developed a video that will be used campuswide to introduce students to the ways in which metaphor is used across disciplines. After viewing the video, students will discuss metaphor in terms of their own discipline and then work in teams to explore how a metaphorical idea is expressed in literature, music, and visual media. Finally, students will be assigned a discipline-specific project requiring the application of metaphor to their own work. Projects will be evaluated on the richness and effectiveness of selected metaphors. Ultimately, the Aesthetics Team plans to use data from the project to ascertain whether a student's understanding of metaphor leads to more creative work and a deeper understanding of the interconnectedness of the arts.

Use of Findings

Faculty have used results to make many changes in their courses. They have, for example, included general education goals on syllabi; altered exams to include essay questions on student self-assessment; administered midsemester course evaluations; and restructured courses in a variety of ways, such as extending the percentage of class time spent to teach particular skills and using parallel assignments to help students better integrate and apply material. The project has also significantly increased faculty-student dialogue and awareness of general education goals.

Success Factors

The project works primarily because it instantly closes the gap between student assessment and curricular reform. Faculty are invigorated by the intellectual challenge of their research, and by the immediate payoff their efforts receive. In addition, the interdisciplinary character of the project promotes vigorous and rigorous discussions about pedagogy and curricular goals.

Clinical Assessment in a Baccalaureate Dental Hygiene Program

Ann McCann

CASE 75: UNIVERSITY OF DETROIT MERCY

Look for: An effort to improve assessment of students' clinical performance that brought faculty together for discussion. Weekly focus on a single aspect of patient care caused faculty to deepen their knowledge of each area and to develop more consistency in their methods of evaluating students.

Background and Purpose

Dental hygiene students engaged in clinical work are evaluated by individual faculty while they provide care to patients. Successful patient care performance requires the students to integrate and apply countless pieces of information learned in the classroom. The complexity of this task is further complicated by the fact that clinical grading systems are competency based, with well-defined standards for successful performance of every aspect of care, that is, multiple criteria for health history, assessment, treatment planning, deposit removal, and professional conduct. Thus confronted with all the possibilities for error, the dental hygiene student feels that it is very difficult to perform at a high level, especially at the beginning of the clinical experience.

The dental hygiene faculty at the University of Detroit Mercy first tried to solve this student frustration by grading "easier" at the beginning of the clinical experience; however, this resulted in decreased inter-rater reliability. Students perceived grading to be capricious and unfair. We then developed a standardized system for grading progressively "harder" over time, but the students were still overwhelmed and fearful about their early clinical experiences. Finally, the faculty decided to develop a method of assessment that would help the students identify areas of focus for their performance in the clinic.

Method

We called the strategy the "weekly clinical concern." For each week, an area of patient care was identified as the weekly concern, or the most important area, and the one faculty would assess most thoroughly. The students would still be graded on all aspects of care, but most of the faculty time during assessment would be spent on the weekly concern. In other words, most errors in performance would relate to the weekly concern.

Weekly topics were identified by the faculty for an entire semester and posted for the students. No new instruments had to be developed since the assessment mechanism was already in place. At weekly meetings, the faculty briefly discussed the assessment procedures for the weekly clinical concern.

Findings

The principal outcomes of this strategy were that the beginning students said they experienced less stress and were able to learn the identified aspects of patient care very well. They studied those areas prior to going into the clinic, and once in the clinic, they received extensive feedback from faculty about their performance.

There were also some unanticipated outcomes. In the clinic, individual faculty have a tendency to focus their assessment on the aspects of patient care in which they are most personally interested and/or with which they are most comfortable. The need to focus on the designated weekly concern forced faculty to assess patient care areas with which they were less comfortable, and they needed to review their knowledge of patient care. The discussions at meetings became more and more lively as faculty found the need to focus on specific areas of patient care.

It soon became apparent to the faculty that they were not nearly as finely calibrated in their assessment procedures as they thought they were and that improvement was needed. Students also came to the same conclusion. They would often work with several different faculty members during any given week, and the differences in the assessment process among the faculty became apparent. Inter-rater reliability is always a problem with clinical evaluation in dental hygiene where multiple raters are used, but our process seemed to be particularly problematic.

Use of Findings

Two changes were instituted that have led to improvement in our clinical assessment process. Based on our positive experiences with providing students with more feedback on performance, we developed a series of competency examinations where the focus was on observing the process of patient care and providing immediate feedback to the students.

The other change involved the development of calibration exercises for faculty to improve inter-rater reliability. Sample student performances were selected for these exercises, some of which involved processes such as the oral examination, and some of which involved patient care products, such as a set of plaster study models (casts of a person's teeth). If a process was involved, we videotaped students during their performance and had faculty evaluate their performance. If a product was involved, we brought in student samples for grading. After grading according to departmental criteria, the faculty discussed their differences and worked toward a consensus. The students were appreciative of our efforts to improve the assessment process and facilitated the calibration process by helping us develop the materials we needed.

Success Factors

This assessment strategy worked because of the strong leadership of the clinic coordinator (myself) and the support of the department chairman. Because both of us wanted it to work, we provided the enthusiasm and the direction for the rest of the faculty. We met on a weekly basis with the faculty and talked about the process frequently to both faculty and students.

Another reason for the success of the weekly clinical concern was that this strategy actually made the assessment process easier. Often the introduction of assessment procedures is perceived as giving teachers more work to do, and so resistance is encountered. In our case, the strategy provided a focus for the assessment, and so minimized the complexity and increased the efficiency of the process.

Finally, the implementation of the weekly clinical concern improved the quality of student-faculty interaction. Since both groups had clear expectations about the focus of the assessment, this strategy lessened the stress of the interaction, especially for the students. Such a positive experience facilitates student learning and makes teaching more rewarding for faculty.

Preparing Faculty for Writing Across the Curriculum

John A. Muffo, Nancy Metz

CASE 76: VIRGINIA POLYTECHNIC INSTITUTE AND STATE UNIVERSITY

Look for: Formal and informal efforts to help faculty in disciplines across the curriculum learn to teach and assess students' writing performance. The need for these faculty development initiatives became apparent after five years of assessment via reviews revealed universal dissatisfaction with writing skills.

Background and Purpose

Since the mid 1980s, all public institutions in Virginia have been required to engage in comprehensive student outcomes assessment. Part of the process at Virginia Polytechnic Institute and State University involves conducting departmental self-studies every five years. By the end of the first of the five-year cycles, most departments had independently identified written and spoken communication as one of the areas in most need of improvement among graduating seniors. The university thus implemented writing-across-the-curriculum (WAC) requirements.

Faculty have found that most students consider sentence construction, grammar, punctuation, spelling, and other writing matters to be important topics for English composition classes only. Thus, students do not feel that correct use of the language should be a consideration when they submit written assignments in other courses, including those in the major. They tend to take such matters much more seriously when their importance is emphasized in courses in their major. In addition, different disciplines have different modes of communication, and these can be refined best in courses in the major. Being exposed to the emphasis that employers put on written communication skills can be a motivating factor as well. Finally, writing about a concept has been shown to be a highly effective way of synthesizing knowledge. The new WAC requirements emphasize the role of writing in advancing the content goals of courses in the major.

Method

Many Virginia Tech faculty reported a need for some assistance from outside their departments in determining the best way to improve student performance in writing. In response, faculty workshops and consulting in writing have been formally provided under the auspices of a new entity, the Writing Program. Informally, a network of interested individuals from a variety of academic disciplines across the institution has developed, aided by an internal electronic-mail discussion list, a series of brown-bag lunches, and afternoon seminars. These formal and informal resources will become even more important as the departments work to get courses approved as "writing intensive" in order to meet the new graduation requirement of three additional writing-intensive courses for every student. Several departments have requested intensive discipline-specific workshops related to this curriculum revision.

Findings and Their Use

A number of departments have adjusted their curricula to require more writing in the discipline. Sometimes this includes a requirement for a number of different writing modes, such as business letters, memoranda, laboratory reports, other research reports, proposals for funding, applications for patents, and the like. One department in the College of Engineering has hired a faculty member from the English department, not to teach a single course but rather to work with a range of faculty and their students on matters related to writing.

A network seems to be developing of individuals in different fields of study who are interested in improving writing in the disciplines. That network has been helpful in discussing other issues related to undergraduate education as well.

Success Factors

The discovery of the need to improve written communication came about because the department faculty themselves collected the outcomes assessment data that led them to that conclusion. Consequently, when the WAC requirements were being planned, many faculty saw this step as necessary to improving the quality of undergraduate education at Virginia Tech, rather than as centrally mandated interference in curricular matters.

It is too early in the process of implementing the WAC requirements to know how they will affect student learning, but it is clear that the Virginia Tech program does exhibit some of the features most predictive of student success. It emerged from broad faculty consensus rather than from administrative prescription. It will be implemented gradually, in realistic stages. Most importantly, it is supported not just by platitudes but by solid funding for workshops and by a long-term commitment to faculty development.

CHAPTER SIXTEEN

DEVELOPING A CAMPUSWIDE APPROACH TO THE ASSESSMENT OF INSTITUTIONAL EFFECTIVENESS

Chapter Guide

The chapter guide lists the cases contained in this chapter by institution and by assessment method. Institutions are organized by Carnegie Classification. The location of each institution and its approximate enrollment follow the institution name. The relevant case numbers follow each entry.

Institutions

Assessment Methods

Chapter Overview

Developing an assessment initiative that involves every academic unit and administrative office within an institution is a mammoth undertaking. Often the impetus for such an effort comes from an external mandate emanating from a state legislature, a coordinating board, or a regional accrediting agency.

The case studies in this chapter illustrate proven strategies for creating campus awareness of the need for outcomes assessment, encouraging faculty and staff to become involved in assessment, and sustaining that involvement over time. These strategies include developing a distinctive new mission statement using assessment data derived from surveys to inform the process (Case 77); conducting an assessment audit through a series of structured interviews with administrative and faculty colleagues in order to inventory existing data and determine how they are being used (Case 78); basing periodic analysis of institutional progress on specified indicators of program effectiveness (Cases 79 and 80); encouraging faculty to become involved in assessment by offering mini-grants to departments that propose innovative approaches (Case 81); and establishing open and effective communication channels to keep internal and external audiences informed about assessment and its role in enhancing institutional quality (Case 82).

Using Assessment to Guide Mission Development

Paul A. Wagner

CASE 77: UNIVERSITY OF HOUSTON-CLEAR LAKE

Look for: Beginning an assessment initiative by developing a new mission statement with a focus on outcomes of degree programs.

Background

At a time when the University of Houston-Clear Lake (UHCL) was experiencing a great deal of administrative turnover and internal strife, it began preparations for its first full Southern Association of Colleges and Schools (SACS) review. UHCL was only sixteen years old when the self-study began, and the university took very seriously the accrediting agency's dictum that this should be an exhaustive self-study and not just an audit. Fully three-quarters of the professional and administrative personnel and faculty were involved in the process.

Method

As at most other universities, faculty assigned tests, term papers, and other assignments to ensure that students were learning what was expected on a course-by-course basis. A few program areas such as accounting, teacher education, and family therapy tracked graduates' performance on various external measures such as licensing examinations. But to the collective chagrin of faculty and administration alike, it was evident that there was no profile for the distinctive features of a UHCL graduate nor, even more startling, of a degree graduate within specific programs.

Absent in nearly all unit plans was a universitywide organizing theme. Nowhere was this fact more conspicuously evident than in the lack of identifiable student outcomes. We set out to identify outcomes appropriate to our degree programs and other offerings. This was accomplished by combining information from three sources. First, the registrar's office assembled data identifying enrollment trends. Student affairs contributed information from surveys of students and graduating students that contained information about student satisfaction with facilities and placement office opportunities. Finally, the Institutional Effectiveness Committee created several new surveys, including one for alumni based upon a value-added model of student outcomes.

Other surveys of faculty, professional staff, administrators, employers, and current students afforded a broad perspective on what brings students to UHCL and what determines their success upon graduation. This information was aggregated and led eventually to the adoption of Total Quality Management throughout the university.

Findings

The UHCL community had long been aware that most students came to the university to improve their employment opportunities. Nevertheless, many faculty, having graduated from major research universities, persisted in their advocacy of liberal arts education as an end in itself. While there is nothing inherently wrong with this notion, research findings at UHCL made it clear that the traditional model of liberal arts education could not serve the customer pool of UHCL.

Identifying the customer pool was very revealing. Just as the liberal arts model was deemed inadequate, so, too, was the perception that currently enrolled students exhaust the customer pool. If career enhancement is the draw, then employer satisfaction with UHCL's graduates is critical to the university's continued success. Employers and potential employers were recognized as primary customers of the university. Other additions to the customer pool included funding agencies, the community, and the professions.

Through this detailed articulation of the UHCL customer pool, the mission of the university emerged in well-articulated form. UHCL is a regional, comprehensive, urban university. Its mission is dramatically different from that of a small liberal arts college, a rural institution, or a major research university. Through its surveys of alumni and others and a new commitment to quality and customer satisfaction, the UHCL has articulated its mission more fully than ever before. No longer is the term "comprehensive university" an empty collection of vague and high-sounding concepts.

Use of Findings

First and foremost, UHCL strives to produce competent professionals for regional employers. The university also provides the region with continuing short-term professional training and extensive applied research. Pure research has not been abandoned. Indeed, it is one way UHCL faculty continue to serve their professions. Nevertheless, ordered priorities are now clear to all. Finally, UHCL continues to serve the traditional liberal arts student quite adequately within budgetary distributions appropriate to the institution's mission.

The UHCL mission is fully reflected in its strategic plan. For example, training in professional ethics was added as a universitywide objective. And there is an emerging sense of what it means to be a UHCL graduate. Each of the four schools has identified outcomes appropriate to each of its degrees. Moreover, these outcomes are reviewed on a regular schedule. Across all schools and inherent in all degrees awarded is a recognition of the special attributes of a professional as opposed to someone simply seeking employment.

Within each school, curricular modifications continue to reflect the professional needs of the UHCL service region. Degree programs in dance, theatre arts, higher education, and educational futures have been discontinued. Programs in software engineering have been initiated (UHCL has a border in common with the Johnson Space Center), and other degree programs are currently being revised to incorporate an explicit professionalism.

In the alumni survey, graduates named nineteen faculty as especially competent. Recalling the professional orientation of our students, it was revealing that, of the faculty named, only two had been selected previously by enrolled students as candidates for the teacher-of-the-year award. What this means has not yet been determined, but it has led to more interest in what counts as effective instruction in a university such as UHCL.

UHCL knows that its students are professionally oriented, with an average age for both graduate and undergraduate students of thirty-two. As degree and universitywide student outcomes continue to emerge, instruction appropriate to the flourishing of UHCL graduates is being further developed. To accomplish this, the shared governance system has created a task force to develop procedures for identifying additional appropriate student outcomes and the most effective procedures for achieving them. The quest for quality is never ending.

Our efforts in quality improvement were recorded and led not only to SACS approval but served as the basis for UHCL's successful bid to secure an IBM Total Quality Management grant. Senior UHCL leadership continues every effort to make the university accountable to each of its customer groups. As long as data are used for system improvement and not as a tool of oppression, the outlook for continuous improvement at UHCL seems assured. Confirmation of this is reflected in the university's receiving from Texas comptroller John Sharp the first "Breaking the Mold" award. UHCL now has an explicit identity and resiliency often lacking even in the nation's so-called comprehensive institutions.

Success Factors

The SACS emphasis on institutional effectiveness was, admittedly, the original impetus in moving UHCL forward in its assessment efforts. The data acquired from the alumni survey opened horizons to the true range of customers served by the University. With new leadership and a young energetic faculty, the appeal of using a team approach to serving a professionally-oriented set of customers became irresistible. Soon adoption of a quality improvement approach became an obvious need to all involved.

Taking the First Step: An Assessment Audit

Trudy Bers, Mary L. Mittler

CASE 78: OAKTON COMMUNITY COLLEGE

Look for: Beginning an assessment initiative with an audit that entails a planned series of interviews with administrators, faculty, and staff to determine what data are being collected, how they are stored, and how they are used.

Background and Purpose

In fall 1992, faculty and administrators at Oakton Community College conducted several related projects that, quite without initial intent, ultimately led to the formulation of an assessment audit. The original projects included revamping existing assessment and testing requirements for students; revising the general education component of all associate degrees; and intensifying our examination of teaching and student learning and progress. As work on these projects progressed, several of us noted the extent to which our lust for data was frustrated by our ignorance of (1) whether certain pieces of student information were collected; (2) if so, by whom; and (3) where such data were stored. While we were most interested in improving our educational programs and services, our awareness of new North Central Association (NCA) criteria regarding outcomes and a 1995 assessment report due to the NCA provided additional motivation for us to devise some way of ascertaining just how student data were gathered and stored at the institution.

Consequently, the assessment audit was designed to compile baseline information about what sorts of data and information about students were being gathered; how these data were stored, accessed, analyzed, and used; and the extent to which duplicative or potentially complementary assessments existed in isolation from each other. The audit was conducted by the authors of this case.

Method

Our initial step was to identify all administrators, faculty, and staff across the institution whom we thought might be gathering, analyzing, or using data, or information, related to students' characteristics, academic abilities and performances, or participation in academic and nonacademic services. We made no prior determination about the value such data collection might have; indeed, we were very careful to ensure that value judgments would not play a part in the process. Our initial and primary goals were to learn who knew what about our students, and how that information was gathered and stored. Thus, we needed to encourage people to talk honestly about their procedures without concern for justification.

As we discussed potential sources of information, each person identified was assigned to be interviewed by one of us personally, one-to-one. We used a common set of questions; recorded summaries of the open-ended, conversational responses; and finally, synthesized our observations and findings.

Personal interviews were somewhat time consuming but far more informative than a survey would have been. For instance, it was not uncommon for an interviewee to remark that while she or he did not collect this or that piece of information, a colleague from another office did. One interview thus led to another; this information highway was not a straight and narrow one!

Findings

The audit revealed important information about the extent to which student assessment, writ broadly, is being carried out at the institution. Among our key findings were these: (1) Overall the institution has a great deal of information about its students, but too often, the information is not shared among offices; the lack of sharing is due essentially to a lack of awareness of the potential use to which the data may be put by others rather than to a deliberate sense of territoriality or an unwillingness to collaborate. (2) Several offices collected student data but made little if any use of them because there was no way to store and manipulate the data easily. (3) Some offices collect student data because "we've always done it," but do not any longer (if indeed they ever did) make use of such data. (4) Many areas were reluctant to carry out assessment projects in which they were interested because of the burden of doing so; college personnel were unaware of the kind and extent of professional assistance available to them through the Office of Research. (5) Initially, several interviewees said they did not do any student assessments, but in conversation they described activities that were assessments. (6) Some offices that work directly with students do not see the value of collecting and analyzing data about students, and some others see only marginal utility in doing so. Yet these same offices expressed dismay that there seemed to be so little collegewide understanding of the kinds of services they provided and the numbers of students they served. (7) The college's ability to gather, integrate, and manipulate data is considerably limited by its current computing resources, particularly its student information system.

Use of Findings

While it began as a project designed simply to elicit information, the assessment audit proved to be a valuable educational tool. The institution now has a more comprehensive understanding of the extent to which student assessment is being carried out already and of the barriers to initiating certain desired assessments. And because problems related to data collection, storage, and manipulation were uncovered, corrective action could be taken.

As the institution moves to implement more rigorous student assessment policies, to respond to increasing requests from internal and external bodies regarding accountability, and to prepare for its next accreditation self-study, more efficient and effective student assessment can be achieved as a result of this project. In addition, the findings of this audit supported the institution's pursuit of a new student information system and made clear some specific features that such a system should have.

Success Factors

We believe the methodology of personal interviews made a substantial contribution to the success of the project and the richness of information about assessment that was compiled. It was clear from our interviews that a paper-and-pencil instrument would have blurred the issue: questionnaire recipients would have indicated that their offices did not engage in the work of assessment when, in fact, they do. Consequently, survey findings would have indicated much less assessment activity than is actually taking place. Ignorance of available services would probably not have been manifested through surveys but was sharply evident during the interviews. And finally, many people were excited that an administrator was taking time to sit down and listen to them talk about what they did, why they did it, what problems they had, and how the institution might make their work easier. People felt cared about and valued. This, in and of itself, made the audit process a success.

Laying the Foundation for Effectiveness Through Assessment

James L. Hudgins, Dorcas A. Kitchings, Starnell K. Williams

CASE 79: MIDLANDS TECHNICAL COLLEGE

Look for: A close relationship between college mission and measures of effectiveness. These measures include broad performance indicators, academic program review, employer involvement in goal setting and in student outcomes assessment, and longitudinal tracking of mathematics and language skills.

Background and Purpose

Over the past eight years, Midlands Technical College (MTC) has utilized the institutional effectiveness movement as a strategy for institutional renewal. For MTC, institutional effectiveness is a comprehensive planning and evaluation process that enables the college to demonstrate that its performance matches its purpose. This institutional perspective has resulted in tangible improvements and promoted a college culture conducive to informed decision making. A key to the success of the model is the collection of truly useful information that can be applied to a number of reporting and operational purposes.

While the process of developing or operationalizing institutional effectiveness programs in higher education varies, it usually contains seven basic steps:

1. Articulate the mission.
2. Establish a planning mechanism.
3. Develop an evaluation system that tells if the college is doing what it says it does.
4. Identify critical areas of success.
5. Establish priority standards upon which the college can judge its effectiveness in the identified critical areas.

6. Determine mechanisms for documenting if established standards have been met.
   - Objective data: enrollment reports, licensure test results, transfer grades, assessment of majors
   - Surveys: written, telephone, interview
   - Peer reviews
7. Utilize results of assessment for decision making.

Method

The MTC assessment process asks three questions: What is the principal mission of the college? What results can be expected from mission achievement? And, What measurements will serve as adequate evidence that these results have been achieved? In order to find the answers to these questions, the college established a strategic planning cycle that requires systematic interaction, consensus, and collaboration on appropriate actions and outcomes and ultimately provides parameters for specific operational decisions. As a basic component of the strategic plan, the college identified six areas critical to institutional success: (1) accessible, comprehensive programs of high quality; (2) student satisfaction and retention; (3) posteducation satisfaction and success; (4) economic development and community involvement; (5) sound, effective resource management; and (6) dynamic organizational involvement and development.

Twenty indicators were designated within these core areas as evidence of the college's effectiveness in fulfilling its stated mission. Because MTC's prime commitment is to student success, the indicators of effectiveness reflect and measure this key value.

Three specific examples of the twenty indicators of effectiveness are assessment of student knowledge and skills acquired in the major area of study; feedback from employers and receiving institutions on the success of employees or transfer students; and student evaluation of the college's role in the achievement of personal or career goals.

Because MTC places heavy emphasis on career education leading to productive employment in the college's service region, special attention is given to assessment of technical and vocational programs. One of the most comprehensive strategies for assuring that students are exposed to a relevant, quality learning environment is the academic program review process for all associate degree programs. The following data elements are included in an academic program review: (1) achievement of program goals; (2) student grade point averages; (3) student mastery of capstone competencies; (4) student mastery of a general education core; (5) program statistics, including enrollment, cost, retention rate, and number of graduates; (6) employment success of graduates; and (7) surveys of students, alumni, employers, and lay advisory committees.

The college is sensitive to the practical workplace skills employers expect and require of technical/community college graduates. In many areas, the DACUM (Developing A CUrriculuM) process is used as part of a program review involving members of the business community in establishing a set of expectations and capstone competencies for each academic area. Each program review uses the DACUM, the primary feature of which is practitioners who develop a curriculum using a nominal group process. The DACUM is only one component of the program review. The program faculty rely on DACUM input when determining course content, methods of information delivery, and mechanisms for assessing capstone competencies. In all cases, program faculty work with education division administrators to develop appropriate standards. Various measures of accountability are built into the process.

Another important assessment strategy for measuring student progress is longitudinal tracking of mathematical and language skills through a series of courses presented in a structured sequence. Sequenced-course objectives allow the MTC tracking system to identify strengths and weaknesses in the curriculum.

Use of Findings

Tracking data, in concert with classroom research, are used to modify and improve curricula. Tracking in the English department of a cohort of one thousand students recently resulted in a course design that allowed students to learn writing through readings. In the math department, tracking led to a faculty decision to define course objectives more clearly. The tracking of students' progression through course sequences resulted in decisions by faculty to increase expectations and make adjustments in the course content to enhance student success in meeting those expectations.

MTC uses these and a variety of other assessment measures to evaluate success in achieving the benchmarks established for each indicator of effectiveness and to make continuous improvements. Two of the most important aspects of institutional effectiveness are using the results of data collection to effect change and making constituencies aware of the college's commitment to accountability. At Midlands Technical College, assessment results are communicated through an array of published reports including an annual *Institutional Effectiveness Report Card*, a detailed update on progress toward annual objectives prepared for the board of trustees; and the *Community Report*, the executive summary of the report card, with additional highlights that demonstrate the college's accountability to the public.

Success Factors

The strategies described here are examples of the complex assessment program at MTC. The commitment and clarity of purpose that led to the design of this program have resulted in an integration of assessment procedures that is now implicit in the institution's routine and culture. Such extensive commitments to

assessment and planning require an obvious investment of personnel and resources. However, colleges can expect practical outcomes. At MTC the benefits
of establishing an institutional effectiveness process have included:

- Clarification of mission
- Improved use of resources
- Identification of priorities
- Improved performance
- Increased return on resources invested
- Enhanced reputation
- Enhanced work environment

The ultimate purpose of assessment is to improve the college for the benefit
of students served. By defining effectiveness and using the results of structured assessment activities for planned improvement, the college is best able to achieve
and identify its success.

Developing Indicators to Monitor Quality

Dennis C. Martin

CASE 80: WINONA STATE UNIVERSITY

Look for: Development of a comprehensive campuswide database to monitor quality, using
some 250 indicators. Sources of data include surveys of students, faculty, and staff
as well as institutional files on personnel, the library, finances, and facilities.

Background and Purpose

Winona State University (WSU) is developing and implementing a comprehensive assessment database to evaluate the quality of education provided to our students. The university-level database will be composed of approximately 250
quality indicators developed through the collaborative efforts of students, faculty,
staff, and administrators. These indicators are tied to specific goals and objectives
set forth in the WSU Long Range Plan and are also in line with the institution's
overall mission.

The comprehensive quality indicator database, once it has been fully implemented, will serve as a barometer of WSU's progress in providing quality education for its students.

Method

The university's Quality Assurance and Assessment Plan was approved in 1993
by all WSU's constituent groups, and data collection has begun on many of the

identified indicators. Data on over 80 of the 250 indicators are currently being collected, and instruments are being developed for gathering information on another 170 indicators. Data collection instruments include the following: the CIRP freshman survey; the ACT-COMP survey administered to graduating seniors; internally developed surveys for enrolled students, faculty, and staff; and several other surveys aimed at specific student populations. Other indicator data are abstracted from the WSU master database, including student profile, demographic, and performance data. Personnel, financial, facilities, and library data are also used.

Findings

The Quality Assurance and Assessment Plan is proving useful in evaluating progress toward fulfilling the WSU mission and goals as well as in providing valuable information for future planning and management decision making. Data from two major surveys previously mentioned—the CIRP freshman survey and the ACT-COMP survey—have now been collected for four years, and some preliminary trend lines have been established. These surveys provide WSU with information on approximately twenty-five key indicators.

Some of our findings reveal that the university has raised admission standards recently and has taken measures to improve its image. Students have increasingly indicated that academic reputation was an important reason for deciding to attend WSU. Measures of other key indicators show an increase in the amount of time students spend studying, in the amount of required reading assigned, in the quality of instruction, and in the amount of time students spend working in a group setting. Specifically: (1) Winona State University has raised its minimum admission requirements from a composite ACT score of 19 or higher, or the upper 60 percent of high school graduating class, to an ACT of 21 or higher, or the upper half of high school graduating class. (2) Specific high school preparation standards for all entering freshmen have been put into effect. These standards require that a student have successfully completed four years of English, three years of math, three years of science, three years of social studies, and three years of additional electives chosen from world language, world culture, or the arts. (3) In fall 1990, 39 percent of incoming freshmen rated academic reputation as an important reason for choosing WSU. Three years later, 45 percent gave this response. (4) During the 1991–92 school-year, 35 percent of WSU students reported studying sixteen or more hours per week. Within a year, this percentage rose to 42 percent. (5) The percentage of students reporting that most or all of their classes require regular reading assignments has increased from 87 percent to over 91 percent. (6) The percentage of WSU students reporting satisfaction with the quality of instruction has risen from 60 percent to 68 percent. (7) In 1992, 47 percent of WSU survey respondents indicated significant personal growth in becoming an effective group member; in 1993, 52 percent reported significant gains.

Use of Findings

The initial results of the WSU data collection efforts have been used to provide a profile of our incoming students. This information was used in adjusting our admission standards, in setting enrollment management targets, and in developing more effective ways to orient and integrate our students into the mainstream of university life. The collection of data on student outcomes has also helped the university determine the current levels of satisfaction on key performance indicators and to set goals for improving student performance while measuring progress toward achieving these goals.

Data currently being collected on 150 quality indicators will provide WSU with a comprehensive set of baseline data that will be used to evaluate and improve all aspects of the educational process. Information on students, faculty, staff, administration, budgets, facilities, educational climate, and numerous other areas will be collected and analyzed over time. Internal and external benchmarks will be established, and processes will be analyzed and adjusted for improved performance.

Primary areas for improvement will be student learning activities. Indicator measures based on the "Seven Principles for Good Practice in Undergraduate Education" (Chickering and Gamson, 1987) and learning outcomes identified in the WSU mission statement will help focus the university's efforts as we utilize some of our initial findings to improve learning processes and outcomes. Additional information from indicator measures will be analyzed and used to improve the educational environment and enhance interpersonal relations among faculty, administration, staff, and students.

Success Factors

The Long Range Plan and the Quality Assurance and Assessment Plan have been carefully aligned with the stated mission and goals of WSU. Data are being collected on quality indicators that have been developed and agreed upon by a wide spectrum of university constituents: faculty, staff, administration, and students. Data collection has been incorporated into ongoing processes whenever possible. Examples of such processes include freshman registration and application for graduation.

Sample Goals and Indicators from WSU
Quality Assurance and Assessment Plan

Student Goals and Objectives

Goal 1. **Students:** the university will recruit and admit well-prepared incoming students from culturally diverse backgrounds, representing traditional and nontraditional age groups.

Sample indicator: number/percentage of incoming undergraduate students at percentile intervals of ACT (or SAT) scores, high school rank, and high school GPAs.

Sample indicator: number/percentage of incoming undergraduate students completing college preparatory programs.

Goal 2. **Curriculum:** the university will offer a strong, student-centered curriculum that disseminates knowledge, develops the basic skills for lifelong learning, supports student affective growth and development, and implements the [Q7] indicators of educational quality identified by the Blue Ribbon Commission on Access in the Minnesota State University System.

Sample indicator: number/percentage of students involved in faculty research.

Sample indicator: number/percentage of courses designed with primary emphasis on multicultural content and learning activities.

Sample indicator: number/percentage of programs requiring a prerequisite math competency to enroll in upper-division courses.

Sample indicator: number/percentage of programs requiring an internship, practicum, or other field-based learning experience.

Sample indicator: number of times per quarter students report using the library.

Sample indicator: number/percentage of students reporting frequent use of computers for academic purposes.

Goal 3. **General education:** the university will provide a strong General Education Program grounded in the liberal arts tradition and supported by all disciplines representing the knowledge, skills, and attitudes essential to a generally/liberally educated person.

Indicators: (in process).

Goal 4. **Instruction:** the university will offer a strong instructional system of curriculum delivery that encourages implementing the "Seven Principles of Good Practice in Undergraduate Education" [Chickering and Gamson, 1987] and supports optimal teaching/learning strategies.

Sample indicator: average number of times per quarter faculty meet with students outside of class.

Sample indicator: percentage of students experiencing class enrollments of 15 or fewer students.

Sample indicator: number/percentage of students reporting participation in student study groups during a quarter.

Sample indicator: average number of hours students study per week.

Sample indicator: average number of hours per week faculty spend preparing for classes.

Sample indicator: number/percentage of students reporting generally receiving instructor evaluations of work within one week.

Sample indicator: number/percentage of students reporting satisfaction with the degree of academic challenge experienced in courses.

Sample indicator: number/percentage of programs with half or more of the required credits at the upper-division course level.

Goal 5.   **Student development:** the university will provide a strong student growth and development program of academic services and co-curricular activities that will enhance students' personal, social, and physical growth as well as their potential for academic success.

Sample indicator: number/percentage of students participating in departmental student orientation activities.

Sample indicator: number/percentage of students reporting satisfaction with the freshman orientation program and activities.

Sample indicator: average number of hours per week faculty spend advising students.

Sample indicator: number/percentage of students reporting satisfaction with the quality of advising they have received.

Sample indicator: number/percentage of students who attend campus-sponsored activities (athletic events, theatre, guest lectures, musical productions, and the like).

Sample indicator: number/percentage of students who report satisfaction with the counseling services they have received.

Goal 6.   **Student learning:** Students will demonstrate the [Q10] knowledge, skills, attitudes, and appreciations that represent what all students should know and be able to do as candidates for graduation.

Sample indicator: student portfolio content demonstrating the quality of student performance in accomplishing eleven learning objectives [Q11] as outlined in the university's quality assurance plan. (Portfolio development plan yet to be determined by appropriate groups.)

Sample indicator: number/percentage of alumni reporting satisfaction with their preparation and abilities in each of the [Q11] learning areas.

Goal 7.   **Student growth and development outcomes:** Students will demonstrate personal, physical, and social growth as developed through formal and informal learning communities, co-curricular activities, and academic service programs.

Sample indicator: number/percentage of students reporting improvement in their abilities to relate positively to others.

Sample indicator: number/percentage of students who report becoming a more effective team or group member.

Sample indicator: number/percentage of students reporting increased leadership skills.

Human Resources Goals and Objectives At the personnel level, quality of educational achievement will be measured in three broad areas relating to the goals established for student development and learning. Indicators associated with each of these goals will assess personnel progress in meeting student-related goals and objectives. The primary goals for personnel at Winona State University that are currently being assessed include the following.

Goal 1.   **Human resources:** the university will hire and retain high-quality full-time culturally diverse faculty, administrators, and staff who have demonstrated excellence in teaching, scholarship, and service.

Sample indicator: retention rates for full-time faculty, staff, and administration.

Goal 2. **Faculty development:** the university will maintain a strong faculty and staff development program that sponsors teaching excellence, research, scholarly activity, creative achievement, and other forms of professional growth and involvement.

Sample indicator: number/percentage of faculty and staff participating in university-sponsored in-service seminars, workshops, and presentations.

Sample indicator: number/percentage of faculty reporting satisfaction with the degree of support furnished for scholarly activities, creative achievements, research, and continuing study.

Goal 3. **Faculty development outcomes:** faculty will demonstrate progress in achieving the outcomes of Professional Development Plans for effective instruction and academic service.

Sample indicator: number/percentage of faculty engaging in continuing preparation and study.

Learning Environment Resources and Support Structures Goals and Objectives

At the level of learning environment resources and support structures, quality of educational achievement will be measured in seven broad areas relating to the goals established for student development and learning. Indicators associated with each of these goals will be measured to assess resource and support structure progress in meeting student-related goals and objectives. The primary goals for resources and support structures at Winona State University that are currently being assessed include the following.

Goal 1. **Campus climate:** the university will create an organizational culture and psychological climate that implements the values of mutual respect, ethical behavior, cooperative decision making, appreciation of differences, and positive relations among all constituencies.

Sample indicator: number/percentage of students, faculty, and staff who report experiencing a sense of community in their university activities.

Sample indicator: number/percentage of students, faculty, and staff reporting satisfaction with the degree of their participation in institutional decision making.

Goal 2. **Facilities and resources:** the university will provide and maintain attractive, environmentally responsible physical facilities containing the level of instructional resources and technology necessary to achieve effective instruction and learning outcomes.

Sample indicator: number of hours per week the library is open for students and faculty.

Sample indicator: number of small interactive classrooms (twenty-five seats or fewer) as a percentage of total classroom space.

Goal 3. **Fiscal resources:** the university administration will furnish the fiscal resources and budgetary provisions necessary to effectively implement quality academic processes and learning outcome goals.

Sample indicator: amount and percent change in the FY budget for faculty positions.

Sample indicator: percentage of total FY budget allocated to library material/resources.

Goal 4.   **Teaching/learning climate:** university faculty, students, and staff will create an interactive teaching/learning climate conducive to optimum learning and positive interpersonal dynamics.

   Sample indicator: number/percentage of students reporting they are generally
encouraged to express their views in classes.

   Sample indicator: number/percentage of students reporting a climate of ethnic,
cultural, and religious acceptance/understanding.

Goal 5.   **Administrative process:** the university administration will effectively support high-
quality educational processes with sufficient economic resources, practice a partici-
pative management style, maintain collegial relationships, and provide effective
leadership for sustaining institutional excellence.

   Sample indicator: number/percentage of faculty and staff reporting satisfaction
with the degree of their participation in the institutional decision-making process.

   Sample indicator: number/percentage of faculty and staff reporting satisfaction
with the accessibility of administrators.

   Sample indicator: number/percentage of faculty and staff who report receiving
acknowledgement and positive reinforcement for performance excellence.

   Sample indicator: number/percentage of faculty and staff who report knowing the mission and goals of WSU.

Goal 6.   **Continuous process improvement:** the university will effectively evaluate the infor-
mation/results produced by the assessment process for the purpose of improving
curricula, instruction, and student learning.

   Sample indicator: number/percentage of departments and academic units
that have written goals, objectives, and indicators specified for each program or
service.

Goal 7.   **University stature:** the university will achieve recognition for academic quality with
programs that meet external standards of excellence, by qualifying for public and
private grants and through the professional achievements of faculty, staff, and administrators.

   Sample indicator: number of programs meeting licensure and certification requirements and standards.

   Sample indicator: number/percentage of students reporting that one of their
reasons for choosing WSU is its positive image as a quality institution.

Encouraging Faculty Involvement Through Mini-Grants

Ben F. Shaw, Jr., Kenneth H. McKinley, Stephen P. Robinson

CASE 81: OKLAHOMA STATE UNIVERSITY

Look for: Use of mini-grants to encourage the faculty at a research university to develop models for assessing students' attainment of specific program outcomes. An annual insti-

tutionwide report, consisting of one-page summaries of assessment findings from each academic program, communicates with external audiences and keeps departments motivated to continue their efforts.

Background and Purpose

Oklahoma State University (OSU) began a comprehensive assessment program as a result of a State Regents' mandate requiring that all institutions of higher education in the state assess students' competencies and satisfaction at the entry, mid, and outcome levels. Entry- and midlevel assessments consist primarily of existing data analysis, testing, and writing assessments.

The three primary purposes of the OSU assessment program are program improvement, public accountability, and accreditation. An assessment council, comprising faculty from each of the six academic colleges at OSU, administrators, and students, was formed to plan and implement the beginning phases of the assessment program. The council was divided into council subcommittees, each with the responsibility of planning and initially implementing activities for assessing student entry-level skills, midlevel skills, program outcomes, or satisfaction. Each subcommittee solicited input from various campus populations and devised a plan for assessing students at the particular level for which it was responsible.

The OSU subcommittee for the assessment of program outcomes asked faculty representing individual departments and degree programs to develop their own models for assessing their students' attainment of stated program outcomes. The Assessment Council offered mini-grants, in amounts based on the number of majors in those academic departments that devised exemplary outcomes assessment models, for implementation and piloting of the models. The OSU Office of University Assessment then used many of these models as templates to assist other departments in planning and developing their assessment activities. Within a year of the initial call for assessment models, all but four or five of the academic departments across campus had submitted and begun implementation of an assessment plan. Eventually, every academic department on campus submitted models that explained how the department would assess student outcomes.

The models were initially reviewed by members of the program outcomes subcommittee to determine the feasibility of each plan and the extent to which the results of that plan would meet State Regents' guidelines.

Method

Most assessment methods in the various departments focused on students who were expected to graduate within one year and on alumni who were within one to five years of graduation. In all cases, both internal and external assessment methods were used. Internal methods were defined as those in which a locally developed instrument or method was administered and analyzed by personnel within the department. External methods were those developed, implemented, and/or analyzed by professionals outside the program.

Actual assessment methods varied greatly among academic programs, but all were aimed at evaluating the level of students' achievement of the programs' stated outcomes. Assessment methods included:

- Senior seminar projects
- Capstone course portfolios
- Surveys of employer satisfaction
- Graduate school admission rates
- Job placement data
- GRE, MAT, and GMAT scores
- Certification/licensure exam scores
- External reviews of internship performance
- Graduation rates
- External review of portfolios
- Locally developed assessment instruments
- Major Field Achievement Tests
- External program and accreditation reviews
- Exit interviews
- Intercollegiate academic competitions
- Performance in selected courses
- Student teaching evaluation
- Alumni surveys

While no program used all the methods listed, each was asked to utilize (1) a multidimensional model that included more than one method and (2) at least one externally validated assessment methodology. The Office of University Assessment provided guidelines for the implementation of assessment activities, and newsletters, seminars, and faculty meetings helped people understand the need for and expected format of outcomes assessment at OSU.

Findings

As can be expected from any assessment initiative that allows for program-based assessment methods, the findings of the OSU outcomes assessment activities varied greatly. The one consistent result of the overall program was summed up by one department head in a newsletter article. He stated: "When all of the [outcomes assessment] data were assembled, a picture quickly developed, much to my surprise, that revealed, at a glance, our strengths and weaknesses. My attitude about the value and usefulness of program outcomes assessment changed completely, and I am now a strong proponent of the process. . . . There is no question in my mind that program outcomes assessment is a valuable tool for identifying program strengths and weaknesses. It won't correct the problems, but it tells you where to start" (Hughes, 1993, p. 4).

Some of the more specific findings that help to illustrate this faculty member's point were listed in progress reports submitted to the Office of University Assessment after one year of assessment activity. The most useful findings were those that helped departments identify curricular deficiencies and other shortages in their degree programs. A sample of these findings is listed below. (Please note that these findings are from different, randomly selected departments and are not related to each other.)

- Exit interviews: students expressed concern about the marketability of their degrees, but were generally satisfied.
- Capstone course project: 85 percent of students achieved an "excellent" rating on capstone course projects when reviewed by a jury of industry professionals. Follow-up interviews revealed that students gained a greater understanding of group and social dynamics than they had before.
- Employer survey: the results indicated a need for additional computer training in the area of specialization. Computer knowledge and application skills were extremely outdated.
- Portfolio assessment: oral communication skills were identified as strong in a majority of students, but writing skills are still weak.
- Internship evaluation: 78 percent of students completing internships received "above average" overall ratings from cooperating professionals. One consistent weakness was found in the interns' ability to explain technical concepts and designs to clients.

The task of compiling such a wide array of findings into a generic report is challenging. The assessment office approach is to have each academic program submit a one-page report listing stated outcomes, assessment methods, and general results. This type of reporting provides interested parties with useful information while allowing the individual programs to maintain and use specific findings for their most valuable purpose—program improvement.

Use of Findings

Along with generating reports for the State Regents, the data gathered from outcomes assessment activities have been used as the basis for making a variety of modifications across campus. Many programs have made curricular changes in established courses, added facilities and equipment, implemented writing assessments at various stages of students' progress, and added or deleted courses from degree programs as a direct result of their outcomes assessment activities.

In most cases, assessment results are analyzed and discussed by the faculty and staff of each of the departments. The department then decides what action to take to address any concerns that are uncovered. Personnel in the Office of

University Assessment serve as resource persons and are periodically called upon to help departments make sense of their findings and put them to the most efficient use. Departments are further kept up to date on the possible uses of assessment data by newsletters and articles sent out by the office.

Success Factors

The carrot that was dangled before departmental faculty and staff, outcomes assessment mini-grant funding, was the initial motivator for participation. The funds provided through the mini-grants gave programs the necessary resources to explore and experiment with the plethora of assessment possibilities available to them. Once a few programs had started their assessment activities, others followed suit, seeing the value of what was happening. Currently, funding seems to have become a secondary concern.

The most influential factors contributing to the success of the outcomes assessment program at OSU have been faculty involvement and administrative support. One of the highest priorities of the Office of University Assessment was to stay in constant communication with all levels of faculty and administrative staff. The activities of keeping faculty and staff up to date as to the purposes and objectives of assessment and providing them with literature and educational opportunities have been very valuable in maintaining faculty and staff ownership and motivation.

Communicating Outcomes Assessment: A Comprehensive Communications Plan

Denise Gallaro, Gail Cooper Deutsch, Donald Lumsden, Michael E. Knight

CASE 82: KEAN COLLEGE OF NEW JERSEY

Look for: Specific suggestions for using open and frequent communication to create awareness of and involvement in outcomes assessment on campus and to inform external audiences about assessment and its role in improving institutional quality.

Background and Purpose

Effective communication is essential when implementing any program that will require institutional change. Outcomes assessment is such a program, one that may generate anxiety and foster resistance if a communications plan is not comprehensively developed and implemented.

Undertaking assessment of program performance implies that some form of change is needed. On many campuses, confusion exists regarding the nature of this change. Is it necessary because faculty are not teaching the subject material, because the curriculum is deficient, or because students are not learning what is being taught? Some perceive assessment as a threat, and some welcome the challenge of change. An effort must be made to bring both groups to an understanding of the many advantages of outcomes assessment.

Communication can be the single most important factor in conveying the purposes of assessment to the faculty, reassuring them that it will be an internal process for internal purposes, and imparting the benefits of resulting program modifications to students and to the community at large.

Method

The first step in planning any communication activity is to define the audience. Both internal and external constituencies must be reached in order to maximize the impact of an assessment program. Goals and objectives for each group must be developed, and the plan itself must be developed and implemented.

For the purposes of communicating outcomes assessment in higher education, faculty, administration, students, and staff are considered part of the *internal audience.* The primary communication goals in addressing these groups are to create an awareness of outcomes assessment and to provide complete information about the policies, procedures, methods, and activities that are part of the assessment program. These factors are then related to the needs of each particular group and the scope of its present and potential involvement with assessment activities on campus. The ultimate objective is to create an assessment mentality in the group.

At Kean College of New Jersey, open communication has proven to be a successful vehicle for acquainting faculty and administration members with the principles of assessment, informing them of assessment's purposes, ensuring ownership of data, and encouraging participation in the assessment process.

Stimulating participation and involvement of faculty is one of the goals of any campuswide project. Open communication has proven to be a means of enhancing faculty understanding of assessment's contribution to teaching and curriculum development. It emphasizes the fact that involvement in assessment affords opportunities for personal and professional growth. Assessment coordinators can promote participation and involvement by regularly reporting to the faculty about the progress of all activities and by responding to all questions. The individual faculty members responsible for the direction of the assessment efforts in their academic programs can report regularly at departmental meetings, so that all program faculty are aware of developments that will affect their major. At information-sharing sessions open to the college community, these faculty can share their experiences in planning and implementing the various stages of outcomes assessment. Such sessions provide faculty with opportunities to share ideas and participate in cross-discipline exchanges.

Students are another key audience in the assessment process. They need to receive the message that assessment has the potential to strengthen their majors and enhance the value and integrity of their degrees. In addition, they must understand their role in the process, for without them, it could not happen. Student involvement can either be passive or active. They may do no more than take the tests and surveys. Or they can be actively involved by becoming a member of the assessment committee in their academic major. Committee membership gives students an opportunity to learn more about the process, and it provides a way for their experiences and opinions to influence the instruments and procedures employed in their departments. Once they understand the assessment process, it works very well to ask students to talk to other students at forums and group meetings and on informal occasions about the benefits of assessment.

One of the most efficient methods of informing faculty, administrators, staff, and students about assessment is through campus media. Assessment coordinators may develop a publication that describes the process in general and efforts of individual programs in particular. In addition, many departments have their own publications in which articles about their program's progress can be placed.

External audiences for outcomes assessment in higher education include employers, graduate and professional schools, business leaders, governmental agencies, prospective students and parents, high school counselors, alumni, and financial supporters. The primary goal of communicating with this diverse audience is to convey the message that the assessment process will enhance the quality of education at the institution, thus adding integrity and prestige to the school's degrees.

Articles in professional journals and other publications, as well as external circulation of internal newsletters, are effective means of communicating with groups as varied as local business leaders, alumni, and educational experts. These articles can be written by staff and/or faculty members. Other publications, such as catalogs and admissions materials, can inform prospective students, their parents, guidance counselors, and alumni of the institution's assessment efforts.

Presentations, workshops, and conferences are worthwhile methods of communicating to external audiences. Through presentations conducted by faculty and staff, members of the corporate community can be informed how the assessment process will ensure that programs are designed to address workplace needs. Presentations describing the assessment process and the benefits derived from it can also be made at higher education conferences and professional meetings and at seminars planned for faculty and administrators at other institutions. Conferences planned for faculty and administrators from other institutions serve to describe the assessment plan and its implementation.

Use of Communications

Good communications are essential for a successful assessment project. They serve to allay fear and resistance by keeping the campus community informed about purposes and progress. They involve staff, faculty, and students in the process of determining the direction of the institution and its individual programs. Good communications inform the outside community of the institution's commitment to program quality and the integrity of its degrees.

CHAPTER SEVENTEEN

HAS ASSESSMENT MADE A DIFFERENCE?

Trudy W. Banta

In *Making a Difference: Outcomes of a Decade of Assessment in Higher Education* (Banta and Associates, 1993), I asked the forty-five chapter authors to focus on the *accomplishments* of assessment. What uses had been made of assessment findings on their campuses? Were instructors teaching more effectively? Were students learning more? Were institutions more effective as a result of assessment? What evidence did we have that a decade of experience with assessment had made a difference?

I discovered that these were not the questions assessment practitioners really wanted to answer. They wanted to talk about the *process* of assessment: how faculty had taken charge of assessment and were doing it for their own reasons despite the pressures of external mandates; how faculty had developed their own interesting approaches to assessment and, in the process, had gained new insights about their own teaching and about the nature of student learning.

In preparing cases for this volume, I encouraged the authors to tell their own stories in their own ways. While there was a common template for presentation, imposed to make the reader's job easier, authors were free to provide their own focus. And as the organization of cases in several chapters in Part Two illustrates, some of the authors concentrated on establishing the *purpose* for assessment, some emphasized the *methods* faculty used, and others were eager to tell about their *findings* and the *use of assessment results* in making improvements in academic programs and student services. Finally, a few of the cases are distinguished by insightful comments about the *factors the authors believe are responsible for the successes of assessment* on their campuses.

Despite the fact that the focus in this book is not upon assessment's bottom line, every author was asked to address the outcomes of the assessment practices he or she described. I would be less than honest if I did not identify assessment outcomes as a source of abiding concern for me. Accordingly, this last chapter provides a summary of what I learned by putting together the information from the concluding sections of the cases in Part Two. Once again the question is, Has assessment made a difference?

Evidence of Increases in Student Learning

Douglas J. Eder, of Southern Illinois University at Edwardsville (SIUE), may have expressed my overall conclusion best in his statement that "the most visible consequences of [assessment] so far are not for the students" (Case 3). Having assembled 165 case studies based on some of the best assessment taking place at campuses across the country, I must say that the number of these cases containing concrete evidence that student performance has improved as a result of assessment is very small. At SIUE and at the University of Montevallo (Case 18), assessment focused on student involvement in research has produced increases in the numbers of (1) proposals submitted and (2) papers presented by undergraduates at regional and national professional conferences. At Montevallo, more students are being placed in Ph.D. programs in psychology as a result of their experience in conducting research, and Montevallo graduates enrolled in advanced degree programs have reported that their undergraduate research experience has helped them appreciably in their graduate studies.

Students in the College of Dentistry at the University of Louisville (Case 15) were encouraged to take their end-of-program board exams more seriously and to engage in focused preparation for the exams. As a result, students' scores on the board exams increased significantly. At Dyersburg State Community College (Case 16), student scores on the National League for Nursing Achievement Test improved after faculty took note of student score deficits and made corresponding curriculum changes. For thirteen years, no DSCC nursing student has failed to pass the national exam.

At Northeast Missouri State University (Case 29), sophomores' gain scores on the ACT College Outcome Measures Project (COMP) exam were actually losses. Faculty changed the mathematics curriculum and gain scores improved dramatically. Students' self-assessments of their abilities to understand and apply mathematical concepts also improved. Similar gains in science scores and related self-perceptions followed changes in science requirements at NMSU.

Although Samford University (Case 11) has no numbers in its report, faculty in the School of Education there believe that using portfolios in assessment has increased students' computer skills and their abilities to plan and to collaborate with other students.

At DePaul University (Case 14), retention of graduate students is higher as a result of their participation in an assessment colloquium. Students learn to engage in self-assessment, to seek feedback from multiple sources, and to set direction in their work and in their personal lives. The DePaul faculty have evidence that their graduates perform more effectively as professionals as a result of their assessment experience because they are being promoted at a faster rate than was the case with previous groups of DePaul students in the same curriculum.

Retention to graduation of honors students at Radford University (Case 27) has increased in part because the faculty initiated a colloquium similar to the one for graduate students at DePaul. The learning outcomes expected of students are discussed in this setting. Having clear expectations, well understood by students, increases the likelihood that students will attain the expectations—one of which is that students will obtain degrees.

Perhaps the most unusual and tangible evidence of the benefits to students that assessment can convey comes from the College of Business at Ball State University (Case 19). Employers play an important role in determining students' grades in the course New Venture Creation by indicating which student proposals for new businesses have the best chance for success. In a few cases, the employer-assessors have been so impressed with the ideas presented for a new venture that they have been willing to invest money to get it started!

Despite the interest among the publics of higher education—parents, students, legislators, governors, accrediting bodies—in concrete evidence of what students know and can do when they complete a college major, outcomes assessment so far has contributed too little such evidence. While assessment has produced some spectacular gains for students at a few institutions, and continues to hold great promise for providing more objective evidence of learning, few campuses are reporting on student outcomes in ways that will satisfy higher education's supporters, much less its detractors.

So has assessment made *any* difference? Absolutely.

Evidence That the Process of Education Has Been Improved

The cases assembled for this volume are filled with concrete examples of changes that faculty and administrators have undertaken on the basis of assessment findings for purposes of improving classroom teaching, assessment techniques, curricula, and student services. In order of frequency of mention, these improvement actions may be characterized as follows:

1. Changes in classroom activities and assignments to promote student learning of specified outcomes
2. Changes in curricula to address student learning needs discovered in the course of assessment

3. Improvements in the assessment of student learning: designing exams, assessing performance in internships, and assigning grades

Changes in Classroom Activities and Assignments

Assessment's most powerful point of impact is the individual classroom. A change in curriculum or in a student service like advising may take years to produce a measurable change in student performance, but a faculty member can adopt a new teaching technique that can immediately help a whole class of students see a concept more clearly.

Assessment findings have helped faculty spot specific learning deficits or problems more quickly. Such findings suggest immediately where action should be taken.

Faculty report that students need more help in improving their communication skills than in any other area of their development. Many of the campus cases included in this volume illustrate how faculty have increased writing assignments, class discussion time, and opportunities for group work in order to improve written and oral communication and listening skills.

Critical thinking and functioning as part of a team are other areas of competence in which reviews of assessment findings have encouraged faculty to spend additional time developing their students' skills. These complex skills can be enhanced by assigning projects that require individuals and/or groups to apply concepts they have learned in solving actual or simulated problems. Offering more opportunities for students to practice these skills is most effective in promoting learning. At Virginia Polytechnic Institute and State University (Case 17), for instance, some upper-division math courses have been modified to provide reinforcement of basic concepts taught earlier, and at many colleges, writing, computing, and critical thinking are being taught "across the curriculum."

Changes in Curricula

As faculty have looked at student performance on comprehensive exams and read student criticisms of curricula on questionnaires, many have recognized that changes in individual classrooms are not enough to produce needed improvements in student learning. Modifications in curricula and course structure also are needed.

The experience of faculty members at Western Carolina University (Case 25) is typical in that assessment findings convinced them that they needed to come to collective agreement about the kinds of skills and knowledge students should develop as a result of the college experience. Explicit statements of competence for students can become guides for teachers as they design their course content and for students as they focus their studies. At King's College (Case 5), the Sophomore-Junior Diagnostic Project serves as a focal point for departmental discussion of what a student major should learn and, thus, helps faculty build consensus about student outcomes.

Shining the light of collective discussion of curriculum on individual courses encourages faculty to keep their content current and responsive to the demands of students and of faculty who teach subsequent related courses. Such discussion also leads often to the realization that instructors are doing very different things in multiple sections of the same course. At Ball State University (Case 1) and the University of Arkansas at Pine Bluff (Case 24), this discovery has led faculty to develop common syllabi for multisection courses.

In many cases, assessment findings have suggested the need for new courses or experiences to be developed or for current courses to be required rather than elective. At the University of Tennessee, Knoxville (Case 2), the performance of speech majors was sufficiently disappointing to faculty in the speech communication department to prompt the design of a new course emphasizing performance and a capstone course offering opportunities to assess and improve performance.

At some institutions, an internship component has been added to the curriculum to give students the opportunity to apply their learning in actual situations. At Kean College of New Jersey (Case 21), content analysis of students' internship evaluations given by fieldwork supervisors revealed weaknesses in students' preparation in statistics and research methods. Several steps were taken to strengthen the curriculum and instruction in these areas. At the University of Montevallo (Case 18), the level of students' research skills prompted faculty to develop a second research course—one incorporating an animal laboratory experience—for undergraduates and to increase the instances of student involvement in faculty research.

Improvements in Assessment Strategies

After many years of intensive work and major investments at many levels, the science of assessing human performance and the art of developing valid and reliable measures for classroom use still seem to many faculty to be at rather primitive stages. Nevertheless, the interest in assessing comprehensive student learning outcomes has produced an almost unprecedented level of activity in the field of measurement, and many creative instruments and methods are being proposed.

The application of Primary Trait Scoring (PTS) to the grading of student work provides one example. PTS was first used to score essays completed as part of the National Assessment of Educational Progress. Barbara Walvoord and her associates from across the country have adapted PTS to make classroom grading criteria and procedures more explicit and systematic (Case 64). Thus, expected student outcomes and the criteria for their assessment can become more public and more comparable across classrooms. Traditional classroom grades then can be used to serve external accountability as well as internal improvement purposes.

Through faculty development experiences provided to prepare instructors for assessing outcomes, faculty have learned how to improve their own classroom assessment methods. The consistent 100 percent pass rates on the national nursing exam by Dyersburg State Community College students (Case 16) are attributed in part to the fact that faculty have learned to add to their own classroom tests good multiple-choice items similar to those students will encounter on the national test. Thus, course exams have become, in effect, practice tests for the national exam. At Kean College of New Jersey (Case 21), content analysis of fieldwork supervisors' evaluations of Kean social work majors has resulted in several improvements in the evaluation form the supervisors are asked to complete.

The skill of self-assessment is becoming recognized as a valuable learning tool in and of itself, and faculty are seeking to develop this skill within themselves as well as within students. At DePaul University, faculty and students work together on self-assessment (Case 14). Faculty believe students become better problem solvers as they learn to seek information from multiple sources and better planners as they learn to set directions for their work and in their personal lives. Self-assessment skills are accorded at least partial credit for enabling DePaul graduates to be more effective professionals and to earn more promotions than their peers from previous years when self-assessment was not emphasized to the extent it is today.

Participating in peer assessment of written and oral performances strengthens self-assessment skills as well as the ability to offer constructive criticism of the work of others. At King's College (Case 5B), the use of peer response in writing, in association with the Sophomore-Junior Diagnostic Project, is credited with increasing student-student interaction skills as well.

From Principles to Practice and Back to Principles

In Part One, we related the campus experiences assembled for this book to the nine AAHE principles for good practice in assessment. The model for those assessment principles is the "Seven Principles for Good Practice in Undergraduate Education" (Chickering and Gamson, 1987), developed in connection with a Wingspread conference held in 1986. As also described in Chapter Four, these seven principles assert that good practice in undergraduate education:

1. Encourages student-faculty contact
2. Encourages cooperation among students
3. Encourages active learning
4. Gives prompt feedback
5. Emphasizes time on task
6. Communicates high expectations
7. Respects diverse talents and ways of learning

The seven principles are based on decades of research on student learning in higher education. They describe conditions that promote, enhance, and increase student learning. It seems quite justifiable to conclude that if outcomes assessment increases the extent to which these principles are applied in classrooms across the country, then assessment is enhancing and increasing student learning. I believe the contents of this book prove that this is happening. The examples that follow give only the barest hint of the weight of evidence that can be gleaned from the 165 cases upon which the book is based.

Student-faculty contact is certainly enhanced and increased by the involvement of undergraduates in faculty research that is taking place at institutions like SIUE (Case 3) and Montevallo (Case 18). Moreover, students have been involved in working with faculty on every phase of assessment, from planning approaches to interpreting findings and suggesting responsive improvements.

Increases in student-student cooperation and collaboration are outcomes of involvement in assessment projects like the development of portfolios by teacher education students at Samford University (Case 11) and the use of peer response in writing in some of the Sophomore-Junior Diagnostic Projects at King's College (Case 5B). At Belmont University (Case 69), students build teamwork skills as they learn to apply quality-improvement strategies to the evaluation of a class they are taking.

As assessment has revealed less than ideal levels of fundamental skills among the student population, responsive faculty have found ways to increase opportunities for students to participate more actively in learning and to spend more time practicing their skills. For example, more writing assignments and more time for class discussion have been found helpful in improving written and oral communication skills. At Virginia Polytechnic Institute and State University (Case 17), upper-division math courses were redesigned to provide students with additional practice of some basic concepts taught in earlier courses. When students' research skills were found wanting at Montevallo (Case 18), a second research course was added.

Good assessment is all about providing feedback to students regarding their performance. The 100 percent pass rates on the national nursing exam at Dyersburg State Community College (Case 16) are due largely to the fact that students find out where the gaps in their learning are by looking at the scores they earn on classroom tests that require them to apply skills and concepts that will be found on the national exam.

The application of Primary Trait Scoring to traditionally graded work (Case 64) combines the principles of setting high expectations and providing prompt feedback. Students first receive explicit statements of expected outcomes, then get detailed information about their attainment levels of these outcomes as they complete assignments and exams.

The diverse array of methods being used to evaluate student learning demonstrates that assessment respects diverse talents and ways of knowing. For instance, a senior capstone course in speech communication at the University of Tennessee, Knoxville (Case 2) employs six methods, from a symposium speech to an oral critique of another student's paper, to assess student competence in eight areas. In addition, assessment findings have prompted many instructors to make adaptations in their teaching and classroom assessment techniques that accommodate diverse learning styles.

While we may not have volumes (or even a full chapter!) of hard data that show just how much assessment has increased student learning, we have every reason to believe that this young science can furnish that data as it matures in the years just ahead. In the meantime, in *Assessment in Practice*, we have produced a second volume, a companion to *Making A Difference*, that presents many examples of the extent to which assessment is contributing to practices demonstrated to enhance and increase student learning.

RESOURCE A: CARNEGIE CLASSIFICATION DEFINITION OF CATEGORIES

The 1994 Carnegie Classification includes all colleges and universities in the United States that are degree-granting and accredited by an agency recognized by the U.S. Secretary of Education.

Research Universities I: These institutions offer a full range of baccalaureate programs, are committed to graduate education through the doctorate, and give high priority to research. They award 50 or more doctoral degrees[1] each year. In addition, they receive annually $40 million or more in federal support.[2]

Research Universities II: These institutions offer a full range of baccalaureate programs, are committed to graduate education through the doctorate, and give high priority to research. They award 50 or more doctoral degrees[1] each year. In addition, they receive annually between $15.5 million and $40 million in federal support.[2]

Doctoral Universities I: These institutions offer a full range of baccalaureate programs and are committed to graduate education through the doctorate. They award at least 40 doctoral degrees[1] annually in five or more disciplines.[3]

Doctoral Universities II: These institutions offer a full range of baccalaureate programs and are committed to graduate education through the doctorate. They award annually at least ten doctoral degrees—in three or more disciplines—or 20 or more doctoral degrees in one or more disciplines.[3]

Master's (Comprehensive) Colleges and Universities I: These institutions offer a full range of baccalaureate programs and are committed to graduate education through the master's degree. They award 40 or more master's degrees annually in three or more disciplines.[3]

Master's (Comprehensive) Colleges and Universities II: These institutions offer a full range of baccalaureate programs and are committed to graduate education through the master's degree. They award 20 or more master's degrees annually in one or more disciplines.[3]

Baccalaureate (Liberal Arts) Colleges I: These institutions are primarily undergraduate colleges with major emphasis on baccalaureate degree programs. They award 40 percent or more of their baccalaureate degrees in liberal arts fields[4] and are restrictive in admissions.

Baccalaureate Colleges II: These institutions are primarily undergraduate colleges with major emphasis on baccalaureate degree programs. They award less than 40 percent of their baccalaureate degrees in liberal arts fields[4] or are less restrictive in admissions.

Associate of Arts Colleges: These institutions offer associate of arts certificate or degree programs and, with few exceptions, offer no baccalaureate degrees.[5]

Specialized Institutions: These institutions offer degrees ranging from the bachelor's to the doctorate. At least 50 percent of the degrees awarded by these institutions are in a single discipline. Specialized institutions include:

Theological seminaries, Bible colleges, and other institutions offering degrees in religion: This category includes institutions at which the primary purpose is to offer religious instruction or train members of the clergy.

Medical schools and medical centers: These institutions award most of their professional degrees in medicine. In some instances, their programs include other health professional schools, such as dentistry, pharmacy, or nursing.

Other separate health profession schools: Institutions in this category award most of their degrees in such fields as chiropractic, nursing, pharmacy, or podiatry.

Schools of engineering and technology: The institutions in this category award at least a bachelor's degree in programs limited almost exclusively to technical fields of study.

Schools of business and management: The schools in this category award most of their bachelor's or graduate degrees in business or business-related programs.

Schools of art, music, and design: Institutions in this category award most of their bachelor's or graduate degrees in art, music, design, architecture, or some combination of such fields.

Schools of law: The schools included in this category award most of their degrees in law. The list includes only institutions that are listed as separate campuses in the *1994 Higher Education Directory*.

Teachers colleges: Institutions in this category award most of their bachelor's or graduate degrees in education or education-related fields.

Other specialized institutions: Institutions in this category include graduate centers, maritime academies, military institutes, and institutions that do not fit any other classification category.

Tribal colleges and universities: These colleges are, with few exceptions, tribally controlled and located on reservations. They are all members of the American Indian Higher Education Consortium.

Notes on Definitions

1. Doctoral degrees include Doctorate of Education, Doctor of Juridical Science, Doctor of Public Health, and the Ph.D. in any field.

2. Total federal obligation figures are available from the National Science Foundation's annual report called *Federal Support to Universities, Colleges, and Nonprofit Institutions.* The years used in averaging total federal obligations are 1989, 1990, and 1991.

3. Distinct disciplines are determined by the U.S. Department of Education's *Classification of Instructional Programs* 4-digit series.

4. The liberal arts disciplines include English language and literature, foreign languages, letters, liberal and general studies, life sciences, mathematics, philosophy and religion, physical sciences, psychology, social sciences, the visual and performing arts, area and ethnic studies, and multi- and interdisciplinary studies. The occupational and technical disciplines include agriculture, allied health, architecture, business and management, communications, conservation and natural resources, education, engineering, health sciences, home economics, law and legal studies, library and archival sciences,

marketing and distribution, military sciences, protective services, public administration and services, and theology.

5. This group includes community, junior, and technical colleges.

Source: The Carnegie Foundation for the Advancement of Teaching, *A Classification of Institutions of Higher Education.* Princeton, 1994.

RESOURCE B: LIST OF CONTRIBUTORS

Case authors' current institutional affiliations are given here. In some instances, the current affiliation will differ from the institution about which the author writes.

JOAN E. AITKEN, associate professor, Communication Studies
University of Missouri-Kansas City

JOHN M. ALEXANDER, head, Department of Languages and Literature
Ferris State University

LARRY D. ALEXANDER, associate professor, Strategic Management
Virginia Polytechnic Institute and State University

VIRGINIA JOHNSON ANDERSON, professor, Biology
Towson State University

BOOKER T. ANTHONY, assistant professor and chairperson, English and
    Communication
Fayetteville State University

ROGER A. BALLOU, dean of students
University of Wisconsin-River Falls

JOHN R. BARKER, institutional research associate
University of Mississippi Medical Center

KATHRYN H. BAUGHER, dean of admissions
Belmont University

MARY H. BEAVEN, professor of management, College of Business Administration
Fairleigh Dickinson University

TRUDY BERS, senior director, Institutional Research, Curriculum, and Strategic
     Planning
Oakton Community College

ELLEN LOWRIE BLACK, associate vice president, Planning, Research, and
     Assessment
Liberty University

SUSAN LOVEGREN BOSWORTH, assessment coordinator
College of William and Mary

KAREN A. BOWYER, president
Dyersburg State Community College

JEAN ANN BOX, chair, Teacher Education
Samford University

JOHN R. BREIHAN, professor, History
Loyola College in Maryland

STEPHANIE L. BRESSLER, assistant professor, Political Science
King's College

JUDITH E. BRISBOIS, deputy for academics, Foreign Languages
United States Air Force Academy

EARL B. BROWN, JR., director, Honors Program
Radford University

R. DALE BULLARD, assistant dean, Student Affairs
University of South Carolina at Sumter

VERNON BURNSED, associate professor, Music
Virginia Polytechnic Institute and State University

JAMES A. CALLIOTTE, director, Student Development Center
Old Dominion University

LYNN CAMERON, associate professor, Carrier Library
James Madison University

JO ELLEN CANTRELL, director, Total Quality Management
Spartanburg Technical College

KAREN W. CAREY, director, Institutional Research
Eastern Kentucky University

ROSEMARIE CARFAGNA, director, Ursuline Studies Program Core Curriculum
Ursuline College

RICHARD A. CHECHILE, professor, Psychology
Tufts University

ROBERT J. CHIERICO, professor, Spanish
Chicago State University

ROGER D. CLARK, professor, Sociology
Rhode Island College

STEVE COHEN, technical director, Curricular Software Studio
Tufts University

RICHARD E. COWAN, chair, Division of Mathematics and Computer Science
Shorter College

ELIZABETH H. CROWTHER, director, Instructional Services
Lord Fairfax Community College

STEVEN M. CULVER, assistant professor, School of Social Work
Radford University

TODD M. DAVIS, director of research, Institute of International Education,
    and associate professor, Higher Education
University of North Texas

CAROL D. DEAN, director, Office of Field Experience
Samford University

RUSSELL K. DEAN, associate provost, Curriculum and Instruction
West Virginia University

GAIL COOPER DEUTSCH, assistant to dean of education
Kean College of New Jersey

PATRICIA DEWITT, director, Institutional Planning and Research
Shorter College

NANCY L. DILLARD, associate director, Baccalaureate Nursing Program
Ball State University

DOUGLAS J. EDER, associate professor, Neuroscience, and director,
      Undergraduate Assessment and Program Review
Southern Illinois University at Edwardsville

VIOLA GRAY ELLISON, director, Comprehensive Testing, and professor, Education
University of Arkansas at Pine Bluff

JOHN W. EMERT, associate professor, Mathematical Sciences
Ball State University

JOHN F. ENNIS, associate professor, English
King's College

NOREEN C. FACIONE, associate researcher
University of California-San Francisco

PETER A. FACIONE, dean, College of Arts and Sciences
Santa Clara University

MORRIS FIDDLER, senior fellow, School for New Learning
DePaul University

RACHEL FILINSON, associate professor, Sociology
Rhode Island College

JOHN FOLGER, professor emeritus, Vanderbilt Institute for Public Policy Studies
Vanderbilt University

DARLENE A. FRANKLIN, assistant professor, Nursing
Tennessee Technological University

JACK FRIEDLANDER, vice president, Academic Affairs
Santa Barbara City College

BARBARA S. FUHRMANN, director, Academic Planning
Virginia Commonwealth University

JOANNE GAINEN, director, Teaching and Learning Center
Santa Clara University

DENISE GALLARO, assistant director, Assessment, Planning, and Research
Union County College

ANITA GANDOLFO, professor, English
West Virginia University

FRED GEER, professor, Education and Psychology
Avila College

RUTH G. GOLD, assessment coordinator
Northern Illinois University

M. CRISTINA GRABIEL, dean of students
Winthrop University

DALE B. HAHN, professor, Physiology and Health Science
Ball State University

DAVID C. HANSON, director, Instructional Support Services
Virginia Western Community College

LINDA K. HANSON, associate professor and chairperson, English
Ball State University

MARIA HARPER-MARINICK, instructional designer, Center for Learning and
    Instruction
Maricopa Community Colleges

CHARLES F. HARRINGTON, director, Institutional Research, and assistant
    professor, Management
University of Southern Indiana

MARIE JOAN HARRIS, vice president and dean, Academic Affairs
Avila College

RICHARD H. HASWELL, professor, English, and coordinator, Writing Assessment
Washington State University

MICHELLE HENRY HEARD, research associate
University of Arkansas at Pine Bluff

ROSALIE HEWITT, acting associate provost
Northern Illinois University

INGA BAIRD HILL, associate professor, Strategic Management
Ball State University

FRED D. HINSON, director, General Education
Western Carolina University

KAY E. HODSON, coordinator, Instructional and Computer Resources
Ball State University

MARTIN HOPE, coordinator, Student Personal Growth and Development Project
Winthrop University

JAMES L. HUDGINS, president
Midlands Technical College

PAT HUYETT, coordinator, Writing Assessment
University of Missouri-Kansas City

PAMELA IRVING JACKSON, professor, Sociology
Rhode Island College

CAROLEE G. JONES, professor, Business Education and Office Administration
Ball State University

SANDRA J. JORDAN, chair, Art
University of Montevallo

FAYE D. JULIAN, professor and head, Speech Communication
University of Tennessee, Knoxville

GREGORY W. JUSTICE, associate professor, Theatre Arts
Virginia Polytechnic Institute and State University

KORREL W. KANOY, professor, Psychology
Peace College

ALBERT M. KATZ, coordinator, Assessment
University of Wisconsin-Superior

DORCAS A. KITCHINGS, director, Assessment, Research, and Planning
Midlands Technical College

MICHAEL E. KNIGHT, coordinator, Assessment of Student Learning and
Development, and professor, Early Childhood and Family Studies
Kean College of New Jersey

PAULA KRAMER, professor and chair, Occupational Therapy
Kean College of New Jersey

DONALD F. KURATKO, Stoops Distinguished Professor in Business and director,
Entrepreneurship Program, College of Business
Ball State University

JAMES H. LARSON, professor and director, Special Projects for Arts and
Sciences College
University of North Dakota

BARBARA M. LAWRENCE, director, Institutional Research
Idaho State University

SAMUEL G. LAWRENCE, assistant professor, Speech Communication
Indiana University Kokomo

ROSALYN LINDNER, chairperson and professor, Sociology
State University of New York College at Buffalo

DELORES LIPSCOMB, assistant provost, Academic Development
Chicago State University

ROGER C. LOEB, professor, Psychology
University of Michigan-Dearborn

CATHLEEN M. LONDINO, associate professor, Communications
Kean College of New Jersey

DAVID L. LUECHAUER, assistant professor, College of Business Administration
Butler University

DONALD LUMSDEN, professor, Communications
Kean College of New Jersey

ANN MCCANN, director, Assessment and Improvement, Baylor College of
Dentistry
Baylor University

Lucille Parkinson McCarthy, associate professor, English
University of Maryland Baltimore County

Tricia McClam, professor, Education
University of Tennessee, Knoxville

Peter R. MacDougall, president
Santa Barbara City College

Kenneth H. McKinley, associate dean, College of Education
Oklahoma State University

W. Jack Magruder, president
Northeast Missouri State University (Truman State University after July 1996)

Catherine Marienau, associate professor, School for New Learning
DePaul University

Dennis C. Martin, director, Institutional Research
Winona State University

William O. Martin, assistant researcher, Quantitative Assessment Project
University of Wisconsin-Madison

Frederic J. Medway, professor, Psychology
University of South Carolina

Nancy Metz, coordinator, University Writing Program
Virginia Polytechnic Institute and State University

Mark Michael, associate professor, Mathematics and Computer Science
King's College

Robert E. Millward, professor, Education
Indiana University of Pennsylvania

Mary L. Mittler, assistant vice president/dean
Oakton Community College

Gary O. Moden, associate provost
Ohio University

Deborah Moore, assistant director, Offices of Institutional Research and
     Academic Assessment
Ball State University

JOHN A. MUFFO, director, Academic Assessment Program
Virginia Polytechnic Institute and State University

ANNE E. MULLIN, assistant professor, English, and director, Writing Lab
Idaho State University

PATRICIA H. MURRELL, director, Center for the Study of Higher Education
The University of Memphis

CATHERINE R. MYERS, professor, English
Manhattanville College

JEAN P. O'BRIEN, chairperson, Human Resources Management, and associate
    professor, Psychology
King's College

ERNIE OSHIRO, director, Assessment
University of Hawaii-West Oahu

CATHERINE PALOMBA, director, Offices of Institutional Research and
    Academic Assessment
Ball State University

CHARLES R. PARISH, professor, Mathematical Sciences
Ball State University

ROBERT A. PATTERSON, director, University Assessment Center
Capital University

BRIAN K. PICKERILL, senior research analyst, Office of Academic Assessment
Ball State University

JAMES W. PICKERING, senior research associate
Old Dominion University

DANIEL J. POJE, assistant dean of the Graduate School and director, Instructional
    Evaluation
The University of Memphis

DEBBIE POWERS, assistant professor, Physical Education
Ball State University

JOSEPH S. PRUS, professor, Psychology, and director, Office of Assessment
Winthrop University

JOHN W. QUINLEY, director, Planning and Research
Central Piedmont Community College

LISA K. REAVILL, assistant dean of students
University of Wisconsin-River Falls

FREDA L. REMMERS, associate professor, Communications and Theatre
Kean College of New Jersey

DANIEL R. RICE, director, Office of Instructional Development
University of North Dakota

R. DEAN RIESS, assistant chair, Mathematics
Virginia Polytechnic Institute and State University

DOROTHY MARIE RIZZO, instructor, Social Work Program
Kean College of New Jersey

GWEN ROBBINS, coordinator, Fitness, Sport, and Leisure Studies, School of
    Physical Education
Ball State University

SHARON N. ROBERTSON, coordinator, Academic Assessment
Northern Virginia Community College

LARRY ROBINSON, vice chancellor and provost
University of Houston-Victoria

STEPHEN P. ROBINSON, director, University Assessment
Oklahoma State University

SUSAN MILLER ROBISON, professor, Psychology
College of Notre Dame of Maryland

JULIA S. ROGERS, director, Institutional Evaluation
University of Montevallo

MICHAEL ROONEY, district director, Student Development Services
Maricopa Community Colleges

JOHN A. ROUSH, vice president, Planning, and executive assistant to the president
University of Richmond

LINDA B. RUDOLPH, commissioner, Department of Human Services
State of Tennessee

MARILYN E. RYAN, associate director, Graduate Nursing Program, and
coordinator, Research and Grants
Ball State University

RICHARD L. SAGNESS, professor, Education
Idaho State University

MARILYN SAROW, assistant professor, Mass Communication
Winthrop University

RICHARD A. SCHALINSKE, director, Institutional Research
Capital University

BRIAN L. SCHULTZ, professor, Economics, and assessment coordinator
University of Wisconsin-River Falls

SUSAN SCIAME-GIESECKE, professor, Speech Communication
Indiana University Kokomo

JEFFREY A. SEYBERT, director, Office of Institutional Research
Johnson County Community College

NAHID SHABESTARY, instructor, Chemistry
Southern Illinois University at Edwardsville

BEN F. SHAW, JR., coordinator, University Assessment
Oklahoma State University

A. KIMBROUGH SHERMAN, associate professor, Decision Science
Loyola College in Maryland

CAROL SHULMAN, president
Dynamic Learning Systems

GARY M. SHULMAN, professor, Communication
Miami University

CATHY A. SIMPSON, coordinator, General Education Discipline Evaluation
Northern Virginia Community College

GARY L. SMITH, dean, Adult Learning and Assessment
Capital University

GEORGE E. SMITH, associate professor, Philosophy, and director, Curricular
   Software Studio
Tufts University

LESLIE S. SMITH, professor, Business and Office Systems Technology
Rappahannock Community College

DONALD F. SOLTZ, research associate, Health Sciences Center
University of Colorado at Denver

FRANK J. SPICUZZA, associate professor, College of Social Work
University of Tennessee, Knoxville

IRENE M. STAIK, professor, Psychology
University of Montevallo

KAREN STERN, assistant professor, Occupational Therapy
Kean College of New Jersey

JUDITH M. STILLION, vice chancellor, Academic Affairs
Western Carolina University

TRINA STOUT, research analyst, Offices of Institutional Research and Academic
   Assessment
Ball State University

ELNORA W. STUART, associate professor, Marketing
Winthrop University

DONNA PRIOR SULLIVAN, dean of freshmen
Lynn University

DONNA L. SUNDRE, associate assessment specialist, Office of Student Assessment
James Madison University

MARGARET TEBO-MESSINA, associate professor, English, and coordinator,
   General Education Assessment
Winthrop University

MELANIE S. THOMAS, instructor, English
Central Missouri State University

SUSAN L. THOMAS, assistant professor, Psychology
Southern Illinois University at Edwardsville

DAVID E. TOWLES, coordinator, Distance Learning
Liberty University

JANICE VAN DYKE, associate professor, Developmental Mathematics
State Technical Institute at Memphis

ARTHUR VAN STEWART, professor, School of Dentistry
University of Louisville

JOHN F. VAN WICKLIN, professor, Psychology, and director, Institutional Research
Houghton College

W. E. VINSON, professor, Dairy Science
Virginia Polytechnic Institute and State University

PAUL A. WAGNER, chair, University Planning Committee
University of Houston-Clear Lake

JUDY JONES WALKER, associate professor, School of Education
Lynn University

RICHARD D. WALKER, professor, Civil Engineering
Virginia Polytechnic Institute and State University

R. DAN WALLERI, director, Research, Planning, and Computer Services
Mt. Hood Community College

BARBARA E. WALVOORD, director, Writing Across the Curriculum, and
       codirector, Project to Improve and Reward Teaching
University of Cincinnati

THOMAS D. WEBB, coordinator, Office of Planning and Institutional Research
Gainesville College

CAROL J. WILLIAMS, associate professor, Social Work Program
Kean College of New Jersey

GEORGE W. WILLIAMS, chair, Chemical Engineering Technology
State Technical Institute at Memphis

SHERYL LEVERETT WILLIAMS, assistant professor, Chemistry
Gainsville College

STARNELL K. WILLIAMS, vice president, Advancement
Midlands Technical College

A. MICHAEL WILLIFORD, assistant professor, School of Applied Behavioral
    Sciences and Educational Leadership, and director, Institutional Research
Ohio University

DEBORAH ALFINO WILSON, assistant director, English Language Center
Central Missouri State University

DAVID A. WISSMANN, associate professor, Sociology
Avila College

RICHARD E. WOKUTCH, professor, Management, Pamplin College of Business
Virginia Polytechnic Institute and State University

SUSAN WYCHE-SMITH, director, Composition
Washington State University

CANDACE CARTWRIGHT YOUNG, professor, Political Science
Northeast Missouri State University (Truman State University after July 1996)

REFERENCES

Aitken, J. E., and Neer, M. "A Faculty Program of Assessment for a College Level Competency-Based Communication Core Curriculum." *Communication Education,* 1992, *41,* 270–285.

America 2000: An Education Strategy. Washington, D.C.: U.S. Department of Education, 1991.

American Association for Higher Education. *Principles of Good Practice for Assessing Student Learning.* Washington, D.C.: AAHE, 1992.

Angelo, T. A. "Ten Easy Pieces: Assessing Higher Learning in Four Dimensions." In T. A. Angelo (ed.), *Classroom Research: Early Lessons from Success.* New Directions for Teaching and Learning, no. 46. San Francisco: Jossey-Bass, 1991.

Angelo, T. A. "Classroom Assessment: Involving Faculty and Students Where It Matters Most." *Assessment Update,* 1994, *6*(4), 1–2, 5, 10.

Angelo, T. A., and Cross, K. P. *Classroom Assessment Techniques: A Handbook for College Teachers.* (2nd ed.) San Francisco: Jossey-Bass, 1993.

Astin, A. W. *Academic Gamesmanship: Student-Oriented Change in Higher Education.* New York: Praeger, 1976.

Astin, A. W. *Four Critical Years: Effects of College on Beliefs, Attitudes, and Knowledge.* San Francisco: Jossey-Bass, 1977.

Astin, A. W. *Achieving Educational Excellence: A Critical Assessment of Priorities and Practices in Higher Education.* San Francisco: Jossey-Bass, 1985.

Astin, A. W. *Assessment for Excellence: The Philosophy and Practice of Assessment and Evaluation in Higher Education.* New York: American Council on Education/Macmillan, 1991.

Astin, A. W. *What Matters in College? Four Critical Years Revisited.* San Francisco: Jossey-Bass, 1993.

Astin, A. W., Green, K. C., and Korn, W. S. *The American Freshman: Twenty-Year Trend, 1966–1985.* Los Angeles: Higher Education Research Institute, Graduate School of Education, University of California, 1987.

Baker, E. L., O'Neil, H. F., Jr., and Linn, R. L. "Policy and Validity Prospects for Performance-Based Assessment." *American Psychologist,* 1993, *48,* 1210–1218.

Banta, T. W. "Use of Outcomes Information at the University of Tennessee, Knoxville." In P. T. Ewell (ed.), *Assessing Educational Outcomes.* New Directions for Institutional Research, no. 47. San Francisco: Jossey-Bass, 1985.

Banta, T. W. "Is There Hope for TQM in the Academy?" In D. L. Hubbard (ed.), *Continuous Quality Improvement: Making the Transition to Education.* Maryville, Mo.: Prescott, 1993a.

Banta, T. W. "Summary and Conclusion: Are We Making a Difference?" *Making a Difference: Outcomes of a Decade of Assessment in Higher Education.* San Francisco: Jossey-Bass, 1993b.

Banta, T. W. "Toward a Plan for Using National Assessment to Ensure Continuous Improvement of Higher Education." *Journal of General Education,* 1993c, *42,* 33–58.

Banta, T. W. "Using Outcomes Assessment to Improve Educational Programs." In M. E. Weimer and R. J. Menges (eds.), *Better Teaching and Learning in College: More Scholarly Practice.* San Francisco: Jossey-Bass, in press.

Banta, T. W., and Associates (eds.). *Making a Difference: Outcomes of a Decade of Assessment in Higher Education.* San Francisco. Jossey-Bass, 1993.

Banta, T. W., and Borden, V.M.H. "Performance Indicators for Accountability and Improvement." In V.M.H. Borden and T. W. Banta (eds.), *Using Performance Indicators to Guide Strategic Decision Making.* New Directions for Institutional Research, no. 82. San Francisco: Jossey-Bass, 1994.

Baugher, K. *LEARN: The Student Quality Team Manual.* Nashville, Tenn.: LEARN, 1992.

Baxter Magolda, M. B. *Knowing and Reasoning in College: Gender-Related Patterns in Students' Intellectual Development.* San Francisco: Jossey-Bass, 1992.

Belenky, M. F., Clinchy, B. M., Goldberger, N. R., and Tarule, J. M. *Women's Ways of Knowing: The Development of Self, Voice, and Mind.* New York: Basic Books, 1986.

Bloom, B. S. (ed.). *Taxonomy of Educational Objectives: The Classification of Educational Goals. Handbook I: Cognitive Domain.* New York: Longmans, Green, 1956.

Borg, W. R., Gall, J. P., and Gall, M. D. *Applying Educational Research: A Practical Guide.* White Plains, N.Y.: Longman, 1993.

Bowen, H. R. *Investment in Learning: The Individual and Social Value of American Higher Education.* San Francisco: Jossey-Bass, 1977.

Boyer, E. L. *College: The Undergraduate Experience in America.* The Carnegie Foundation for the Advancement of Teaching. New York: HarperCollins, 1987.

Brandt, D. S. "Assessment: Mandate or Privilege?" In D. J. Lee and G. G. Stronks (eds.), *Assessment in Christian Higher Education: Rhetoric and Reality.* Lanham, Md.: University Press of America, 1994.

Bruner, J. S. *Acts of Meaning.* Cambridge, Mass.: Harvard University Press, 1990.

Calliotte, J. A., and Pickering, J. W. *Old Dominion University Freshman Survey.* Unpublished instrument. Norfolk, Va.: Old Dominion University, 1988.

The Carnegie Foundation for the Advancement of Teaching. *Campus Life: In Search of Community.* Princeton: The Carnegie Foundation for the Advancement of Teaching, 1990.

Chickering, A. W., and Gamson, Z. F. "Seven Principles for Good Practice in Undergraduate Education." *AAHE Bulletin,* 1987, *39*(7), 3–7.

Cohen, S., and others. "A Method for Evaluating the Effectiveness of Educational Software." *Behavior Research Methods, Instruments, & Computers,* 1994, *26*(2), 236–241.

Cohen, S., Tsai, F., and Chechile, R. "A Model for Assessing Student Interaction with Educational Software." *Behavior Research Methods, Instruments, & Computers,* 1995, *27*(2), 251–256.

Cross, K. P., and Angelo, T. A. *Classroom Assessment Techniques: A Handbook for Faculty.* Ann Arbor: National Center for Research to Improve Postsecondary Teaching and Learning, University of Michigan, 1988.

Cunningham, B. W. "The Effect of Noncognitive Variables on the Prediction of Academic Difficulty and Attrition of Freshman Student Athletes." Unpublished doctoral dissertation. Norfolk, Va.: Old Dominion University, 1993.

Davies, G. "The Importance of Being General: Philosophy, Politics, and Institutional Mission Statements." In J. Smart (ed.), *Higher Education: Handbook of Theory and Research*. Vol. 2. New York: Agathon Press, 1986.

Deming, W. E. *Out of the Crisis*. Cambridge, Mass.: Massachusetts Institute of Technology, Center for Advanced Engineering Study, 1986.

El-Khawas, E. *Campus Trends*. Higher Education Panel Report Number 77. Washington, D.C.: American Council on Education, 1987.

El-Khawas, E. *Campus Trends*. Higher Education Panel Report Number 82. Washington, D.C.: American Council on Education, 1992.

Erwin, T. D. *Assessing Student Learning and Development: A Guide to the Principles, Goals, and Methods of Determining College Outcomes*. San Francisco: Jossey-Bass, 1991.

Ewell, P. T. *The Self-Regarding Institution: Information for Excellence*. Boulder, Colo.: National Center for Higher Education Management Systems, 1984.

Ewell, P. T. "Outcomes, Assessment, and Academic Improvement: In Search of Usable Knowledge." In J. Smart (ed.), *Higher Education: Handbook of Theory and Research*. Vol. 4. New York: Agathon Press, 1988.

Ewell, P. T. "Assessment and Public Accountability: Back to the Future." *Change*, 1991a, *23*(6), 12–17.

Ewell, P. T. "To Capture the Ineffable: New Forms of Assessment in Higher Education." In G. Grant (ed.), *Review of Research in Education*. No. 17. Washington, D.C.: American Educational Research Association, 1991b.

Ewell, P. T. "A Matter of Integrity: Accountability and the Future of Self-Regulation." *Change*, 1994, *26*(6), 25–29.

Ewell, P. T., and Jones, D. "Data, Indicators, and the National Center for Higher Education Management Systems." In V.H.M. Borden and T. W. Banta (eds.), *Using Performance Indicators to Guide Strategic Decision Making*. New Directions for Institutional Research, no. 82. San Francisco: Jossey-Bass, 1994.

Ewell, P. T., and Jones, D. P. "Actions Matter: The Case for Indirect Measures in Assessing Higher Education's Progress on the National Education Goals." *Journal of General Education*, 1993, *42*, 123–148.

Farmer, D. W. *Enhancing Student Learning: Emphasizing Essential Competencies in Academic Programs*. Wilkes-Barre, Pa.: King's College, 1988.

Gilligan, C. *In a Different Voice: Psychological Theory and Women's Development*. Cambridge, Mass.: Harvard University Press, 1982.

Greer, B., and Semrau, G. "Investigating Psychology Students' Conceptual Problems in Mathematics in Relation to Learning Statistics." *Bulletin of the British Psychological Society*, 1984, *37*, 123–125.

Griffith, J. V., and Chapman, D. W. *The Learning Context Questionnaire*. Davidson, N.C.: Davidson College, 1982.

Halpern, D. F., and others. "Targeting Outcomes: Covering Your Assessment and Needs." In T. V. McGovern (ed.), *Handbook for Enhancing Undergraduate Education in Psychology*. Washington, D.C.: American Psychological Association, 1993.

Hansen, R., McCann, J., and Meyers, J. "Rote Versus Conceptual Emphasis in Teaching Elementary Probability." *Journal for Research in Mathematics Education*, 1985, *16*, 364–374.

Holsti, O. R. *Content Analysis for the Social Sciences and Humanities*. Reading, Mass.: Addison-Wesley, 1969.

Hughes, R. K., "Outcomes Assessment—A Convert." *Synergy* (Oklahoma State University, Office of University Assessment), 1993, *3*(1), 4.

Hunt, L. *Writing Across the Curriculum*. Spokane, Wash.: Whitworth College, 1992.

Hutchings, P. "Principles of Good Practice for Assessing Student Learning." *Assessment Update*, 1993, *5*(1), 6–7.

Illinois Board of Higher Education. *Report of the Committee on the Study of Undergraduate Education,* September, 1986.

Jacobi, M., Astin A., and Ayala F. *College Student Outcomes Assessment: A Talent Development Perspective.* ASHE-ERIC Higher Education Report No. 7. Washington, D.C.: Association for the Study of Higher Education, 1987.

Jones, D. *Data and Information for Executive Decisions in Higher Education.* Boulder, Colo.: National Center for Higher Education Management Systems, 1982.

Kaminsky, L., and others. "Evaluation of a Shallow Water Running Test for the Estimation of Peak Aerobic Power." *Medicine and Science in Sports and Exercise,* 1993, *25*(11), 1287–1292.

Kinnick, M. "Increasing the Use of Student Outcomes Information." In P. T. Ewell (ed.), *Assessing Educational Outcomes.* New Directions for Institutional Research, no. 47. San Francisco: Jossey-Bass, 1985.

Knight, M. E., Lumsden, D. L., and Gallaro, D. (eds.). *Outcomes Assessment at Kean College of New Jersey: Academic Programs' Procedures and Models.* Lanham, Md.: University Press of America, 1991.

Leslie, L., and Brinkman, P. *The Economic Value of Higher Education.* New York: Collier Macmillan, 1988.

Light, R. J. *Harvard Assessment Seminars: Explorations with Students and Faculty About Teaching, Learning, and Student Life: Second Report.* Cambridge, Mass.: Harvard University, Graduate School of Education, 1992.

Light, R. J., Singer J. D., and Willett, J. B. *By Design: Planning Research on Higher Education.* Cambridge, Mass.: Harvard University Press, 1990.

Linstone, H. A., and Turoff, M. *The Delphi Method: Techniques and Applications.* Reading, Mass.: Addison-Wesley, 1975.

Lipsey, M. W., Cordray, D. S., and Berger, D. E. "Evaluation of a Juvenile Diversion Program: Using Multiple Lines of Evidence." *Education Review,* 1981, *5,* 283–306.

Lloyd-Jones, R. "Primary Trait Scoring." In C. Cooper and L. Odell (eds.), *Evaluating Writing: Describing, Measuring, Judging.* Urbana, Ill.: National Council of Teachers of English, 1977.

Loacker, G. and Mentkowski, M. "Creating a Culture Where Assessment Improves Learning." In T. W. Banta and Associates (eds.), *Making a Difference: Outcomes of a Decade of Assessment in Higher Education.* San Francisco: Jossey-Bass, 1993.

Marcia, J. "Ego Identity Development." In J. Adelson (ed.), *Handbook of Adolescent Psychology.* New York: Wiley, 1980.

Mentkowski, M., and Doherty, A. *Careering After College: Establishing the Validity of Abilities Learned in College for Later Careering and Professional Performance.* Final Report to the National Institute of Education: Overview and Summary. Milwaukee, Wis.: Alverno College, 1984.

Miller, R. I. "Using Change Strategies to Implement Assessment Programs." In T. W. Banta (ed.), *Implementing Outcomes Assessment: Promise and Perils.* New Directions for Institutional Research, no. 59. San Francisco: Jossey-Bass, 1988.

Miller, R. I. *Major American Higher Education Issues and Challenges in the 1990s.* Higher Education Policy Series 9. London: Jessica Kingsley, 1990.

National Center for Higher Education Management Systems. *A Preliminary Study of the Feasibility and Utility for National Policy of Instructional "Good Practice" Indicators in Undergraduate Education.* Boulder, Colo.: National Center for Higher Education Management Systems, 1993.

Pace, C. R. *Measuring the Quality of College Student Experiences.* Los Angeles: University of California, Higher Education Research Institute, 1984.

Pace, C. R. "Perspectives and Problems in Student Outcomes Research." In P. T. Ewell (ed.),

Assessing Educational Outcomes. New Directions for Institutional Research, no. 47. San Francisco: Jossey-Bass, 1985.

Pace, C. R. *College Student Experiences Questionnaire.* (3rd ed.) Los Angeles: University of California, Graduate School of Education, 1990.

Pascarella, E. T., and Terenzini, P. T. *How College Affects Students: Findings and Insights from Twenty Years of Research.* San Francisco: Jossey-Bass, 1991.

Perry, W. G., Jr. *Forms of Intellectual and Ethical Development.* Troy, Mo.: Holt, Rinehart & Winston, 1970.

Pickering, J. W., Calliotte, J. A., and McAuliffe, G. J. "The Effect of Noncognitive Factors on Freshman Academic Performance and Retention." *Journal of the Freshman Year Experience,* 1992, *4*(2), 7–30.

Pintrich, P. R., Smith, D.A.F., Garcia, T., and McKeachie, W. J. *The Motivated Strategies for Learning Questionnaire.* Ann Arbor: National Center for Research in Postsecondary Teaching and Learning, University of Michigan, 1991.

Readability Program for the IBM PC. Rockville, Md.: Scandinavian PC Systems, March 1988.

Rest, J. *Defining Issues Test Manual.* Minneapolis: University of Minnesota, 1990.

Rice, D. R., and Larson, J. "Developing the Assessment Plan at a State University: Strategies and Lessons Learned." In *1994 A Collection of Papers on Self-Study and Institutional Improvement.* Chicago: Commission on Institutions of Higher Education of the North Central Association of Colleges and Schools, 1994, pp. 120–126.

Riggs, M. L., and Worthley, J. S. "Evaluation of Student Outcomes Assessment Pilot Projects in the California State University." In California State University Institute for Teaching and Learning (ed.), *Student Outcomes Assessment: What Makes It Work?* Long Beach: California State University Foundation, 1992.

Robbins, G., Powers, D., and Burgess, S. *A Wellness Way of Life.* (2nd ed.) Madison, Wis.: W. C. Brown and Benchmark, 1994.

Senge, P. M. *The Fifth Discipline: The Art & Practice of the Learning Organization.* New York: Doubleday, 1990.

Special Study Panel on Education Indicators for the National Center for Education Statistics. *Education Counts: An Indicator System to Monitor the Nation's Educational Health.* Washington, D.C.: National Center for Education Statistics, 1991.

Strail, M. L. *College Student Inventory.* Coralville, Iowa: Noel/Levitz Centers, 1988.

Study Group on the Conditions of Excellence in American Higher Education. *Involvement in Learning: Realizing the Potential of American Higher Education.* Washington, D.C.: U.S. Department of Education, 1984.

Stufflebeam, D. L. "The CIPP Model for Program Evaluation." In G. F. Madaus, M. S. Scriven, and D. L. Stufflebeam (eds.), *Evaluation Models: Viewpoints on Educational and Human Services Evaluation.* Boston: Kluwer-Nijhoff, 1983.

Terenzini, P. T. "Cross-National Themes in the Assessment of Quality in Higher Education." *Assessment Update,* 1993, *5*(3), 1–2, 4, 13.

Walleri, R. D., and Seybert, J. A. "Demonstrating and Enhancing Community College Effectiveness." In T. W. Banta and Associates (eds.), *Making a Difference: Outcomes of a Decade of Assessment in Higher Education.* San Francisco: Jossey-Bass, 1993.

Walvoord, B. E., and others. *Thinking and Writing in College: A Naturalistic Study of Students in Four Disciplines.* Urbana, Ill.: National Council of Teachers of English, 1991.

Webster, E. "Evaluation of Computer Software for Teaching Statistics." *Journal of Computers in Mathematics and Science Teaching,* 1992 *11,* 377–391.

Whitehead, A. N. *The Aims of Education and Other Essays.* New York: Free Press, 1967. (Originally published 1928.)

Wingspread Group on Higher Education. *An American Imperative: Higher Expectations for Higher Education.* Racine, Wis.: Johnson Foundation, 1993.

Wolff, R. A. "CSU and Assessment—Second Down and Eight Yards to Go: A View from the Scrimmage Line." In California State University Institute for Teaching and Learning (ed.), *Student Outcomes Assessment: What Makes It Work?* Long Beach: California State University Foundation, 1992.

Wright, B. D. "An Assessment Primer." *Metropolitan Universities: An International Forum,* 1993, *3*(4), 7–15.

INDEX

A

Academic Advising Council, 240–243

Academic Performance Survey (APS), 21

Accountability (Principle 9), 2, 56; and attrition, 236; context for, 56–58; examples of, 58–61; and quality improvement, 269

Accreditation, 33, 57, 59; assessment mandated by, 76–79, 302, 319–322, 323, 324, 335; and employment-related satisfaction, 99; and standardized exam performance, 180

ACT Assessment Exam, 169

ACT College Outcome Measures Project (ACT-COMP), 28, 158, 169, 182, 329, 343; scores on, analysis of, 184–186

Active learning, 266

Administration: goals and indicators for, 334; intervention of, to improve professional student performance, 124–128; support of, for assessment, 36, 62–65, 143, 186, 199, 225–226, 237, 240, 247, 250, 338; views of, on assessment, 51

Advising, academic, 234, 240–250, 260–261, 309

Advising audit, 240–243

Advisory group, 240–243

African-American student body. *See* University of Arkansas at Pine Bluff

Aitken, J. E., 13, 68, 82

Alabama institutions. *See* Samford University; University of Montevallo

Alexander, J. M., 210–213

Alexander, L. D., 53

Alumni involvement, in civil engineering program, 147–149

Alumni research, 37, 38, 46, 272–275. *See also* Surveys, graduate/alumni

Alumni Survey Steering Committee, 37–38

Alverno College, 36, 37, 51, 66

America 2000: An Education Strategy, 18

American Assembly of Collegiate Schools of Business (AACSB), 76, 78, 79

American Association for Higher Education (AAHE), 1–2, 3, 10, 17, 23, 29, 35, 43, 50, 56, 62, 68, 69, 347

American College Testing, 119, 242

American Council on Education, 51

American Council on Teaching of Foreign Languages (ACTFL), 111, 112

American Dairy Association, 145

American Dental Association, 125

American Imperative, An: Higher Expectations for Higher Education (Wingspread Group on Higher Education), 4

American Sociological Association, 140

Anderson, V. J., 278–280

Angelo, T. A., 25

Anthony, B. T., 213–216

Application, assessment of, 15

Arizona. *See* Maricopa Community Colleges

Arkansas. *See* University of Arkansas at Pine Bluff

Assessment: administrators' views on, 51; comprehensive, fourteen-step program for, 149–152; and decision-making, 50–55; formative, 293–295; as learning process, 31–32; outcomes of, 342–349; setting the context for, 76–79; strategies of, improvements in, 346–347. *See also* Classroom assessment; Communication skills assessment; Critical thinking skills assessment; General education assessment; Institutional assessment; Major field assessment; Principles of assessment; Student